Agricultural Policies in
the USSR and Eastern Europe

Other Titles in This Series

Westview Special Studies on the Soviet Union and Eastern Europe

Agricultural Policies in the USSR and Eastern Europe
edited by Ronald A. Francisco,
Betty A. Laird, and Roy D. Laird

The nations of Eastern Europe and the USSR seem destined to face, increasingly, a choice between satisfying citizen demand for improved diets and satisfying the leaders' own ideological imperatives. The 1970s have been a decade of paradoxes in agriculture for these nations. Between 1970 and 1979, enormous production advances have been made, and the average diet now contains enough calories; yet, key food items remain in short supply. Enormous investments have been made in the state and collective farms, but returns, especially in labor productivity, have been disappointing.

The authors see the agrarian problem in communist systems as only the most conspicuous aspect of the more comprehensive problem of low efficiency--the price paid for the pursuit of ideological goals.

Ronald A. Francisco is assistant professor of political science and Soviet and East European area studies at the University of Kansas. Betty A. Laird is an independent research analyst specializing in rural affairs and Soviet agriculture. Roy D. Laird, professor of political science and Soviet and East European area studies, also at the University of Kansas, is founder of the continuing conference on Soviet and East European agricultural and peasant affairs.

Agricultural Policies in the USSR and Eastern Europe

edited by Ronald A. Francisco, Betty A. Laird, and Roy D. Laird

with a Conclusion by Karl-Eugen Wädekin

Westview Press / Boulder, Colorado

*Westview Special Studies on
the Soviet Union and Eastern Europe*

Published in 1980 in the United States of America by
        Westview Press, Inc.
        5500 Central Avenue
        Boulder, Colorado 80301
        Frederick A. Praeger, Publisher

Library of Congress Catalog Card Number: 79-3687
ISBN: 0-89158-687-3

Composition for this book was provided by the editors.
Printed and bound in the United States of America.

Contents

Tables and Figures

Figures

Preface

The present volume is the fifth to result from the efforts of North American and European scholars who have met periodically over the past two decades to exchange views on their study of Soviet and East European agricultural problems and prospects. Both the first and the fifth conferences were held at the University of Kansas, in 1962 and 1978, respectively. In between, meetings were held at the University of California, Santa Barbara; Munich, Germany; and the University of Washington, Seattle.

We believe that the published findings from the sessions have been a help in understanding an important facet of the world economy, and that the volumes offer a useful record of Soviet and East European agricultural affairs over the past two decades. The four preceding volumes, plus two other related works in which we have been involved are as follows:

Laird, Roy D. (ed.). Soviet Agricultural and Peasant Affairs. Lawrence, Kansas: The University of Kansas Press, 1963.

Laird, Roy D. and Crowley, Edward L. (eds.). Soviet Agriculture, The Permanent Crisis. New York: Frederick A. Praeger, 1965.

Karcz, Jerzy F. (ed.). Soviet and East European Agriculture. Berkeley and Los Angeles: University of California Press, 1967.

Jackson, W. A. Douglas (ed.). Agrarian Policies and Problems in Communist and Non-Communist Countries. Seattle: University of Washington Press, 1971.

Laird, Roy D., Hajda, Joseph, and Laird, Betty A. (eds.). The Future of Agriculture in the Soviet Union and Eastern Europe, Boulder, Colorado: Westview Press, 1977.

Francisco, Ronald A., Laird, Betty A., and Laird, Roy D. (eds.). The Political Economy of Collectivized

xv

Agriculture: A Comparative Study of Communist and Non-Communist Systems. New York: Pergamon Press, 1979.

We hope and believe that what appears in the pages that follow is an important extension of the earlier work.

Again, Darlene Heacock, the incomparable lady who makes the University of Kansas Soviet and East European Area Center run, deserves our enormous thanks, as does Pam McElroy of the Department of Political Science, who labored over the tables, Nancy Kreighbaum who patiently manipulated the ATMS, and Deborah Francisco whose literary help has been above and beyond the call. Karl-Eugen Wädekin, as the European coordinator for the conference, added immeasurably to its success. We too must thank the University of Kansas, Earl Nehring of the Political Science Department, the Hesston Foundation, and the Institute for the Study of World Politics for assistance that makes such work possible.

The Editors

Agricultural Policies in
the USSR and Eastern Europe

Part 1

Soviet Union

Introduction

Roy D. Laird

Significant changes have been made in Soviet agriculture since Khrushchev's ouster in 1964. There are important continuities between the Khrushchev and the Brezhnev leadership that need to be noted, but some of the contrasts are striking. Thus an examination of some of the more important similarities and differences is offered here by way of an introduction to the studies in the volume dealing with Soviet agricultural policy at the end of the 1970s.

Differences

Leadership style: The difference here is enormous. Clearly, Brezhnev has paid enormous attention to agriculture, but largely as the leader of the Kremlin team, low-keyed, and often behind the scenes. Khrushchev was almost constantly on the move, visiting numerous farms, often making pronouncements, and sometimes coming forth with earthy remarks. One day he could announce some major national program, and the next criticize a farm's leadership on a specific local matter.

Rubles and kopeks: The huge subsidies now being poured into Soviet agriculture (admitted to have reached 22 billion rubles annually in 1978) have to be the most important of all of Brezhnev's innovations. Investment in agriculture did increase somewhat under Khrushchev, but remained well below either the levels needed or the levels adopted in recent years.

Innovations: On balance, Khrushchev's schemes for improving agricultural output were of the get-rich-quick-at-minimal-expense variety. Planting corn almost everywhere, even plowing up the virgin lands of Kazakhstan, involved relatively little cost to the national treasury. In contrast, the Brezhnev emphasis on intensifikatsia (increasing yeilds on existing fields) has required enormous new investments. However, the massive land amelioration scheme for the non-chernozem region of the Northwest does seem sound, and promises to increase grain output substantially.

3

Incentives: Although peasant incomes still lag behind those of the urban industrial workers, rural incomes have advanced significantly, and guaranteed annual minimums have been introduced. Similarly, the introduction of stable, long-term state purchase plans for the portion of the farms' output slated for the state must help to encourage output increases.

Storage capacity: A truly mammoth, much-needed expansion of the grain-storage capacity has been introduced. Soviet grain output tends to fluctuate enormously from year to year. Normally post-harvest losses are serious. Ironically, largely because of poor and inadequate storage, post-harvest losses tend to soar during the best years, so that the carry-over of grain from the good years to the lean years is always much less than it might be.

Private plots: Of course, the ultimate goal of communism includes the total abandonment of all private economic activity. Perhaps because he was in too much of a hurry, Khrushchev moved to curtail the peasant families' production, even though private agricultural activity produces some 20 to 30 percent of the nation's food. In stark contrast, Brezhnev not only has spoken up concerning their present importance to the food supply, but he has introduced policies to encourage the peasants to increase private output.

Similarities

In spite of the importance of such changes as listed above, much remains the same. The drive for increased farm specialization, and the introduction of inter-farm cooperatives may be innovative, but along with other Brezhnev practices, such as that of outside authorities mandating above-plan purchases of a farm's produce , they all add up to even tighter outside control of the farms.

Although the pace has slowed, farm amalgamations still continue. Each year there are fewer farms, while those that remain become ever more huge.

Western critics long argued that Soviet agriculture needed enormous additional investments; these investments as well as some other needed economic changes have come about. Nevertheless, many of the shortcomings and inefficiencies of Soviet agriculture have to be rooted in the fact that it is one of the most politicized farming systems in the world. Politics always gets top priority, often at the expense of good economics or correct farming practice. Be it the selection of a new chairman (who really is appointed by the oblast party officials under the nomenklatura system), or a revised national model charter to guide life on the farms, the bottom line is maintaining strong controls from above. This fact must always be kept in mind when examining Soviet agricultural policies.

1
Capital Intensity in Soviet Agriculture

Folke Dovring

A CAPITAL-INTENSIVE SECTOR

Soviet agriculture is now one of the most capital intensive enterprises of its kind in the contemporary world. Official data give the stock of productive capital in agriculture as 77 billion rubles in 1965 and 168 billion in 1975,[1] which comes to 21.4 percent and 20.8 percent respectively, of total "productive" capital, the concept needed for comparison with national product data in the Soviet system of such statistics. The figures for capital in agriculture do not include any estimate for the value of land, even though such estimates have been available in the USSR for some time.[2]

Soviet agriculture now receives more than its share of investible resources. Agriculture's share in national income (Soviet concept) was 22.5 percent in 1965 and 16.8 percent in 1975, reflecting the high prices of agricultural products. In the tenth Plan (1976-80) agriculture's formation of new capital is supposed to continue growing somewhat faster than in the whole economy, although at a slower rate than before.[3]

The increasing drain on capital resources has not escaped attention in recent Soviet debate. Table 1.1 is an illustration.

From these numbers it appears that investment in 1965-70 was followed by substantial increases in output, if not at the same rate as the growth in investment, despite the fact that the last year of the period (1970) was a good one for agriculture. The five years 1970-75 appear much more disappointing. Correcting for the good base year 1970 would improve the performance of the subsequent five-year period somewhat, only to weaken that of the preceding period. The end year 1975 was that of the big drought, but the over-all

5

TABLE 1.1
Growth in Energy and Capital Supply to Agriculture
and of Gross Production of Kolkhozy and Sovkhozy,
1970-75 (in Percent of 1965)

	1970	1975
Energy capacity (HP) of agriculture	139.0	197.4
Energy supply to labor on kolkhozy and sovkhozy	145.0	218.2
Agricultural productive capital (incl. livestock, end of year)	147.0	247.0
Availability of agricultural productive capital		
Per worker	156.0	265.0
Per 100 ha agric. area	146.0	245.0
Gross production of kolkhozy and sovkhozy	128.0	133.0
Gross income of kolkhozy	127.4	137.7

Source: P. Ignatovskii, "Kontsentratsiya
sel'skokhozyaistvennogo proizvodstva,"
Voprosy ekonomiki, no. 6 (1977), pp. 15-26
(table, p. 20).

index of agricultural production for that year was not as bad
as that for grain crops. Any way one reads the evidence, the
conclusion of low and falling marginal productivity of capital
still stands.

The following will trace the quantities of durable
investment and working capital going to agriculture from other
sectors. Subsequently, we will look at the labor embodied in
both groups of external inputs, and at the fuel used both
directly in agriculture and indirectly as embodied in external
inputs. Some international comparisons will be added to
illustrate the level of capital intensity in Soviet
agriculture. Finally, an attempt will be made to interpret
the economic meaning of the material presented.

FIXED CAPITAL

Annual additions to capital stock in Soviet agriculture are covered in recent statistics, as shown in tables 1.2 and 1.3. These numbers relate to capital "for productive purposes," and do not include expenditures for rural social overhead capital, which are included in other data in the same sources. This overhead capital is in general of the magnitude of about 20 percent of the figures shown in these tables.

The statistics now also sometimes show a third concept of capital in agriculture, one which includes investment in some of the industries and services which supply external inputs to agriculture.[4] This concept, labelled "po vsemy kompleksu rabot," usually exceeds that for "productive purposes" by 11 to 12 percent; when combined with rural social overheads, the total may exceed the figures in the tables by about one-third.

It is evident from the data that agriculture's claim to a share in national product for fixed investment has been rising steadily from the early fifties until recently. A downward flexion in the last couple of years is as yet very slight.

How much the permanent stock of fixed capital increases over the years depends, obviously, also on the rates of depreciation. Some estimates can be inferred from data on stock and new investment; a few others are available from various sources. The former approach is pursued in table 1.4. Year-to-year differences between the data in the table's first column are identified in the second column, showing by how much the stock of capital increased during the year. The third column then shows the investment during the year (from table 1.3), and the difference between columns two and three becomes an estimate of depreciation during the year, which can be expressed as percent of national income (shown in table 1.3).

The data in table 1.4 include livestock. Index numbers showing capital stock in agriculture with and without livestock are so different that it is evident that the aggregate value of livestock has changed only slowly; the increases in cattle, hogs, and so forth, have been balanced in part by the decline in draft animals. Hence we can conclude that most if not all of the depreciation represents contributions from other sectors, external inputs, even if to some extent generated by local rural industry.

The estimates in table 1.4 show depreciation of agricultural productive capital to have been of the magnitude of 6-9 billion rubles per year, and from 1.5 to over 3 percent of the national product. These findings can be compared with a few numbers from other sources. The capital balance sheet for the year ending January 1,1974, as given in Narodnoe Khozyaistvo, 1974 (page 82), shows depreciation in agriculture with 9 billion rubles, which includes capital for rural social

TABLE 1.2
Investment in Soviet Agriculture "for Productive Purposes,"
by Plan Periods etc., and Comparison with National Income

Periods	Investment (million rubles)	National Income (billion rubles)	Investment as Percent of National Income
1918-40	6,020	...	...
1941-50	7,540	...	...
5th Plan 1951-55	12,754	374	3.4
6th Plan 1956-60	23,984	613	3.9
7th Plan 1961-65	37,759	865	4.4
8th Plan 1966-70	59,667	1,229	4.9
9th Plan 1971-75	99,059	1,674	5.9

Sources: SSSR v tsifrakh v 1977 godu, pp. 166, 189, and
Narodnoe Khozyaistvo, various years.

TABLE 1.3
Investment in Soviet Agriculture "for Productive Purposes" in
Individual Recent Years, and Comparison with National Income

Year	Investment (million rubles)	National Income (billion rubles)	Investment as Percent of National Income
1965	9,477	193.5	4.9
1966	10,154	207.4	4.9
1967	10,840	220.5	4.9
1968	12,120	244.1	5.0
1969	12,634	261.9	4.8
1970	14,276	289.9	4.9
1971	16,430	305.0	5.4
1972	17,984	313.6	5.7
1973	19,856	337.8	5.9
1974	21,579	354.0	6.1
1975	23,293	363.3	6.4
1976	24,260	385.7	6.3
1977(prel.)	24,800	403.0	6.2

Sources: SSSR v tsifrakh v 1977 godu, pp. 166, 189, and
Narodnoe Khozyaistvo, various years.

9

TABLE 1.4
Stock and Flow of Fixed Capital "for Productive Purposes" in Soviet Agriculture

Year	Stock—End of Year (billion rubles)	Change During Year (billion rubles)	New Investment During Year (billion rubles)	Difference (billion rubles)	Depreciation as Percent of National Income
1965	77	...	...	...	...
1970	106	29	59.7	30.7	2.5
1971	113	7	16.4	9.4	3.1
1972	122	9	18.0	9.0	2.9
1973	137	15	19.8	4.8	1.4
1974	153	16	21.6	5.6	1.6
1975	168	15	23.3	8.3	2.3
1976	183	15	24.3	9.3	2.4
1977	...	...	24.8	...	...

Sources: Narodnoe Khozyaistvo SSSR, Nation's years; SSSR v Tsifrakh v 1977 godu, p. 166.

overhead, as is evident from the figure for total investment shown in SSSR v tsifrakh 1977, (page 166). Vladimir Treml et al. show depreciation in agriculture as 4.63 billion in 1966 and 7.06 billion in 1972,[5] which comes to 2.25 percent of national income for both of those years. Although not identical with the figures computed in table 1.4, they are sufficiently close to the same magnitude to confirm that depreciation of fixed capital in Soviet agriculture in recent years has been in excess of 2 percent of national income (Soviet concept) year after year.

These rates require some comments. During a period of capital build-up as rapid as that we have been witnessing, it would be normal if rates of depreciation were relatively low compared with new additions to stock, for during a rapid build-up, large portions of the stock on hand are relatively young. This is why, in addition to the depreciation charges, the annual totals for new investment also must be considered when we try to gauge the burden placed upon the economy by intensive investment in agriculture. But discussing depreciation alone, for the moment, the rates are high when the general situation is considered, for a very large part of all new investment is in buildings and other permanent installations, and they cannot depreciate very rapidly when they are new. The rates of depreciation of machines are much higher, as shown for three categories in table 1.5.

These data confirm an earlier finding of very high rates of scrapping of Soviet farm machines.[6] The rates are still very high in the period 1970-75. A tendency toward lower rates of scrapping in 1976-80, which would be in keeping with the general theme of the tenth Plan, is not very strong in tractors and combines, but more so in trucks. The latter feature may be related to the emphasis on tractor-drawn transportation units (traktornye pritsepy) which might lessen the intensity of use of the truck fleet. Other than that, it remains to say that the high rates of scrapping likely reflect high rates of use. There may be some lack of care for the machines, but the main explanation for high rates of scrapping is shown by the data on petroleum fuels in Soviet agriculture, as we shall see in the following section.

WORKING CAPITAL

The various goods and services which agriculture receives as current production inputs from other sectors of the economy are not treated in any routine statistical presentation of costs of production. For most items we get separate data but in physical units, and so it is difficult to construct comprehensive cost data such as those including transportation and servicing of the inputs by agents outside agriculture.

TABLE 1.5
Machinery in Soviet Agriculture

Year	Stock, End of Year	Net Increase During 5 Years	Supplied to Agriculture During 5 Years	Scrapping = Col. 3 - Col. 2
Tractors (natural units in thousands)				
1955	844	...	...	...
1960	1,122	278	747	469
1965	1,613	491	1,093	602
1970	1,977	364	1,467	1,103
1975	2,336	359	1,700	1,341
1980 (Plan)	2,850	516	1,900	1,384
Grain Combines (in thousands)				
1955	338	...	...	...
1960	497	159	389	230
1965	520	23	387	364
1970	623	103	469	366
1975	680	57	449	392

1980 (Plan)	800	120	538	418

Trucks (in thousands)

1955	544	...	...	...
1960	778	234	483	249
1965	945	167	355	188
1970	1,136	191	717	526
1975	1,396	260	1,100	840
1980 (Plan)	2,160	764	1,350	586

Sources: Narodnoe khozyaistvo, various years; SSSR v tsifrakh v 1977 godu; articles in Planovoe khozyaistvo 1976, no. 5, pp. 28-39 and 1976, no. 9, pp. 21-27 and Materialy XXV S''ezda KPSS, Moscow 1976, p. 144.

The gap is filled for certain years by the input-output tables. We may cite the two most recent ones, from 1966 and 1972. Summing vertically all that agriculture buys as production inputs other than labor and capital, and subtracting intra-agriculture transfers (mainly stockfeed from crop farming to animal husbandry), we obtain totals of 10.8 billion rubles in 1966 and 24.5 billion in 1972. Some of these purchases are from food industries, especially flour mills but also meat industries, and thus contain inputs recycled from agriculture itself. These items amount to 810 million in 1966, 3879 million in 1972. Looking at these items in terms of rubles, we have no basis for knowing how much of their value represents farm value of the same goods (e.g., as feed equivalent) and how much represents cost-of-production in the food industries; this is a bookkeeping matter entirely out of our view. To resolve this conflict in the simplest possible way, we propose to subtract half of these items, and thus arrive at estimates of 10.4 billion in 1966 and 22.6 billion in 1972, as current external inputs into Soviet agriculture.

Working capital is, as a financial matter, a revolving fund; its increase of 12.2 billion in six years is in any event noteworthy.

More important, agriculture's current external inputs represent a continuous claim on productive resources in other sectors, the size of which is indicative of how far agriculture draws on capital, manpower, and energy in the rest of the economy. In 1966, 10.4 billion and in 1972, 22.6 billion represent 5.0 percent and 7.2 percent, respectively, of national income (Soviet concept) for these two years. The tendency toward rapidly rising cost is even more striking here than in the case of fixed capital. The pricing of inputs is too little elucidated by the sources to allow these conclusions to be more than indicative.

Details item by item show that large material items such as petroleum and electricity have less than doubled in the six-year period, basic chemicals, mainly fertilizers, have just about doubled, while service items such as repairs have more than doubled, as did also the inputs from food industries discussed above.

The tenth Plan gives only scattered clues, for the same reasons as in the routine statistics. Electricity is scheduled to increase by a factor of 1.8 in five years, and mineral fertilizers by 1.56. The basic thrust of the tenth Plan being in the direction of more efficient use of inputs, repair services and spare parts are likely to gain even more weight in the future, to offset the slower growth in machine fleets and their lower rates of attrition and scrapping.

EMBODIED LABOR

One way of gauging and interpreting capital intensity is to compute the amount of labor in other sectors, the productive nonagricultural sectors, in this case, that go into producing and servicing the external inputs to agriculture. This problem has gained some attention in the Soviet Union in recent years, and authority for this is cited all the way to Marx and Lenin. Research on "previous" or "incorporated" labor is as yet tentative; results are piecemeal; they cannot yet be raised into aggregate estimates for the whole agricultural economy, and there seem to be internal contradictions within the research itself.[7] A further difficulty is that this research appears oriented more to normative data (the "socially necessary" amount of labor) as a means to setting goals for improved productivity, rather than to measure what goes on in the present.[8]

This leaves us with the input-output tables of 1966 and 1972, and the possibility of estimating aggregates of incorporated labor by a shortcut method. This method assumes that the goods and services delivered to agriculture from other sectors of the economy are a representative cross section of the nonagricultural economy, an assumption which has proved realistic in the United States.[9] We then compute the external inputs to agriculture as a percentage of the national product in the nonagricultural sectors. In the case of Soviet accounts, the data to be used are those for national income (Soviet concept) and for the labor force in the "productive" sectors of the economy.

The nonagricultural share of national income is simply the total national income minus the part credited to agriculture. For 1966 this nonagricultural national income comes to 157 billion rubles, and for 1972, 254 billion.

The share of nonagricultural "productive" sectors in the labor force is found by adding up the number of workers and service personnel (rabochie i sluzhaschie) in the sectors so designated. These numbers come to 51.9 million in 1966 and 61.9 million in 1972.

Taking first the current external inputs discussed in the previous section, the amounts of 10.4 billion in 1966 and 22.6 billion in 1972 are 6.6 percent and 8.9 percent, respectively, of the nonagricultural national income as shown above. Applying the same percentages to the nonagricultural labor force in "productive" sectors, we obtain as answers 3.4 million worker years in 1966 and 5.5 million in 1972, thus an increase of 2.1 million in six years, with the appropriate reserve for changes in relative prices of the inputs.

Turning then to investments, let us look first at the data on depreciation as discussed in the section on fixed investments. For the years 1966 and 1972 we may accept those published by Treml et al., of 4.63 and 7.06 billion rubles, respectively, which come to 2.95 percent and 2.78 percent, respectively, of the nonagricultural national income in those two years. Applying these percentages to the numbers of nonagricultural "productive" workers and service people, we find as answers 1.5 million and 1.7 million worker years, respectively. Adding those numbers to those for current inputs, we find the embodied labor in external inputs to Soviet agriculture to have been 4.9 million and 7.2 million worker years, respectively, in 1966 and 1972, for an increase of 2.3 million in six years.

Alternatively, we may consider the total of new investment rather than depreciation as a gauge of the total drain on national resources caused by the rapid build-up of agriculture. With 10.2 billion in 1966 and 18.0 billion in 1972, these investments, which are nearly all generated outside agriculture,[10] represented 6.5 percent and 7.1 percent respectively of the nonagricultural national income in those years. Applying these percentages to the labor-force data for the same sectors, we obtain 3.4 and 4.4 million worker years, respectively. Summing again with the labor embodied in current inputs, we get 6.8 and 9.9 million worker years, or an increase of 3.1 million in six years.

These numbers can then be compared with those for direct labor in agriculture, which amounted to 25.4 million in 1966 and 23.5 million in 1972, thus a decline of 1.8 million in the same six years. This does not include those who work only on family plots, numbering about 4 million. A table in Narodnoe khozyaistvo, 1975 (p. 110) appears to indicate 28.7 million as total labor use in Soviet agriculture in 1972.

Apparently, the total labor input in Soviet agriculture may have increased rather than declined. The sharply rising figures for external inputs in fact have been accompanied by a slow--recently very slow--decline in the agricultural work force. It is interesting to note that the share of women in agricultural work, which has long been high, appears to be declining slightly, indicating some stabilizing of the number of men working in agriculture.[11]

Comparing the above numbers with those for the total work force in the Soviet Union, which was 97 million in 1966 and 110 million in 1972, we find that direct labor in agriculture was 26.2 percent and 21.4 percent, respectively, of this total. Adding the indirect labor (that embodied in external inputs), we find first, with only the depreciation variant, (25.4 ÷ 4.9 =) 30.3 million, or about 31 percent of all workers in 1966, and (23.5 ÷ 7.2 =) 30.7 million, or 28.0 percent of all workers in 1972.

Substituting the total-investment variant for the depreciation-based numbers, we obtain instead (25.4 ÷ 6.8 =) 32.2 million, or 33 percent in 1966, and (23.5 ÷ 9.9 =) 33.4 million, or 30 percent of all workers in 1972.

16

Already the direct-labor share of agriculture in the total
work force is greater than its share in national income,
throughout the last decade and more. Adding the indirect
labor embodied in external inputs of agriculture, the
conclusion is of a sector that is very heavily capitalized in
relation to the direct work force it still carries.

FUEL AND EMBODIED ENERGY

Fuel and energy use are another set of indicators of
capital intensity. Soviet agriculture absorbs large amounts
of petroleum-refinery products and electricity, while other
fuels (coal, gas, peat, and wood) figure in modest quantities.
For recent years, we want to discuss the data from the 1966
and 1972 input-output tables, a more recent balance sheet of
fuel and energy use for 1965 and 1975,[12] and some indications
from the tenth Plan.

Starting with oil, the input-output tables give
indications from which the consumption of petroleum products
(mainly diesel oil) may be computed, as shown in table 1.6.

The 1965 and 1975 balance sheet data in Vestnik statistiki
1978:1 give no direct data on oil consumption in agriculture,[13]
but do contain some clues which may be used for estimates.
Based on these clues, Soviet agriculture in 1975 used 13.2
percent of all oil consumed in the country, or 10.2 percent of
all oil produced in the same year. This estimate comes to 50
million tons of oil used in Soviet agriculture in 1975, which
is well in line with the estimate for 1972.

Turning to electricity, the input-output tables as
reconstructed by Treml et al. indicate numbers as shown in
table 1.7. Computations like these are beset by pricing
problems, which make the comparisons, especially over time,
indicative at best.

The analysis in Vestnik statistiki (see note 12) indicates
that agriculture took 2.8 percent of the electricity in 1965
and 5.3 percent in 1975. With totals of 507 and 1039 billion
kwh for those two years, agriculture's use comes to 14.2
billion kwh in 1965 and 55 billion in 1975, indicating a
recent quantum jump, unless the input-output estimate for 1972
is incorrect.

The tenth Plan foresees use of electricity in Soviet
agriculture to be 130 billion kwh in 1980, against 74 billion
in 1975. The difference against the just-quoted estimate of
55 billion in 1975 indicates that the Plan, here as elsewhere,
uses the extended concept of agriculture, including both rural
social overheads and some of its backward linkages. Whether
the use "for productive purposes" in agriculture proper will

17

TABLE 1.6
Direct Use of Petroleum in Soviet Agriculture, 1966 and 1972

		1966	1972
1.	Total crude oil production[a] (million tons)	265.1	400.4
2.	Crude oil as Gross Value of Output (GVO) (million rubles)[b]	1,895.2	6,072.3
3.	Of which, going to refinery	1,208.5	4,749.3
4.	Line 3 as percent of Line 2	63.7	78.3
5.	Line 4 times Line 1 = Crude oil refined (million tons)	164	310
6.	Refinery output as GVO[b] (million rubles)	8.262.0	16,091.7
7.	Of which, to agriculture (million rubles)	1,286.7	2,240.0
8.	Line 7 as percent line 6	15.6	13.8
9.	Line 8 times line 5 - oil to agriculture (million tons)	25.6	41.5
10.	Line 9 as percent of line 1	9.7	10.7

Sources: [a] Narodnoe Khozyaistvo, appropriate years;

[b] Vladimir G. Treml et al., "The Soviet 1966 and 1972 Input-Output Tables," in Soviet Economy in a New Perspective (see note 3).

TABLE 1.7
Direct Use of Electricity in Soviet Agriculture,
1966 and 1972

		1966	1972
1.	Gross Value of Output (GVO) (million rubles)	7,527.30	14,030.40
2.	Agriculture's share (million rubles)	185.90	317.30
3.	Line 2 as percent of line 1	2.47	2.26
4.	Total electricity generated (billion kwh)	545.00	857.00
5.	Line 3 times line 4 = agriculture's share (billion kwh)	13.50	19.30

Source:Data for total electricity from Narodnoe
khozyaistvo SSSR v 1975 godu.

rise in the same proportion of 1:1.8 as in the totals just
quoted, is unclear; if it applies, the total for "productive"
purposes might be about 100 billion kwh in 1980.

The above relates to direct energy: what is consumed on
farms, or the agricultural sector however defined, as fuel and
as electricity. Indirect energy, that spent in producing both
the direct energy and other input goods is also a matter of
economic concern, not the least when supply restrictions begin
to be felt, even in the USSR. There are three main categories
that we may investigate, namely motor fuel, electricity, and
agricultural chemicals, mainly fertilizers.

The very large oil consumption in Soviet agriculture is
almost all for operation of agricultural machines and
propulsion of vehicles. For these we have useful indications
on indirect energy from the United States. First there is the
overhead of the oil industry itself, which consumes energy in
various operations, foremost in refining. This overhead was
recently estimated at 22.3 percent, meaning that for every 100
units of oil-refinery products consumed in a final-use sector,

another 22.3 units (or their energy-unit equivalent of other fuels) have been consumed by the oil industry directly or indirectly.[14] Then there are other backward linkages: energy consumed in the making and servicing of machines, and so forth, all the way back to the steel mill and the iron mine, as well as forward to transportation from factory to final user of the machine. When these overheads are added to those of the oil industry, the total indirect use of oil comes to the equivalent of about three-quarters of the oil in direct final use. Thus, every one hundred units of oil-refinery products consumed in final use have caused the indirect use of another seventy-five units, or thereabout.[15] Raising the above estimates by 1.75, we obtain the following level of both direct and indirect energy use (in oil-equivalent terms) by and for Soviet agriculture:

1966 25.6 million tons times 1.75 = 44.7 million tons
1972 41.5 million tons times 1.75 = 72.5 million tons
1975 50 million tons times 1.75 = 87.5 million tons

Those numbers come to 6.4 percent, 8.7 percent, and 10.0 percent, respectively, of all energy used in the years covered.

For electricity, the problem is different. The energy content of electricity is not comparable with that of fuels because electricity is a more efficient form of energy. For comparison one uses instead data on the fuel used to generate electricity, which is now usually about three times the energy content of the electricity. When all the backward linkages are included (the energy used in building and servicing the power stations and their basic grids, and in making the materials of which they are built, etc.), the total energy used to generate electricity comes to about four times the energy content of the electricity (see note 14). For Soviet conditions, we may use the figures for direct fuel use in power stations in Narodnoe khozyaistvo for 1974 (p. 218) and 1975 (p. 238) which indicate the number of grams of coal burned per kwh generated: 415 in 1965, 405 in 1966, 354 in 1972, and 340 in 1975. Adding one-third to each of these numbers (for backward linkages, on the same level as in the United States), we obtain the coefficients used below to compute the coal-equivalent amounts of energy embodied in the production of electricity for direct use in Soviet agriculture:

20

1965 14.2 b kwh times .550 = 7.8 million
      tons of coal-equivalent

1966 13.8 b kwh times .540 = 7.5 million
      tons of coal-equivalent

1972 19.3 b kwh times .470 = 9.07 million
      tons of coal-equivalent

1975 55.0 b kwh times .450 = 24.7 million
      tons of coal-equivalent

For 1980, 100 billion kwh, with the same coefficient of fuel use as in 1975, would mean 45 million tons of coal-equivalent fuel. For all the years 1965-75, the fuel used in electricity generation for agriculture comes to about .50 percent of all the energy consumed in the USSR in those years. This compares with about another 1.00 percent for direct use of coal and minor fuels.

These estimates exclude all uses which are indirect altogether, such as those of chemicals. The bulk of these are the chemical fertilizers. Again we may refer to indicators from U.S. research. Based on 1967 data, commercial fertilizers embodied 24 million British thermal units (Btu) per ton of pure nutrient content.[16] Applying this coefficient to Soviet data, we obtain the following:

	Million Tons of Pure Content	Times 24 m Btu = Trillion Btu	Percent of National Energy Budget
1965	6.3	151	0.61
1970	10.4	250	1.23
1972	12.5	300	1.14
1975	17.7	425	1.06
1977	18.6	447	....

For 1980, the Plan foresees 115 million tons of chemical fertilizers. Reducing this to pure content in the same proportion as in 1977, we obtain 26.5 million tons of pure content in 1980, for an energy expenditure of 635 trillion Btu.

Summing up the findings, we have, for the early 1970s:

Petroleum and related indirect consumption	8-10 % of national energy budget
Coal and minor fuels	1 % national energy budget
Electricity	.5 % national energy budget
Fertilizers	1 % national energy budget
Total of the above	10.5-12.5 % national energy budget

These estimates are still likely to be on the low side because they do not include several items of indirect energy use such as construction, chemicals other than fertilizers, transportation not on the charge of the farms themselves, and several services not connected with the items investigated.

INTERNATIONAL COMPARISONS

Total use of external inputs into Soviet agriculture in the early 1970s amounted to over 2 percent of the national income for depreciation (or about three times as much if all new capital is counted instead of depreciation) plus current external inputs (working capital) of about 7 percent of the national income. Thus Soviet agriculture absorbed 9 percent (or 13 percent, if all new capital is included) of the national income in those years.

This finding is remarkable because it is normal, in market economies, that agriculture's external inputs are of the order of 3 percent of the national product (the first Simantov constant).[17] Even if some adjustment is made for the difference of national accounting concepts,[18] yet there is no way of escaping the conclusion that Soviet agriculture is from two to three times as capital intensive as countries on a similar level of per capita income but subject to the discipline of market prices.

The conclusion is borne out by the analyses of indirect labor and of fuel and energy. It is quite evident that Soviet agriculture's external inputs absorb several million worker-years of labor in the nonagricultural sectors, which is again two to three times the amount of indirect labor absorbed by United States' agriculture through its external inputs, which is of a magnitude of two million man-years.[19]

On energy, the conclusion is equally compelling: 10 percent or more of the national energy budget is more than twice the amount spent in the United States, and points to a

22

substantially higher level of energy use per unit of farm
output in the Soviet Union than in almost any other country.
The Soviet economy as a whole is about as energy intensive as
the United States economy--both are big energy squanderers
when compared with Western Europe and Japan. But in the
agricultural sector, the USSR comes out as even more wasteful
than in the economy as a whole. The details show that the
main culprit, in Soviet agriculture, is in the use of power
machines. With 40-50 million tons of liquid fuel as direct
consumption, the USSR is clearly ahead of the United States,
even though Soviet agricultural output has not yet reached the
quantity level of U.S. agriculture.

ECONOMIC INTERPRETATION

The high level of external inputs in Soviet agriculture
means, first of all, a high level of costs of production. The
large percentages of nonagricultural products required as
inputs means, directly, a denial of factory capacity which,
under a more economic agricultural system, could have been
available to other investment and other consumption.
Indirectly, it also means a larger claim to investment in the
sectors generating agriculture's external inputs, both the
current ones and those for capital formation in agriculture.
Thus the total consequences of agriculture's capital intensity
are even greater than appears at first sight. The latest
variant of Soviet accounting, of investment "po vsemu
kompleksu rabot" marks an attempt at grasping some of those
consequences, without yet reaching more than a fraction. This
capital-intensive agriculture is in fact a heavy burden on the
system and reduces the system's ability to expand in other
directions. Ultimately, of course, the bill is paid by the
consuming public in the form of a level of living that is
quite a bit lower than it might have been if resources
committed to agriculture had been used more efficiently.

The evidence about overconsumption of motor fuel, and of
high rates of machine depreciation, points to the farm
management system as the chief explanation for the waste that
goes on. Substitution of capital for labor has been pushed,
without regard for the fact that the farm labor made
economically redundant still lingers on in the farm work
force, doing extremely low-productive work.

It is interesting to note that the years of debate around
the tenth Plan also have produced some renewed interest in the
"mechanized zveno" which, after a rash of interest around
1960, was held back largely for ideological reasons.[20] This
also coincides in time with a new tendency in the journals to
ask for the "ultimate result" of the economic process.[21] How
far this type of economic rationality will be allowed to work
its way through current Plan fulfillment, will be interesting
to watch.

1.   Data on capital stock and national income from Narodnoe khozyaistvo SSSR v 1975 godu (Moscow: Centralnoe Statisticheskoe Upravlenie), pp. 57, 58, 564.
2.   See among others S. Cheremuskhin, "O stoimostnoi otsenke zemli," Ekonomika sel'skogo khozyaistva, no.   12 (1967). Cf. also Michael D. Zahn, "The Applications of Economic Rent in the Union of Soviet Socialist Republics," (M.S. thesis, University of Illinois, 1975).
3.   See among others G. Loza and I. Kurtsev, "Rost proizvoditel'nykh sil sel'skogo khozyaistva v desatoi pyatiletke," Voprosy ekonomiki, no. 7 (1976), pp. 67-77. Cf. also U.S., Congress, Joint Economic Committee, "Soviet Agriculture: Recent Performance and Future Plans," by David W. Carey in Soviet Economy in a New Perspective, A Compendium of Papers (Washington, D.C., 14 October 1976), p. 590.
4.   Narodnoe khozyaistvo, (1975), pp. 57 sq, 564; cf. SSSR v tsifrakh v 1977 godu, p. 165. Cf also Carey, Soviet Agri., pp. 585 sq.
5.   Vladimir G. Treml et al., "The Soviet 1966 and 1972 Input-Output Tables," in Soviet Economy, (see note 3 above), pp. 357 and 373.
6.   Folke Dovring, "Progress on mechanization in Soviet agriculture," in James R. Millar, ed., The Soviet Rural Community, (Urbana: University of Illinois Press, 1971) pp. 259-75, especially pp. 266 sq.
7.   Foremost are two articles by a group of scholars working for the All-Union Institute of Agricultural Economics (VNIIESKh): by V. Mashenkov and four associates in Vestnik statistiki, no. 3, (1976), pp. 20-24, and by V. Mashenkov and two of the same associates in Ekonomika sel'skogo khozyaistva, no. 3 (1978), pp. 54-62. The differences between the findings of embodied labor in animal production are so large that this can only underscore the authors' own comments on the recent and as yet tentative nature of this research. Among others, see also a research note by a Ukrainian writer, A. Bugutskii, in Voprosy ekonomiki, no. 6 (1974), pp. 104-109.
8.   On this distinction, see Folke Dovring, "Underemployment in traditional agriculture," Economic Development and Cultural Change 15 (January 1967): 163-73, and idem, "Underemploymnent, slow motion, and X-efficiency," ibid, 27 (April 1979): 485-490.
9.   Folke Dovring, Productivity of Labor in Agricultural Production (University of Illinois College of Agriculture, Agricultural Experiment Station Bulletin 726, [September 1967]).
10.   Note that even investments carried out through the labor of local kolkhoz and sovkhoz workers is often counted as external;   the   numbers   of   workers   in   agriculture are

"srednegodovye," meaning average numbers present for agricultural work, which excludes most investment activities.

11. M. Fedorova, "Ispol'zovanie zhenskogo truda v sel'skom khozyaistve," Voprosy ekonomiki, no. 12 (1975), pp. 55 sq. The share of women in the work force of kolkhozy fell from 56 percent in 1960 to 51 percent in 1974, while their share in work days spent in collective work fell less, from 49 percent to 47 percent, because their level of employment rose more than that of the men, without yet catching up.

12. V. Voropaeva and S. Litvak, "O toplivno-energeticheskom balanse SSSR," Vestnik statistiki, no. 1 (1978), pp. 3-12.

13. According to tables on page 9 of the article cited in the preceding note, agriculture consumed 6.1 percent of all fuel consumed in the country in 1965, and 6.3 percent in 1975. Further, this included in 1975 2.8 percent of the coal, 1.0 percent of the natural gas, 0.6 percent of the fuel oil (toplivnyi mazut), and 35.7 percent of the diesel fuel. The direct meaning of the latter figure is nowhere revealed in official sources. The small fractions of coal, gas etc. represent together no more than 1.1 percent of the fuel used in the country, which leaves oil in agriculture as 5.2 percent, which comes to 13.2 percent of all the oil used in the country, or 10.2 percent of the oil extracted the same year or, in a round figure, 50 million tons.

14. Clark W. Bullard, Peter S. Penner, and David A. Pilati, Net Energy Analysis: Handbook for Combining Process and Input-Output Analysis, (Urbana-Champaign: University of Illinois, Center for Advanced Computation (CAC) Document No. 214, [October 1976]), p. 48.

15. Bruce Hannon, Robert Herendeen, F. Puleo, and Anthony Sebald, Chapter 3, in R. H. Williams, ed., The Energy Conservation Papers, A report to the Ford Foundation (Cambridge, Mass.: 1975). Similar results were obtained recently from analysis of Illinois farm records from 1972-76.

16. Bullard, Penner, and Pilati, Net Energy Analysis, p. 50 (line 2702) gives 187,051 Btu as the total energy requirement per dollar's worth of chemical fertilizers, 1967 prices. Applying this to the dollar value of fertilizer production in 1967, one obtains 308 trillion Btu which, divided by the physical volume of pure nutrient content yields a coefficient of 24 million Btu per ton of nutrient. This represents cost ex-factory; costs of transportation and distribution from factory to farm are not included. The proportions of nitrogen, phosphate, and potash are roughly the same in the USSR as in the United States.

17. Basic findings in A. Simantov, "The dynamics of growth and agriculture," Zeitschrift für Nationalökonomie, 27, no. 3, pp. 328-51. Elaboration on the Simantov constants in Folke Dovring, Income Growth and Sector Proportions (University of Illinois Department of Agricultural Economics,

AERR 97, [December 1968]). Application to one major country in Folke Dovring, "Macro constraints on agricultural development in India," Indian Journal of Agricultural Economics, 27 (January/March 1972): 46-66. An example of abnormally high levels of external inputs into agriculture in another centrally operated economy in Folke Dovring, Land Reform in Hungary, AID Spring Review, June 1970 (SA/LR/C-10, also PB 195-324), p. 41.

18. Cf Rush V. Greenslade, "The Real Gross National Product of the USSR, 1950-1975," in Soviet Economy, (see note 3 above), pp. 269-300.

19. Folke Dovring, Labor Used in Agricultural Production, (see note 9 above).

20. T. Orlova, "Model' rascheta mekhanizirovannogo zvena," Ekonomika sel'skogo khozyaistva, no. 11 (1977), pp. 68-71. Cf Folke Dovring, "Soviet farm mechanization in perspective," Slavic Review 25 (June 1966): 287-302.

21. L. Abalkin, "Konechnye narodokhoziaistvennye rezultaty," Voprosy ekonomiki, 1976, no. 11, pp. 3-13.

2
The Low Productivity of Soviet Agricultural Trade

F. A. Durgin, Jr.

INTRODUCTION

"Soviet agriculture is something of a monument to inefficiency" states Campbell R. McConnell, the author of one of the most popular economics texts in use on U.S. campuses today.[1] It is, in the words of Robert W. Campbell, America's foremost sovietologist, "...unreliable, irrational, wasteful, unprogressive--almost any perjorative adjective one can call to mind would be appropriate."[2] I single McConnell and Campbell out, not for attack, but simply because they, more eloquently than anyone else, sum up the prevalent Western view of Soviet performance in the countryside.

As all of us in the field are well aware, there is indeed a formidable body of evidence that seems to support the above dismal assessments: Plan failures, large grain imports, low crop yields, high losses during harvests, high levels of private-plot activity, overly large farms, lower levels of living in the countryside and the concomitant mass migration of rural youth to the cities, and low productivity of labor. Although low productivity of labor is just one small part of that overwhelming body of evidence, I have singled it out because it appears to be the strongest, and is the most widely cited piece of evidence used to support the generally accepted view that Soviet agriculture is highly inefficient. The objective of this paper is to (1) point out that labor productivity figures are not infallible indicators of inefficiency and (2) to point out certain rather high costs which, although they are not generally perceived as being so, are associated with the achievement of high productivity of labor.

27

THE EFFECTS OF THE LAW OF DIMINISHING RETURNS

It would indeed be difficult to find a study of Soviet agriculture that failed to discuss the low productivity of labor in the Soviet countryside. It would be equally difficult to find a study that did not use the United States as its benchmark and point out that the productivity of Soviet Agricultural labor is only a small percentage that of the United States--only 20-25 percent even by Soviet estimates.[3] It would also be rare to find a study that did not conclude on the basis of that evidence that Soviet agriculture was highly inefficient. But is this low productivity of Soviet agricultural labor prima facie evidence of inefficiency, or is it merely a manifestation of the law of diminishing returns, a law discovered in agriculture over 150 years ago, and as fundamental to the science of economics as the law of gravity is to physics?

Except under conditions of ceteris paribus on the physical and technical planes, productivity of labor figures are not necessarily evidence of the relative efficiency of agricultural labor under differing economic systems. Involved here is the law of diminishing marginal and average returns, and on the basis of that law, and a priori reasoning, one can easily deduce that the productivity of Soviet agriculture labor is considerably less than that of the United States. In the early 1970s each Soviet worker had on an average only a third as much land, far less fertile soil, and some 10-20 percent as much capital equipment and used in the neighborhood of a ninth as much power as his U.S. counterpart. He is also assisted by a far less favorable climate. These formidable obstacles, not withstanding the productivity of Soviet agricultural labor, according to a study by Earl R. Brubaker, are greater than those in Italy and roughly on a par with those prevailing in France and Germany.[4]

On the basis of the law of diminishing returns, one can also deduce that the productivity of labor in the Soviet private sector is lower than that of the public sector. The private sector receives about 40 percent[5] of the nation's total agricultural labor input, but has only 3 percent of the land and 5-10 percent of the productive assets. Consequently this 40 percent expenditure of labor on the private sector produces only 20 percent[6] of the nation's agricultural output. Corresponding figures for the cooperative and state sectors combined are some 60 percent of the total labor input and some 80 percent of the output. As can be seen, the productivity of labor in the private sector is less than half that of the public sector. Similarly, given the relative scarcity of the land factor in the private sector, one can also deduce that the heavy labor input produces phenomenal returns per hectar on the private sector, thus the familiar phrase, "the Soviet peasants, on their private lots which account for less than 3 percent of the total sown area, produce 20 percent of the nation's total agricultural output."

Proceeding around the remaining corners of the production function, one can also deduce that, given its relative scarcity, the return to capital on Soviet farms exceeds that on U.S. farms. And in this respect, whether measured in physical or value terms, the Soviet farm produces far more per unit of capital than does a U.S. farm. In 1970, the Soviets cultivated 258 acres of sown area per tractor vs. only 65 per tractor in the U.S. They harvested 573 acres of grain with every combine vs. only 53 in the U.S., and they serviced some 499 acres with each truck used in agriculture vs. only 98 in the U.S. In value terms they produced $17,171 worth of output per tractor vs. only $7,558 in the U.S., and $29,890 worth of output per truck used in agriculture vs. only $11,741 in the U.S.[7]

But to say that Soviet arms are more efficient than their U.S. counterparts in their use of tractors by a factor of four in physical terms, and 2.3 in value terms, and more efficient in their use of trucks by a factor of 4.5 in physical terms, and 2.5 in value terms, as everyone well recognizes, is absurd. The dynamics of the law of diminishing marginal and average returns are such that the "efficiency index" can be raised to infinity by simply reducing the amount of tractors, trucks, and combines used in agriculture, while at the same time, of course, reducing total output. But however meaningless productivity of capital figures may be as evidence of a Soviet superiority in the use of capital, they are no more meaningless than the fact that that same year each Soviet farm worker produced only $834 worth of output as compared to the $7,746 produced by his U.S. counterpart.

I will not argue that indices of the productivity of land, labor, and capital have no value in assessing the comparative economic efficiency of differing systems. They are indispensable for determining whether the systems being compared have attained a reasonable degree of efficiency-- i.e., a situation in which the returns to all three factors are equal in all sectors. And in this respect one can conclude only that both the Soviet and U.S. systems are inefficient. In 1970 the Soviet agricultural sector with 17.2 percent of the nation's capital stock produced 21 percent of the nation's national income, whereas in the U.S. the agricultural sector with 4.7 percent of the nation's capital stock produced 3 percent of the nation's national income.[8]

SOME HIDDEN COSTS ASSOCIATED WITH IMPROVING THE PRODUCTIVITY
OF LABOR

The low Soviet capital/output ratio vis-à-vis the
remaining sectors of the economy does suggest strong support
for the generally accepted thesis of a Soviet "neglect" of the
countryside. This neglect, however, may not be as flagrant as
the figures seem to suggest. It is clearly of no avail to
replace labor with capital and technology in a sector plagued
by labor surpluses if the vocational training facilities, the
plant and equipment, and the housing and community facilities
necessary to train, employ, and house the released workers are
not in place. And as these prerequisites for effective
investments in the agricultural sector were not in place in
the capital-short USSR, every ruble of investment in the
agriculture sector would have had to be accompanied by several
rubles of investment in other sectors, a fact that
considerably inflates the real vs. the apparent marginal
capital/output ratios. If capital is used to replace manpower
that cannot be used elsewhere, then not only has that capital
been wasted, but it can generate high costs in other sectors
as is illustrated by the U.S. experience.[9]
The above not withstanding, I recognize that one might
still make a strong case that the Soviet levels of investment
in the countryside have in fact been suboptimal. But however
large the costs of this "neglect" of agriculture may have
been, there is an abundance of evidence that seems to suggest
that they are no larger than the many high private and social
costs associated with the government largesse toward
agriculture in the U.S. As a result of a myriad of government
subsidy and subsidy-like programs, capital has been pumped
into the U.S. agricultural sector over the past few decades at
costs to the farmer that have been way below its equilibrium
price or true cost to society. Subsequently each U.S.
agricultural worker is now backed by three times as much
capital as his industrial counterpart and ten or so times as
much as his Soviet counterpart.[10] The corollary of this is a
familiar story: labor productivity soared, as did output. But
hand in hand with these increases went the creation of large
surpluses of agricultural products[11] and large surpluses of
agricultural entrepreneurs and laborers.
Between 1935 and 1965 the rural population fell by more
than 20 million persons. Each year over the course of the
period 1950-63, the replacement of labor with machinery and
technology precipitated the abandonment of an average of
145,000 farms a year and an outward migration of over a
million persons a year to nonrural areas.[12] Several millions
of these migrants headed for the large cities of the North
where they took up the tenements that were being abandoned by
middle America in its own government-subsidized trek out of
the cities, and because they had no skills that could be used

in urban industry and commerce, the rural migrants were forced into the ranks of America's many, urban unemployed, poor, hungry, and sick, and provided the critical mass for the urban explosions that ripped across America in the 60s, the burnt-out rubble of which can still be seen in so many of our cities.

The connection between the large costs, both human and economic, associated with this rubble on the one hand, and the soaring productivity of agricultural labor on the other, has been completely overlooked in every comparison of U.S. and Soviet agricultural performance that I have seen. We students of Soviet agriculture, however, must bear in mind that in any attempts we make, either explicitly or implicitly, to compare the performances of Soviet and U.S. agriculture, a large part of the cost side of the U.S. agriculture ledger will be found, not on the farms, but rather in the cities. The benefits of the capital intensification of U.S. agriculture turn up in the tables on labor productivity. A large share of the costs, however, are found in the tables on urban unemployment, poverty, hunger, crime, and violence, and the high public expenditures for welfare and law and order that are associated with urban unemployment and poverty.

THE EFFECTS OF INSTITUTIONS ON LABOR PRODUCTIVITY

In addition to differing degrees of capital intensity, soil fertility, and climate, another factor underlying the large differential in the productivity of U.S. and Soviet agricultural labor is institutional. The commonly accepted view in this respect is that collective-type farming does not offer the incentives provided by capitalist-type farming-- hence the differential. I will not argue the point of incentives. Harry G. Shaffer has dealt with it effectively.[13] The point I want to make is that the differences in labor productivity on U.S. and Soviet farms stem primarily (after abstraction for capital intensity etc.) from the methods of labor utilization.

Sovkhoz workers are full-time, year-round employees, while on the kolhoz the size of the work force, which is also year-round, is determined not by activity analysis, but rather by historical accident. On U.S. farms, on the other hand, the number of year-round, full-time employees is kept to a minimum, with migrant and/or temporary labor used to satisfy seasonal and peak demands for labor. A result of this is that in our farm-to-farm comparisons (those conducted on a micro plane) the U.S. farm appears far more efficient in its utilization of labor than does the Soviet, and it is indeed far more efficient if we view the maximization process from the viewpoint of the farm enterprise only.

31

Labor expenditures on Soviet-type farms run high because they (wages and distributions to labor) run for the entire year and cover the year-round living costs of year-round work forces. On U.S.-type farms, however, labor costs are lower because they (wages) run for only part of the year and cover the worker's living costs for only that period of time during which he is employed. The effect of Soviet-type institutions is to transform labor costs, which are variable on U.S.-type farms, into fixed costs, very high fixed costs in fact. But labor costs, when viewed from a social or macro point of view are fixed, and a U.S.-type farm, contrary to appearances, does not eliminate them. It merely externalizes them and transforms them into an even higher set of costs, those associated with high levels of underemployment among the rural labor force.

SOME COSTS PRODUCED BY INSTITUTIONAL DIFFERENCES

In 1960 underemployment in rural areas was equivalent to the full-time unemployment of 2 million persons.[14] In 1966 it was equivalent to 2.5 million unemployed.[15] In 1973 it was estimated as equivalent to the year-round unemployment of 3 million persons, and its cost in terms of lost wages was estimated to be some $22 billion.[16] If to this $22 billion one adds the government's $2.6 billion in payments to farmers, the reported net farm income of some $33 billion for 1973 (a banner year for U.S. agriculture) turns out to be a net social farm income of only $8.5 billion, or a mere 2 percent return on assets tied up in U.S. farming.[17] In 1972 net farm income was only $18 billion, clearly not enough to cover some $20 billion in opportunity costs of lost labor and some $3.9 billion in government payments. The 1972 figures thus show a net social loss of some $5.9 billion even before the deduction of agriculture's share of the urban costs which were explained in the discussion of the law of diminishing returns. While U.S.-type farming may appear to be highly efficient when compared with Soviet-type on the micro plane, that verdict does not come through quite as clearly when a comparison is made on the macro plane.

The corollary of this high rate of underemployment is low income and widespread rural poverty, together with its attendant high social costs and human suffering among rural laborers in general and extremely harsh working conditions for the migrants in particular.[18] I will not deal with these here. They have been described in innumerable government and private studies.[19] They have been widely portrayed in the media.[20] And they are highly visible to anyone traveling through the U.S. countryside. It takes an enormous amount of self-discipline not to see them. They are just one of the

32

costs of "efficiency" in the utilization of the U.S. rural
work force, which have been ignored in all of our comparisons
of U.S. and Soviet farming.

CONCLUSION

One of the high costs associated with Soviet farming has
been the low productivity of agricultural labor. That cost,
however, may simply be the price paid for avoiding the
possibly higher set of human and social costs that might have
been (and were, in the case of the U.S.) associated with rapid
capital intensification of agriculture.

ADDENDUM

The start-up costs, both economic and human, associated
with the Sovietization of the Russian countryside are among
history's highest. Half a century after they were incurred,
they remain in the scales (as they should) because they were
of an unmortizable nature. Consciously or subconsciously,
therefore, they have loomed, and continue to loom, large in
all of our U.S.-Soviet farm comparisons, and have obscured our
view of the social and human costs associated with U.S.-type
farming. These latter, consequently, are never factored into
our comparisons. Most of us feel (and perhaps quite rightly
so) that the high initial human costs, and the subsequent
economic costs of "hair-brained schemes" in the Soviet
countryside outweigh, and by such an infinitely large margin,
the accumulation over the years of all of the hidden costs
that are associated with a U.S.-type agriculture, that the
omission of the latter can in no way affect the comparisons.
Costs, however, may accumulate more rapidly than we realize,
and unless some of the human and social costs associated with
U.S.-type farming are thrown into the scales along with the
Soviet-type, we will never be able to convince disinterested
scholars that our findings (however correct they may prove to
be ultimately) were anything more than a bundle of assumptions
and an article of faith. History, one day, will examine our
comparisons and will surely ask, "Where did you post the U.S.
costs when you found that Soviet agriculture was less
efficient than U.S. agriculture?" And unless we Western
scholars are in a position to demonstrate that we did post
them, we just will not have a case we can be certain history
will bother to finish examining, let alone accept.

NOTES

1. Campbell R. McConnell, Economics: Principles, Problems and Policies, (New York: McGraw Hill Book Company, 1957), p. 900.

2. Robert W. Campbell, The Soviet-Type Economies-Performance and Evolution (Boston: Houghton Mifflin Co., 1974), p. 65.

3. Narodnoe khozyaistvo SSSR za 60 let (Moscow, 1977), p. 96. While the Soviets claim a figure of 20-25 percent, I would not want to have to defend any figure in excess of 10 percent.

4. Earl R. Brubaker, "A Sectoral Analysis of Efficiency under Market and Plan," Soviet Studies, 23, (January 1972): 440. A large factor is certainly the extreme parcelization of the land in these three nations.

5. Nancy Nimitz gave a figure of 42 percent for 1963. The thrust of her paper was that it was increasing. Nancy Nimitz, "Farm Employment 1928-1963," in Jerzy F. Karcz, ed., Soviet and East European Agriculture (Berkeley and Los Angeles: University of California Press, 1967).

6. Howard J. Sherman, The Soviet Economy (Boston: Little, Brown, and Company, 1969), p. 170, citing a Soviet source, gives a figure of 17 percent for 1966.

7. All of these figures have been derived on the basis of figures given in U.S., Congress, Joint Economic Committee, "Comparison of Farm Output in the U.S. and USSR," by F. Douglas Whitehouse and Joseph F. Havelka, Soviet Economic Prospects for the Seventies (Washington, D.C.: Government Printing Office, 1973), and figures given in the Statistical Abstract of the United States, 1976, and Narodnoe Khozyaistvo SSSR, 1972.

8. Campbell, The Soviet Type, p. 101.

9. It is of interest to note that despite the low Soviet agricultural capital/output ratio, the USSR is the world's second largest exporter of tractors and fertilizers.

10. That this level by far surpasses the optimum can be seen in a comparison of the rates of return on capital invested in U.S. agriculture and manufacturing. Over the eight-year period 1971-77 the return to equity in agriculture averaged out to 4.78 percent per year vs. 13.86 percent for all manufacturing. 22 June, 1978, Congressional Record, p. E-5918.

11. The consumer was clearly not soverign here.

12. 2.2 million migrated in the single year 1953. Statistical Abstract of the United States, 1976, p. 631.

13. Harry G. Shaffer, "Soviet Agriculture: Success or Failure," in Harry G. Shaffer, ed., Soviet Agriculture: An Assessment of Its Contribution to Economic Development (New York, London: Praeger Publishers, 1977), pp. 56-105.

14.   U.S.,   Congress,   Committee on Agriculture and Forestry, <u>Hearings before   the   sub-committee   on   Rural Development of the Committee on Agriculture and Forestry</u> (1971), Part II, p. 144.

15.   Secretary of Agriculture Orvill Freeman, Speech at a conference on rural poverty at Twin Bridges, Arlington, Virginia,   30   January   1967.   Reprinted in 27 February 1967, <u>Congressional Record</u> p. A-921.

16.   Luther Tweeten and Neal O. Walker, "Economic Cost of Poverty" in Robert O. Coppedge and   Carlton   G.   David,   eds., <u>Rural Poverty and the Policy Crisis</u> (Ames: Iowa   State University Press, 1977), p. 46.

17.   The assets of all U.S. farms that year were estimated at 387.3 billion. <u>Statistical Abstract of the United States,</u> <u>1975</u>, p. 619.

18.   Read, for example, Wayne King's account of the migrant crew leader (verified by photograph) who owns a machine gun that he periodically fires into the trees to keep the workers intimidated. <u>New York Times</u>, 28 August 1977, p. 1.

19.   As an example of each see U.S., President, National Advisory Commission on Rural Poverty, <u>The People Left Behind</u> (Washington D.C.: U.S. Government Printing Office, 1967), and U.S. Chamber of Commerce, <u>Rural Poverty and Regional Progress</u> <u>in a Urban Society</u> (1969).

20.   Can anyone forget Edward R. Murrow's searing <u>Harvest</u> <u>of Shame</u>, or the scenes from rural America depicted in CBS's <u>Hunger In America</u>?

3
Soviet Policies on Agriculture, Trade, and the Consumer

Keith Severin

INTRODUCTION

This paper was prepared for the purpose of provoking thought and stimulating discussion at the Fifth International Conference on Soviet and East European Agriculture and Peasant Affairs. It was hoped that suggestions for further research would be fruitful. Therefore, it seems best, in the opinion of the author, to retain the original informal presentation for the wider reader audience.

It was evident at the conference that a number of participants who conduct research on the USSR have had direct and recent experience in the Soviet Union. This is good and is, in all likelihood, true of today's "Soviet researchers," in general. (It was not the case, though, in 1962, when the first in the series of conferences was convened.) And we should all benefit as a result, since students of the USSR's economy ought better to be able to interpret their primary source material, largely Soviet publications. Unfortunately, however, it seems that full advantage is not being taken of these opportunities we now have.

Bringing personal observations to bear on current research gives invaluable insight and perspective to the practical problems that confront both policymakers and others who deal with the USSR and its representatives in nonacademic pursuits. Such research helps assess the probable outcome of Soviet policies and signal their effect on the society and economy of the USSR.

SOVIET POLICIES ON AGRICULTURE, TRADE, AND THE CONSUMER

From the point of view of his role as a consumer, the Soviet citizen, through the sixty years of his country's existence, has probably experienced more ups and downs and change than anyone else. The period of the revolution, the time of famine and collectivization in the 1930s, and the deprivations during and after World War II were all difficult. His lot, while by no means up to Western standards or even that of some of his East European neighbors, has been improving. The Soviet consumer has been progressively better off each succeeding year, so he has reason to believe that his government's pronouncements of still better things to come will be realized. To him, the past is indeed prologue.

Just how plans for the future will be met raises a series of interesting and rather complex questions, which this paper is directed toward. Obviously, the Soviet leadership is highly concerned. Indeed, the July 3rd plenum (1978) showed how much spadework has already been done for the period 1981-85. Recent events--the death of Fydor Kulakov and the international travels of the Chinese leader Hua Kuo-feng--may also mean that politics may enter into the picture to a larger extent than usual. Before giving a brief background, however, I would like to pose several questions in the way of a summary.

SUMMARY

The 1981-85 targets for the output of grain and of meat in the Soviet Union seem consistent with one another. But how realistic is the 238-243 million ton goal for grain? The meat target of 19.5 million tons for 1985 implies a slowdown in the planned rate of per capita output during the period, only about 1.5 percent increase annually compared with the 2.2 percent Plan figure for 1976-80.

Perhaps more importantly, the rate in growth of output will most likely not keep pace with that of growth of per capita income, further boosting the surplus of consumer purchasing power. Will the regime persist in its policy of maintaining stable retail prices for food items, even those that have some elasticity of demand? How much more can the regime afford to subsidize the well-being of its citizens in the area of food?

Will imports continue to make up about the same proportion of total grain utilization? If so, this carries an implicit assumption about the availability of hard currency.

Can improvements in the utilization of grain for feed be made so as to reduce requirements per unit of output? How will the shortage of protein feedstuffs be approached? To what extent will the "industrialization" of livestock production increase efficiency? Will the current relaxation in the state's position on private ownership of livestock improve the efficiency of output?

To what extent might improvement in forage crop production in the USSR help take up the slack in feed deficiencies for cattle?

What will U.S.-USSR relations--trade relations--be in the first half of the next decade? Will the Soviets have most-favored-nation treatment?Might they seek other (non-U.S.) sources of supply for feedstuffs, especially corn and soybeans? Perhaps they can secure a substantial part of their needs from trading partners that will provide the USSR a better, overall balanced trade.

Will the Soviet scheme of things mean a continued relative deemphasis of agricultural trade with its East European partners in the Council of Mutual Economic Assistance (CMEA)?

What connotations do the recent moves toward internationalism by the People's Republic of China carry regarding future Soviet policy and resource allocation?

How long will Brezhnev remain on the scene? What will the top Soviet leadership be in the 1980s? What will be its attitude toward consumers, agriculture, and trade? Did the outlook change with the passing of Kulakov who very likely had a paramount role in the July plenum?

These questions are all germane when one looks at how the consumer will fare in the future in the USSR. The answers depend on many of the customary things such as weather and input necessities as well as economic policies. But in this instance, international politics and even human mortality weigh more heavily than usual.

BACKGROUND - PRE-BREZHNEV

Until Khrushchev passed from the leadership scene, Soviet policies concerning agriculture and trade basically either exploited the consumer or ignored him. Beyond the occasional time, prompted by political expediency, when private plots were given some sanction, the consumer received lip service at best.

The Stalinist era emphasized heavy industry development. Agriculture paid the bill, through supplying export grain that could be ill-afforded and the entire process of collectivization. Malenkov's tenure in the Kremlin provided only brief relief for the consumer. Khrushchev will undoubtedly be remembered more as a man for agriculture than any other Soviet leader. But what did he really accomplish that redounded to the consumer? (This may be an unfair question, given the relative state of development of the entire Soviet economy, and it is certainly open to conjecture.) The fifteen-year reign of the exhuberant

Khrushchev was marked by the "plow-up" program in 1955-56 when the expansive virgin lands were brought into cultivation. This was a logical, quick way to achieve an increase in grain output. The Soviets had land, tractors, plows, and the grain drills to undertake this extensive, high-risk project. They did not have adequate fertilizer and the other necessary, more technical inputs to increase output in the traditional agricultural zone of the country. While the harvest in the new lands cannot be a sure thing (although the 1978 grain crop in Kazakhstan looks to be of record proportions), it did provide the country, if not the consumer, with a needed commodity for export.

From the time the new lands began producing in volume, say 1957, until the poor crop of 1963, the USSR's net grain exports averaged close to 7 million tons annually. In 1962 they fell to 3 million tons and then for the next three years the USSR was a net importer of grain. However, in 1967 things were reversed again and through 1971 the Soviets were exporters on a net basis. Their hard spring wheat (SKS-14) was a decided factor in the international market in the late 1960s and it enjoyed an excellent reputation with the buyers in Western Europe. The small crop of 1972 put the Soviets on the importing side of the ledger where they have since remained.

Khrushchev's biggest ploy to gain consumer support was probably his "catch-up program" that was enunciated in 1957. He announced that his country and its system would do away with the capitalists peacefully by burying them--surpassing them in the output of milk, meat, and butter. (It was instructive to compare the text of his catch-up speech as it appeared in Pravda with what was later printed in the official compendium of Khrushchev's speeches. By 1964, some changes in the rhetoric had been made, and the Soviet consumer was faring about the same as in earlier days.)

As a part of his catch-up campaign, Khrushchev's corn program, though not properly conceived nor executed for his country's agroclimatic conditions, has had some carry-over effect. In the 1950s corn seeding became nearly universal in the Soviet Union. In 1962 it topped out with 37 million hectares--30 million for roughage and 7 million for grain. Before Khrushchev's program, the Moldavians were about the only ones in the USSR who knew what corn was.

The corn program has broadened Soviet contacts with the West. For example, breeding programs, coordinated with international bodies, as well as commercial seed firms, have been developed. Soviet officials told a U.S. agricultural exchange team that one of the things they plan to do to implement that part of the July plenum that deals with increasing feed production is to apply "corn-for-grain technology" to the total area seeded to corn. They contend that in the event of a good growing season, therefore, at least part of the 15-18 million hectares of corn seeded for silage and greenchop would yield grain.[1] The U.S. team observed that the Soviets appear to be making good progress in their drought-resistance breeding program for corn.

THE BREZHNEV ERA

At the time of Khrushchev's departure from the Kremlin in October 1964, the Soviet Union was ready for a change. The leadership was caught up in a wave of ever-increasing pressure from the outside world. For exmple, they could not prevent the Voice of America from being transmitted into the USSR and being heard. Therefore, a controlled relaxation of some constraints began to occur. Agriculture was still quite predominant in the economy, but it had been stagnant for several years. Moreover, the crop in 1963 had been so poor that grain imports were necessary, the hog herd was severely reduced, bread had been in relatively short supply (its quality was poor, too), and reportedly, even the vodka was not up to par. Therefore, in many ways the country was ready for a change, and Brezhnev was to provide it.

The advocacy of consumerism by Brezhnev is well known, and it was given considerable impetus in the March 1965 plenum. That meeting of the central committee set forth the guidelines for agriculture for the rest of the decade. From the important eight to ten announcements from the plenum, which still maintains its hallmark stature, it was easy to deduce that incentives to increase output were being given to agriculture. Among them, state purchase prices for meat and milk were increased; bonuses for above-Plan delivery of grain were to be paid; investment in agriculture was to be stepped up markedly; procurement goals for grain and livestock products were reduced; and the private ownership of livestock was made less restrictive. These last two noted items were to benefit the consumer, which should be expected from the plenum that "ushered in a new stage in the development of the Leninist agrarian policy of the Party." As a manifestation of this policy, agriculture's budget for 1965 was planned at a deficit of 5.2 billion rubles. (Ten years later, continued investment and reduced profit taking by the state resulted in a net deficit of 16.6 billion rubles for the agricultural sector.) Thus the 1965 plenum was a clear commitment by Brezhnev to elevate the priority of agriculture vis-à-vis industry and thereby bring about an improvement in the diet of the Soviet citizen.

Ironically, although perhaps not too much so when all is considered, Khrushchev's first major speech, in September 1953, also had hit upon the necessity to improve agriculture, because its abundance was a prerequisite for solving the problems of building a communist society. Khrushchev's approach to achieving this abundance, though, was to extend agriculture. Brezhnev, on the other hand, and who admittedly was operating a later stage of development, chose to intensify it.

At the Twenty-Fifth Party Congress, in March 1976, another blow was struck for the consumer, but in an oblique way. While no growth in the per capita consumption during 1976-80 was foreseen, it was stated that the main task continued to be raising the material and cultural well-being of the citizenry. Average per capita consumption was set to grow 3.2 percent annually, the same as in 1971-75 and certainly less than the 4.7 percent that had been achieved during the 1966-70 Plan, which had been Brezhnev's first. Perhaps in setting a low target for 1976-80, account was taken of how poor harvests (1972 and 1975) could affect output and, therefore, consumption. The 1976-80 planned growth figure for agriculture was 5.5 percent, as compared with the planned 3.5 percent and an actual -0.6 percent of the preceding five-year period.

The tenth five-year Plan was notable in that the rate of investment for the entire economy was to be slowed sharply from the previous plan period. Agriculture, therefore, would expect an average annual investment of only 3.4 percent, less than half the 9.7 percent rates in the two preceding Plans. The planned smaller investment in agriculture translated into a slowdown in deliveries of the major forms of inputs including equipment and fertilizer, especially the former. The planned situation regarding investment was not as bleak as it appeared, however, because Brezhnev expressed determination that more attention should be paid to quality of inputs--all inputs, including labor--rather than strictly to quantity. With the aim of increasing productivity, the Soviet leader reiterated a statement made in 1973 concerning the need to bring industrial methods into more active use in agriculture. The Plan for 1980 is that 80 percent of the eggs, 30 percent of the pork, and 14 percent of the milk and beef produced in the USSR are to result from "industrialized" methods. This carries a strong implication of dependence on an assured supply of feed.

Before we move on to more recent happenings in the USSR, it is interesting to note the recognition that one of the practical aspects of consumerism has been receiving. As stated earlier, Khrushchev said that an abundance of milk, meat, and eggs is necessary to help overcome problems in building communism. At the Twenty-Fifth Party Congress, two and a half years ago, Brezhnev remarked that a shortage of consumer goods could result in the Plan not being fulfilled because of a lack of incentive. More recently, in the May-June 1978 issue of the Economic Series of _Izvestia_ of the USSR Academy of Science, an article by N. A. Shokin said much the same thing, only in theoretical terms. The article deals with

42

the necessity, at least in the long term, of improving public welfare and not letting consumption suffer continually to the benefit of capital accumulation. The author emphasizes that socioeconomic factors play a definite role in raising the level of labor productivity and, consequently, economic efficiency. He states also that the growth of monetary income does not in itself mean a rise in the real standard of living. This has very interesting connotations for the period ahead, particularly if per capita income continues to outstrip per capita availability of those food items that have some elasticity of demand. In that regard, Shokin advocates that public demand and purchasing power should be equated to "available resources." The ramifications of this could be significant. He concludes that the worst impact on society a deficit of consumer goods can have is to create speculation in scarce commodities and the use of private plots for speculative purposes. These are all interesting thoughts, and all the more so because of their currency and apparent officiality.

THE PLENUM OF JULY 1978 - ITS AIMS

"On the Further Development of USSR Agriculture" was the title of the report Chairman Brezhnev presented on July 3 to the central committee CPSU. The report basically put down the groundwork, and gave several important targets, for the eleventh five-year Plan. Since the plan period won't begin until 1981, why the meeting so early? Why the long lead time? The opinion most commonly offered is that because so much of the economy's total performance hinges on the success of agriculture, it is necessary to get the initial stages of planning underway at the earliest moment in order that policymakers can set appropriate priorities for the entire economic Plan, as well as for some of agriculture's needs. In this regard, in late August the central committee issued a decree to the several machine building industries to prepare themselves for a plenum in March 1979 when plans for their development in 1981-85 and 1986-90 would be discussed. Foremost here is the view to upgrade the level of productivity and automation so as to reduce the number of workers in manual, nonautomated jobs. There can be little doubt that Soviet agriculture received much attention at these meetings, since it still requires considerable hand labor for tasks that are mechanized in other parts of the world and detracts from productivity. Cotton is but one prime example.

The Soviet countryside took almost immediate steps last summer to consider how to meet the tasks set out in the decree issued after the plenum. Before the end of July, slogans, banners, and signs about the plenum were prominent at farms far away from Moscow. By early August, the press carried reports of plenums of oblast committees in Uzbekistan and other republics. These meetings in Central Asia are significant, since cotton is among the leading exports from the USSR and its production is not fully mechanized.

Few precise goals were actually given by Brezhnev for 1981-85 at the plenum. He did say, however, that meat production will receive top priority, meaning that the consumer is apparently still in mind. The target for meat output in 1985 is 19.5 million tons, which, while consistent with the average annual grain target of 238-243 million tons, is modest. The increase in per capita production of meat implied for the Plan period depends on the level of output achieved in 1980, the last year of the current Plan period. At best, however, it is doubtful that the new rate of increase can exceed that achieved heretofore under Brezhnev which has been about 2.5 percent per year.

It is important to note that in all likelihood the growth in meat output per capita will be exceeded by increases in income. The average annual increase in per capita disposable income in the current five-year Plan is set at 3.7 percent. In 1966-70, it was 6.8 percent and in 1971-75 it was 4.9 percent. Thus, it can be seen in comparing the growth rates for meat output and income that a surplus of purchasing power has existed during Brezhnev's reign. There is no plan to reduce demand pressure though, as it appears that the policy of not raising retail prices will be maintained. (In June 1962, Khrushchev decreed a 30 percent increase in retail meat prices, and it created strong consumer protest.) Procurement prices for milk, wool, mutton, potatoes, and some vegetables will be raised in January 1979, but there will be no price increase at the retail level. The cost of the subsidy for the difference between procurement and retail prices for meat and milk alone is estimated at 100 billion rubles for the current five-year Plan period. This gap is easily seen widening in the years to come. The retail price of beef is reportedly 1.65 rubles per kilo,compared with the price to the state of 3.21 rubles. The subsidy for butter amounts to 1.24 rubles per kilo, and for cottage cheese it is 35 kopecks.

In the July plenum Brezhnev was rather explicit in his lengthy remarks on the livestock sector. Mainly he hit at the persistent feed inadequacies. He was critical of the techniques used to harvest and store roughages, saying that 20 to 30 percent of the nutritive value is lost. Grain is used inefficiently in rations that are short on protein by as much as 20 to 30 percent, with the result that rates of gain are low. Also, the mixed feed industry is still relatively underdeveloped to meet its needs. The expected solutions to these perennial problems were proposed. Beyond them though, recent U.S. exchange teams to the USSR were impressed that very active consideration is being given to what Chairman Brezhnev said. For example, the plan is to increase soybean acreage by 300,000 hectares in the western part of the country and on irrigated land. The Soviets are actively seeking help on this from U.S. specialists. It is recalled that in December 1977 a decree was issued with the aim of expanding soybean output. Also, rape and lupine are being investigated as sources of oilseed meals. Another example is that the nagging problem of being unable to produce seed for grain sorghum is being worked on, in both the technical and applied aspects, again using specialists from the U.S. and other Western countries.

Private plots are a significant source--"a vital source"--of food, according to one point made by Brezhnev in his plenum speech. He reiterated his position of October 1976 that individuals should be able to obtain young livestock and the feed for them from state and collective farms. Last year in Brezhnev's speech on the draft of the new constitution, private plots seemed to be assured a continued existence, which should help both production and procurement planners. The July plenum took this to more concrete terms when the chairman addressed the need for a new form of rural housing. He said that families living on farms should have separate, individual dwellings with garden plots and buildings for livestock. (I noted in August on a state farm near Ufa that this policy was already being implemented.) This seems to spell the demise of further construction of apartment buildings on farms.

The grain target for 1981-85 seems rather unrealistic, as noted above. Achievement of an annual average production of 238-243 million tons looks rather difficult. Good weather must be assumed, as well as the availability of fertilizer and other inputs that will contribute materially to higher yields. The planned fertilizer-delivery growth rate for 1981-85 is lower than that for the current five-year period, and there is some real doubt whether the 1980 target will be met. No mention of reducing fallow or bringing more land into cultivation has been made.

The 238-243 million-ton grain target looks consistent with the 19.5 million-ton meat goal for 1985. But what if grain production falls short? Will imports be made? As long as the present policy and leadership prevail, the answer seems to be, "Yes." The decision to use foreign trade as the means to make dietary improvements in the lives of the Soviets has been seen in the 1970s. This followed the apparently serious announcement by the current leadership that such policy would be one of the goals of the ninth five-year Plan (1971-75). Supply-utilization data for grain in the 1970s show this was the policy.

Food, seed, and industrial usages of grain this decade have remained constant for all intents and purposes. However, in order to keep the feed element in the equation as close as possible to the requisite level, large volumes of grain were

45

imported as the consequence of the crop shortfalls in 1972 and 1975. Of course, stock reductions were made, too, but the important thing is that the crop shortfalls were in the main compensated for by imports. Even last year when the grain crop was 196 million tons, net grain imports were high--21 million tons--the same as after the small crop in 1972. It is recognized, naturally, that the livestock herd in 1977 was substantially larger than six years earlier, and estimated feed use of grain was 20 percent higher--120 million tons compared with the earlier figure of 98 million. In this regard a Soviet official recently noted that the level of what they may import in a given year should not necessarily be tied to grain production that year. The inference is that imports could be used for stock replenishment, a most logical possibility, all factors considered. Partly for this reason, as well as for increased feed requirements, the USDA is currently estimating 1978-79 net Soviet grain imports at 14 million tons, along with a near-record crop of 220. Should the estimated supply-distribution prove correct, total grain utilization would be at an all-time high of 233 million tons, including 125 million for feed. It is clear, therefore, that the principle of using imports to help bring about an improvement in the Soviet diet has been adhered to since its enunciation in the ninth five-year Plan.

As to the possible sources of grain imports by the Soviets, the U.S.-USSR Grains Agreement is beginning its third year of operation. Signed in 1975 and negotiated with the view of bringing some stability to the world market when the Soviets buy grain, the agreement came into force October 1, 1976, and runs for five years. Basically, the Soviets are to purchase a minimum of six million tons--half wheat and half corn--from the United States each year. Should they choose to buy more than eight million tons, however, the agreement stipulates that they must consult. Given the U.S. domestic supply situation the last two years, the Soviets, at the fall consultations, were informed that they could purchase up to 15 million tons without consultation. In 1976-77 the purchases amounted to just over 6 million tons--the minimum--and in the year just ended, the total was nearly 15 million tons--3.5 wheat and the remainder, corn. The value of those exports for those two years was $1 billion and $2.9 billion, respectively.

Circumstances are favorable at the present for the USSR to continue to rely on the United States as the main source of their grain import needs. Beyond the fact that the U.S. has ample supplies and is a big producer with all-season ports that have considerable capacity, the SALT talks have gone well, which is a consideration. Also, during the summer of 1978, when overall relations between the two countries were strained, agricultural relations were as good as they have ever been.

Moving on from imports, it would be well to note a couple of items that can influence the grain balance relationships in the USSR. Winter wheat is the crop that takes precedence in the USSR. Any crops grown in rotation with it are subordinated to its cultural requirements. (This is one reason why grain sorghum acreage is limited in some areas where it would at first appear to be a good feed crop to be grown.) Efforts are also being made to extend the area of winter-wheat production northward. To the extent that a successful winter-wheat crop can be grown--and it does outyield spring wheat and is less risky--a larger acreage can be devoted to spring barley. Obviously, this helps the grain balance.

The USSR has some 370 million hectares of pastures and meadows that could be improved, not including land above the Artic Circle. Soviet specialists contend this could be done easily by improving the stands through clipping, fertilizing, liming, interseeding, irrigating, and so forth. In the last decade, reportedly, some 17 million hectares of such lands have been improved. These pastures and meadows, however, are generally remote and, in the opinion of some, not suited to the current Soviet system of keeping livestock. Here, though, the Soviets say they are interested in fast, temporary fencing techniques. Still, a large, untapped resource that could augment forage supplies exists. The Soviets say they have at least as much interest in raising and improving forages as they have in producing grains for feed.

THE NEW LEADERSHIP??

Here is the 64-ruble question everyone is asking. With the passing of Brezhnev a whole era will have gone, for as Ambassador Foy Kohler said, "Brezhnev is the last of the Stalinists." But, as noted, Brezhnev has done much for the Soviet citizen. In my own mind, and to a large degree based on what I have seen in my travels in the Soviet Union over the last fifteen years, I contend that Brezhnev wants to go down in Soviet history as second only to Lenin. This is evident in many ways; the way he is being propagandized, how he shows up next to Lenin at the memorial in Ulyanovsk, the role he played in the defense of the hero city of Novorossisk in the Malaya Zemlya, how he is portrayed in the Tretyakov Gallery, and, of course, his real achievements where the consumer is concerned. Succeeding him could be difficult.

Whoever follows Brezhnev will indeed have a challenge--at least he will have to decide whether to ignore or implement what Brezhnev said at the plenum in July. "The resolution of the big and complex tasks put forward by the Central Committee in the field of agriculture will make it possible to raise the well-being of the people to a new stage."

47

NOTES

1.   While there are other differences in technology between growing corn for grain and corn for roughage, the main one is that fields seeded for roughage have a much higher plant density in order to maximize green mass.

4
The Crop Policy of the Soviet Union: Present Characteristics and Future Perspectives

Chantal Beaucourt

Crop production is one of the key problems of the Soviet economy: harvest fluctuations are a heavy burden on its growth, and for the last few years, the massive purchases of grain from Western countries have increased the deficit in the Soviet balance of payments vis-à-vis the West. The problem is rendered even more acute by the fact that enormous resources have been allocated to the agricultural sector in the last fifteen years. The recent party plenum devoted to the perspectives of agricultural development, as well as the measures taken since, attest to the importance that Soviet leaders attach to this problem. They also give us interesting insight into the orientation of Soviet agricultural and crop policy in the 1980s.[1]

Here, we shall examine these evolutions in the light of broad traditional orientations of Soviet crop policy. In particular, we shall look at how grain and meat production and consumption will adjust in the next decade, what repercussions this will have on ensuring an adequate supply for the USSR's East European partners, and finally, the impact on the Western grain market. We shall then see that Soviet forecast for grain and meat consumption and the production objectives follow a trend that allows the country to meet its population's "normative" needs in these products by 1990.

PRINCIPAL ELEMENTS OF SOVIET CROP POLICY

The Objectives

Basically, Soviet crop policy has been, and is, conditioned by two permanent objectives: the desire for self-sufficiency and the search for stability in production.

Soviet economic leaders have always considered cereals, and wheat in particular, to be a "strategic" product, for which national self-sufficiency must be guaranteed. After World War II the concept of self-sufficiency was extended to cover the needs of East European countries. This concept has two important consequences for the Soviet economy. First, to the extent that economic criteria alone do not guide decision making and planning choices, certain measures to increase crop production are adopted irrespective of cost. Thus, for instance, the virgin lands campaign in the 1950s gave rise to much controversy on this point. Second, this goal explains the orientation of Soviet grain trade: as long as its partners cannot totally cover their consymption needs, they have priority on Soviet wheat shipments.[2] This trade orientation, however, has a two-fold impact on Soviet financial resources. On the one hand, the East European countries pay for Soviet cereals in rubles, and this trade thus deprives the USSR of hard currency required for buying the Western capital goods it needs. On the other hand, to honor its commitments to its partners in the case of poor harvests, the USSR is forced to augment its resources by a corresponding increase in hard currency imports of grain. (See table 4.1.) But neither the structure of crop trade, nor grain redistribution within the USSR can explain Soviet intervention in the East-European grain "market."[3]

The second fundamental objective of Soviet crop policy--harvest stability--ensues partly from the first to the extent that production in difficult or uncertain conditions is accepted for reasons of self-sufficiency. Cereals make up about one-third of Soviet agricultural production, and thus, wide fluctuations in harvests have a considerable impact on overall economic growth (table 4.2).

The Strategies

While the objectives have remained basically unchanged, the general conditions for their realization have undergone considerable modification since the 1960s. There are, in fact, two ways of seeking self-sufficiency: one is to subordinate consumption demand to supply policies; the other is to seek an adjustment of internal resources to consumption needs. Soviet crop policy has successively followed first one and then the other.

Up to 1964, the first orientation predominated. Crop self-sufficiency was assured by a supply policy that was harsh for the consumer. The development of production was hampered by the limited material and financial means devoted to agriculture; exports had priority over internal consumption.[4] The pressure on the consumer, particularly strong during the Stalinist period since exports were kept up even during years of famine, was let up somewhat

TABLE 4.1
Geographical Distribution of Soviet Grain Trade (in Million Metric Tons)

	1971		1972		1973		1974		1975		1976	
	Wheat	Grain	Wheat	Grain	Wheat	Grain	Wheat	Grain	Wheat	Grain	Wheat	Grain
Total exports to:	7.61	8.64	3.89	4.56	4.19	4.80	5.26	7.03	2.66	3.57	0.808	1.468
GDR	1.85	1.91	1.047	1.066	0.88	0.978	1.078	1.42	0.577	0.72	...	0.187
Poland	1.90	2.13	0.956	1.180	0.96	1.069	1.605	1.89	0.763	1.01	...	0.269
Czechoslovakia	1.18	1.49	0.898	1.091	0.76	1.094	0.412	0.67	0.505	0.58	...	0.056
Hungary	0.37	0.43	...	...	...	...	...	...	...	...	...	...
Total Eastern Europe	5.31	5.95	2.901	3.33	2.59	3.141	3.095	3.99	1.845	2.31	0	0.512
Korean Dem. Republic	...	...	...	...	...	...	...	...	...	...	0.213	0.213
Cuba	...	...	...	...	...	...	...	...	...	...	0.389	0.537
Total imports from:	2.30	3.50	8.1	15.5	15.2	23.9	2.70	7.1	9.14	15.9	6.686	20.638
U.S.	...	...	2.41	...	9.84	...	11.32	...	3.81	7.1	2.052	11.962
Canada	1.80[a]	...	3.99	...	3.53	...	0.41	...	2.19	3.0	2.038	3.099
France	0.20	...	0.53	...	0.34	...	...	...	...	0.20	...	0.339
Hungary	...	...		0.100	0.15[b]	0.543	0.117	0.137	0.674	0.85	0.020	0.421
Argentina	...	...	...	...	...	...	...	...	0.810	1.764	0.961	1.261
Net exports to:	+5.3	+5.1	-4.2	-11.0	-11.0	-19.1	+2.6	...	-6.48	-12.3	-5.878	-19.170
Eastern Europe	5.31	5.95	2.901	3.230	2.44	2.598	2.978	3.85	1.171	1.46	-0.020	+0.091

a +0.30 Wheat Flour
b Romania : 0.183

51

TABLE 4.2
Variations in the Grain Crop and GNP Growth - USSR

					Preceding Year = 100						
	1963	1964	1965	1966	1970	1972	1973	1974	1975	1976	1977
Annual rate of growth GNP (in constant prices)	104	109.3	106.9	108.1	109	103.9	108.9	105.4	104.5	105	104.5
Agricultural production[a] (in constant prices)	92.5	114.5	101.9	108.7	104.5	96	116	97.6	94.7	104.1	102.9
Grain crop	77	141	80	141	111.5	92.8	132	88	71.5	160	87.5

Source: Narodnoe khozvaistvo SSSR.

[a] Gross output. The gap between GNP and the share of GNP created in agriculture (in current prices) are about the same. It would be much greater if agriculture and food industry were excluded from GNP. We must also take into account that the impact of the variations in the grain crop on food production lasts for two years.

52

under N. S. Khrushchev; the cultivation of the virgin lands[5] resulted in a "take-off" for crop production. Nevertheless, exports were increasing considerably as well, whereas human grain consumption was decreasing; this decrease was compensated for only by a very slight growth in meat consumption.

We can consider 1964-65 as an intermediate period during which Khrushchev's policies were reexamined, particularly after the catastrophic harvest of 1963,[6] and where the new orientations characterizing the "Brezhnev era" were defined. This stage culminates in 1966 in a new concept of agricultural development, which modifies considerably the implications of the self-sufficiency objective. Indeed, the effort is now directed toward raising crop production to a level sufficient for satisfying growing demand.

In fact, the crop policy of the eighth and ninth five-year Plans is in line with the two broad options adopted in March 1966 during the Twenty-Third Party Congress: (1) To the extent that "raising the standard of living" was chosen as one of the fundamental objectives of the eighth five-year Plan, it followed that the need for grain would greatly increase. In a "quasi-developed" economy, better consumption means, as a first step, an improvement in the quantity and quality of agricultural products supplied; in particular, the consumption of meat increases. Given the relative scarcity of substitution goods and protein products in the USSR, feed grain needs increase proportionately.[7] (2) Simultaneously, the emphasis placed on "efficiency" and the choice of an intensive type of development incited the planners to concentrate material and financial resources on the agricultural sector, perennially lagging in the Soviet economy. The "industrialization" of this sector concerned, in the first instance, grain production. Machines, fertilizers, and land improvement were intended to increase the volume and stability of harvests. It was hoped that all this would raise grain production sufficiently to cover a rise in internal demand and external requirements, also relatively high.

The Results of 1965-75

In order to evaluate the results of this new orientation in the policy of self-sufficiency, we must distinguish clearly between two periods: (1) From 1966 to 1970, the country's crop needs increased considerably along with meat consumption, which went from forty-one kg per capita in 1965 to forty-eight kg in 1970. At the same time, crop production progressed rapidly as well and enabled the USSR not only to satisfy its internal needs, but also to dispose of large surpluses for export. The Soviet Union resumed its role of net grain exporter, and even while maintaining shipments to its partners, it supplied certain Western countries.[8] (2) From

1971 to 1975, conversely, the targeted crop production figures set out in the ninth five-year Plan were far from being reached, whereas consumption continued to increase as much as foreseen.[9]

Where the harvests expected by the planners should have sufficed, by a wide margin, to satisfy both internal and external needs, and to ensure self-sufficiency, Soviet economic leaders thus found themselves faced with a "gap" of some 13 million tons per year on average for the period.[10] This time, however, in contrast to pre-1965 policies, in order to keep up with foreseen consumption growth, cattle slaughter was limited and massive grain imports were resorted to. During 1971-75, the USSR had to import some 37 million tons of grain[11] to cover its own needs. At the same time, harvest fluctuations increased and led to much wastage because of inadequate transport and storage facilities.[12] Moreover, increased production was tied to high investment costs; 131 billion rubles were poured into agriculture instead of the 128 billion originally planned. This had important consequences for the grain supplied to Soviet partners: shipments of Soviet grain decreased regularly from 1971 to 1975, and the proportion of grain and wheat of Soviet origin in the total supply of East European countries similarly diminished. Thus, these countries became less dependent on shipments from the USSR for their grain supply (table 4.3).

FUTURE PROSPECTS

Thus, since 1965, the agricultural problem and in particular, grain policy, have been set in new terms dealing with both production and needs. But the planners had not found a solution, and it was interesting to see how Soviet leaders would handle the situation[13] at the onset of the new five-year period. The elaboration of the tenth Plan could have been an occasion for radical modifications in policy orientations. In fact, the two fundamental objectives of crop policy-bloc self-sufficiency and harvest stability are maintained. This appears clearly in L. Brezhnev's reports at the party's Twenty-Fifth Congress and last July's plenum as well as in the reports of various East European leaders during the adoption of their respective five-year Plans. Not so long ago, A. Kosygin referred to the "security of self-sufficiency for grain" and this security is one of the main goals of CMEA's long-term integrated agricultural program. Similarly, the general framework for self-sufficiency is unchanged. The emphasis is on satisfying rapidly increasing needs through increased production resulting from adequate means devoted to the agricultural sector: "we must strongly uphold the CP's

TABLE 4.3
The Degree of Grain Dependence of the Six European Countries

	1971	1972	1973	1974	1975	1976
All grains (as a percentage of C)[a]						
Import Total	12.0	11.9	10.3	10.9	11.3	16.2
Net import	10.0	8.9	7.1	7.0	7.7	11.3
Total import from USSR	7.8	4.0	3.9	4.8	3.8	0.6
Net import from USSR	7.8	3.9	3.3	4.6	1.9	...
Wheat (as a percentage of C)[a]						
Import total	18.8	15.5	14.1	12.5	13.2	16.4
Net import	16.7	10.5	9.9	6.8	5.9	8.7
Total import from USSR	18.1	10.1	8.8	10.1	7.3	0
Net import from USSR	18.1	9.8	8.3	10.0	4.6	0

[a] C = Apparent consumption (Production - net exports).

55

principle of a systematic increase in investments for agriculture; their share in overall investment will not be less, in 1981-85, than in the tenth five-year Plan."[14]

There does appear, however, a new element in crop policy, the impact of which may not be felt deeply during the tenth Plan but which could profoundly transform the USSR crop situation and trade prospects in the next decade; this element is the effort to improve distribution.

Mid-term Prospects: 1976-1980

Whether we look at the "fundamental orientations for development in 1976-80" or at the objectives finally adopted in October 1976, agriculture remains a high priority sector for Soviet development during 1976-80. This period must be characterized by "decisive efforts" to resolve the agricultural problem. This "priority to agriculture" policy is implemented by a higher percentage of investment devoted to the sector: more than 26 percent in the current Plan as against 22 percent in the ninth five-year Plan.[15] At the same time, in L. Brezhnev's own terms, crop production is the "key sector": "the most important task of agriculture," he specifies, "is to increase, by all possible means, crop production, and the stability of harvests."

The target for increased crop production is ambitious: by more than 20 percent during the whole period[16] whereas the growth rate attained in 1971-75 was 8.3 percent (the Plan had set 16 percent). Nonetheless, meat production and livestock grain consumption are not to increase by much.[17] The consumer, though, should not suffer too much since his meat consumption is to increase at the same rate as that in the previous five-year Plan.[18]

At first sight, it would thus appear that by attaining its production target, the USSR would be able to provide for its own grain consumption even if the harvest followed the "minimum" line in the production plan. Besides, the 1976 and 1977[19] harvest results and the favorable forecasts for the 1978 season augur well for the realization of this alternative in the crop production plan. There are two factors, however, that must not be neglected: on the one hand, the USSR needs to replenish its stocks, probably close to exhaustion at the beginning of the period; on the other, it wants to meet the import needs of its partners. Thus, even if the production target is met, the USSR will be forced to import from the West, at least the minimum it is committed to by virtue of its contract with the USA. Moreover, the possibility of harvest fluctuations as great as those of past years cannot be excluded; this could prompt the Soviet Union to import even greater amounts during a bad harvest.

Soviet Crop Prospects in the 1980s

In order to assess the longer-term situation, we have proceeded as follows. We started by trying to determine the grain production and consumption goals that Soviet planners set for themselves in 1980-90. We then estimated their chance of success in terms of what implications these goals had at the level of yields. Finally, we tried to anticipate the impact on foreign grain trade if the USSR in fact balances production and consumption.

For the eleventh five-year Plan, L. Brezhnev announced a rather modest target rate for production growth--around 2 percent per annum.[20] But to obtain, by 1990, a harvest of 292 million tons which corresponds to a level of production of one ton per inhabitant,[21] the growth rate with reference to 1985 would have to be about 2.4 percent per annum. These are hardly spectacular performances. In fact, this means that, assuming sown areas remain unchanged, crop yields will reach 18.8 centners per hectare in 1981-85 and 22-23 centners per hectare in 1986-90.[22] There are many ways to increase crop yields: increase fertilizer, produce more efficient machinery in greater quantities, improve and reclaim land, and so on.

Although Soviet production and use of mineral fertilizers have been increasing rapidly, from the global perspective, the quantity used per hectare sown to grain in the seventies was estimated at half that required. In 1976-80 planners hope that more intensive use of fertilizers will account for more than half of the increase in the Soviet crop harvest. However, the optimum level still will not have been reached, and if we concur with certain Soviet experts that each additional ton of fertilizer increases the output by 1.1 - 1.4 tons of grain, there still will be considerable potential for greater production.

In 1980, 115 million tons of mineral fertilizer are to be supplied to Soviet agriculture, of which 47 million are destined for cereals (the latter also receive one-third of all organic fertilizers). In 1981-85 the use of mineral fertilizers should rise to 135-50 million tons. Moreover, these fertilizers could be used with greater efficiency and their quality improved. Today 20 percent of the chemical production is considered of "quality" standards, but only 8 percent of the mineral fertilizer is in this category,[23] and the losses of production in transport and storage range over 6 percent.[24]

The development of agricultural machinery could be very beneficial. The deficit in the production of cereals due to the lack of machinery during the harvest is estimated at 35-40 million tons.[25] From another source we learn that grain combines work at only two-thirds of their capacity and cannot be transferred from one region to another where needed because of the lack of transport.[26] In any case, such transfers of agricultural machinery from southern regions, to the Urals, and then to Siberia, are expensive and delay harvest.

On improved land, the yield per hectare is estimated to be three times as high as the yield on nonimproved land. But there is little improved land and it accounts for only a quarter of the production. In 1976-80, however, in view of the important investments devoted to irrigation and drainage, improved land must account for two-fifths of the additional agricultural production; 3.9 million hectares of irrigated land should produce 14 million additional tons of grain, and the 7 million planned hectares of improved land, 22 million additional tons of grain.[27]

The possibilities of increasing grain yields and areas sown to grain have been estimatd by Soviet experts (Institute for Study of Soils, V. V. Dokucaev, Institute for Study of Soil Resources, s.o.p.s. of Academy of Sciences); their evaluations by region and type of soil are the result of lengthy research and allow us to conclude that, with technological improvements in conjunction with adequate measures (particularly soil drainage in the forests zone) the expected grain yields could be, from twelve to fifteen centners per hectare depending on the type of soil, and twenty-four centners per hectare on average for the Soviet Union.[28] The inclusion of fallowed land, in dry regions, could allow a grain yield of 50-55 centners per hectare i.e. an increase of 55-60 million tons of winter cereals.[29]

As a result, the harvest could reach an average of 310 million tons, (280-335 million tons) and could meet entirely the population's requirements, even in the long term (twenty to thirty years) but with the minimum demographic projection. Furthermore, increase of area sown to grain could ensure a volume of production sufficient to cover the population's requirements with the maximum estimate of demographic growth. Although it is admitted that these results will be very costly, particularly for irrigation and land improvement, we can presume that recourse will be made to at least some of the above measures to improve yields.[30]

Of the various elements that make up internal grain consumption, only one should undergo considerable change, that is animal consumption. In fact, the evolution in the grain-demand structure, already apparent in the last decade, is being accentuated.[31] Total human consumption shifts little if at all. The reduction in per capita grain consumption, which falls from 140-44 kg in the 1975-80 period to 120 kg in 1990 compensates for population growth.[32] The volume of grain needed for seed should not change by much either if we accept the figures given by L. Brezhnev, indicating relatively little increase in area to be sown to grain in the 1980s. In contrast, livestock feed needs will increase considerably, especially in the latter half of the decade. Despite the effort to satisfy the needs for high-protein feeds (in

58

particular, by increasing the production of soya and lucerne), livestock feed will be composed mainly of grain, as during 1976-80.[33] We can thus estimate that the cattle grain consumption will follow meat production trends. With the eleventh Plan, the latter should increase rapidly.[34] If by 1990 the USSR succeeds in covering its population's "normative" needs for meat (it would then need 24 million tons), the grain needs for livestock should increase even more rapidly.

Impact on External Trade

We can regroup these elements into balance-sheets to try to determine the extent to which the country's grain needs will be met during the next decade and with what consequences on the crop market. If we keep to the figures presented in table 4.4, it appears that the realization of crop production and consumption goals will ensure the USSR's self-sufficiency in the course of the next decade. The USSR would even dispose of a surplus of at least 2 to 7 million tons per year during 1981-85 and 7 million tons during 1986-90.[35]

To assess the real situation however, we must take into account two elements of contrary effects that could force a complete revision of these initial observations. On the one hand, the volume of crop needs set forth in our first hypothesis can be considered as a maximum level to the extent that it is calculated on the basis of a rate of "losses" equivalent to that of the current period and of an equally constant structure of livestock feed and yield.[36] But if, for instance, the rate of "losses" is reduced from 15 to 10 percent, available resources are augmented by 13 to 15 million tons. On the other hand, the evaluation of trade prospects may turn out to be erroneous due to the fact that the calculations are based on annual averages.[37] Under current transport and storage conditions in the Soviet Union, the more abundant the harvest, the higher the losses,[38] and there can be no compensation between good and bad harvests. If harvest fluctuations of the magnitude observed during 1971-75 persist in the course of succeeding five-year periods, they will render the USSR again greatly dependent on the Western market during poor harvest.[39] Thus, harvest instability is, once more, the crucial factor in defining trade needs.

Eight out of the eighteen economic regions of the USSR produce about 85 percent of the grain (on average, for each of the three last five-year periods), and are responsible for 100 percent of the variations in the grain crop relative to the average production (table 4.5). But in fact four of them have

TABLE 4.4
Past and Projected USSR Grain Balances, 1971-90 (in Million Metric Tons)

	1971-1975 (Annual Average)	1976-1980 (Annual Average)	1980	1981-1985 (Annual Average)	1985	1986-1990 (Annual Average)	1990
Gross output[a] Internal consumption[b]	181.5	217.5	235	238-243	260	270	292
Human and industrial consumption	50	50.5	51	50	48.5	47	44.5
Feed	97	105.0	112	124 (106)[d]	136 (117)[d]	150 (128)[d]	167 (143)[d]
Seed	25	26.0	26	26	26	26	25
Waste	27[a]	32.5	35.5	36	39	40 (27)[f]	43.5 (29)[f]
Total	199	214	224.5	236	249.5[e]	263	279 (216.5)[h]
Balance[g]	-17.5[b]	+3.5[c]	+10.5[c]	+2→+7(+18)[h]	+10.5	+7 (+42)[h]	+13.0(+75.5)[h]

[a] With a rate of losses estimated at 15 percent of gross production.

[b] Of which net exports = stock changes = -10.0 million tons.

[c] If we take into account the need to replenish the stocks, the balance becomes negative; we must also include the USSR export requirements for its partners which reduces this balance correspondingly.

[d] Hypothesis where the grain requirements per ton of meat diminishes (ratio 6 : 1) The figures in parentheses reflect projected levels under the hypothesis.

[e] The level of grain needs in 1985 has been estimated at 900 kg per capita by Soviet experts. It corresponds to a total grain consumption of 252 million tons.

[f] The losses are here estimated at 10 percent of gross production. The figures in parentheses reflect this level.

[g] Except in 1971-75 and excluding stock changes and export requirements.

[h] Optimum possible net production and/or surpluses, assuming hypotheses in "d" and "f" are valid.

TABLE 4.5
Impact of the Variations in the Soviet Grain Crop (in Million Metric tons)

	1966-1970	1971-1975		1976-1980		1981-1985		1986-1990	
		Actual	Hypothesis (a)	1 st Hypothesis (b)	2 nd Hypothesis (c)	1 st Hypothesis (b)	2 nd Hypothesis (c)	1 st Hypothesis (b)	2 nd Hypothesis (c)
Average annual gross output (in million of tons)	167.6	181.5	181.5	217.5	217.5	241	241	270	270
Minimum output	147.9	140.1	161	192.3	171	213	187	239	209
Maximum output	186.7	222.5	203	242.7	264	269	295	302	331
Magnitude in variations (in percent of annual average)	23.2	45.4	23.2	23.2	45.4	23.2	45.4	23.2	45.4
Internal grain consumption [d] (in millions of tons)	171.0	199.7	199.7	214	214	236	236	263	263
Gap between requirements and the minimum production [e] (in millions of tons)	-23.0	-59.6	-38.7	-22.0	-43	-23	-49	-24	-54

Sources: Economic Survey of Europe in 1976, Part. II, p. 59, O.N.U.

(a) Based on the indicator of the intensity of annual variations 1966-70, and on the same difference with respect to the average.

(b) First hypothesis: magnitude in variations - 1966-70.

(c) Second hypothesis: magnitude in variations - 1971-75.

(d) Excluding export requirements.

(e) i.e., stock changes and net imports.

61

a decisive influence on these variations, the Urals, the Volga, Kazakhstan, and Western Siberia, which produce about 40 percent of all cereals in the USSR (43.4 percent in 1966-70, and 39.3 percent in 1971-75) because their production is the most vulnerable. The variations account for 60 to 75 percent of all variations of the grain crop (minimum or maximum level, relative to the average for the five-year period). These regions contain almost all the virgin lands, where production seems difficult to stabilize.

If we examine, on the other hand, the results of the production of the non-black-soil zone, the magnitude in variations was important in 1966-70 but very small in 1971-75; however, on average for the last period, the production hardly changed. The enormous investment allocated to the region should allow production to reach 31 million tons in 1980 and 43 million tons in 1990, i.e., a little more than 15 percent of Soviet production (about 11 percent over the last ten years). The impact on crop stability could be, in this case, important.

In the short term, however, despite all the measures taken to augment production, the variations have continued to intensify, and it is unlikely that much--or at least sufficient--progress can be made in this area.

In the longer term, if no direct and effective action can improve crop production stability, a new element in crop policy may remedy the situation: the stabilization of internal supply based on the accelerated development of transport and storage facilities. In effect, this appears currently to be the fundamental orientation of Soviet crop policy. The emphasis on developing transport and storage capacity attests both to the leader's awareness of the handicap created by the deficiency of these capacities and to their readiness to do something about it. "The problem of transporting agricultural products is acute," admits L. Brezhnev in particular; "however difficult it may be, it is time to resolve it in a cardinal way."[40] Storage capacities were to increase by about 40 million tons during the tenth five-year Plan.

If we refer to certain experts' conclusions (see table 4.5) the gap between the needs and production capabilities has continually widened; even if the current goal were attained, it would still fall short of the mark.[41] If, on the other hand, the process continues and is accentuated in the next decade, a considerable improvement in Soviet supply stability can be expected as of 1985. The question is whether Soviet leaders are ready to pay the price and what share of the large investments to be allocated to agriculture in the eleventh five-year period will be devoted to these objectives. If this challenge is met, it is possible that the average annual surpluses could become really available for the country, and the USSR could, at least by 1986-90, become once more a grain exporter.

However, the prospects for Soviet grain trade and possible ingress into Western grain markets also depend on the USSR's partner's capacity to cover their own grain requirements. The long-term, integrated, agricultural development program of the CMEA countries foresees that the whole zone must satisfy its grain consumption needs through the next decade, and in fact, despite a big growth of domestic demand, the six East European countries are already less dependent on external trade for their supply.

It is quite evident that estimates of the USSR's exports to its partners are closely linked to the realization of the objective above. As long as these countries' self-sufficiency is not attained, the Soviet Union will partly cover their needs, even if it must resort to imports. Of course, in 1976, Soviet grain deliveries, and of wheat in particular, to the six East European countries were substantially reduced. But to deduce a change of policy from a particularly bad and exceptional situation would be, in our opinion, unfounded. As of 1977, the USSR resumed its exports to these countries, and it is hardly possible for it to abandon them totally without leaving its partners in dire economic straits.

CONCLUSIONS

1. However gross the above estimates, those elements we do have indicate that the Soviet Union will totally satisfy its own grain needs on the average during the next decade, thanks to the enormous resources allocated to agriculture. In fact, the production schedule for the 1980s is relatively modest, enough to be attained, and the final grain- and meat-consumption target is also moderate enough to permit self-sufficiency. Nonetheless, the future of Soviet grain purchases depend, on the one hand, on the USSR's continued self-sufficiency, which supposes that transport and storage problems will be resolved, and, on the other hand, on the self-sufficiency in grain of the six East European countries. If difficulties appear in one or the other, the Soviet Union could be forced to import from the Western countries.

2. In addition, these analyses provoke two important questions. First, even if the program is realized, will it be sufficient to satisfy the consumer? In 1980 Soviet and Romanian meat consumption per capita will be among the lowest in East Europe. As of 1985, the production target of 19.5 million tons set by L. Brezhnev should raise per capita consumption to seventy kg and in 1990 to around eighty-two kg, approximately the current average level for Economic Cooperation and Development (OECS) countries. Second, what is the rationale behind such a costly operation, conducted with such determination? Soviet planners have decided to maintain,

as a minimum, in 1981-85, the high percentage of total investment that has been devoted to agriculture in recent years. When we look at the sums to be invested in the non-black-soil zone alone--35 billion rubles during five years--it seems that the leaders still favor large-scale operations. Nonetheless, given the very difficult conditions of cultivation, results are uncertain.

3. Should we therefore deduce that political concerns always overshadow economic interests in the eyes of the leaders? For the regime, a resolution of the agricultural problem eliminates that of the peasants. The difficulties they have in "maniuplating" the peasant masses, in L. Brezhnev's own terms, pushes them to speed up agricultural industrialization, thus bringing closer city and country (see note 13). In addition, grain plays an important role not only in the development of international economic cooperation "but also in the economic competition between the two systems."[42] In reality, inadequate Soviet supply and massive grain purchases in the West do not enhance the Soviet Union's prestige abroad. Finally, grain deliveries are, for the Soviet Union, an important means of control of the economic activity of the socialist countries. But the situation does not completely satisfy Soviet economists.[43]

If economic criteria predominate, we can admit that Soviet trade with its partners would be limited to some specialized products, cotton, sunflower seeds, and so forth. If, on the contrary, Soviet leaders wish to maintain, at all costs, their control over the East European countries' grain supply, it is conceivable that the USSR will continue to supply the latter with cereals for human use while obtaining from them additional meat.

4. If the political rationale predominates in decisions concerning cereal programs, the question is, in the most favorable hypothesis where the USSR again becomes a net grain exporter and its partners cover their own consumption, whether it would not be tempted to use its surpluses for more direct action in the less developed countries. The resales recently made in certain of the latter demonstrate the possibility of such an operation. We cannot exclude the eventuality that the policy, followed with such determination by L. Brezhnev for now more than fifteen years, will bear its fruits should a stabilization of internal supply be attained.

The final question is that of L. Brezhnev's successors. It seems that his policy was not unanimously approved at the last plenum. What is certain is that he will no longer be present in the 1980s. Was it to ensure his policy's permanency that the objectives of the eleventh Plan were set and announced in such an unusual and premature fashion?

NOTES

1. At about the same time, the long-term, integrated agricultural development program of the Council for Mutual Economic Assistance (CMEA) countries was adopted. However, at the time of writing, few details have trickled down to the press.

2. The USSR, in fact, covers the greater part of its partners' cereal deficit and accounts for almost all of their wheat imports. Thus, between 1971-1974, 66 percent of Soviet cereal and wheat exports went to East Europe; these shipments represented 46 percent of the grain imports and 78 percent of the wheat imports of the countries of Eastern Europe.

3. See Chantal Beaucourt, "Agriculture and Economic Integration Policies of East European Countries in the 1976-1980 Plans," in Revue d' !Etudes Comparatives Est-Ouest, October 1978, CNRS.

4. With this policy, the level of consumption was dictated by that of production and external trade; thus trade did not play a compensation role, but on the contrary, internal supply was determined by the volume of crop exports decided upon.

5. It was only in 1955 that per capita crop production attained the level of 1913, and in 1956 it overtook the latter. In 1950 per capita meat consumption was only 26 kg as opposed to 29 kg in 1913.

6. In 1963, per capita crop production was 10 percent lower than that of 1913. By resorting to increased imports--which caused the USSR to become, for the first time, a net grain importer--the leaders managed only to maintain a consumption level 20 percent lower than that of the preceding year. In addition, they had to undertake massive cattle slaughter that led to a 20 percent reduction in meat production in 1964.

7. In fact, it is estimated that the lack of protein necessitates a 30 percent increase in the consumption of feed per unit of production. Ekonomika sotrudnichestvo stran - clenov sev, no. 3 (1967), p. 80.

8. Crop production was 29 percent higher than that of the preceding five-year period; meat production was up by 23 percent, and net grain exports over the whole period consisted of 13.8 million tons.

9. Production increased by 8.3 percent in five years instead of the planned 16.4 percent.

10. The planned harvest of 195 million tons per annum reached 181.5 million tons (on average for the period). The shortfall of 13.5 million tons corresponds exactly to the level of gross annual imports. Furthermore, meat production increased by 21 percent versus the projected 23.5 percent. There again, the deficit was made up by increased imports.

11. The USSR exported 28.5 million tons of grain of which 18.7 million went to East European countries. Thus, more than 37 million of the total 65.5 million tons imported went to satisfy domestic needs.

12. Between 1971 and 1976, we count two "record" harvests and two "catastrophic" ones. The difference in the yields of the best and the worst harvests of the ninth five-year Plan reached 6.8 centners per hectare and in some areas even more: 10.3 centners per hectare in the Volga region, 8.7 in the central non-black-soil zone.

13. Certainly, the Soviet leaders were not expecting a "miracle"; at the Twenty-Fifth Congress L. Brezhnev reiterated the fact that the agricultural problem was not one of those that can be solved in a few years.

14. Report by L. Brezhnev at the July 1978 Plenum, reported in Pravda, 4 July 1978.

15. The volume of agricultural investments increases less than in the preceding period. However, this sector is privileged if we consider that for the first time in the history of Soviet Plans, the total investment rate is set particularly low relative to the growth target. This emphasis appears even stronger if we examine the funds invested in "related" branches. The global volume of investments devoted to agriculture is thus estimated at 40 percent versus 34.3 percent in the ninth five-year Plan, 30.1 percent in the eighth and 26.6 percent in the seventh. Izvestia akademii nauk SSSR, Economic Series, no. 6 (1975), p. 47.

16. Relative to the preceding five-year period. Greater than half of this increase should be due to a more intensive utilization of fertilizers. The extension of sown areas and the restructuring of sowing should, on their side, help to augment production by 27 million tons. Finally, the building of new storage capacities could ensure better treatment of the harvests.

17. As L. Brezhnev himself admits, grain will still be at the base of animal feed. Meat production in 1976-80 is to rise from 7 to 11.5 percent, whereas it grew by 20.6 percent in 1971-75 (with respect to the preceding five-year period). We must note, however, that in 1975 actual production slightly exceeded the target as a result of livestock slaughter after the bad harvest. As a result, 1976 saw a setback in production.

18. That is, by 14.3 percent. In fact, meat consumption rose in 1975 by more than expected (+18.7 percent) because of livestock slaughter; in 1976 it decreased despite meat imports.

19. For these two years the average harvest was only slightly lower than the forecasts. The USSR could have once more become a net exporter of some million of tons of grain in the event that the harvest attained the "maximum" alternative of the Plan.

20. With respect to the preceding five-year period. Versus 3.7 percent per annum in 1976-80.

21. This level, postulated by L. Brezhnev for 1990, is that which the planners have long considered as adequate to cover all the country's needs. We have also relied on the "middle" demographic hypothesis put forth by the Foreign Demographic Analysis Division, Department of Commerce, USA.

22. Rate of growth of production for the period, relative to the preceding five-year Plan:

	Plan	Actual
1961-65	7.2%	...
1966-70	28.6%	...
1971-75	16.3%	8.3%
1976-80	20.2%	...
1981-85	10.3%	...
1986-90	12.5%	...

23. Socialisticheskaya industriya, 19, no. 4 (1978).

24. Soc. indust., 24, no. 5 (1978); see too, Planovoe khozyaistvo, 3 (1978): 45 and 55 and 10 (1978): 67.

25. Ekonomika sel'skogo khozyaistva, no. 10, (1977), p. 70.

26. Ekon. sel'. khoz., no. 7, (1978), p. 9.

27. Ibid.

28. See also: Izvestia akademii nauk, Geographic Series, no. 4 (1978), p. 36, and Douglas B. Diamond, W. Lee Davis, "Comparative Output and Productivity of U.S. and Soviet Agriculture." See comparisons with the North American experience, "At first glance," conclude the authors, "the U.S. record (...in North American areas similar to the U.S.S.R., between 1950-1958 and 1967-1975) surely must be encouraging to Soviet planners."

29. Ekon. sel'. khoz. no. 12 (1977), p. 18.

30. L. Brezhnev announced a yield of 20 centners per hectare, most likely by 1985. The expected harvest for 1985 can thus be estimated at about 260 million tons.

31. Compared to 16.8-17.2 centners per hectare in 1976-1980 and 14.7 centners realized in 1971-1975.
Evolution of yields (increase with respect to the average of the preceding five-year period).

1966-70	34 %
1971-75	7 %
1976-80	14-17%
1981-85*	10.5 %
1990-85*	10-14 %

* 1990 compared to 1985

32. To define these needs, we took as a base the per capita levels of meat and grain consumption foreseen for 1980 and 1985 and the consumption target set for 1990. The rates of conversion of grain into flour which have been used are based on data given to a French delegation to the USSR in 1976.

33. Grain converted into flour equivalent.

34. We note, however, that for the first time in many years, per capita consumption should hardly decrease during this five-year period.

35. East European leaders are quite aware of the importance of the problem of livestock protein feed. They estimate the average annual shortfall of cattle protein feed to be 6 million tons in the CMEA. At the twenty-eighth CMEA council session, the permanent agriculture commission was given the task of preparing a draft agreement on the subject. Ekonomika sotrudnichestvo stran-clenov sev, no. 5 (1976), p. 80.

36. In 1976-80 meat production should rise by 7 to 11.5 percent (compared to the preceeding five-year period). In 1981-85 it should grow by about 19 percent if we accept, on the basis of the 1985 target of 19.5 million tons of meat, a production of about 18.5 million tons.

37. On the condition that the stocks are replenished at the outset and that annual stock variations cancel themselves out during the period.

38. In 1973, storage capacity for grain equaled 98.5 million tons, whereas 120 million tons was needed. All possible means were used to store cereals, in particular, freight trains. (Ekonomika sel'skogo khozyaistva, no. 3 [1975], p. 47.) "Losses during the harvest, the transport and storage of cereals can reach 20 to 25 percent of the crop." (Voprosy Ekonomiki, no. 7 [1977], p. 90.)

39. We can foresee, however, that the cattle feed composition and the output per animal will evolve and that the livestock grain needs will be "relatively" smaller. In this case, the first hypothesis, based on a constant figure for grain consumption per ton of meat, must be taken as a maximum variable of this consumption. However, the estimates for 1981-85 correspond, in the first hypothesis, to a level of grain consumption per capita of 900 kg, which is that adopted by the planners. The second hypothesis can thus be envisaged only in the latter half of the decade.

40. Or, at the end of the period, at a level which we can consider as maximum.

41. Conversely, it appears that if, in 1971-75 the variations in the harvests had not exceeded those of 1966-70, the USSR could have avoided a massive recourse to the market with the same internal supply.

42.   Karl-Eugen Wädekin, "A Survey of Soviet Agriculture in 1974," Radio Liberty Research Supplement, 9 May 1975.

43.   Ekonomika Gazeta, no. 26 (February 1978).

5
Factors Affecting
Social Mobility for Women
in the Soviet Countryside

Ethel Dunn

In 1976 45 percent of the total population of the USSR was female, and 40 percent of all Soviet women lived in rural areas.[1] Since the Revolution, increasing numbers of women have migrated to the cities, impelled by forces of two world wars, revolution, collectivization, and their own changing views of what constitutes the good life. Soviet sources uniformly stress the beneficial effects of the Revolution and Soviet policies on the status of women, but consistent information on the status of Soviet rural women is hard to come by. In this paper, I will attempt to test the hypothesis that Soviet policies in regard to rural women failed to achieve equality for them, and that in order even to have access to the equality proclaimed by Soviet ideology (equality of opportunity being the most significant feature of this ideology), women have had to leave rural areas entirely. Most of my data concern the population of the European USSR-- Russians, Belorussians, Ukrainians, and Baltic nationalities. I have used certain Central Asian and non-European data to highlight what I consider to be the greater degree of success of Soviet policy in non-European areas relative to the European USSR.

In The Peasants of Central Russia, Stephen P. Dunn and I wrote: "...the peasant is a man in transition....He feels the influence of the larger culture, whose elements are diffused to him through a screen made up of geographical, economic, and social (class) factors. This screen filters out certain elements completely...and lets others seep through after varying delays and in more or less simplified forms...."[2] In our conclusion we added: "...and the terms within which this transition occurs are determined not only by the point from which he starts out--the traditional culture--but by the state's attitude toward him."[3] The suspicion with which the Soviet regime regarded peasants was based on an ideology that asserted the primacy of the proletarian and the class nature

71

of the new state. In spite of sixty years of the union of peasants and proletariat, M. T. Iovchuk, rector of the Academy of Social Sciences under the Central Committee of the CPSU, corresponding member of the Academy of Sciences USSR, and member of the Central Committee of the CPSU, writes of "irregularities in the development of the consciousness and cultural level of various strata of the rural population...chiefly in psychology....[T]he underlying economic cause of this preservation of individual psychology is involvement of part of the rural population with the personal subsidiary economy, which leads to serious consequences [among which are] acquisitiveness, a market orientation, etc..., involving at times part of the rural intelligentsia and the families of rural activists."[4]

It seems Stephen P. Dunn and I had our gender wrong; woman has remained the peasant in transition, in spite of enormous efforts to change her. People with leadership potential have consistently been offered access to education in order to enlist their support of the Soviet system. Giving women this opportunity was a powerful stimulus for change. Although the class nature of the party is persistently reaffirmed, Brezhnev himself has stated that supplementing the ranks of the party with kolkhozniks "answers the interests of further strengthening of the union of the working class and the peasantry."[5] P. I. Simush says that at the beginning of 1976, about 2,170,000 kolkhozniks were members or candidate-members of the party. A significant portion of these (34 percent in 1972) were members of a new stratum in the rural population--equipment operators of various types, and 17.2 percent were agronomists, zootechnicians, engineers, technicians, and other specialists.[6]

It is not clear to what extent rural women have been included in this process. Western researchers, like Lapidus, Moses, and Hough, stress that the career patterns of female party members differ markedly from those of males. Lapidus says: "Most women worked in health, education, and welfare, supervising academic institutions and cultural affairs, or in departments of propaganda and agitation."[7] Moses notes the presence of a woman, M. T. Poberei, of rural origin on the All-Union Central Committee in 1971, and asserts that this is as a result of a policy decision to have women or agriculture specialists on the central committee. He acknowledges in a footnote Hough's contention that ideological party secretaries have also been responsible for health and social welfare policies in their regions, but he still thinks that women's services in agitation and propaganda (Poberei's specialty) are primary.[8] In 1975, 23.8 percent of the party and 52.1 percent of the Komsomol were women.[9] Hough, citing himself, says: "A mere 5 percent of all women between ages of 31 and 60 are party members, compared with some 22 percent of all men in that age group."[10] If this assertion is correct for rural

72

areas as well, it virtually precludes high representation among rural women. Wädekin says that in rural areas in 1961, barely 1 percent of field workers and 2-3 percent of workers in livestock were party members.[11] Certain efforts have been made in recent years to have party members involved in increased agricultural production, but in 1977, in Aban raion of Krasnoyarsk Krai, only 6 of 525 milkmaids were members of the party, and only about 18 were Komsomol members.[12] These figures are particularly interesting if we remember that Komsomol and party membership represent a ticket for both educational and professional advancement in the Soviet Union.[13] Peasant women have always had difficulty in combining their roles as wives and mothers with their professional aspirations, although Soviet sources point out that only the Revolution made it possible for them to have professional aspirations at all. A few educational data will serve to indicate both the original limits of rural women's aspirations and the extent to which in the 1970s, these limits continue to operate.

In 1927, according to a survey made by A. M. Bol'shakov in Goritsy raion of Tver guverniia (now Kalinin Oblast), boys named thirty-six desirable professions, while the girls named only eighteen. Only 2.9 percent of the boys and 6.8 percent of the girls wanted to remain peasants. Between 1967 and 1974, a questionnaire consciously replicating Bolshakov's study was distributed to 1700 schoolchildren in the fourth to tenth grades in Rzhakskaia raion of Tambov Oblast. Even though girls now named forty-four professions (against fifty-four by boys), 28.8 percent wanted to be doctors, 24.3 percent teachers, and 8.2 percent educators of small children. Of the 8,408 tenth graders who received diplomas in Tambov Oblast in 1974, 61.7 percent continued schooling, with only 1,204 entering kolkhozy, sovkhozy or other agricultural enterprises.[14] V. G. Kostiuk and M. N. Traskunova report that in 1973, the girl graduates of rural schools in Novosibirsk Oblast were more strongly oriented than boys toward continued study: 74 percent of the boys and 90 percent of the girls planned to go on studying--10 percent of the boys and 5-7 percent of the girls by means of evening or correspondence courses; 24 percent of the boys and 3 percent of the girls planned to go to work at once. In 1973 not a single girl planned to work in agriculture, although in fact girls did do so, just as they did in fact enroll in agricultural educational institutions, although not a single girl chose a rural professional-technical school.[15]

The mobility of Central Asian women is many times lower than for the rest of the Soviet Union. R. A. Ubaidullaeva attributes this to larger families and the fact that only 20 percent of preschool children in Central Asia are placed in childcare facilities, as compared to 40 percent for the USSR as a whole.[16] She considers the liberation of female labor resources in agriculture to be a pressing problem, complicated by the lack of special skills and industrial work habits. Her study of new industrial enterprises in Namangan, Andizhan, Fergana, Kokand, and Leninsk in the Fergana valley of Uzbekistan, revealed that of 5,867 persons hired, only 5-7 percent were kolkhoznitsy; 60 percent of these were apprentices, meaning that their wages were lower than they had been on kolkhozy. Nevertheless, when the kolkhoz was within commuting distance of an industrial enterprise, women sought industrial work, even though about 50 percent of the women in industry were engaged in manual labor, 15 percent of it classified as heavy. In the machine-building, building materials, food, and lumber-processing industries, the skill level of women is significantly lower than among men. A comparison of the free time of women in light industries-- which might serve as an index of their ability to upgrade their skills--revealed that they had 19.5 free hours a week in Uzbekistan and 18.3 hours in Tadzhikstan, as compared with 34 hours and 24 hours for men in the respective republics.[17] Other authors note that in Uzbekistan, trade, public catering, communal housing, and consumer services (entry-level urban professions, so to speak) employ a high percentage of young men, whereas there are 1.5 times fewer young men in agriculture than young women.[18] At the same time, only 4.6 percent of eighth graders in Uzbekistan went into professional-technical and secondary specialized schools, but almost 80 percent of them went into the ninth grade (compared to 60 percent for the country as a whole).[19] Between 1970 and 1976, the percentage of women in the rural population of Uzbekistan declined from 63 to 61, from 50 to 47 in the Kazakh SSR, from 62 to 61 in the Kirgiz SSR but remained stable in the Tadzhik SSR, at 63 and in the Turkmen SSR at 52.[20] At the end of 1975, Uzbekistan had 190 of the 416 intereconomic enterprises, organizations, and units in Central Asia and Kazakhstan; none of the 29 enterprises processing only agricultural produce in the USSR were located in this area.[21] These intereconomic enterprises are expected to ease the problem of seasonal unemployment and underemployment in rural areas,[22] but from what has been said above, it seems unlikely that this avenue is open to Central Asian women. Indeed, we may hazard a guess that rural women in general are not being as readily employed in some of these enterprises as men, since in 1974, only 8.8 percent of female blue- and white-collar workers were employed in the agricultural sector (8.3 percent in sovkhozy and subsidiary enterprises), and this represents a decline from 1960.[23]

This curious statistic is probably explained by the exodus of part of the most educated portion of the rural population-- young women, although Central Asia is an exception. I have devoted some attention elsewhere to the migration of peasant women in the European USSR out of rural areas,[24] caused by their inability to continue their education or utilize their skills in villages. Soviet sources generally stress that rural women in the younger age groups are more highly educated than their male peers. M. Fedorova apparently includes non-Slavic areas in her statement that among employed rural women in 1970, "more than half had only primary and less than primary, with 32.5% possessing primary. In the most work-capable age groups (25-29 and 30-34) 66-67% of rural women working in the public sector had incomplete secondary and primary education. Even in the 20-24 age group, the percentage of the latter was 50."[25] In 1972, depending on the republic, 90-98 perent of women were engaged in manual labor, with not more than 0.5-0.6 percent of the tractor-and-combine drivers on kolkhozy and sovkhozy being women.[26] Contrary to the expressed desire of the State Committee for Professional and Technical Education of the Council of Ministers USSR, 82 percent of the tractor and vehicle drivers trained in 1973 were male. Moreover, relatively small numbers of equipment operators for fieldcrops, orchards, vineyards, or livestock farms were being trained. Since rural professional and technical schools (SPTUs) were set up in 1953, the percentage of girls accepted had not exceeded 9.5 percent, whereas in 1973, girls were 55.1 percent of the students enrolled in urban professional and technical schools. Of the 320,000 accepted in the PTUs in 1973, half were rural. An additional 58,000 persons were accepted by rural secondary PTUs; almost two-thirds of the students in both places were studying urban specialties. In the Azerbaidjan, Tadzhik, Georgian, and Armenian SSRs, half the women working in July were not employed at all in December,[27] apparently because of lack of work, or less than optimum labor needs.

Rural women appear, then, to be undereducated, and underemployed. The need for equipment operators of every type, but particularly for tractor-and-combine drivers, is so great that, since 1968, a special effort has been made to train women, even though there is a "mistaken" opinion among rural people that "the profession of equipment operator is not a feminine one."[28] In April 1976 there were 4,074,000 equipment operators of various types on kolkhozy, sovkhozy, and interfarm economic enterprises.[29] It is not clear how many of these are women. Monich reports a survey of sixty-one kolkhozy in the Belorussian SSR in 1967 among 2,530 tractor and truck drivers that showed that there were altogether five women.[30] In Millerovo raion, Rostov Oblast, there is a well-publicized woman's tractor brigade, headed by L. A. Tikhomirova, Hero of Socialist Labor and Deputy to the RSFSR Supreme Soviet. Hers was the first women's tractor brigade on the Don in 1968. She reported at the 1975 All-Russian Meeting of Women Equipment Operators in Krasnoyarsk that in her raion, 245 women were working in 27 brigades and links. In December of 1975, there were supposed to be 28 women's brigades, with more than 300 women; 208 have grade classifications (52 as first- and second-class equipment operators). However, of the 3,094 equipment-operators trained in Millerovo raion in the ninth five-year Plan, only 52 were women, and of the 625 persons who acquired a second mechanical skill, including 103 sent to the local rural professional technical school, only 45 were women.[31]

Uzbekistan is a republic in which the majority of rural residents are women, and, like many other republics, it has fewer equipment operators than available equipment, leading to an underutilization of technology. Ever increasing numbers of equipment operators are being trained, but before 1970, few of them were women. Between 1966 and 1970, SPTUs of the republic trained 3,938 Uzbek girls. Short-term courses organized by the Uzbek branch of Sel'khozttekhnika in 1969-1970 trained and retrained 78,500 equipment operators, including about 4,000 girls able to drive cotton-picking machines. In Samarkand Oblast in 1970, 576 persons, including 186 girls, acquired the skill of tractor driver in five rural schools in the oblast. In 1975, the Komsomol of Uzbekistan announced a drive to train 100,000 young equipment oeprators for agriculture, and in fact attracted 120,000 including 12,640 girls and women.[32]

Komsomol or party initiative in training women equipment operators is widespread, especially in organizing courses directly on kolkhozy or sovkhozy. In 1973, for example, the Komsomol organization of Balkovskii sovkhoz, Tselinnyi raion, Kalmyk ASSR admitted ten girls--former secondary-school students, shepherd's helpers, a sales girl, and a store manager--to a course for tractor drivers. When they began work, their brigade leader was first a man, and then later a woman. They were given special uniforms, including one for dress wear, and a special trailer for rest periods, as well as a guarantee of year-round work (all things that most male equipment operators cannot count on). Clearly, the profession is a stepping stone for other careers, inasmuch as the woman brigade leader has now been given administrative work with the Komsomol, one girl is in her first year of study at an institute in Saratov, and another entered a sovkhoz tekhnikum.[33] In recent years there has been an attempt to provide a second skill for members of the rural intelligentsia, many of whom may be in need of additional income.[34] In Karagatskii raion, Novosibirsk Oblast, the Trudovoi sovkhoz enlisted seventeen women--bookkeepers, teachers, and medical workers in courses for tractor drivers, at the request of the Party and the sovkhoz administration. On Znamenskii sovkhoz, sixteen women were enrolled; nine finished the course, the others having dropped out for family reasons of various sorts. The woman reporting this incident, who did finish the course, has five children, the eldest eighteen, and the youngest in third grade. The oldest is

76

currently working as a cowherd, but hopes to drive a tractor later.[35]

A certain campaign is being mounted to create prestige for the job of female equipment operator: an effort is made to attract women with promises of tracors with their personal names on them as a reward for successful competition, or automobiles for successful completion of their assigned task, which is made to look as attractive as possible.[36] Much fanfare surrounds competitions for the best equipment operators, especially women who hold their own with men.[37] Upper-class, student agricultural brigades get their share of publicity in connection with the Pasha Angelina Prize,[38] given in memory of the first woman tractor driver (from Donetsk Oblast).[39] In 1977 there were said to be more than 19,000 holders of the prize.[40] It is difficult to know what percentage of the total these laureates represent. A current report from Voronezh Oblast stated that according to the local department of agriculture, about five hundred women were working with tractors in the oblast.[41] Stories on the working conditions for women equipment operators frequently mention the back-up system which exists for them (but not always for their male counterparts) when and if the new tractors break down. In some places, women's brigades are assigned a bus to take them to and from work. In Kirov Oblast, about 225 girls were attracted by these conditions, but in Lipetsk Oblast more than 1,000 combines were idle part of the time for lack of operators.[42]

In recent years there has been an attempt to create "family teams" of equipment operators, on the theory that the family that works together will stay on the farm, daughters being as capable of helping fathers as sons.[43] Husband-and-wife teams also operate successfully.[44] Newspaper reports suggest that family teams could be more of a mass movement than that of young women equipment operators, who are frequently trained and sent back to work on farms only during busy seasons: Orenburg Oblast in July 1977 was said to have five thousand family teams; more than eight hundred family teams were employed on the Don, and more than four thousand women equipment operators were working to bring in the harvest.[45]

Inducing young people to stay in rural areas is crucial to the success of Soviet agriculture, since equipment operators have aged along with the rest of the employed rural population: In 1966 44.2 percent of the operators on kolkhozy and 48.8 percent of those on sovkhozy were under thirty years of age; in 1972, only 23 percent on kolkhozy and 21 percent on sovkhozy were under thirty, and 33 percent were over forty. Young people under nineteen are used primarily as manual laborers,[46] probably because Soviet law does not allow them to operate machinery without supervision until then.[47] In 1975, according to V. I. Kochemasov, deputy chairman of the Council of Ministers, RSFSR, only 4 percent of the graduates of secondary schools in Tiumen Oblast who went to work in agriculture utilized the skills taught in the schools; in Novogorod Oblast,[48] the figure was 11 percent, and in Vologda Oblast 16 percent. In Vokhomskii raion, Kostroma Oblast, five hundred kilometers from Kostroma, in 1977 five times as many young men as women were employed on kolkhozy and sovkhozy; [49] of fifty-seven graduates only two wished to be milkmaids.

If traditional attitudes can be blamed for the slowness with which rural women have acquired technical skills, in agriculture, it must be noted that advancement in rural areas comes only with education, and statistics alone suggest that women are not attracted to agricultural professions. Although the proportion of women students in agricultural higher educational institutions increased from 30 percent in 1970-71 to 33 percent in 1975-76, at the secondary specialized agricultural institutions the proportion has fluctuated between 36 and 37 percent.[50] Without specialized training, it is highly unlikely that women will be advanced to leadership positions. One source states that as of 1975, 97.2 percent of the directors of sovkhozy and 89.3 percent of kolkhoz chairmen had higher and secondary specialized education, although there are regional variations.[51] As of 1 April 1976, the figures had risen to 98.1 percent and 91.5 percent respectively.[52] Almost all are members of the party.[53] Robert C. Stuart, using the 1959 census, noted a pattern of female kolkhoz chairmen in the twenty to twenty-nine age bracket, and speculated that this would mean "a slightly expanded role for women as kolkhoz managers in the future."[54] L. V. Ostapenko, commenting on Vyshnii Volochek raion, Kalinin Oblast in 1967-68, said[55] that there was not one woman heading a sovkhoz or kolkhoz, but in 1976, Morozov kolkhoz in Il'inskoe village, forty kilometers from Kalinin, where 124 persons were employed, was headed by a woman.[56] In 1966, there were no female kolkhoz chairmen in Leningrad, Rostov, Sverdlovsk, Novosibirsk, and Omsk Oblasts,[57] but Leningrad Oblast, in the early 1970s, did have a female director of a "poultry factory" in Gatchina raion and a female sovkhoz director in Volosovskii raion.[58] Orienting women toward careers in agriculture at the administrative level appeared to have paid off in Altai Krai, where in 1975, 8,786 women administrators and specialists (a third of the administrators) were employed--2.5 times as many as in 1965.[59] In the Mountain Altai, more than 60 women became directors and chief specialists of enterprises, 680 specialists in agricultural production, and 205 secretaries of primary and shop party organizations.[60] As of April 1, 1976, 521 of 27,737 kolkhoz chairmen (1.8 percent), and 1,163 of their special assignment deputies out of 17,888 (6.5 percent) were female; 295 of 18,876 sovkhoz directors (1.5 percent) and 2,072 of 40,769 heads of sovkhoz departments or farms (5

percent) were women.[61] Whether the campaign to advance women
in administrative posts (and it must be remembered that such a
campaign is only one in a series) will be successful in
inducing young women to remain in rural areas, remains to be
seen. As Monich has pointed out for Belorussia,[62] and
Ostapenko for Kalinin Oblast,[63] rural women are heavily
burdened by the necessity of managing a household plot, and
are in fact severely disadvantaged if foodstuffs such as
vegetables, berries, eggs, and milk must be purchased rather
than produced, simply because such items are not consistently
available in local stores.[64]

Throughout the Soviet Union it is still women who put
fresh foods on the family table. Some writers suggest that
male administrators simply do not have the time,[65] and that
this division of labor is rational and sensible.[66] The job of
kolkhoz chairman requires long hours, many of them away from
home,[67] and while the pay was, even in 1971, three times more
than that earned by ordinary kolkhozniks,[68] numerous studies
have shown that it is the conditions of rural life as such
rather than inadequate pay or poor working conditions that
cause young people to migrate to cities. Dissatisfaction with
the cultural life of the village is, in the long run, not as
significant as dissatisfaction with educational opportunities,
especially childcare facilities,[69] and with health care.

An indication that women are rejecting rural life in
increasing numbers can be seen from the statement by S.Ia.
Chikin, Deputy Minister of Public Health for the RSFSR, that
in 1975 women comprised 54.3 percent of the physicians in
rural areas.[70] In 1973 there were 37,100 physicians of all
kinds in rural areas of the RSFSR (two per ten thousand
residents),[71] and in 1974 about 30,000 (fifteen per ten
thousand) in the Ukraine.[72] Table 5.1 shows that the
proportion of women physicians and dentists[73] has declined in
most Soviet republics since 1959. Lithuania, Latvia, Estonia,
and Armenia are exceptions, but it should be noted that the
Baltic republics have the lowest percentage of rural women in
the Soviet Union, and that, in recent years, Armenian women
have moved to the cities at an accelerated rate. A study of
rural migration patterns in Staraia Russia raion of Novgorod
Oblast in 1966-67 indicated that 3.1 percent of the migrants
were employed in education and public health before migrating
and 2.6 percent after.[74] A study in the Ukraine in 1967-69
found that 15.6 percent of the sample were employed in public
health, education, science, culture, trade, and public
catering before migrating, and 8.9 percent were so employed
after migrating. Among women the figures were 26.6 percent
and 16.3 percent as compared to 8.6 percent

TABLE 5.1
Percentage of Women Physicians and Dentists in Selected Years
and by Republics
(in Percent of Total Number)

USSR	1959	1970	1975
Chief physicians and administrators	54	53	...
Doctors	79	74	70
Dentists	83	77	...
RSFSR			
Chief	61	61	
Doctors	82	77	71.2
Dentists	87	83	
Ukrainean SSR			
Chief	47	46	
Doctor	75	70	
Dentist	76	71	
Belorussian SSR			
Chief	42	35	
Doctor	73	68	
Dentist	87	80	
Uzbek SSR			
Chief	39	39	
Doctor	68	59	56
Dentist	61	53	
Kazakh SSR			
Chief	54	49	
Doctor	76	74	71
Dentist	79	75	
Georgian SSR			
Chief	35	33	
Doctor	68	69	
Dentist	75	71	
Azerbaidzhan SSR			
Chief	40	29	
Doctor	70	64	
Dentist	58	46	
Lithuanian SSR			
Chief	46	54	
Doctor	68	74	
Dentist	95	90	

80

TABLE 5.1 (cont.)
Percentage of Women Physicians and Dentists in Selected Years
and by Republics
(in Percent of Total Number)

USSR	1959	1970	1975
Moldavian SSR			
Chief	46	36	
Doctor	67	66	
Dentist	74	63	
Latvian SSR			
Chief	55	58	
Doctor	78	77	
Dentist	84	91	
Kirgiz SSR			
Chief	47	41	
Doctor	70	69	64
Dentist	68	47	
Tadzhik SSR			
Chief	37	38	
Doctor	69	55	55
Dentist	71	55	
Armenian SSR			
Chief	38	48	
Doctor	72	69	72
Dentist	49	54	
Turkmen SSR			
Chief	36	28	
Doctor	67	60	56
Dentist	69	54	
Estonian SSR			
Chief	48	63	
Doctor	74	77	
Dentist	88	96	

Sources: Itogi Vsesoivzhoi perepisi naseleniya 1970
(Moscow, 1973), vol. 6, pp. 168, 173, 178, 183,
188, 193, 198, 203, 208, 213, 218, 223, 228, 233,
237, 243; Vestnik statistiki, no. 1 (1977), p.88;
Chikin, "Voprosy podgortovki," p. 21.

and 4.0 percent for men. After migrating, 63.7 percent in this category earned a hundred rubles a month or less, whereas before, 81.5 percent had.[75]

Iu. V. Arutiunian, on the basis of a study of rural Russian and Tatar families, states that there is less desire to migrate where people are satisfied with their family life and their work. In the Tatar ASSR, 18 percent of the Tatars and 20.5 percent of the Russians in his sample wished to migrate. In happy families, only 13.4 percent did. This attitude rubs off on children: in families with very good relations, 36 percent of the children moved to cities, and in families where relations were satisfactory, 47 percent. Among high-level specialists, 14 percent asserted that the family hindered professional mobility.[76] In Kalinin Oblast, 20 percent of the women employed in physical labor and 32 percent of those employed in mental labor had experienced professional advancement in the five years prior to 1969. In Krasnodar Krai the corresponding figures are 14 percent and 30 percent.[77] M. G. Pankratova, who was part of Arutiunian's team, demonstrates that the attitude of women to the family and its role in professional advancement is more negative than that of men in every age group, and that this tendency is most marked among women twenty-three to twenty-seven years of age, where "the percentage of nonparty women is comparatively high." Eighty percent of them have small children. In Kalinin Oblast, one-third of the mothers had their children in childcare facilities, but 6 percent had no one to look after them.[78]

If a woman in a rural area must tend her garden plot and raise her children without the modern conveniences that Western housewives take for granted, the question of whether women should work outside the home is a good one. Soviet researchers have found that the answer depends on the status of the respondent: only among women engaged in manual labor did more women than men think that women should not work. Husbands were more likely to help a wife employed at skilled labor than unskilled,[79] but Arutiunian writes: "In families where the wife earns more than the husband (based on data in the Tatar ASSR), 30% are not satisfied with family life, whereas in 'normal' families the figure is 25%; 17% and 12% respectively complain of quarrels [about money, the children's education, drinking, and interference by inlaws]. In such families, divorces are more frequent."[80]

A survey of divorce actions brought by women in two raions of Orel Oblast in the late 1960s revealed that 47.9 percent cited drunkeness and bad conduct on the husband's part. Prominent among reasons given in actions brought by men are dissimilarity of character and views (27.3 percent), wife's infidelity (19.3 percent), and the wife's refusal to live and work in the village (2.6 percent). Seven percent of the actions brought by the wife and 9.7 percent of those brought by the man cited the fact that the marriage was arranged and

the couple were not previously acquainted.[81] V. T.
Kolokol'nikov studies 637 divorces brought over a three-year
period in the early 1970s in all seventeen rural raions of
Grodno Oblast (Belorussia). Alcoholism remained the chief
cause for divorce in the opinion of the wife (44.3 percent),
and in addition, the primary manifestation of interference by
parents and other relatives cited by the husband (11.3
percent) concerned drunkenness. Incompatability of character
(22.2 percent), marital infidelity (15.3 percent), alcoholism
(10.6 percent) and loss of affection for unexplained reasons
(12.3 percent) were the chief causes for divorces from the
man's view.[82] Research showed that 148 of the men already had
a second family at the time of the divorce hearing (23.2
percent) as compared to 11.6 percent (70) of the women; 12.5
percent (80) of the men had permanent ties with another woman,
and 6.6 percent of the women had another man.[83]

Soviet students of the changing rural family generally
cite divorces brought by women as a positive example of
women's liberation, but, as Kolokol'nikov suggests, women are
less successful than men in creating a new life for themselves
in the event of divorce.[84]

In Central Asia, divorces are less frequent and
traditional attitudes toward women in many cases still
survive: the Turkmen poet Toushan Esenova was particularly
indignant that four recent cases of kaitarma (failure by the
bridegroom to pay the full brideprice [kalym]) involved
members of the intelligentsia--fathers who believe that they
are honoring their daughters, and daughters who think that
they are especially valuable, since nonpayment of kalym
supposes a very high price. The woman in such a case lives
with her parents--the bridegroom being allowed only the
honeymoon--and she dresses in a manner characteristic neither
of unmarried nor of married women. All parties believe that
this is a permissible national custom. After an investigation
of the problem within the central committee of the Turkmen
party, the Presidium of the Supreme Soviet of the Turkmen SSR
issued an ukaz, reinstating, after twenty years' absence from
the criminal code, a prison sentence as punishment for the
detention of married women in the parental home. Obviously,
it is still necessary to combat traditional views in Turkmen
society. Esenova remarks that in 1973, only about 15 percent
of the 55,000 women employed in Ashkhabad were Turkmen. "I
am," she wrote, "of course, not for having absolutely every
woman go to work instantly, sit on tractors, stand at factory
work benches, at laboratory tables, at drawing boards, and
behind store counters. Really, we have quite a few large
families, and raising the new generation is a task no less
complicated and responsible that the construction of a house
or sewing clothes....But all the same, the figures make one
stop and think."[85]

The thoughts, perhaps, are about the limits of women's liberation. Many Soviet women, including Central Asian women, are making their own choice, by limiting the family to two children.[88] It remains to be seen whether they must also absolutely choose to live in cities. The trend toward urbanization which is so marked in European Russia is just beginning in Central Asia, but it has begun. The exoticism of Esenova's articles can be duplicated in many areas of the Soviet Union where the traditional roles of women conflict with the regime's stated policy, and where essentially this policy has been slowed down by the people's selective acceptance of cultural change.

Soviet policy toward rural women seems to have hit a snag: women want to work because the society in which they live values work and, on an ideological level, encourages them to express their creativity in this way. At the same time, educationally, rural women have been given a humanistic orientation, and, for the most part, they do not see themselves as rural technicians. The regime has had great difficulty creating and maintaining schools and childcare facilities in rural areas, and, because of the inadequate rural consumer service network (including health care facilities), the modern Soviet rural woman shows a preference for the city. This process must be reversed in some areas of the Soviet Union (chiefly in the Ukraine, the RSFSR, Belorussia, and the Baltic area) and accelerated in others, such as Central Asia, which experience rural underemployment.

NOTES

1. Vestnik statistiki 1977, no. 1, p. 83.
2. Stephen P. Dunn and Ethel Dunn, The Peasants of Central Russia (New York: Holt, Rinehart, & Winston, 1967), p. 2; restated on pp. 130-131.
3. Ibid., p. 131.
4. Problemy agrarnoi politiki KPSS na sovremennom etape, vol. 2 (Moscow, 1975), p. 229.
5. Quoted in Agrarnaya politika KPSS v usloviiakh razvitogo sotsializma (Moscow, 1976), p. 285. Between the Twenty-Fourth and Twenty-Fifth Party Congress, more than 11 percent of newly accepted party members were kolkhozniks. P. I. Simush (Sotsial'nyi portret sovetskogo krest'ianstva [Moscow, 1976], p. 43) notes that at the Twenty-Fifth Party Congress, 13.9 percent of the party were kolkhozniks. However, the number of Communists in rural areas is said by L. A. Kozlova to be "more than 5.5 million; of these, about 2.6 million are employed directly in agricultural production." (Agrarnaya politika KPSS, p. 161). As V. I. Bakhovkin makes clear, the declining number of kolkhozniks may be explained by

increases in other strata (workers and white-collar personnel, and sovkhoz workers)--in other words, by a change of class (ibid., p. 28.).

6. P. I. Simush, Sotsial'nyi portret, p. 189. In Moscow Oblast in 1975, 15.6 percent of agricultural workers, including 24.6 percent of the equipment oeprators and 10 percent of the livestock breeders belonged to the Party, but in the Ukraine, more than a third of the more than 480,000 members candidate members of the party working directly in kolkhoz and sovkhoz production were equipment operators (Problemy agrarnoi politiki KPSS, pp. 13, 243).

7. Gail W. Lapidus, "Changing Women's Roles in the USSR," in Women in the World, eds. Lynne B. Iglitzin and Ruth Ross (Santa Barbara: ABC-Clio Press, 1976), pp. 310-11.

8. Joel C. Moses, "Women in Political Roles,m" in Women in Russia, eds. Dorothy Atkinson, Alexander Lallin, and Gail Warshofsky Lapidus, (Stanford: Stanford University Press, 1977), pp. 344, 348, 35 n.

9. Zhenshchiny v SSR: Statisticheskii sbornik (Moscow, 1975), p. 51.

10. Jerry F. Hough, "Women's Issues in Soviet Policy Debates" in Women in Russia, p. 362.

11. Karl-Eugen Wädekin, "Soviet Rural Society: a Descriptive Stratification Analysis," Soviet Studies, 22 (April 1971): 521.

12. Pravda 25 April 1977, p. 2.

13. See, for example, the career of a seventeen-year old Kazakh woman tractor-driver, given in Problemy agrarnoi politiki KPSS, vol. 2, p. 256. For other examples of the extent to which the work record of women equipment operators correlates with their access to education and party membership see Sel'skaya zhizn' 6 May 1977, p. 2; Pravda 17 August 1977, p. 2; 15 August 1977, p. 2, showing the picture of a young Tadzhik woman who operated a cotton-picking combine for ten years on a kolkhoz and is presently a Communist, Deputy to the Supreme Soviet of the USSR and a student by correspondence at the Tashkent agricultural institute; Sel'skaya zhizn' 21 May 1977, p. 1; Pravda 28 July 1977, p. 1, photo of Uzbek woman brigade leader, surrounded by an admiring team of male cotton-picking combine drivers; Sel'skaya zhizn' 28 June 1977, p. 2, photo of Azerbaijani woman Komsomol cotton-combine driver, one of the best on her kolkhoz; Sel'skaya zhizn' 29 April 1977, p. 1, photo of corn-harvester woman Communist deputy to the Kradnodar Krai Soviet).

14. Literaturnaya gazeta 26 March 1975, p. 12.

15. V. G. Kostiuk and M. M. Traskunova, "Nekotorye sotayal'nye aspekty obrazovaniia i professional'noi orientatsii sel'skoi molodezhi (na materialakh issledovanii v Novosibiskoi oblasti)," Izvestia Sibirskogo otdeleniia Akademii nauk SSSR, Seriya obshchestvennykh nauk 1975, no. 6, vyp. 2, pp. 115, 118-119.

16. In 1975, 40.8 percent of the Uzbek children in permanent preschool facilities lived in rural areas; in the Kazakh SSR, 52.1 percent, in the Kirgiz SSR, 35.2 percent in the Tadzhik SSR 13.7 percent and in the Turkmen SSR, 234.5 percent (Narodnoe obrazovanie, nauka i kul'tura v SSSR (Moscow, 1977), pp. 125, 126, 132-133, 135).

17. R. A. Ubaidullaeva, "XXV S"ezd KPSS i aktual'nye problemy ispol'zovaniya zhenskogo truda v respublikakh Srednei Azii," Obshchestvennye nauki v Uzbekistane, no. 12 (1976), pp. 15-18.

18. T. B. Musaeva and R. T. Khasanova, "K voprosu ratsional'nogo ispol'zovaniya trudovykh resursov molodezhi," Obshchestvennye nauki no. 10 (1977), p. 32. Norton T. Dodge ("Women in the Professions," in Women in Russia, p. 216) notes that in 1970, women dominated trade, procurement and supply, and food service at the administrative level in the USSR as a whole.

19. Musaeva and Khasanova, Obshchestvennye nauki, p. 31.

20. Vestnik statistiki no. 1 (1977), p. 81.

21. Narodnoe khozyaistvo SSSR v 1975 godu, (Moscow: Centralnoe Staticheshoe Upravlenie, 1976), p. 422. "Agrarian-industrial enterprises" may not be included in this table. V. Pleshkov ("Ekonomiko-statisticheskii analiz deyatel'nosti agrarno-promyshlennykh predpriyatii i ob'edinenii," Vestnik statistiki no. 7 (1977), pp. 9-10, 12) lists 583 of them, mostly engaged in wine making and canning as of 1976; at least three are in Turkmenia and Tadzhikistan.

22. See Stephen P. and Ethel Dunn, Kulturwandel im sowjetischen Dorf (Berlin, 1977), pp. 76-77, 88-89.

23. Vestnik statistiki no. 1 (1975), p. 86.

24. See Stephen P. and Ethel Dunn, Kulturwandel, pp. 60-74; Stephen P. and Ethel Dunn, "Ländliche Zuwanderer im sowjetische Städte," Berichte des Bundesinstituts für ostwissenschaftliche und internationale Studien, 53 (1977); 1-24; Ethel Dunn, "Russian Rural Women," in Women in Russia, pp.176-81.

26. Ibid.

27. Ibid, pp.60-61.

28. Agrarnaya politika KPSS, p. 201.

29. Nar. khoz. 1975, p. 448.

30. Zinaida I. Monich, "The Professional and Paraprofessional Component in the Structure of the Rural Population (based on data from the Belorussian SSR)," Soviet Sociology, vol. 12, no. 3 (1973), pp. 12-13.

31. Sel'skaya zhizn' 13 December 1975, p. 2.

32. D. Kurbonova, "Zabota Partii o podgotovke mekhanizatorsikh kadrov v Uzbekistane," Obshchestvennye nauki v Uzbekistane 1976, no. 11, pp. 17-19.This is a significant effort, but hardly a mass movement. In the early 1940s, more than 21,000 women in Uzbekistan learned to drive tractors (O.

P. Umurzakova, Zakonomernosti sblizheniia byta i traditsii sotsialisticheskikh natsii (Tashkent, 1971), p. 93.

33. Krest'ianka no. 7 (1976), pp. 8-9.

34. In 1975 the average monthly wage for workers in education was 126.9 rubles; in public health 102.3 rubles, in the field of culture, 92.2 rubles, other white-collar personnel, 114.0 rubles (compared to workers in sovkhozy and other agricultural enterprises, 126.7 rubles, and industrial workers 160.9 rubles. Nar. Khoz. 1975, pp. 546-547.

35. Krest'ianka no. 8 (1976), p. 8.

36. Krest'ianka no. 10 (1976), p. 8. See also the photo-story datelined Tselinograd Oblast, showing an ethnically mixed group of six young women tractor drivers with new machines, Izvestia 12 March 1977, p. 1; the story of a Tadzhik woman equipment operator, Pravda 14 March 1977, p. 1.

37. For example, Izvestia 28 June 1977, p. 5; Pravda 17 June 1977, p. 1.

38. Uchitel'skaia gazeta 26 July 1977, p. 3.

39. The photo-story in Sovetskaya kul'tura 2 August 1977, p. 2 notes that Pasha Angelina's granddaughter continues the family tradition.

40. Sel'skaya zhizn' 29 March 1977, p. 2; see also photo-story in Izvestia 30 March 1977, p. 1.

41. Sel'skaya zhizn' 2 May 1977, p. 2. Fedorova (p. 63), apparently referring to the early 1970s, noted about 7,000 women equipment operators on kolkhozy and sovkhozy of the SFSR, with 56,000 girls studying, and more than 3,000 women equipment operators in the Ukraine. This last figure may be contradicted by the statement of M. M. Kobyl'chak, First Secretary of the Kirovograd Oblast Committee of the Communist Party of the Ukraine that between 1965-75 more than 1,200 girls received training as rural equipment operators (Problemy agrarnoi politiki KPSS, p. 266).

42. Sel'skaya zhizn' 27 April 1976, p. 2.

43. Sel'skaya zhizn' 5 August 1977, p. 1, 2 August 1977, p.1, 12 July 1977, p. 2; Izvestia 29 July 1977, p. 2.

44. Izvestia 3 July 1977, p. 1. This interview with N. V. Pereverzeva, a Hero of Socialist Labor and Delegate to the Twenty-Fifth Party Congress from Rostov Oblast, stresses collectivism rather than competition.

45. Sel'skaya zhizn' 12 July 1977, p. 2; Pravda 9 March 1977, p. 2.

46. Problemy agrarnoi politiki KPSS, vol. 1, pp. 234, 237.

47. This is at least the implication of the remark by V. P. Polianichko, secretary of the Orenburg Oblast Committee of the CPSU that capable youths "do not have the right to work on tractors and automobiles. And if 15 or 16 year old boys and girls are not allowed at machines, at 17 and 18 they will understand that it is easier to do nothing." (Uchitel'skaya gazeta 19 March 1977, p. 2)

48. Perhaps this and the fact that when they were given machines, they were antiquated, is the reason why "some young people underestimate the importance of work in material production and consumer services, being oriented primarily toward work with a humanitarian slant." (Uchitel'skaya gazeta 19 March 1977, p. 1-2.)

49. On the other hand, five young women workers who came from Kostroma to help with the harvest in 1976 married local young equipment operators (Pravda 19 July 1977, p. 6). Estonian milkmaids at least work with machines, have husbands willing to take over the household while their wives study by correspondence, and are ultimately rewarded by being named delegates to party congresses (Sel'skaya zhizn' 8 March 1977, p. 2). If Kostroma farms were mechanized completely and not by halves, young women would not remain in the city after receiving their education (Sel'skaya zhizn' 26 August 1977, p. 3).

50. Compare E. Dunn, "Russian Women," p. 177, table 2 and Vestnik statistiki no. 1 (1977), p. 89.

51. Problemy agrarnoi politiki KPSS, vol. 2, p. 52.

52. Nar. khoz. 1975, pp. 445, 447.

53. Robert C. Stuart, The Collective Farm in Soviet Agriculture (Lexington, Mass.: Lexington Books, 1972), p. 174 (table 8-10).

54. Stuart, The Collective Farm, p. 164.

55. L. V. Ostapenko, "The Effect of Woman's New Production Role on Her Position in the Family (based on data from a study in Vyshnii Volochek Raion, Kalinin Oblast)," Soviet Sociology, vol. 12, no. 4 (1974), pp. 90-91.

56. Krest'ianka no. 10 (1976), pp. 22-23.

57. Izvestia 26 November 1967, p. 2.

58. V. I. Starodun, Zhenshchina i obshchestvennyi trud (Leningrad, 1975), p. 66.

59. Problemy agrarnoi politiki KPSS, vol. 2, p. 64.

60. Sel'skaya zhizn' 6 July 1977, p. 3.

61. Nar. khoz. 1975, pp. 444, 446. In the Turkmen SSR in 1974, of 271 female deputy kolkhoz chairmen, 147 had been on the job more than five years, and 59 had been on the job since 1964. One of their jobs was involving more women in the cultural and economic life of the kolkhozy, a task in which they were not always supported by their immediate male superiors (Sovetskaya kul'tura 9 July 1974, p. 2). As concerns the women kolkhoz chairmen, the best publicized are real veterans--P. A. Malinina, twice Hero of Socialist Labor, chairman of the Twelfth of October kolkhoz, Kostroma raion, Kostroma Oblast for twenty-five years, a delegate to the Twenty-Fifth Party Congress (Krest'ianka no. 6 (1976) pp. 7-9); Ol'maskhon Atabekova, Hero of Socialist Labor, chairman of the Frunze kolkhoz, Lenin raion in southern Kirgizia (Pravda 24 August 1977, p. 2, photo-story). The career of I. F. Anisimova appears typical of the younger generation: a native

88

of the Gomel area, she graduated from the Kiev agricultural academy as an economist, married and raised a family on the Viatsa Noue kolkhoz in Moldavia, became a party organizer on the kolkhoz, was granted a degree of Candidate of Economic Sciences in 1967, was named chairman of the kolkhoz in 1968, but at present is the director of a sovkhoz tekhnikum (B. Glushko, Put' novoi zhizni [Kishinev, 1976], pp. 43, 46-48).

62. Monich, "Rural Population," in Soviet Sociology, pp. 55-57.

63. L. V. Ostapenko, "The Effect of Woman's New Production Role," Soviet Sociology (1974),; Ostapenko, "The Village of Gadyshi Today," Soviet Sociology, vol. 10, no. 1 (1971).

64. Their per capita consumption of meat, fish, and eggs in the USSR increased in 1975 as compared with 1974, but the consumption of fruits and vegetables, which was below the norm, remained the same; see Stephen P. and Ethel Dunn Kulturwandel im sowjetischen Dorf, p. 124, table 13; Nar. khoz. 1975, p. 594. It is not clear from this table whether the discrepancy in consumption pattern between urban and rural areas has been corrected.

65. Iu. V. Arutiunian, Sotsial'naya struktura sel'skogo naseleniia SSSR (Moscow, 1971), pp. 186-87, p. 216 (tables 55-56, 71); the time men have to give to household chores in rural areas appears to correlate with whether or not they think women should work, and how significant a factor the wife's income is. See E. Dunn, "Russian Women," pp. 181-82.

66. I. F. Suslov, Ekonomicheskie interesy i sotsial'noe razvitie kolkhoznogo krest'ianstva (Moscow, 1973), pp. 204, 164, 169.

67. I. M. Slepenkov and B. V. Knyazev (Rural Youth Today [Newtonville, Mass.: Oriental Research Partners, 1977] p. 57) report a study of 818 specialists conducted (apparently in the late 1960s in Kradnodar Krai which revealed that kolkhoz chairmen and sovkhoz directors spent about one-third of their work time away from their farms, with as much as 76 percent of the time being spent on meetings and conferences. Agronomists spent 10-12 percent of their time going from field to field and from team to team, with another 15 percent of the time spent writing reports.

68. Suslov, Ekonomicheshie intersy, p. 208 (table 54).

69. V. Kalmykova, an inspector for the Ministry of Education, reporting in 1977, said that there are a little more than 15,000 preschool institutions on sovkhozy, and if one considers that some sovkhozy have more than one, this means that thousands of sovkhozy have not manifested the necessary concern for working mothers and their children. On kolkhozy, there were 12,500 preschool facilities for 29,000 kolkhozy. In 1976 almost 25 million rubles set aside for construction of preschool facilities went unused (Sel'skaya zhizn' 28 April 1977, p. 2). The apparent reason for the

unused funds is the refusal of some agencies like Brianskkolkhozstroi--where about one hundred sovkhozy and two hundred kolkhozy have no preschool facilities--to approve the plans (Uchitel'skaya gazeta 7 April 1977, p. 3).

70. S. Ia. Chikin, "Voprosy podgotovki i rasstanovki meditsinskikh kadrov v RSFSR," Zdravookhranenie Rossiiskoi Federatsii 1977 no. 1, p. 21.

71. V M. Ivakina, "Statisticheskie materialy o deiatel'nosti uchrezhdenii zdravookhraneniia, kadrakh i razvitii seti v RSFSR za 1973 god," Zdravookhranenie Rossiskoi Federatsii no. 11 (1974) p. 40. G. P. Kobets, "Osnovnye napravleniya sovershenstvovaniya zdravookhraneniya v sel'skom raione," Sovetskoe zdravookhranenie, no. 3 (1975) p. 11.

72. V. P. Kryshtopa, "Problemy sblizheniya urovnei meditsinskoi pomoshchi gorodskomu i sel'skomu naseleniiu Ukrainskoi SSR," Sovetskoe zdravookhranenie, no. 3 (1975) p. 11.

73. In 1970 there were only four thousand dentists in rural areas of the RSFSR, and many hospitals in the Ukraine, Belorussia, Armenia, and Turkmenia with none at all (see Stephen P. Dunn and Ethel Dunn, Kulturwandel im sowjetischen Dorf, pp. 106-114).

75. V. V. Onikienko and V. A. Popovkin, Kompleksnoe issledovanie migratsionnykh protsessov. Analiz migratsii naseleniia USSR (Moscow, 1973), pp. 68 (table 9, 77 (table 12), 78 (table 13).

76. Iu. V. Arutiunian, Sotsial'naya struktura, p. 224.

77. Ibid., p. 213.

78. M. G. Pankratova, "The Function of the Family as Understood by the Modern Rural Resident," Soviet Sociology vol. 15, no. 4 (1977) pp. 48-50.

79. For details, see E. Dunn, "Russian Women," pp. 181-182.

80. Sotsial'noe i natsional'noe: Opyt etno-sotsiologicheskikh issledovanii po materialam Tatarskoi ASSR, eds. Iu. V. Arutiunian et al. (Moscow, 1973), pp. 218-22.

81. Kollektiv kolkhoznikov: Sotsial'no-psikhologicheskoe issledovanie, ed. V. N. Kolbanovskii, (Moscow, 1970), p. 216.

82. V. T. Kolokol'nikov, "Brachno-semeinye otnosheniia v srede kolkhoznogo krest'ianstva (Iz opyta konkretno-sotsiologicheskogo issledovaniia v Brestskoi i Grodnenskoi oblastiakh Belorusskoi SSR)," Sotsiologicheskie issledovaniia no. 3 (1976), p. 82.

83. Ibid., p. 85.

84. These data indicate a perhaps not entirely desirable approximateion of urban life (see Stephen P. Dunn and Ethel Dunn, "The Study of the Soviet Family in the USSR and in the West," Slavic Studies Working Paper No. 1 (Columbus, Ohio, AAASS, 1977), pp. 36-38.

85. Literaturnaya gazeta, 22 May 1974, p. 12, 18 May 1975, p. 12.

86. See Dunn and Dunn, "The Soviet Family," pp. 39-46.

Part 2

Eastern Europe

Introduction

Ronald A. Francisco

The decade of the 1970s in Eastern Europe, like the two previous ones, has been dominated by the Soviet Union. This is particularly true in agricultural policy. Yet it is possible to contend that the USSR's impact on Eastern European farm policy in the 1970s arose more from its absence than its presence. In the first few years of the decade Eastern European nations were told that the USSR could no longer supply their need for imported grain. Most East European nations spent the rest of the 1970s attempting to adjust to this new reality.

Their responses were not, it seems, coordinated closely by Moscow. Yet as the following chapters show, nationally derived policies 'throughout Eastern Europe are remarkably similar. Almost all have sought to maximize their ability to gain self-sufficiency in food and grain supplies and to sustain growth in their livestock sectors (the latter goal has assumed considerable political significance). Actually determining effective policy to meet these goals, however, has proved difficult.

Eastern European nations are constrained by their limited arable land and other resources. Nonetheless, most East European governments have adopted concerted programs to raise productivity and total production to the highest possible levels. Most have invested heavily in agriculture. Some, like Hungary, bought heavily in the West to support a rapid modernization and mechanization of agriculture. Others, like East Germany and Czechoslovakia, upgraded farm wages and benefits substantially and brought the agricultural sector into virtual equality with the industrial sector. Yet whatever ambitious programs have been able to achieve, one thing remains painfully clear: Eastern Europe is constrained less by its natural or financial limits than by its ideological shackles.

This is most evident in the remarkably widespread adoption of agro-industrial integration programs. These attempts at vertical integration of food producing and processing sectors fit nicely into Marxist-Leninist dogma about the inherent superiority of industrial organization in all branches of production. This attractive feature is offset, however, by difficulties of implementation and nagging doubts about the potential effectiveness of these schemes. Although many nations are officially committed to agro-industrial integration, few have made great strides in implementing their programs. Whatever the reasons for this hesitancy may be, things are hardly likely to improve. While the 1970s began with a Soviet default in grain exports, the 1980s will, it seems certain, follow with a decreased Soviet ability to supply oil to Eastern Europe. Hence, governments in these states face massive questions not only about how to achieve more self-sufficiency, but about how to fuel the machinery and agro-industrial complexes that are designed to lead them to this goal.

6
The Origins and Development of Agro-Industrial Development in Bulgaria

Paul Wiedemann

On the occasion of the April 1970 plenum of the central committee of the Bulgarian Communist party, Todor Zhivkov, the first secretary, outlined plans for the "concentration and development of agriculture on an industrial basis." This was to be the official pronouncement of a further transformation of Bulgarian agriculture, with actual and planned developments over the 1971-75 and 1976-80 five-year Plans that are more far-reaching than those of the previous quarter century. The policy of agro-industrial development and horizontal integration that evolved led to the formation of very large agrocomplexes, and shortly thereafter to the improvement and expansion of the application of industrialized methods of production in the agricultural sector.[1]

During this phase of development these agro-industrial complexes also began developing processes of forward and backward integration with the processing industry and with industries and firms producing manufactured inputs. While this process of agro-industrial development was developed across the agricultural sector, the process of vertical integration (and the beginnings of industrioagricultural development) was inaugurated in a small group of complexes (the industrioagricultural complexes). At the same time the long-standing role of state economic organizations in vertically integrated operations in the livestock-breeding sector was expanded.

This paper will set out the broad outlines of the creation and the development of the agro-industrial complexes (APKs) and the industrioagricultural complexes (PAKs) in Bulgaria, and will place emphasis on the question of why the Bulgarians choose to initiate yet another stage in the Bulgarian agricultural development policy and why, given this decision, the characteristic feature of the third stage of Bulgarian agricultural development was the development of APKs and PAKs. An attempt will then be made to evaluate the process of agro-industrial development using the traditional measures of output and yield.

THE CREATION OF THE APK

Stages One and Two

The present process of concentration, intensification, and industrialization in Bulgarian agriculture can be considered the third (and certainly most sophisticated) stage of the postwar transformation of the traditional Bulgarian countryside. The first stage of Bulgarian agricultural development began with the collectivization of 1954-6 when, on the Soviet model, both collective and state farms were established, and during this stage their numbers steadily increased. The second stage of Bulgarian agricultural development began at the end of 1958, with a reduction in the number of collective farms by three-quarters, while at the same time there was some consolidation of both collective and state farms into state farms.[2]

The aggregate dimensions of the change in the face of Bulgarian agricultural development are illustrated on table 6.1. While the area of the farms was expanded and their organization consolidated,[3] a massive shift occurred in the technology of production employed in the agricultural sector. Following the Soviet model of development, labor was transferred out of agriculture and capital was substituted for labor in the production function employed in agriculture. These processes of cosolidation, mechanization, and intensification were, however, judged to be inadequate as a basis for the development of Bulgarian agriculture in the 1970s.

The development of agro-industrial complexes (APKs), and the third stage of Bulgarian agricultural development, officially began at the Communist party plenum in April 1970. In its initial phase the key words were agriculture concentration--a process that already had been adopted widely in the industrial sector before 1970--and industrialization of agricultural production. Plans then called for the creation of a type of fusion between agricultural production units (which would by then be highly concentrated and put on an industrial base) and industrial enterprises in the food industry.

In this first stage of their development the new complexes can be seen to represent an extension of previous Bulgarian experience of horizontally integrating pre-existing state and collective farms into larger production units. A dominant theme in the period of the creation of the APKs was the industrialization of agricultural production. In part, this

TABLE 6.1
Factors of Production in Bulgarian Agriculture at the
Beginning of the First, and End of the Second, State of
Development

	Units	1948	1970
Percentage of total work force employed in agriculture	%	82.7	36.5
Tractors in agriculture in physical units	units	5231	...
in 15HP units	units	4615	84000
Fertilizer application: natural fertilizer	kg/dka	469	71,408
chemical fertilizer	kg/dka	97	17,524
Cultivated land in state or collective farms: of which:	mil. ha	2.4[a]	3.9
in collective farms	mil. ha	2.3[a]	3.3
in state farms	mil. ha	.07[a]	.6

Sources: Kh. Khristov and J. Stoyanov, "Sŭstav i.
Kvalifakatsiya na Rabotnata Sila v. Selskoto Stopanstvo",
Novo Vreme 2/1971, p. 53; Sotsialisticheska Bŭlgariya v
Tsifri i Fakti (Sofia: Izd. na BKP, 1969), pp. 77, 82; L.A.D.
Dellin, Bulgaria (New York: Praeger, 1957), p. 303;
Statisticheski Godishnik na Narodna Republika Bŭlgariya 1972
(hereafter SGNRB1972), p. 198.

[a] Data for collective farms excludes private plots.

[b] For 1950. For 1948 the area was .18 mil. ha for TKZSs
and .03 mil. ha for DZSs.

emphasis on the industrialization of agricultural production is simply a continuation of the emphasis on mechanization and the more intensive use of physical capital inputs in general that characterized agricultural production in the 1960s.

As Bulgarian agricultural production became more concentrated, the farms became more specialized. In this situation of a more concentated and more specialized sector, the industrialization of agricultural production meant the introduction into agriculture of the large-scale, more technologically sophisticated techniques that have proven successful in the development of industry in Bulgaria.

The APKs were created by horizontally integrating 744 collective farms (TKZSs) and 56 state farms (DZSs) into 161 new units (APKs)[4] which were composed entirely of collective farms, entirely of state farms, or mixed. It is certainly arguable that such a new organizational form is well suited for a country (and indeed a whole region of Europe) where highly qualified specialists engaged in agricultural production are at (and paid) a premium and that it creates a production base and a physical size sufficiently large to allow the rational utilization of certain modern techniques previously either eschewed, or at least under-utilized.

Table 6.2 shows the dimensions of the change in the average size of the old state and collective farms and the new complexes that took place as the number of production units was reduced by 82 percent. The average arable land per complex was 4.6 times larger, average gross fixed capital was 5.1 times larger, and the number of employed persons was 4.3 times larger. But the changes that have been introduced into the organization and management of agricultural production with the creation of the APK extend far beyond such narrow confines.

The new management structure of the APK is an amalgam of that of the old TKZSs and DZSs (which, when the APK is completely horizontally integrated, cease to exist) with some new features of its own. It is to combine "the principle of centralization in planning, the safe-guarding cf state discipline and of one-man management in the labor process"-- all features of the Bulgarian state farms--with "all the positive sides exhibited in co-operative ownership, such as the successive application of the principle of economic accounting, the tighter connection of the personal income of the producers with the final result of their work, participation of workers themselves in the management of production, and the strengthening of the socialist principle, the principle of the choice of the management cadre."[5]

With the development of the APKs, the state commands concerning the necessary agricultural produce are now given from the Council of Ministers through the state committee for planning directly to the individual APKs. They in turn carry out the planning activity for all of their "individual

TABLE 6.2
State and Collective Farms and APKs, 1970 and 1971.

YEAR	Type of Farm or Complex	All Farms or Complexes					Per Farm or APK			
		No. of Farms or Complexes (units)	Total Arable Land[b] (th.ha)	Total Gross Fixed Capital[c] (mil.leva)	Total Employed Persons (th.units)	National Income (Current prices) (mil.leva)	Arable Land (ha.)	Gross Fixed Capital (th.leva)	Employed Persons (units)	National Income (Current prices)[d] (th.leva)
1970	State Farms[a]	156	635	574	152	239	4070	3679	978	1532
	Collective farms	744	3270	2581	920	1404	4390	3470	1237	1887
	State and collective farms	900	3905	3155	1072	1644	4340	3506	1192	1827
1971	APKs	161	3910	3443	1064	2114	24,286	21,385	6609	13,134

Source: Statisticheski Godishnik na Narodna Republika Bŭlgariya 1972 (Sofia: TsSU, 1972, p. 93); and unpublished TsSu data.

a State farms are those under the Ministry of Agriculture and the food industry.
b Total arable land excludes private plots.
c Captial stock is valued at (undepreciated) original cost. It is measured in current prices.
d National income excludes income and output from private plots.

enterprises" (the term now used to include the member farms, reorganized within the APK, as well as new service sectors), with the number of control figures depending on the specialization of the complex. There are also central norms on wages and profitability, limits on capital investment, and schedules of tax liabilities for the complexes. Control figures also cover bank credit for capital investment and the amount of material and technical supplies, and there are control indices for irrigation and drainage work and for the introduction of new techniques into production.[6]

The Creation of the Complexes

Discussion in Bulgaria of the APKs had begun by late 1968, and the first APK was formed from five state farms in November 1968.[7] The idea became increasingly more widely discussed and several other "experiments" were made--twelve by the end of 1969.[8] After Zhivkov's April speech the formation of APKs proceeded so rapidly that by the autumn the number stood at 102,[9] and by January 1971 it had reached 138--though only fifty-one had been officially approved[10] by the recently created Committee for Economic Co-Ordination, an organ of the Council of Ministers which decided if the newly created APKs were economically viable.

By the late summer of 1971 the number had risen to 156,[11] unofficial reports put the number at 160 in the autumn, and by the end of the year there were 161. The number increased to 171, and through merging--a process that continued throughout the 1970s--fell to 170 by the end of 1972. (See table 6.3 below.)

In terms of the technology of production, with the creation of the APKs not only was there a four- to five-fold concentration in the size of the primary unit of agricultural organization and management, but there was also an extensive (and generally much greater) concentration, as well as increased specialization, in the basic production units. In 1970 grain production was carried out on over 45,000 separate tracts of land averaging some 40 ha, and vegetable production was carried out on over 17,000 separate tracts of land.[12] As the APKs were developed the size of the basic grain production track rose to between 200 and 500 ha, the basic size of new orchards and vineyards to between 1,000 and 1,500 ha--and for both grains and orchards and vineyards these maxima were sometimes greatly exceeded. The basic size of vegetable tracts rose to 315 ha.

For livestock-breeding the most important change in terms of the technology of production was the greatly increased emphasis on the application of industrial-type production techniques in the fattening of pigs, calves and broilers, and in the production of eggs. Press reports discussed the construction of fattening complexes with capacities of up to 200,000 pigs and 20,000 calves,[13] but the more scientific discussions generally gave maxima of half this size. This further increase in the scale of microproduction units, with increased application of capital-intensive production methods in agriculture and specialization of production within the units was not, however, a new idea in April 1970. Such developments had already been underway since 1964 in the form of inter-collective and state-collective enterprises, and by the end of the 1966-70 Plan several pig-fattening farms and large (500 cows) dairy farms were in operation and construction of some twenty-one poultry combines, fourteen pig combines, and six calf-fattening enterprises was underway.

In its early years the APK is best seen as an agrocomplex in which both collective and state farms were combined in a new form of organization and management, many of the characeristic features of which were continuations and extensions of trends carried over from the DSOs in the1960s. The APK served as a means for facilitating the further development of proven, modern technology, for introducing new technologies, for spreading the fixed costs of production, for further harmonizing socioeconomic conditions throughout agriculture, for rationalizing parts of the production process in agriculture, for making the agricultural sector more amenable to planning, and for making the output of the agricultural sector better suited as an industrial input. But why inaugurate the program in April 1970, and why agro-industrial development?

WHY

Why Stage Three?

The search for the motivation behind the introduction of a third stage in Bulgarian agricultural development is a fascinating one--even if at the conclusion of the search one remains less than absolutely certain as to the precise ranking and weighting of the contributing factors. Or even if one has managed to isolate all of the key variables.

One of the key decision factors would be the performance of the agricultural sector in the last years of the fifth (1966-70) five-year Plan. The first years of the Plan had been successful, but many basic indicators (e.g., output, material expenditure, the capital-output ratio) had now taken a significant turn for the worse. At this time fruit growing was, at best, only marginally profitable, vegetable production was losing an average of some 6 percent and livestock breeding suffered much greater losses. Agricultural production had fallen in 1967 and 1968, and by 1969 had still not regained its 1966 level, although it had recovered from the (drought-reduced) 1968 harvest.

Inventories of livestock were down at the beginning of 1969 as compared with the two previous years, meat production only marginally better than in 1966, and significantly down on 1967 and 1968. In 1970, only poultry had improved over 1969. Tobacco production was lower than in any recent year (having been affected by disease), and Bulgaria was the only Southeastern European socialist country not to have had a bumper harvest in fruit.[15]

At the end of 1969 total agricultural product stood 13.9 percent higher than at the end of 1965--i.e., the annual growth rate had averaged only 3.5 percent, rather than the planned growth rate of some 7.5 percent over these four years. The growth that did occur was concentrated primarily in 1966, and when investigating causal factors for the new policy on the development of Bulgarian agriculture it is tempting to ascribe importance to the failure to fulfill the Plans for agriculture for 1967, 1968, and 1969. The same eyes would consider as supporting circumstantial evidence the fact that the net performance in 1967 was worse than in 1966, and in 1968 worse than in 1967.[16]

It is important to note that this was in no way due exclusively either to country-specific or system-specific factors: the years were ones of unfavorable weather conditions in the Balkans in general. But the critical examination which (must have) accompanied such unfavorable performance in a high-pressure economy undoubtedly was a catalyst in the process which lead to the April 1970 conviction that the second stage of Bulgarian agricultural development had yielded all its fruit.

Intimately connected with the performance of the agricultural sector is the state of Bulgaria's balance of payments, and particularly her balance of payments with convertible-currency countries. It is generally agreed that by and large "Bulgarian machinery and equipment and industrial consumption goods are marketable only within the CMEA."[17] Without the foreign currency earnings from agricultural exports to the West the imports of high-technology machinery and equipment, and hence the progress of Bulgaria's industrial development program, would be hindered. It would be hindered not only because of the reduced degree of access to Western capital goods, but also because of the increased need to export Bulgarian machinery (within CMEA) to finance imports. Although we have not found it anywhere explicitly set out, CMEA specialization certainly makes Bulgaria Comecon's largest fruit bowl and vegetable patch, and Bulgaria has signed agreements to supply agricultural products to other CMEA countries. Thus any shortfall in agricultural production tends either to hit exports to the West or to increase domestic shortages (see below).

Following a policy in which it attempted to increase the value added in each unit of exports, Bulgaria has been increasing the share of processed agricultural products in total agricultural exports. This is a policy that is rational under the pricing policy toward agricultural versus manufactured products prevailing within the CMEA countries, and is also rational from the point of view of consideration of the income elasticity of demand for unprocessed and processed agricultural products. But it is only possible for this policy to succeed if the agricultural sector is supplying the requisite inputs to the processing industry.

In addition to the need to stimulate agriculture for exports, it was essential to stimulate agriculture to allow the attainment of the program for raising the standard of living outlined by Todor Zhivkov in a speech at the central committee plenum of December 1972. Specific objectives-- "scientific norms"--were announced for each of a number of products (primarily unprocessed food items), and detailed targets were established for 1975 and 1980 (and later for 1990).[18]

One can take the more narrowly economic view that the primary factor underlying the inauguration of this policy was a view on the part of the planners that a higher standard of living was a precondition for the higher quality of the labor force necessary to allow attainment of Plan targets across the economy in the 1971-75 and 1976-80 plans,[19] or one can view the entire program as part of a delayed response on the part of Bulgaria to the East European-wide pressure from below for a changed attitude towards personal consumption expenditure. In either case, they represented a widely publicized policy statement on the part of the party, the attainment of which required improved performance from the agricultural sector.

A further important factor in the decision to announce a new policy of agricultural development could be the desire to create a new framework within which to make policy changes that clearly needed to be made in the agricultural sector and which could more easily be made as part of a comprehensive policy. Transferring land (and villages) between farms would be one example, the reorganization of the structure of production of cultures in a given area to reduce transportation expenses and to increase the efficiency of supply of agricultural materials to the processing industries another, as well as numerous measures of specialization, mechanization, and industrialization in agriculture. More generally, the pronouncement of a new policy of agricultural development would allow the planners to create yet another "campaign," would give them another special reason to exhort the people, allow yet a further attempt to extract X-efficiency from the agricultural labor force.

105

Why Agro-Industrial Development?

This question, in its turn, is connected with the planners' increasing their wagers on a past winner: a movement toward the large-scale, mass-production techniques in agriculture that have proven successful in developing Bulgarian industry. These techniques had proven their merit in industrial application and it was felt that they could provide decisive in the search for increased efficiency in agricultural production necessary to improve both the level of domestic consumption and its pattern (the 1972 norms having included a move up the food chain), as well as to provide (in fresh or processed form) further exports. They would now be applied within the framework of the APK. It is clear that neither the physical nor organizational base of the individual farms as they existed was suitable for this industrialization; but the former had been appreciably improved over the latter 1960s and the latter was transformed with the creation of the APK.

The same line of reasoning sees the APK as a strengthening of the contact between industry and agriculture--perhaps as a necessary condition for this strengthening. The increasing sophistication of the production techniques used in those industries concerned with the post-production stages of the agricultural reproduction process imposes demands (with respect to quality, consistency, regularity, and so forth) on units in the earlier stages of the process--requirements which are part and parcel of industrial techniques of production, but much less so of smaller, more loosely coordinated units.

Accepting all this, it would seem only logical to create in agriculture the logical counterpart of the individual state economic enterprises (the DSOs) that had existed in industry since 1964. The planners could therefore draw on years of practical experience in the amalgation of individual production units--both horizontally and vertically--into larger-scale complexes. And, of course, in Bulgarplod, Rodopa, Vinprom, and others the extension of the state economic organizations into agriculture and the food industries had already existed for some years.

Allied to the successful experience of the DSO is the fact that Bulgarian economists generally were agreed with their Western colleagues that the development of science and technology held the key to a successful policy of economic development. Thus, in the same period that John Kenneth Galbraith was writing that technology and organization are what determine the shape of economic society,[20] the Bulgarian economist Jordan Kostadinov was calling the application of technological progress via the integration of agriculture and industry a "law of socialist development."[21] On the practical level, the evidence too was beginning to suggest to Bulgarian planners that the point had been reached where the basic agricultural production units--and these were still the individual collective and state farms, since the inter-farm enterprises had been neither extensively nor enthusiastically developed--were too small to capture fully the benefits of modern production techniques. In the Bulgarian view they were simply too small to provide the strong economic and technical base necessary for the further specialization and the development of concentration on a large scale that the perceived development of science and technology required. On the one hand, for 1970 the full output of all the existing intercollective processing enterprises could have been produced with the underutilized capacity in existing state processing enterprises. While on the other, the newest machinery and production techniques--agroairplanes, large microregions specialized in growing one crop or large complexes specialized in fattening one type of animal--could simply not be rationally applied within the existing organizational framework of the individual farms; and other modern techniques (such as the application of even the simplest form of on-farm computer technology) were totally excluded.

Considerations of efficiency would appear to suggest as a logical corollary to the Bulgarian development policy that stressed specialization, concentration, and industrialization, one fostering production units whose optimal size exceeds the capacity and capabilities of the pre-existing, individual farms. This was presented as an incontestable fact in official Bulgarian policy statements at the beginning of the 1970s and seems economically a quite rational policy. This further emphasis on the economies of scale argument gains a new dimension when one realizes that the economies of scale being discussed are economies of scale in human capital--the human infrasructure capital in the form of specialists and management cadre, both of which are in very scarce supply in agriculture.

These inputs are the basis of a modern agricultural organization, and they gained increasing importance in the process of agro-industrial development. It must be noted, however, that the development of APKs in Bulgaria in practice did not show particular economies of scale in the use of human capital. Nor does production function analysis for the 1970s show an especially large marginal product of specialists employed in Bulgarian agriculture.

One could further add that it is a basic Marxian idea that large-scale farming is much superior to small-scale farming, just as large-scale industry is superior to small-scale industry,[22] and call on this to justify the blind faith in large-scale techniques of production that dominates the literature.[23] But it is our belief that in Bulgaria at least the policy of increasing the scale of farming can be at least as well explained by pragmatic factors such as the desire for the efficient use of airplanes and helicopters in fertilization and spraying and other capital equipment in irrigation, harvesting, and livestock breeding and fattening as by ideological factors.

At the same time that this view on the economies of scale dominated discussion at one level, specialized food processing units were being created at the farm level that were characterized by their small size and by waste and inefficiency in resource utilization. Problems existed in controlling the creation of small processing units on the farms, and steps to rationalize the state canning industry were sometimes thwarted by the small farm processing units acting counter to the policy of the state enterprises. The state canning factories were criticized for having many shortcomings, including an excessive variance in their cost of production and their profitability, and they suffered from excessive fluctuations in the receipt of the necessary raw material inputs.[24] One detailed study of the state canning industry talks of the losses in the quality of the product, the squandering and spoiling of raw materials, the misapplication of techniques of production, and the loss of time in production as being "unbearable."[25]

It is not clear to what extent horizontal and, more importantly, vertical integration, would necessarily be able to alter such a state of affairs, as it is in large part at least a biological and environmental problem beyond the sphere of the organization of agricultural production. But horizontal and vertical integration can be regarded as one means of meeting the more stringent demands with respect to the quality and standardization of output and the regularity of delivery on those enterprises supplying it with inputs which the food-processing industry, expanded both to increase the value added in Bulgarian food exports and to allow a higher standard of living with a more varied selection of food products, would impose in the 1970s.

These are the same type of requirements that were standard in Bulgarian industrial production, but that were much less representative of production in the smaller, loosely coordinated production units that characterized Bulgarian agricultural production before the complexes were developed. By closer relations between agriculture and the food industry, the latter's growth being such that in 1969 for the first time the value of the output of the food industry exceeded the value of the output of the agricultural sector,[26] agriculture would be brought into closer production relations with enterprises whose average size was four times as large as the average state and collective farm, yet where the average number of workers and employees per enterprise was only two-fifths as large.[27] If, however, agriculture and the food industry were to be brought together in a closer, organizational relationship, it is clear the planning and control in agriculture must improve.

Further insights into the decision to carry out agro-industrial development can be gained from moving from micro-level considerations to the level of macrolevel planning. The process of agro-industrial development can be argued to be a means of attaining a fuller utilization of all resources employed in agriculture. Better planning on the complex level could work to reduce seasonal fluctuations in the utilization of both human and physical capital, and the fuller development of post- (and pre-) production industries as vertical integration develops should increase off-peak employment opportunities.

Given the scarcity of high-quality human capital in the agricultural sector, the concentration of specialists at a higher level in the agro-industrial complex could represent a more efficient utilization of this capital. Development of the complex would also create, through complex-level investment, a new form of "national" property which would merge the collective property and state property already existing (and therefore effectively work to abolish collective agriculture). Planners could acquire a more direct control over agriculture that is much more comparable to that that they exercise in the nonagricultural sector. The line of control would become much more direct from the planners to the horizontally integrated complexes, and this control strengthened further in the vertically integrated complexes with a two-level system of management.

Agro-industrial development brings the elements into a group of subsystems and groups these subsystems tightly together with a strong central control. This could be seen to be true whether one saw the APK as the central control or, on a more macrolevel, as just one of the 170 subsystems.

Lastly we must look at the pattern of related developments abroad. Although the mass of the units being created may differ from country to country, and although the same term may have different meanings in different countries, almost all of the socialist countries of Eastern Europe, as well as the Soviet Union, have embarked on a path of integration in the agricultural sector.[28] By the time of the April 1970 speech the development of agrocombines, agro-industrial combines and industriocombines was already proceeding in neighboring Yugoslavia, and developments were also progressing in the GDR and the CSSR. Details of these developments are set out in Everett Jacob's contribution to this volume.

It is to developments in these countries that is the obvious place to look when searching for inspiration for the Bulgarian policies. But one should look even more to the Soviet Union, and it is clear from even the most fragmentary knowledge of Bulgarian economic development that Bulgaria has traditionally followed the Soviet model, with important variations in speed and style, of agricultural development.[29] And, most recently, it had necessarily followed the Soviet example in forming the intercollective farms and enterprises. Few Bulgarian agricultural specialists were aware of the details of developments in agrobusiness in the West, but the general trend was well known and Bulgarian practice could be said to be following on this experience.

Then there is the weight of impartial experts. Here we can take the example of the 1967 FAO study, <u>Agriculture et Industrialisation</u>.[30] The FAO cited figures for three typical canning factories--one with a capacity of 100-200 pounds per hour, one with a capacity of 1000 pounds per hour, and one for 10,000.[31] The "typical" results were quite unequivocal: by all measures, the bigger the better.

But Bulgarian economists on all levels--in the Ministry of Agriculture and the food industries, on the complexes, at the institutes--argue that the role of practice abroad, except in its broad socialist outlines, has been negligible in Bulgaria. In arguing that the formation of the APK is a continuation of the pre-existing development strategy, one can refer not only to the example of the DSO--which is more relevant in vertical integration, the development of the PAKs, and the creation of the industrioagricultural organization (the PAO)--but also to the whole history of the development of socialized agriculture in Bulgaria. The process of horizontal integration is the logical sequitur of the processes of collectivization and concentration which had gone before. The industrialization of agricultural production that is the hallmark of the present stage in the development of the APK is also a logical development of the processes of mechanization, chemicalization, amelioration, and the general intensification that characterized the second stage of Bulgarian agricultural development.

The intercooperative enterprises and state-collective complexes that had been modelled on their Soviet counterpart had introduced into practice the principle of interfarm cooperation., Examination of their results during 1968 and 1969 could be interpreted as showing that, indeed, this "dress rehearsal" had been successful and that one must move further along this line. Or they could be interpreted as showing that such a step in the direction of further cooperation was by its very nature too feeble to produce the desired results. Successful development along this line of grouping a number of farms for undertaking joint investment projects requires a clear line of management control that the loosely organized interfarm amalgamations could not provide (but that the APK, and especially one with full legal independence, could provide). Either interpretation yields the same conclusion.

Many of the arguments presented in this section would lead to the conclusion that short-run factors--i.e., in the terminology of control theory, not the control variables of

the economic system, but signals from outside the system--
caused the fundamental long-term changes in the structure and
management of agriculture. But a number of long-term factors
have also been cited that, of themselves, would have led to a
reassessment of pragmatically oriented policy. And it is our
conclusion that in many respects the policy changes of the
first years of the third stage were a refurbished (with modern
technology) stage two--i.e., a re-tuning of the controls. As
argued below, the evidence on factor allocation to agriculture
over the 1970s would further support the inference that this
was indeed the policy of the planners.

HORIZONTAL AND VERTICAL INTEGRATION

Further Development of the APK

In this same spirit we can gain a perspective on the
development of the agricultural sector during the 1970s by
viewing the developments in Bulgarian agriculture in the 1960s
as a process of horizontal combination. With the creation of
the APKs, Bulgarian agriculture entered a new stage, that of
horizontal integration. Starting at the same time, but
particularly as the process of horizontal integration was
formally complete with the creation of the 171 complexes,
agriculture began developing the process of vertical
coordination between agriculture and the industrial sector on
a much more extensive level than had existed previously.

This process has been expressed by Georgi Kostandinov:
"horizontal integration will have to prepare for the future
full integration with industrial firms, for the gradual
vertical integration with industrial, selling, and trading
organizations. In the course of this process of development
the agro-industrial complex will develop into an
industrioagricultural complex."[32] Thus the agricultural
sector would enter the fourth stage, that of vertical
integration. This is what happened in 1973, when three more
of the complexes were merged and seven others converted into
industrioagricultural complexes (PAKs) within the
industrioagricultural organization (PAO).

During the early- to mid-1970s the APK can be seen as a
new form of the organization of production designed to
facilitate the further development of proven, modern
technology as applied to agriculture, the introduction of new
technology into agriculture, the spreading of the fixed costs
of production, the further harmonization of socio-economic
conditions throughout agriculture, the rationalization of
parts of the productive process, the reduction of the
seasonality of employment of the agricultural labor force, and
the creation of an agricultural sector that was better suited

111

to planning, and the output of which was better utilized as an industrial input.

The basis of planning before the APKs had been that control figures were given to the regional national councils for all TKZSs in their region and to the department for DZSs in the Ministry of Agriculture and the food industry, and they in turn distributed figures to the farms under their jurisdiction. Under the new system a whole intermediate level of planning was removed in 1975 when all the APKs were given full legal and economic control over all their constitutent farms. Thus not only had the distinctions between the TKZSs and DZSs been reduced over the first years of agro-industrial development, but from February 1975 the APK was officially established as the basic agricultural management and control unit for the entire country and the economic and legal independence of the collective and state farms (which had continued on the majority of APKs) was terminated.

Norms and quotas for agricultural production are now given by the state committee for planning directly to the APKs. With the further development of the APK into closer integration with the DSOs, the role of the centralized control figures is reduced and replaced by an extension of the contract system. This is further extended by direct management and control of the agricultural sector by the PAO under industrioagricultural integration. When the third stage of Bulgarian agro-industrial development is viewed from the level of macro-economic planning, the logical development would now be toward vertical productive (as opposed to vertical contractual) integration, in which there would be direct management and control by the DSO (representing the processing, packing, transport, and marketing sectors) of the agricultural units.

Examination of the data on the size of the APKs in Table 6.3 shows that the labor force employed on the complexes fell by some 20 percent over the 1971-76 period, while the gross capital stock rose by 21 percent and the area of arable land fell by 9 percent. These changes in relative factor proportions, at the same time that the number of complexes fell by 9 percent (or 15 percent from the 1972 high of 171 to the 1976 end of year number of 146), represent a significant increase both in the capital-intensity of production in the APK sector, and in the average degree of capital concentration in the basic agricultural production units.

The pace at which the capital-intensification proceeded was not, however, a steady one. As table 6.4 suggests, the rate of annual change was extremely varied, and in the case of no factor of production was the rate of change linear or even monotonic in its development over the period. As one should

TABLE 6.3
Development of APKs, 1971-1976

ALL APKs   PER APK

YEAR	No. of APKs (units)	Total Arable Land (th. na)	Total Gross Capital (mil leva)	Total Employed Persons (th. units)	Total Product (current prices) From all Activity (mil. leva)	Total Product (current prices) Only from Agriculture Activity (mil. leva)	Arable Land (th. na)	Gross Fixed Capital (mil. leva)	Employed Persons (units)	Total Product From all Activity (th. leva)	Total Product Only Prom. Agricultural Activity (th. leva)
1971	161	3910	3443	1,064	3,879	3,125	24.3	21.4	6609	24,093	19,410
1972	170	3965	3721	1,128	4,314	3,417	23.3	21.9	6635	25,376	20,100
1973	160	3631	3682	996	4,240	3,272	22.7	23.0	6225	26,500	20,450
1974	153	3631	3796	972	4,265	3,277	23.7	24.8	6353	27,876	21,418
1975	152	3595	4004	890	4,468	3,402	23.7	26.3	5855	29,395	22,382
1976	146	3544	4154	852	4,451	3,410	24.3	28.4	5836	30,486	23,356

Source: SGNRB 1977, pp. 268-70.

a See table 6.2.

TABLE 6.4
Development of APKs (Percentage Change)

| PERIOD | ALL APKs | | | | | | PER APK | | | | |
| | No. of APKs | Total Arable Land | Total Gross Capital | Total Employed Persons | Total Product | | Arable Land | Gross Fixed Capital | Employed Persons | Total Product | |
					From all Activity	Only from Agricultural Activity				From all Activity	Only from Agricultural Activity
1971-2	+5.6	+1.4	+8.1	+6.0	+11.2	+9.3	-4.1	+2.3	+.4	+5.3	+3.4
1972-3	-5.9	-8.4	-1.0	-11.7	-1.7	-4.2	-2.6	+5.0	-6.2	+4.4	+1.7
1973-4	-4.4	0.0	+2.3	-2.4	+0.6	+0.2	+4.4	+7.8	+2.1	+5.2	+4.8
1974-5	-0.6	-1.0	+5.5	-8.4	+4.8	+3.8	0.0	+6.0	-7.8	+5.4	+4.5
1975-6	-3.9	-1.4	+3.7	-4.3	-0.4	+0.2	+2.5	+8.0	-0.3	+3.7	+4.4
Annual Average 1971-76	-2.5	-1.6	+3.4	-3.3	+2.4	+1.5	0.0	+5.4	-1.9	+4.4	+3.4
Annual Average 1972-76	-2.8	-2.1	+2.3	-4.9	+0.6	-0.04	+0.8	+5.9	-2.4	+4.0	+3.2

a See table 6.2

114

expect from a process of agro-industrial development, the rate of growth of nonagricultural output also exceeded that of agricultural output on the APKs for all periods except 1975/1976, although even with this growth the agricultural/nonagricultural split was still 77/23 (as opposed to 81/19 in 1971).

As the average size of the APKs grew in the 1970s, the average APKs were also becoming more "standardized." The disaggregation of the APKs by the size of the arable land on figure 6.1 shows that whereas 37 percent of the complexes had an arable acreage of between 20 and 27.9 thousand hectares in 1971, complexes with this acreage remained the median in 1976 but accounted for only 27 percent of the complexes. In absolute terms this was a reduction of twenty complexes and of the entire reduction of twenty-four APKs that occurred from the end of 1971 to the end of 1976. A similar trend is evident for other factor inputs.

Two further points are evident from figure 6.1: first, when seven APKs were converted into PAKs in 1973, there was not an appreciable alteration in the size distribution of APKs. The larger agro-industrial complexes that were transformed into industrioagricultural complexes were replaced, through mergers, by other equally large APKs. Second, when the new policy of transforming all the APKs into legally and financially fully independent management units (and terminating the legal and financial independence of the TKZSs and DZSs) began to be carried out in 1975, this major change--major in the sense that only forty-three APKs had been given full independence over the first four years of agro-industrial development--also did not significantly alter the size distribution of the complexes.

Disaggregating still further, to the okrug level, we can compare the APKs in the okrug with the smallest average-sized APKs to those in the okrug with the largest average-sized APKs, and compare both to the median-sized APK. (See table 6.5.) It is clear that the changes that took place were not in the mountainous and hilly okrugs where one tends to find the smallest APKs, but rather in the areas with extensive areas of good soil and flat land in south-central Bulgaria around Pazardzhik and Plovdiv and even more so in northeast Bulgaria around Ruse and Tolbukhin. In the latter areas if one excludes the okrug of Silistra, where one complex has been created covering the entire okrug, then the relationship of the relative size of APKs in okrugs with the largest APKs and in okrugs with the smallest APKs has altered by some 2 to 3 percent per year. If one includes Silistra, where the arable land is 6.2 times the average, gross fixed capital stock 5.7 times the average, and the labor force 5.5 times the average, then the picture is one of a very appreciable widening of the range in the size of APKs across okrugs and quite the opposite

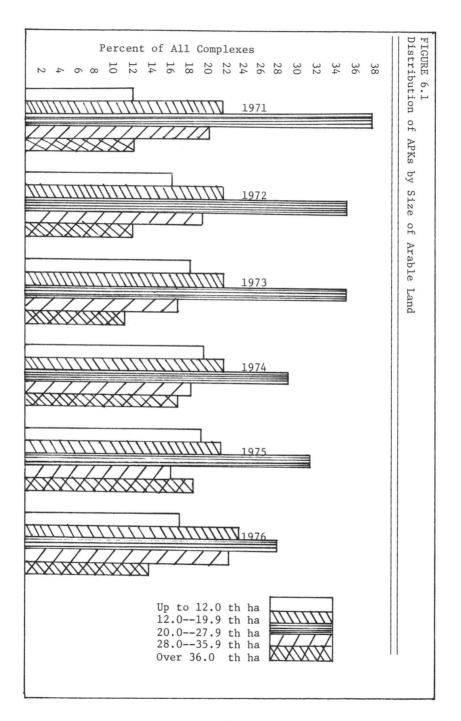

FIGURE 6.1
Distribution of APKs by Size of Arable Land

Percent of All Complexes

1971

1972

1973

1974

1975

1976

Up to 12.0 th ha
12.0--19.9 th ha
20.0--27.9 th ha
28.0--35.9 th ha
Over 36.0 th ha

TABLE 6.5
Relative Size of APKs, 1971 and 1976

Ratio of Okrugs	Arable Land	Gross Fixed Capital	Employed Persons
	1976		
Largest APKs Smallest APKs	27.14	25.12	10.26
(Second-largest APKs) (Smallest APK)	(7.12)	(8.74)	(3.70)
Largest APKs Average-sized APKs	6.26	5.67	5.50
(Second-largest APKs) (Average-sized APKs)	(1.64)	(1.97)	(1.98)
Smallest APKs Average-sized APKs	0.23	0.22	0.54
	1971		
Largest APKs Smallest APKs	6.14	7.91	4.28
Largest APKs Average-sized APKs	1.48	2.02	1.64
Smallest APKs Average-sized APKs	0.24	0.25	0.522

Sources: SGNRB1977, p. 503; SGNRB1972, p. 474.

conclusion to the one drawn from the aggregate data onthe sizedistribution of complexes shown on figure 6.1.

DEVELOPMENT OF THE PAK AND PAO

After the process of horizontal integration had stabilized in 1972, seven of the APKS were converted into PAKs, thus inaugurating the process of vertical integration. The seven complexes were further specialized in sugar beet production, a crop in which Bulgarian production had previously already been relatively highly specialized and concentrated and which experience in other countries suggests as a logical choice for vertical integration. Management and control of the PAKs is carried out by the industrioagricultural organization (the PAO) "Bulgarian Sugar" and thus the system of management has now been reduced from four to two levels.

At the time Bulgarian planners talked of the extension of the development of PAKs and PAOs into other sectors of agriculture and the food industry, but a necessary first step was the creation of a three-level management and control system across the country. This was created when, in February 1975, the central committee plenum gave full legal and economic independence to the APKs.

Only then, with the creation of a three-layer planning and control hierarchy in agriculture, was the further development of the PAK and the PAO possible. This further possible development of agriculture would be based on the PAO--the equivalent unit to the DSO in the nonagricultural sectors--and would allow the extensive application of the principle of decomposition in the planning, management, and control of agriculture.

The pattern of development of the PAKs over 1973-76 is illustrated in table 6.6, and it is clear that the complexes that were created in 1973 were appreciably larger than the average APK by all measures--110 percent larger in arable land, 94 percent larger in gross fixed capital, and 73 percent larger in employed persons. Moreover, they were more efficient in the utilization of their given factor inputs in that the average capital-output and labor-output ratios were smaller. Over the four years, with the merging of APKs, the difference in the average size of the two types of complexes was slightly reduced by all measures, and the APKs became relatively more efficient in their use of inputs relative to the PAKS.

Over the four years the capital and land-intensity of production rose relatively faster in the APKs than in the PAKs, and the degree of labor intensity fell less rapidly in the APKs. Therefore at the end of 1976, and after further merging of APKs, the difference in the average size of the two

118

TABLE 6.6
Development of PAKs, 1973-1976

ALL PAKs | | | | | PER PAK

YEAR	No. of PAKs Units	Total Arable Land (th.na)	Total Gross Capital (mil.leva)	Total Employed Persons (th.units)	Total Product (current prices)		Arable Land (th.na.)	Gross Fixed Capital (mil.leva)	Employed Persons (units)	Total Product (current prices)	
					From all Activity (mil.leva)	Only from Agricultural Activity (mil.leva)				From all Activity (mil.leva)	Only From Agricultural Activity (mil.leva)
1973	7	334	312	80	378	299	47.7	44.6	11.4	54	42.7
1974	7	334	336	74	378	297	47.7	48	10.6	54	42.4
1975	8	371	396	77	443	343	46.3	49.5	9.6	55.4	42.9
1976	8	371	427	78	456	364	46.3	53.4	9.8	57	45.5

Source: SGNRB1977, pp. 271-275.

a See Table 2.

119

types of complexes was slightly reduced by all measures, and the APKs had become relatively more efficient in their use of inputs relative to the PAKs.

We have stressed the difference between APKs and PAKs in terms of the hierarchy of management, planning, and control. But one should also examine the varying degree to which their output has remained primarily agricultural, or has become appreciably more concentrated in the nonagricultural sectors, in the course of agro-industrial development. Table 6.7 illustrates clearly just how similar the activity of the APKs and PAKs is in terms of the origin of their total product, and indeed that the PAKs have a slightly higher share of their output arising from agricultural sector than do the APKs. This emphasizes that it is the scale of production, and even more importantly the system of production (i.e., the system of planning management, planning, and control), that characterizes the PAKs and the PAO and separates them from the APKs.

The role of industry in the attempts to develop the agricultural sector, and especially in attempts to transform the traditionally inefficient livestock-breeding sector, go back to before the introduction of PAKs and even APKs. At the time when the idea of the APK was just beginning to be seriously discussed again in socialist writing in the 1960s-- and before any important Bulgarian research was published on the subject--the state economic organization (DSO) 'Rodopa' began integrating backwards into agriculture.

Fully eight years before the first experiment was begun in vertically integrating agricultural complexes with industrial units, industry had created its own very large units (and taken over other units from the agricultural sector) and had a completely unified industrial-type management system. Indeed this management system then was even more vertically integrated than the PAO Bulgarian sugar is today. Here the introduction of the most modern technology--and the development of the weakest sector of agriculture--was placed squarely in the lap of industry.

In certain cases, when an APK was created, a part of one of the farms was taken over by the DSO Rhodopa and immediately vertically integrated into its operations. While this policy has not been vigorously pursued, it is mentioned to allow a contrast between the speed and scale of vertical integration in the state organizations active in livestock breeding with the pace and scale of efforts at vertical integration that often characterized operations within the APKs. Thus when what was at that time the largest APK in the country (in Vratsa) set up its own processing enterprise for fruit and vegetables, the size of the operation was equivalent to that of the earlier intercollective enterprises and no closer to the scale of operations in the state enterprises than before the creation of the complexes.

TABLE 6.7
Structure of Output of APKs and PAKs (Total Product)

YEAR	APKs of which, from:					PAKs of which, from:				
	From all Activity	Agricultural Activity	Industrial Activity	Construction Activity	Other Activity	From all Activity	Agricultural Activity	Industrial Activity	Construction Activity	Other Activity
	(mil.leva)					(current prices)				
1973	4240	3272	661	100	207	378	299	57	9	13
1974	4265	3277	664	113	211	378	297	58	14	9
1975	4468	3402	747	120	199	443	343	73	14	13
1976	4451	3410	745	120	176	456	364	64	15	13
	(percentage)					(share)				
1973	100.0	77.2	15.6	2.4	4.9	100.0	79.1	15.1	2.4	3.4
1974	100.0	76.8	15.6	2.6	4.9	100.0	78.6	15.3	3.7	2.4
1975	100.0	76.1	16.7	2.7	4.4	100.0	77.4	16.5	3.2	2.9
1976	100.0	76.5	16.7	2.7	4.0	100.0	79.8	14.0	3.3	2.8

Source: SGNRB1977, pp. 268, 271-2.

Assuming similar technology, this is to say that from the point of view at least of economies of scale in processing, the APK was no more efficient at processing operations than the collective farms had been. But Vratsa was a legally and economically independent APK and therefore had the opportunity to apply a different management system than the farms. And this new management system was to prepare the complex "for the future full integration with industrial firms, for the gradual vertical integration with industrial, selling, and trading organizations. In the course of this process of development the agro-industrial complex would develop into an industrio-agricultural complex."[32]

TRADITIONAL EVALUATION

The greatest measure of the performance of the agricultural sector in the 1970s would be the growth in total product which, as is well known, is gross in the sense not only of containing undepreciated capital stock, but also of including intermediate output. In terms of economic efficiency, such growth rates do not have any meaning. In resource allocation terms such growth rates have only the crudest meaning, in the sense that positive growth rates indicate that a larger quantity has been produced--whatever the cost in resource terms.

Such measures are, however, common in the Bulgarian literature and a comparison of growth rates in output for the period 1966-70 with those for the period 1972-76 shows that total gross output (in current prices) in the APKs and PAKs grew at an average annual rate of 5.3 percent which compares quite favorably with the average annual growth rate of 3.1 percent for total output DZSs and TKZSs over 1966-70.[33] Thus in the grossest terms the new agricultural policy was a success in that it at least produced higher growth rates of gross output than had taken place over the 1966-79 FYP.

By turning to an examination of resource inputs over the period of APK development, one can determine the resource cost of their growth in agricultural production. Examining the APKs and PAKs together[34] (table 6.8) we see that the cost of the 5.3 percent average annual growth rate in total product and the 5.4 percent per year average annual growth rate of national income (equal to 95 million leva per year)--which is the net material product on socialist definitions--was a growth rate of 5.5 percent per year of gross fixed capital with a basically static land area.

In the process the planners managed to extract 2 percent of the labor force per year (equal to 22 thousand workers per year), but also increase the number of specialists by 2 percent (equal to the much smaller quantity of 768 specialists per year.[35] This compares with the higher average annual growth rate of gross fixed capital stock in the DZS and TKZS sector of 8.9 percent over 1966-70, but under conditions of a slight reduction in land input (-0.5 percent per year) and a much higher rate of labor redeployment of 4.1 percent per year.[36] In absolute terms the average annual increase in gross capital investment per year was almost identical, but this investment was made within the framework of considerably more marked capital-labor and capital-land substitution in 1966-70 than in 1972-76.

Yields on the DZSs and TKZSs over 1966-70 are compared with yields on the APKs and PAKs over 1971-76 and 1973-76, respectively, on table 6.9. For both the plant-growing sector and the livestock-breeding sector the results are not unequivocal as to the organizational form under which the yields were the highest, a noticeable point being that the APKs are the best producers of sugar beet--even better than the PAKs of Bulgarian sugar.

The annual changes in output and factor inputs over the period of agro-industrial development are shown on table 6.9. Since the annual change in the amount of arable land (column 1), the annual change in the amount of gross fixed capital (column 2), and the annual change in the number of employed persons and specialists (columns 3 and 5) are all measured in different units, a direct comparison of inputs and outputs is not immediately possible, but one can at least compare the turning points in the annual changes for each factor input with the turning point for the value of total output. In the case of gross fixed capital the turning points coincide perfectly: i.e., whenever the input of capital goes up from one year to the next, so does the value of output; and vice versa.

This suggests, as one would of course expect, that the input of gross fixed capital is certainly having a direct effect on the output of the agricultural sector. For land, both of the important turning points coincide, conforming to the traditional view of the role of land in agricultural development. For both employed labor and for specialists employed in agriculture only one of the turning points coincide: that is, in every period except for the first, whenever the number of persons employed in agriculture who are extracted from the agricultural sector increased from one year to the next, the growth of agricultural output also increased, and when there was a decrease in the number of employed persons deployed from agriculture, there was a decrease in the growth of agricultural output. A similar inverse relationship holds for the input of specialists as well.

The data on the changes in the level of factor inputs over the period also shows that there was not a constant monotonic change in factor inputs, i.e., a continual growth in the input of gross fixed capital and of specialists, over the period as

TABLE 6.8
Development of APKs and PAKs, 1971–1976
(All APKs and PAKs)

YEAR	No. of Complexes (units)	Total Arable Land (th. ha)	Total Gross Fixed Capital (current prices undeprec- iated) (mil. leva)	Total Employed Persons (th. units)	Total Product (current prices From all Activity) (mil. leva)	National Income[a] (current prices From all Activity) (mil. leva)
1971	161	3910	3443	1064	3879	2114
1972	170	3965	3721	1128	4314	2372
1973	167	3965	3994	1076	4618	2512
1974	160	3965	4132	1046	4643	2447
1975	160	3965	4400	967	4911	2716
1976	154	3915	4581	930	4907	2684

Sources: Columns 1-5, as tables 6.3 and 6.6
Column 6: SGNRB1977, p. 123; SGNRB1976, p. 125; SGNRB1975, p. 111
SGNRB1974, p. 107; SGNRB1973, p. 107; SGNRB1972, p. 93
SGNRB1971, p. 93.

a Estimated from total product data on the basis of the relationship between total output
and national income characteristic of the entire agricultural sector in each year.

Other Notes as table 6.2

TABLE 6.9
Yields On State And Collective Farms And APKs And PAKs, 1966-1976.

Product	Units	Yields: State Farms		Yields: Collective Farms		Yields: APKs		Yields: PAKs	
		Annual Average 1966-70	1970	Annual Average 1966-70	1970	Annual Average 1971-76	1976	Annual Average 1973-76	1976
wheat	kg/dka	242.5	263.8	280.0	304.7	349.4	394.6	383.2	416.8
barley	"	202.5	222.4	257.9	306.5	308.9	336.6	385.0	390.7
maize for grain	"	324.7	303.9	408.6	400.3	412.2	414.3	387.4	362.0
beans	"	86.2	79.2	102.2	101.8	87.8	90.3	75.8	83.3
sunflower seeds	"	153.3	126.2	170.5	148.6	167.4	160.6	168.0	153.1
cotton	"	-	-	99.7	85.6	94.2	12.5	82.0	-
oriental tobacco	"	102.4	100.9	101.9	103.3	123.3	139.2	173.2	199.0
sugar beets	"	2841.2	2337.7	1727.0	3136.0	3091.2	3368.3	2771.2	3283.0
tomatoes	"	542.7	2339.1	3019.8	2857.8	2862.0	2688.7	2671.3	2620.7
green peppers	"	1610.9	1581.2	1998.4	1912.0	2075.7	2012.8	1524.7	1532.9
onions	"	764.0	760.2	928.4	1017.5	828.3	690.6	1068.1	1010.2
potatoes	"	1156.9	1069.6	1237.9	1176.3	1225.8	1271.8	907.9	979.9
apples	"	476.3	439.2	877.0	778.2	861.2	1192.2	459.6	796.5
cherries	"	202.6	237.2	320.1	421.2	288.3	266.7	307.8	266.7
wine grapes	"	536.4	475.8	637.8	595.8	621.8	788.4	706.6	805.8
dessert grapes	"	542.4	360.9	696.8	610.9	670.2	709.3	722.4	685.7
cows' milk	l/cow	2656	2649	2693	2740	2681	2611	2835	2808
wool	kg/sheep	2.943	3.245	2.704	4.262	4.334	4.403	5.605	5.591
eggs	units/layer	192	198	181	188	192	194	184	184

Sources: SGNRB1977, pp. 270, 272-5; SGNRB1971, pp. 219-233, 231;
SGNRB1969, pp. 199-203, 211.

one would expect under a policy of planned resource allocation that emphasized the industrialization of agriculture and the introduction of more advanced systems of management. Rather, the fluctuations in the increase in the inputs of physical capital of specialists, as well as the fluctuations in the extraction of labor from agriculture suggest that, despite all the arguments cited above, agriculture has continued to be a residual sector in the process of economic development in Bulgaria.

Viewed in isolation, however, such results on factor inputs such as these could lead to completely misleading conclusions--in this case concerning the perverse effect of both total labor force and trained specialists on agricultural production--due to the intertemporal pattern of change of other factor inputs. To attempt to develop a more acceptable framework for our attempt at developing a composite picture of the efficiency of factor utilization in agriculture in the 1970s, labor extracted from agriculture has been valued at the average wage rate in industry for the relevant year, this wage rate being taken as a proxy for the value of the marginal revenue product of labor employed in industry. (See table 6.10.)

In a planned economy there is, of course, no reason whatsoever why the marginal productivity relationships of market economies should hold; but it is not clear what other valuation should be employed. The same evaluation process is used for the input of specialists into agriculture. In this case the ratio of the income of the fifth-richest individual out of every one hundred working in the agricultural sector to the median income in the sector (the P_5/P_{50} ratio) is taken as equal to approximately two on the basis of an extrapolation of data on income distribution in Bulgarian agriculture.[37] This in turn is used to derive a ratio of the marginal revenue product of specialists to the marginal revenue product of the total work force in agriculture of approximately two.[38] Questionable as this evaluation might be, measurement of the land input in money terms would seem to require even more contortions and heroics.

We have, therefore, grouped the APKs and PAKs together (on table 6.10) and in so doing produced a situation where the aggregate change in land input over the period is equal to 0.11 percent, i.e., approximately zero. The grouping of both types of complexes could be argued to be acceptable on the theoretical level because of the marked similarity in the branch composition of their output (see table 6.7); but there is the significant difference in the scale of production discussed earlier, as well as the differences in the composition of intra-branch output. The grouping is nevertheless carried out here since it allows us to avoid the problems of evaluating land in money terms. But it should be noted that the increase of land input in 1971-72 and the

TABLE 6.10

Changes in Factor Utilization For APKs And PAKs, 1971-1976
(All APKs and PAKs)

Period	Arable Land (th.dka.)	Gross Fixed Capital (mil.leva)	Employed Persons (th.units)	Employed Persons (mil. leva)[a]	Specialists (units)[b]	Specialists (th.leva)[c]	Change in Total Output: Total Product From All Activity (mil.leva)	Change in National Income: National Income From All Activity (mil.leva)
1971-2	+550	+278	+64	+102	+1228	+1957	+435	+238
1972-3	- 7	+273	-52	- 88	+ 433	+ 733	+435	+166
1973-4	0	+132	-30	- 52	+1416	+2454	+ 25	+ 13
1974-5	+ 10	+268	-79	-142	+ 767	+1379	+268	+145
1975-6	-511	+181	-37	- 67	+767	+1389	- 4	- 2

Sources: [a] SGNRB1977, p. 78; SGNRB1976, p. 78
[b] and [c] SGNRB1977, p. 106; SGNRB1976, p. 108.

Other sources as in Tables 6.2 and 6.8.

Notes: For a and b see text.

decrease in land input in 1975-76 will lead to an overvaluation of the factor productivity of other factors in 1971-72 and an undervaluation of the factor productivity of other factors in 1975-76.

The result of comparing the values of the increase in gross output each year with the cost of the increase in factor inputs is shown on table 6.11, and the balance of incremental changes for agro-industrial development over the period 1971-72 to 1975-76 as a whole would seem to be a very small, but nevertheless positive, excess of some 250 million leva. Considering the change in net output over the period, agro-industrial development made a loss in terms of the value of incremental change in net output and the cost of the incremental change in factor inputs throughout the period of some 606 million leva.

CONCLUDING COMMENTS

In studying Bulgarian agriculture we would most certainly not agree that "we now witness a new flight into the never-never land of left-wing oppositionism in the rapid formation of huge agricultural-industrial complexes."[39] At the same time, and even granting the view of the Bulgarian economist Violeta Popova that "concentration is an objective process-- not only in agriculture, but in all branches of material production"--and that "is a characteristic of nearly all spheres of our life," no cost curves continue to fall forever. And it is entirely possible that they turn up long before one achieves a five-fold increase in the average size of farms. Particularly in the short-run, when the economic preconditions for agro-industrial development are not all present.

Study of the Bulgarian literature has not revealed an optimal size for the integrated complexes based on detailed analyses of variants of the costs of production; and it has not been possible to find econometric investigations in the literature to serve as a basis for policy prescriptions. It seems important to us that in the arguments for the introduction of programming methods in the planning of agricultural production, the Bulgarian computer specialist and economic modeller K. Murgov left the question of the objective function open.[40] Economic analysis shows that capital investment in the APKs rose in 1971, with the creation of the APKs, over 1970--but fell again by 1976 to below both the 1971 and 1970 figures. Over the period the share of agriculture in total gross fixed capital stock fell as the complexes were developed by a total of some 10 percent (to 18.34 percent in 1976).[41]

TABLE 6.11
Value Of Output And Cost Of Inputs In APKs And PAKs, 1971-76
(in Millions of Leva)

Value of Growth	1971/2	1972/3	1973/4	1974/5	1975/6
In total output	+435	+304	+25	+268	-4
In factor inputs	+382	+186	+82	+127	+115
balance[a]	+53	+118	-57	+141	-119
In national income	+258	+140	-65	+269	-32
In factor inputs	+382	+186	+82	+127	+115
balance[a]	-124	-46	-147	-142	-147

Sources: Same as Table 6.10

[a] Balance is equal to the growth in total output or national income minus the growth in factor inputs.

Also worrying was the development of agriculture's share of productive machinery and equipment in the economy's aggregate total. Such capital is part and parcel of industrial development, but its share fell from 12.9 percent in 1970 to 12.3 percent in 1971 to 9.8 percent in 1976. Furthermore, of the (falling) share of total investment going to agriculture, the share of the investment that was made in machinery and equipment also fell--from 26.29 percent in 1970 to 25.94 percent in 1971 to 23.96 percent in 1976. The traditional habit of spending the investment on large buildings was continuing to assert itself despite the industrialization campaign.

From the actions of Bulgaria's planners we have suggested that rather than involving a highly capital-intensive program of economic development, the APK was part of a campaign to use changes in planning, management, and control to substitute for increased inputs of physical capital.

The result of development throughout the 1970s that can be ascribed to the new system of planning, control, and management was increased efficiency in the utilization of capital investment as measured by capital introduced into production in any given year. Long gestation periods are a traditional problem in Bulgarian economic development and especially so in agriculture. Yet over 1971-76 not only did the relationship between capital investment and capital introduced into activity improve for agriculture, but so did the relationship between this ratio for agriculture and the ratio for industry.

While investment in physical capital, the hallmark of the second stage of Bulgarian agricultural development, is still crucial in the present stage of agricultural development, it is investment in human capital that can be considered the sine qua non of the new stage in agricultural development. Without this investment, all the attention to physical factors-- natural resources and investment in physical capital--will fail to generate an efficient sector of the national economy which employs the latest technological progress and becomes a partner with industry in the development of the country.

While they can therefore be seen to be crucial to stage three, the share of specialists in agriculture fell from 7.6 percent in 1970 and 7.5 percent in 1971 to 6.5 percent in 1976. And the growth rate of specialists coming into agriculture fell from 5.72 percent per year over 1966-70 to 1.85 percent per year over 1971-76. This pattern of development is particularly unfavorable given our interpretation of agro-industrial development as creating a new system of planning, management, and control. Even with this low level of growth of specialists, however, the APKs were criticized as becoming top-heavy.

131

Under these conditions of factor allocation, introduction of the new system of planning, management, and control was not an economic success. But it did create the preconditions for moving to a more decentralized system of planning and control that allowed the introduction of the principles of decomposition in planning and control into agriculture and their application to the management of vertically integrated organizations.

Detailed economic evaluation of the costs and benefits in agricultural integration could, however, be considered of only secondary importance in at least two cases. One could be where the whole focus of the policy was on the longer-term goal of (particularly backward, to incorporate sources of raw materials) vertical integration in industry. A concentrated, directly controllable source of inputs, fully capable of frictionless injection into a highly capital-intensive industrial production process can be considered a sine qua non of future vertical integration.

The statement that "today the most important changes and achievements in agriculture are bound up with the development of industry"[42] refers to the industrialization of agriculture, but is also valid when interpreted as referring to the integrating of agriculture into the industrial structure. A loss in microefficiency may be considered a small cost to pay when the ultimate goal is "the development of the national economy as a unified industrioagricultural complex",[43] with country-wide control of all levels of production.

A second instance could be where the economic considerations were secondary to the social; where economic integration served primarily as a vehicle for the further socioeconomic development of the countryside. Thus on this argument, the improvement in economic infrastructure and rural development would be given primary consideration in an evaluation, or at least equal importance with the strictly economic evaluation. But our reading of the Bulgarian experience is that, for all their importance, these have been regarded as subsidiary goals to that of horizontal integration and industrialization of agricultural production, and hence the latter must be at least primarily evaluated in their own economic terms.[44]

NOTES

1. Rabotnichesko Delo, 29 April 1970.
2. For discussion of the changes in the number of farms see Ivan Stefanov, Wirtschaftsentwicklung und Wirtschaftsplanung in Bulgarien (Kiel: Mohr, 1971); Georgi Kostadinov, Selskoto Stopanstvo v Ikonomikata na NRB i Prekhodŭt Kŭm Kompleksite (Sofia: Partizdat, 1971); and

"Agrarindustrie in Bulgarien," Wissenschaftlicher Dienst Südosteuropa nos. 5-6 (1970), pp. 79-81.

3. The figures conceal the doubling of the size of the state farms, at the expense of the collectives, in 1967 and 1968.

4. Statisticheski Godishnik na Narodna Republika Bŭlgariya 1971 (henceforth abbreviated SGNRB1971) (Sofia: TsSU, 1971), pp. 239, 241.

5. Ivan Kalupov, Ikonomika i Organizatsiya na Selskoto Stopanstvo (Sofia, 1972), p. 22.

6. For more details see Paul Wiedemann, The Organization of Bulgarian Agriculture (Glasgow: ISEES, 1976).

7. Kooperativno Selo, 24 November 1968; cited in "Bildung land-wirtschaftlich-industrieller Kombinate," Osteuropaische Rundschau no. 2 (1969), p. 46.

8. Jordan Kostadinov, Khorizontalna i Vertikalna Integratsiya na Selskostopanskoto Proizvodstvo (Sofia: Izd. na el. Lit, 1970), p. 49.

9. Stefanov, Wirtschaftsentwicklung.

10. D. Vladov, "Kontsentratsiyata na Selskostopanskoto Proizvodstvo," Novo Vreme (July 1970).

11. Rabotnichesko Delo, 2 July 1971.

12. Ivan Prumov, Bulgarian Agriculture Today (Sofa: Sofia Press, 1976), p. 67.

13. Zemedelsko Zname, 15 January 1971.

14. Prumov, Bulgarian Agriculture Today, p. 48.

15. Rabotnichesko Delo, 27 November 1966; SGNRB1970, pp. 223, 225, 227, 228; Wiedemann, Organization of Bulgarian Agriculture.

16. Sava Dŭlbokov, "Natsionalniyat Dokhod i Razvitieto na Ikonomikata na Nashata Strana prez Petata Petiletka," Ikonomicheska Misŭl no. 6 (1966), pp. 3-15; SGNRB1972, p. 191.

17. Mark Allen, "The Bulgarian Economy in the 1970's," East-European Economies Post-Helsinki (Washington: GPO, 1977), p. 691.

18. Todor Zhivkov, Za posledovatelno Izpŭlnenie Resheniyata na Desetiya Kongres na BKP za Povishavane Zhiznenoto Ravnishte na Naroda (Sofia, 1971).

19. Allen, "Bulgarian Economy," p. 686.

20. John Kenneth Galbraith, The New Industrial State (Boston: Houghton-Mifflin, 1967). The Russian translation was circulating in Bulgaria in 1970.

21. Kostadinov, Khroizontalna.

22. Naum Jasny, The Socialized Agriculture of the USSR: Plans and Performance (Stanford: Stanford University Press, 1949), p. 6.

23. See, for example, Domenico Mario Nuti, "Large Corporations and the Reform of Polish Industry," Jahrbuch der Wirtschaft Osteuropas, vol. 7 (Munich-Vienna: G. Olzog, 1977), pp. 345-406.

24. Georgi Gergov, "Nyakoi Aspekti na Ikonomicheskata Otsenka pri Proizvodstvoto na Rastenievŭdni Produkta," Planovo Stopanstvo no. 7 (1971) pp. 12-21; Boris Mikhov, "Problemi na Konstentratsiyata na Konservnata Promishlenosti i Neinoto Intenzivno Razvitie," Planovo Stopanstvo no. 2 (1970), pp. 14-24; Georgi Kostadinov, "Vŭprosi na Kontsentratsiyata; Integratsiyata na Selskoto Stopanstvo i Teritorialniya Kompleks," Ikonomicheska Misŭl no. 4 (1970), pp. 3-13.

25. Panaiot Daskalov, "Proizvodstveni Nasoki v Konservnata Promishlenost," Ikonomicheska Misŭl no. 1 (1969), pp. 22-34.

27. SGNRB1972, pp. 118, 133, 140, 142, 192, 240, 242.

28. cf. Karl-Eugen Wädekin, Sozialistiche Agrarpolitik in Osteuropa, vol. II (Berlin: Duncker and Humblot, 1978), chapter 8.

29. The importance of the Soviet example is, of course, strengthened by the presence of a large number of Soviet agricultural specialists working in Bulgaria.

30. United Nations, Food and Agricultural Organization, Agriculture et Industrialisation (Rome: 1967).

31. Ibid., p. 21.

32. Kostadinov, Khorizontalna, p. 214.

33. SGNRB1977, pp. 268, 271; SGNRB1971, pp. 190-1.

34. The grouping of APKs and PAKs together for analysis can be justified on the theoretical grounds on the basis of the great similarity in the structure of their output (as shown on table 7); and on practical grounds, the grouping together of APKs and PAKs produces a change in total arable land over the total 1971-76 period approximately equal to zero, which in turn allows us to avoid the problem of the evaluation of land. See the later discussion in the text.

35. SGNRB1977, p. 106; SGNRB1976, p. 108.

36. SGNRB1971, pp. 197, 239, 241.

37. Paul Wiedemann, "The Distribution of Income and Earnings and Economic Welfare in Bulgaria and Yugoslavia," Southeastern Europe no. 1 (1976), pp. 1-18.

38. The data in table 6.9 show that the importance of the error resulting from this extrapolation is appreciably reduced by the relatively small importance of the resulting value of the input of specialists in the value of total inputs.

39. R. V. Burks, "Bulgaria--Two Views," Problems of Communism no. 1 (1971), p. 95.

40. See Paul Wiedemann, "A Note on Modelling a Bulgarian Agro-Industrial Complex with Special Reference to the Appropriate Objectives". Oxford Agrarian Studies no. 2 (1974).

41. SGNRB1977, p. 114; SGNRB1972, p. 82.

42. I. Lutsov, "Nauchno-tekhnicheskiyat Progres i Vrŭzkite mezdha."

43. Selskoto Stopanstvo i Promishlenostta," Novo Vreme no. 10 (1970), pp. 46-7. Kostadinov, Khorizontalna, p. 13.

44. The author would like to thank Karl-Eugen Wädekin for his thorough reading of an earlier draft of this paper, but the author alone is responsible for all errors of fact or interpretation.

7
Romanian Agricultural Policy in the Quest of "the Multilaterally Developed Society"

Trond Gilberg

SOCIALIST AGRICULTURE--A PERENNIAL PROBLEM

For three decades, political leaders and economic planners in the communist systems of Eastern Europe have attempted to utilize the agricultural sector as the chief supplier of revenue and manpower for the rapidly expanding industrial sector, and in this process, practically every regime in the area had succeeded in creating serious shortcomings, indeed crises, by the 1970s. The deliberate shortchanging of agriculture is consistent with the ideological preconceptions of Marxism, insofar as this ideology emphasizes the need for rapid industrialization, urbanization, and the creation of the most progressive social stratus, the industrial proletariat.

The consistent "skimming off" of revenue produced in the rural sector has indeed enabled the agrarian societies of the area to launch a most ambitious development program in the preferential industrial sector without reliance on massive outside investment. Thus, the planned relative reduction of the importance of the once dominant agricultural sector has been the mainstay of the modernizing strategies followed throughout all of Eastern Europe. Given such a perspective it is not surprising that the impressive achievements throughout much of the rest of the economy have not been matched on the fields and farms of socialist agriculture.[1]

While the utilization of the agricultural sector as a supply of revenue and manpower is a rational strategy for the rapid industrialization of society in the short run, there are ultimately several self-defeating aspects to this policy. Firstly, the move of millions from the rural areas to the cities and towns will ultimately increase the demand for foodstuffs from that part of the citizenry which is no longer engaged in food production, and the agricultural sector therefore becomes a crucial mainstay of the modernization process itself; without increased production of this basic necessity for the urban population, the development process itself is in dire jeopardy. Secondly, economic development is likely to raise the standard of living, thus increasing the demand for more and better foods, thus putting further demands on the "residual" agrarian sector of the economy. And thirdly, the economic structures of <u>all</u> East European countries, suffering from overemphasis on the heavy and extractive industries, now create a situation whereby the agricultural sector becomes the producer of goods and commodities in short supply, while each country's industrial plants frantically attempt to sell similar goods to each other, since their products usually are qualitatively inferior and thus uncompetitive on the Western market. In this manner, the neglect of agriculture over time becomes a crucial economic fact decisively influencing the performance of the entire economy and may result in the collapse of the regime itself (if not the system.)[2]

The interrelated problems resulting from economic decisions made thirty years ago and consistently upheld in the period up to the 1970s have been further aggravated by well-known ideological tenets that have reduced the regime's options when it comes to remedial actions. Even official statistics admit that productivity on the private plots of collective farmers is superior to that of state--and cooperative entities alike, but ideological givens clearly preclude any attempt to restructure East European agriculture in line with the productivity tables. The fundamental givens of Marxism-Leninism have in fact stipulated a hierarchy of agricultural organization that continues to exist regardless of performance, and in this hierarchy, the state and collective farms are by definition superior to private plots and farms remaining in the hands of individuals. Most East European planners are therefore faced with the unpalatable fact that the most productive sector of agriculture is defined as "residual," presumably destined to disappear as society moves towards socialism and communism. It is only very recently (and only in a few countries) that political leaders have been faced with the need to recognize the indefinite survival of private agriculture even under socialism.[3]

The difficulties discussed above are many and serious, but still they represent only part of the problem complex encountered by the rulers of the managed political and socioeconomic systems of the area. Socialist planning in practice is a negation of accidental development and happenstance, yet it is precisely in agriculture that chance enters into actual performance as a major factor in the form of weather conditions and climate. During the 1970s poor weather during the planting, growing, or harvesting seasons has been responsible for serious losses and underfulfillment of plans, with subsequent problems of supply and remuneration reverberating throughout the entire socioeconomic and

138

political system of several countries. Such vagaries of "wind and weather" have contributed significantly to the continuing economic problems of Eastern Europe in the 1970s.

ROMANIAN AGRICULTURE IN THE 1960S: PROGRAMS AND PRIORITIES

The general problems besetting socialist agriculture are present in considerable degree in Romania as well. As discussed elsewhere,[4] the leadership of the Romanian Communist party (PCR), first under Ana Pauker and subsequently under Gheorghe Gheorghiu-Dej, followed a traditional approach to the agricultural sector, essentially treating it as a "necessary evil" on the march to socialism and communism qua industrialization. Such outlooks resulted in inadequate investments and poor utilization of machines and manpower. Thus, during the 1950s, investments in agriculture constituted merely 10 to 14 percent of all investments. During the last five years of Gheorghiu-Dej's reign, the same pattern continued, and while the Romanian economy developed rapidly in the industrial field, agriculture, traditionally the most important of all economic sectors in this erstwhile "Balkan granary," fell further and further behind. This discrepancy continued even after the completion of the collectivization process in 1962, during the period 1962-65, agricultural investments remained at roughly 19 percent of the total amount allocated for all economic activities. From such inadequate investment poor performance followed; production in most fields remained considerably below plans each year.[5]

The change of leadership that was ushered in by the death of Gheorghe Gheorghiu-Dej in 1965 did not alter fundamentally the agricultural policies of the PCR. Nicolae Ceausescu, the new First Secretary of the party, was equally committed to rapid industrialization, and the triangle of inadequate investments, low production, and frequent reorganizations continued to plague the regime. During the period from the time that Ceausescu assumed power in 1965 to November 1974, at the time of the PCR Eleventh Congress, the collective farms experienced several reorganizations: the National Union of Agricultural Cooperatives was altered twice; the machine-tractor stations were frequently reorganized; and a total of four men attempted to till the unenviable job of Minister of Agriculture. At the same time, the tendency to underinvest in agriculture was as noticeable as ever, and the perennial failures to meet the production plans had a direct impact upon the reorganizations and the personnel changes in this troubled field.

One of the reasons for the continued tendency to de-emphasize agriculture was the fact that the new first secretary had to consolidate his hold on political power in the PCR in the face of entrenched hierarchies and individuals, many of whom had considerably better revolutionary "credentials" than the new leader; many of these individuals had also made their careers as "metal eaters" in the heavy and extractive industries and consequently resented any idea of policy change that could have deprived them of their considerable power and privilege in the political and socioeconomic hierarchies of Romania. This process of Ceausescu's power consolidation took several years, and was not completed until the tenth PCR congress in August 1969.[6]

Another principal reason for the continuation of traditional policies in this field stemmed from the ideological outlook of Nicolae Ceausescu himself. The new first secretary, (who was later to become general secretary) was a modernizer, fully convinced that Romania's path to greatness went through rapid industrialization rather than through agricultural development, and he willingly continued the programs of his predecessors, which called for only minimal increases in agricultural development. Thus, during the period 1965-69, investment in agriculture hovered around 16 percent of total investment. The supply of skilled manpower to this hard-pressed sector lagged far behind the impressive staffing of industrial positions. Due to the considerable discrepancy in wages, salaries, and benefits between urban and rural occupations, a massive emigration of able-bodied men drained the countryside of its most productive elements. The rapid industrialization of Romania swallowed such productive elements and many others, with the result that the rural workforce increasingly was made up of old men, women, and children. Machinery was underutilized, and the failure of the chemical industry to meet its production plans for fertilizer ensured low production per acre throughout the country.[7] In short, the classical syndrome of a malfunctioning economic sector continued during the early stages of Ceausescu's rule as well.

CEAUSESCU AND THE "MULTILATERALLY DEVELOPED SOCIETY": A NEW ROLE FOR AGRICULTURE?

The tenth PCR congress was a major victory for Nicolae Ceausescu. His power at the political center was consolidated. During 1967/68, a territorial reorganization of the country had provided the PCR head with the opportunity to staff the new county party organizations with his own men, thus ensuring his hold over that part of the PCR apparat. After August 1969, then, Nicolae Ceausescu could begin to implement his particular vision of Romanian society, and this vision was summed up in the concept "the multilaterally developed society."

The basic contours of the "multilaterally developed society" have been discussed in considerable detail elsewhere[8] and will not be treated in detail here. What warrants particular attention for the purposes of this paper is the Ceausescu vision of agriculture in this higher society. It was this vision that led to much greater emphasis on solving the problems of agriculture and perhaps also to elevating this sector to a higher position in the hierarchy of economic tasks in Romania during the 1970s, and especially in the period after the Eleventh PCR Congress in November 1974.

In the context of the "multilaterally developed society," agriculture assumes a position of considerable economic importance. Since this level of societal development constitutes the immediate stage prior to socialism, economic performance in the "multilaterally developed society" must have the basic mix and productivity needed for the latter stage. One of the fundamental tenets of Marxism-Leninism is still the assumption that socialism will embody the most productive economy known to man, and this economy will allow each socialist citizen to live better than his or her capitalist counterparts in the nonsocialist world. The standard of living, as measured by consumption, is therefore a crucial consideration for anyone preparing to declare the achievement of "multilateral development," and it is clear that agricultural production constitutes an important element of the elevated standard of living of this developmental stage. Consequently, the residual economic sector of the 1950s and 1960s has become a crucial field of concern in the 1970s, especially after the Eleventh Party Congress, when Ceausescu reported on the giant strides made towards "multilateral development" and the eventual achievement of socialism.[9]

Secondly, the very concept of multilateralism in economic development required increased concern for agricultural production. A multilaterally developed economy implies a system in which all economic sectors have reached a uniformly high level of performance, and, in the Romanian context, such a concept could mean only that agriculture must catch up with the performance of the rest of the economy. Given the low level of this particular sector in the total economic context, the development of the agrarian part must be particularly rapid since the concept of multilateralism demands continued expansion of all other sectors as well. Agriculture, in other words, must somehow catch up with the industrial sector without a major rearranging of economic investment and general priorities. As will be seen below, this "catch-up" mentality had a considerable effect upon the specific agricultural programs adopted in the 1970s.[10]

While the internal logic of the Ceausescu line in ideological matters demanded a reevaluation of the agricultural sector, the dynamics of the modernization process

141

posed other challenges to long-standing economic practices and forced the PCR leadership to focus more intently upon the erstwhile "residual" occupations of farming and forestry. As evidenced by the census of 1977, Romania made giant strides towards modernity (as defined by both Western scholars and East European planners and policy makers) in the decade 1966-77. The population is now equally split between rural and urban residence, a considerable jump in urbanization since the mid-1960s.[11] Furthermore, the very nature of urbanization changed during the decade; the most striking example of this is the increase in the number of cities with more than two hundred thousand inhabitants.[12] Cities of that size are major urban conglomerations that depend upon a productive, cash-oriented agricultural sector for their food supplies, and they can no longer rely upon the exchange and barter arrangements of smaller towns in their relationships with the rural hinterland. Such a dramatic development further highlighted the long-standing trends of out-migration of the most productive elements of the rural population and focused attention on the need to reverse this trend, thus ensuring adequate food supplies for the big-city population centers.

The Ceausescu regime was confronted with other fruits of its modernization program as well, with profound effects on agricultural policy. As discussed by several scholars, the PCR's development program has consistently emphasized education as a crucial ingredient in the quest for rapid socioeconomic development. The Romanian leadership has now learned a lesson that is even more evident in the more highly developed societies of Eastern Europe: an educated citizenry develops expectations, makes demands, questions decisions, and criticizes implementation. One of the expectations most frequently expressed is the idea that the massive economic burdens placed on the population during the last generation must now bear the fruit of increased consumption, of which food consumption is the most conspicuous and important element. During the 1970s, for the first time in its history, the PCR was confronted with a citizenry that openly voiced its demands for more food of higher quality, a demand that has grown more, rather than less, insistent as the decade has developed. One of the most drastic demonstrations of popular dissatisfaction in this field was the miners' strike in the Jui Valley during the summer of 1977,[13] but similar activities had been undertaken elsewhere earlier in the decade. During the summer of 1977, workers in several Bucharest factories also struck for shorter periods of time, at least partly in protest against the inadequate food supplies in the capital and elsewhere.[14] Add to this the problems created by severe floods in 1970 and 1975, periodic droughts during several growing seasons, and the disastrous earthquake of early 1977, and it becomes apparent that the present political leadership in Romania is confronting the twin problems of rising expectations and lagging agricultural performance in their full measure. The very stability of the regime hinges upon solutions to these problems, and the realization of this in Bucharest has brought a renewed urgency to the efforts of updating the agricultural sector as Romania heads towards the 1980s.

This realization of the crucial part played by agriculture in the total economic performance of the Romanian system is further supported by the fact that continued heavy investments in Western industrial technology and know-how depends upon the ability of Romanian agriculture to maintain its exports of foodstuffs and raw materials to the highly developed economies of Western Europe and North America. The Romanians have failed, by and large, in their efforts to expand export of finished industrial goods and machinery to the West, and have been forced to rely on their traditional export commodities such as grain to generate hard currency and thereby buying power. The old adage that one cannot sell what one has not produced neatly summarizes the Romanian focus on agricultural production at this crucial juncture of economic development. [15]

Faced with such a multitude of serious problems, Nicolae Ceausescu and his advisers have produced an agricultural program that is characterized by the following major features:

1. A modest increase in investments that has nevertheless maintained the basic ratio between agriculture and industry in this field.

During the 1970s there has been a steady increase in actual absolute investments in agriculture, as reflected by the figures in table 7.1. (in relative terms, however, there has been an actual decline). At the same time, there has been a considerable increase in investments in the chemical industry, which is the chief supplier of fertilizer for the agricultural sector. Thus in 1971, 5.80 billion lei were set aside for investments; in 1972, the figure was 8,62 billion lei, and in 1973, 9.74 billion lei. [16] By 1975 and 1976, the actual expenditures in this industry were 10.01 billion lei and 8.89 billion lei, respectively. [17]

2. An educational program designed to improve the skill level of agricultural experts and other specialized personnel.

An integral part of the new agricultural program promoted by Nicolae Ceausescu has been an effort to ensure better educational training for cadres working in agriculture, and also a larger pool of skilled manpower for this economic sector. Table 7.2 illustrates this effort.

143

TABLE 7.1
Investments in Agriculture, 1970-76   (Total Figures
and Percentage of all Investments)

Year	Investments in Agriculture (million lei)	Percent of All Investments
1970	12,789	15.9
1971	14,152	16.0
1972	14,492	14.9
1973	14,510	13.7
1974	15,815	13.2
1975	17,996	13.1
1976	21,236	14.0

Source: Anuarul Statistic al Republicii
Socialiste Romania, 1976, pp. 278-79;
 1977, pp. 332-33.

TABLE 7.2
Graduates in Professional Schools, 1971-76

Year	Total	In Agriculture	Agric./Total
1971/72	70,867	9,623	13.6%
1972/73	78,915	7,045	8.9%
1973/74	84,820	7,631	9.0%
1974/75	91,117	7,087	7.8%
1975/76	77,359	3,112	4.0%

Source: Anuarul Statistic al Republicii
Socialiste Romania, 1976, p. 428-29;1977, p. 468.

During the same period, trained agricultural personnel entered
this sector from "post-lycee schools" to the tune of 226 in
1971/72, 258 in 1972/73, 271 in 1973/74, and 351 in 1975/76.[18]
During the 1970s over 3,000 individuals with "maistri"
training[19] also graduated. From institutes of higher learning
came 1861 graduates in 1971/72,[20]1,826 in 1972/73, 1,563 in
1974/75, and 1,764 in 1975/76.[20]
    During the last few years, there has also been a major
effort to train party cadres in the countryside in economic
management and production skills, and there has also been an
expansion[21] of educational opportunities for the average
worker.[21]
    3. A concerted effort to raise prices for

144

agricultural commodities.

In line with the investment program the Romanian regime has made major efforts to raise procurement prices for agricultural commodities as an incentive for increased production. Thus during the present decade the price for cereals has been revised upwards several times; similar revisions were made for vegetables, fruits, and meat, and a recent reworking of the price schedule once again increased the amount paid for important agricultural commodities. This belated realization of the need for an adequate pricing mechanism is of the greatest importance for the collective farms, since individual income here still is tied in with production and sales to a high degree.

4. A consistent attempt to increase wages and pensions of collective farmers and employees of the state farms and mechanization stations.

During this decade the regime has also made concerted efforts to raise the level of wages and pensions in the agricultural sector. As of January 1, 1970, pensions were fixed at 110 lei for individuals with one to four years' service in the collective farms; those who had five to nine years received 150, while ten to fourteen years' service would bring 180 lei, and those who had served over fifteen years could count on 200 lei per month.[22] In April 1977 this fixed schedule was dismantled, and pensions were henceforth to be stipulated according to income earned, work performed, and length of service. This measure was clearly designed to enhance incentives for greater productivity and also length of service which had hitherto been a considerable problem in the agricultural sector.[23] It was later estimated that the new measures would make it possible for certain specialized workers to obtain pensions of up to 650 lei per month, while the less highly paid would get at least 350 lei. (Industrial workers, by comparison, were given over 1,000 lei per month in many categories).[24] A recent policy change also included private farmers in the pension system.[25]

Wages for collective and state farmers have been increased regularly throughout the 1970s as evidenced by table 7.3. It should be pointed out that industrial workers had the opportunity to earn extra bonuses and so forth to a much larger extent than agricultural personnel; on the other hand, the collective farmer presumably had the advantage of consumption from his private plot.

In addition to such measures, the regime has attempted to raise the wages and benefits for mechanics and other key personnel in agriculture, and significant improvements were made in the housing put at the disposal of technical cadres assigned to the countryside.[26] All in all, the 1970s have experienced a major regime effort to equalize the living

TABLE 7.3
Average Income in Romanian Agriculture and in All
Occupations, 1970-76 (Lei)

Year	Agric.	Average of all Occup.	Agric./Average
1971	1,372	1,471	93.3
1972	1,408	1,498	94.0
1973	1,488	1,563	95.2
1974	1,543	1,663	92.8
1975	1,737	1,813	95.8

Source: Anuarul Statistic al Republicii
Socialiste Romania, 1976, p. 76.

conditions in town and countryside and to make the wage scales
and fringe-benefit systems more equitable.
    5.   An   integrated   program   designed to stimulate
production of key commodities on private plots and
independent farms.
    Nicolae Ceausescu and his advisers seem to have reconciled
their ideological leanings with the need to accept the
collective farmers' private plots and the independent farms
that still exist in Romania (the latter primarily in the
mountain regions). During the 1970s Ceausescu has reduced the
tax burden on such property; furthermore, easier credit
possibilities have been established for private farmers, and
this category of producer has also enjoyed the procurement
price increases that have been enacted. Perhaps even more
important, the PCR leader has publicly acknowledged the
contribution of private agriculture to the total economic
effort in this sector, especially in fields such as vegetable
and fruit growing and meat and egg production.[27] Such
recognition, after years of assurances of the eventual demise
of   individual   agriculture,   must   be   a   rather welcome
development   for   Romania's   embattled   independent
"entrepreneurs."
    6.   A belated effort   to protect valuable agricultural
land from the ravages of rapid development.
    During the decades of rapid industrialization and
urbanization, much agricultural land was swallowed up by the
expanding need for roads, water and sewer systems, and
building. During this decade, the regime launched a campaign
to limit such use of good agricultural land, and decreed that

industrial plants and the necessary infrastructure services such as roads and power lines must be assigned to less fertile areas, if at all possible.[28] By the same token, efforts have been made to stop the unchecked growth of cities, towns, and villages, and there are now attempts to systematize and regulate such growth, thereby establishing a balance in the utilization of the surface soil that is being exploited by a steadily growing population.[29] These two programs taken together represent further proof of the regime's realization that the continued development of the entire economy depends upon the preservation of the agricultural base and a better, and more rational, utilization of it in the decades to come.

    7. A continuing effort to gain better control over agricultural activities through organization and indoctrination.

While the measures discussed above are essentially pragmatic and oriented towards improving benefits and thus raising output in agriculture, the Romanian regime has attempted to reach its goals in this sector by means of political measures as well. During the 1970s, there have been several efforts to improve the organizational structure of state and collective farms, and a number of coordinating bodies have been set up to ensure better sharing of manpower, machinery, and know-how in this sector.[30] In 1973 Ceausescu also established a number of commissions of mixed party-state membership for the purpose of furthering economic performance generally; the agricultural sector was also affected by this. The pace of reorganization was in fact rather dizzying, and it is only recently possible to say that some semblance of permanence has been achieved in this endeavor. Should the expected output fail to materialize in the near future, it is likely that further reorganizations will follow.[31]

In addition to the reorganization efforts, Nicolae Ceausescu has sponsored two other programs designed to enhance the productivity of Romanian agriculture during the 1970s. Starting in 1973 and continuing to this day, there has been a major effort to transfer trained cadres from the capital to the countryside, where their expertise can be better utilized in actual production. This program has apparently transferred several thousand highly trained individuals to the farms and fields. Their contribution to production cannot be directly measured at this point, but the central political leadership is clearly convinced that this policy will ultimately produce positive results.[32]

The other major program carried out during this decade has been the ideological offensive started in the summer of 1971 and still going strong. This offensive, which has been analyzed in some detail elsewhere,[33] was designed to raise the ideological level of the general population as well

147

TABLE 7.4

Planned and Actual Investments in Romanian Agriculture, 1971-76
(million lei)

Year	Planned Investment	Actual Investment	Shortfall
1971	13,700	13,000	5.2%
1972	(Figures are not clear on the shortfall in agriculture; in the total economy it was 3,400 mill. lei)		
1973	10,600	10,126	
1974	12,200	11,863	2.8%
1975	(Figures are not clear; planned investment for the whole economy was 142,700 mill; actual was 136,900 mill. lei)		
1976	(Planned total investment 159,500 mill. lei actual investment 149,000 mill. lei)		

Sources: See list of sources for table 7.6.

148

TABLE 7.5
Total Planned and Actual Agricultural Production, 1971-76
(million lei)

Year	Planned Production	Actual Production	Shortfall
1971	91,400	81,000	10,400 (11.4%)
1972	97,800	89,000	8,000 (9.0%)
1973	106,800	90,000	16,800 (15.7%)
1974	113,000	90,000	23,000 (20.3%)
1975	Not specified in plan	93,400	....
1976	119,300	110,000	9,300 (7.8%)

Sources: See list of sources for table 7.6.

TABLE 7.6
Agricultural Production in Selected Commodities, 1971-76 (in Tons)

Year	Item	Planned Prod.	Actual Prod.	+|-(%)
1971	Wheat, Rye	5,575,000	5,641,000	+66,000 (1.2%)
1972	Wheat, Rye	...	6,097,000	...
1973	Wheat, Rye	...	5,531,000	...
1974	Wheat, Rye	18,500,000[1]	5,007,000	...
1975	Wheat, Rye	20,000,000[1]	15,219,000[1]	-4,781,000[1] (23.9%)[1]
1976	Wheat, Rye	7,225,000	6,779,000	-446,000 (6.2%)
1971	Maize	9,060,000	7,762,000	-1,298,000 (14.3%)
1972	Maize	...	9,548,000	...
1973	Maize	...	7,223,000	...
1974	Maize	18,500,000[1]	7,159,000	...
1975	Maize	20,000,000[1]	15,219,000[1]	-4,781,000[1] (23.9%)[1]

Year	Crop			
1976	Maize	11,935,000	11,707,000	-228,000 (1.9%)
1971	Sunflower Seed	976,000	788,000	-188,000 (19.3%)
1972	Sunflower Seed	...	848,000	...
1973	Sunflower Seed	1,018,000	758,000	-260,000 (25.5%)
1974	Sunflower Seed	1,014,000	671,000	-343,000 (33.8%)
1975	Sunflower Seed	1,062,000	724,000	-338,000 (31.8%)
1976	Sunflower Seed	1,080,000	806,000	-274,000 (25.4%)
1971	Sugar Beets	4,800,000	4,301,000	-499,000 (10.4%)
1972	Sugar Beets	...	5,309,000	...
1973	Sugar Beets	6,595,000	4,365,000	-2,230,000 (33.8%)
1974	Sugar Beets	7,350,000	5,000,000	-2,350,000 (32.0%)
1975	Sugar Beets	8,560,000	4,902,000	-3,658,000 (42.7%)
1976	Sugar Beets	7,200,000	6,900,000	-300,000 (4.2%)

TABLE 7.6 (cont.)
Agricultural Production in Selected Commodities, 1971–76 (in Tons)

Year	Item	Planned Prod.	Actual Prod.	+1-(%)
1971	Potatoes	3,925,000	3,300,000	-625,000 (15.9%)
1972	Potatoes	...	3,136,000	...
1973	Potatoes	4,132,000	2,656,000	-1,476,000 (35.7%)
1974	Potatoes	4,385,000	3,560,000	-825,000 (18.8%)
1975	Potatoes	4,550,000	2,319,000	-2,231,000 (49.0%)
1976	Potatoes	4,735,000	4,231,000	-504,000 (10.6%)
1971	Vegetables	3,640,000	2,508,000	-1,132,000 (31.1%)
1972	Vegetables	...	2,447,000	...
1973	Vegetables	3,830,000	2,631,000	-1,199,000 (31.3%)
1974	Vegetables	3,925,000	2,725,000	-1,200,000 (30.6%)
1975	Vegetables	4,045,000	2,364,000	-1,681,000 (41.5%)

1976	Vegetables	3,950,000	3,313,000	-637,000 (16.1%)
1971	Fruit, Grapes	3,105,000	2,048,000	-1,057,000 (34.)%
1972	Fruit, Grapes	...	2,339,000	...
1973	Fruit, Grapes	3,493,000	2,541,000	-952,000 (27.3%)
1974	Fruit, Grapes	3,395,000	2,047,000	-1,348,000 (39.7%)
1975	Fruit, Grapes	3,535,000	2,218,000	-1,317,000 (37.3%)
1976	Fruit, Grapes	3,572,000	2,733,000	-839,000 (23.5%)
1971	Meat (Live Weight)	1,438,000	1,370,000	-68,000 (4.7%)
1972	Meat (Slaughter Weight)	584,000	489,000	-95,000 (1.6%)
1973	Cattle[a]	...	5,895,000	...
1974	Cattle[a]	...	5,897,100	...
1975	Cattle[a]	6,600,000	6,126,000	-474,000 (7.2%)
1976	Cattle[a]	6,620,000	6,349,000	+271,000 (4.1%)

TABLE 7.6 (cont.)
Agricultural Production in Selected Commodities, 1971-76 (in Tons)

Sources: The data presented above have been derived from a variety of sources, as follows: for 1971: Scinteia, 17 December 1971; ibid., 2 February 1972; for 1972: Scinteia, 17 December 1971; ibid., 16 July 1972; Agerpres, 14 February 1973; for 1973: Scinteia, 30 November 1972; ibid., 6 February 1974; for 1974: Scinteia, 2 December 1973; ibid., 7 and 11 February 1975; for 1975: Scinteia, 20 December and ibid., 1974; 4 February 1976; for 1976: Scinteia, 20 December 1975 and 6 February 1977.

I have also relied upon the following issues of Radio Free Europe Research, Romanian Situation Reports: 21 December 1971; 4 January 1972; 8 February 1972; 17 February 1972; 1 March 1972; 18 July 1972; 15 February 1973; 7 December 1973; 14 February 1974; 15 January 1975; 14 February 1975; 18 February 1976; 5 March 1976; 29 April 1976; 17-23 February 1977; 22-28 December 1977; 23 February-1 March 1978.

It should be pointed out that in several cases, e.g., 1973 and 1974, there is a discrepancy between the figures of the official communique and the figures of the statistical yearbooks, that were published up to a year later. This discrepancy is especially noteworthy in figures for cattle raising. Generally, the yearbook figures tend to be higher than those of the communique whenever such discrepancies do occur. I have chosen to use the figures of the official communiques.

^aActual number of animals.

[1]All cereals computed together.

as party cadres in city and countryside alike. From such improved consciousness it was believed, greater production would flow. In the same vein, the 1970s saw an unprecedented attempt to utilize nationalism and the epic of the struggle for Romanian independence as a vehicle for economic mobilization. This latter aspect was particularly evident during the celebrations of the centennial of Romanian independence in 1976-77.[34] This ongoing ideological offensive is a strong indicator of the PCR's continued commitment to political mobilization on a scale unknown elsewhere in Eastern Europe in this decade. But it should also be noted that the pragmatic elements of this campaign are becoming more evident as the 1980s draw near; now, ideology and nationalism seem to be increasingly valued as means to the end of higher production and better performance, in agriculture as well as in other economic sectors, rather than as ends in themselves. If this shift becomes permanent, the PCR and Nicolae Ceausescu may be searching for instrumental legitimacy rather than ideological or charismatic authority in the next decade. Such a shift should have some impact upon future agricultural policies as well (for details, see conclusion below).

AGRICULTURAL PERFORMANCE DURING THE 1970S

The many attempts by the PCR to enhance agricultural production during the decade of the 1970s have met with mixed results. There has been an increase in absolute production, and the years 1973 and 1976 produced record cereal crops, but at no time did the agricultural sector fulfill the production Plans. This problem was partly caused by the inability of the agricultural sector actually to invest all the funds originally allocated for it in the annual Plans. Table 7.4 examines this problem in some detail.

The consistent lag in investments predictably resulted in production shortfalls as well. Table 7.5 examines the problem in terms of total agricultural production, and table 7.6 surveys the underfulfillment of the annual Plans in selected commodities.

As seen from table 7.6, the production achievements of Romanian agriculture in the 1970s leaves a great deal to be desired. This rather dismal record continued in 1977 as well. Actual production that year of key commodities fell well below Plan.

	Plan in Tons[35]	Actual Production in Tons[36]
wheat and rye	7,290,000	6,540,000
maize	12,120,000	10,103,000
sugar beets	8,480,000	6,249,000
sunflower seeds	1,109,000	807,000
potatoes	4,790,000	3,738,000
vegetables	4,110,000	3,065,000
fruits	2,050,000	1,393,000
grapes	1,706,000	1,464,000
meat (live weight)	2,470,200	
milk	51,610,000 (hectoliters)	

The report on Plan fulfillment did not deal with actual meat production but stated instead that at the end of 1977, there were 6,301,000 cattle in Romania, a figure that represented a drop of 50,000 since January 5, 1977. There were 9,732,000 pigs (a decrease of 461,000 during 1977). On the other hand, there were 75,000 more sheep and goats at the end of the year than there had been in January (14,849,000 on December 31, 1977).[37]

The figures presented above show that the year 1977 was another difficult period for Romanian agriculture. The Plan was not fulfilled in any of the categories listed above; the shortfall was as follows:

wheat and rye	750,000 tons (10.3%)
maize	2,017,000 tons (16.6%)
sugar beets	2,231,000 tons (26.3%)
sunflower seeds	302,000 tons (27.2%)
potatoes	1,052,000 tons (22.0%)
vegetables	1,045,000 tons (25.4%)
fruits	657,000 tons (32.1%)
grapes	242,000 tons (14.2%)

Given such a performance over time, it is natural that the analyst is a bit skeptical about the possibilities of Plan fulfillment in 1978. For the record, the 1978 Plan calls for the following production figures this year:

wheat and rye	7,385,000	tons
maize	13,215,000	tons
sugar beets	8,580,000	tons
sunflower seeds	1,133,000	tons
potatoes	4,850,000	tons
vegetables	4,300,000	tons
fruit	2,180,000	tons
grapes	1,776,000	tons
meat (live weight)	2,673,000	tons
milk	61,640,000	hectoliters
wool	43,830	tons
eggs	6,415	million units
cattle	7,100,000	heads
pigs	11,560,000	heads [38]
sheep and goats	17,000,000	heads

Final production figures for 1978 will probably be available in late January or early February 1979.

The problems encountered by Nicolae Ceausescu and his economic planners in the agricultural sector are clearly related to investments, education of personnel, and material incentives such as procurement prices, wages, and pensions. Up to now, these incentives have been lacking to a considerable extent, resulting in low productivity and a host of related phenomena such as poor utilization of raw materials, machinery, and manpower; furthermore, there is a great deal of shirking of duties, absenteeism, and outright theft, and many of the collective farmers openly demonstrate their unwillingness to work in the fields or the barns, as was the case during a recent "harvesting drive," when school children and soldiers labored in the fields while the peasants stood idly by, occasionally jeering at the "do-gooders"[39] who had been commandeered into the countryside. Such manifestations of poor work discipline appear to be very widespread, and the regime is faced with the unpalatable choices of either turning the other cheek or, conversely, increasing the level of coercion to a drastic extent. The third alternative, which is only recently being considered, even in very small doses is a restructuring of the entire approach to the agricultural sector whereby much greater emphasis is put on increasing remuneration, improving the labor force (in terms of age, sex, and education), and generally changing the image of this area of activity from that of second-class to the center of economic concerns in Romania. So far only some of these measures have in fact been taken, and most of these are predominantly exhortative rather than substantive. It is nevertheless true that the PCR and Nicolae Ceausescu now have recognized the existence of fundamental problems in this field. Given the traditional

157

approach of communist elites to the agricultural sector, this is no mean achievement.

LOOKING TO THE FUTURE

Early this year, the Romanian press published guidelines for the 1981-85 five-year Plan, and this document, however preliminary in nature, provides some insight into the thinking of the political leadership concerning the agricultural sector and its position in the total economy. The guidelines establish the following priorities:

1. Industrial production will increase by 11.5 percent annually, so that by 1985, total industrial production will be some 55 to 60 percent over the level of 1980.

2. Agricultural production is scheduled to rise annually by 6.5 to 8.6 percent; by 1985, 23 to 25 percent more agricultural goods will be produced than in 1980.

3. Increased efforts will be made to undo two of the most fundamental bottlenecks in Romanian agriculture, namely the supply of chemical fertilizer and the development of irrigation systems.

4. Labor productivity is to increase considerably in agriculture as well as in other economic sectors.

5. The real income of the peasantry is scheduled to increase by 5.4 percent per year, but increases in labor productivity in the entire economy is scheduled to go up 9.2 percent annually, implying that everyone must work harder than before.

6. Investments in the total economy will be raised by 12.8 percent annually. By 1985, 37 to 42 percent more will be invested than in 1980.

7. Livestock production is to reach the level of the most advanced countries by 1985.[40]

In many ways, the draft Plan is a surprising document. Given the attention focused on Romanian agricultural problems during the last few years, and given Ceausescu's statements indicating a real effort to upgrade the agricultural sector, one might have expected a greater emphasis on this area of activity in the 1980s. Instead, the draft Plan is remarkably similar to its predecessors of the 1950s, 1960s, and 1970s in that it clearly emphasizes industrial production and development. Indeed, the Plan specifies that by 1985 industry must account for 70 percent of the national income, and the share of machine building in total industrial production is scheduled to rise to 36 percent by the end of the target period.[41] The "ethos" of the Plan is clearly heavily industrial, once again reducing agriculture to a secondary, "residual" status.

158

There are two plausible explanations for this continued economic emphasis. First of all, the current problems in Romanian agriculture are of such a magnitude that no early and drastic improvement can be expected; to pump large investments into such a depressed sector of the economy is likely to result in substantial waste rather than dramatic improvements. Under such circumstances, a slower, but steadier, increase in investments and other remedial policies for agriculture may be more beneficial.

Secondly, the current Romanian leadership has remained basically unchanged for considerable period of time, despite "rotation of cadres" at the top, and dramatic policy changes cannot be made overnight. Nicolae Ceausescu and his colleagues have amply demonstrated their earlier devotion to the idea of modernization qua industrialization, and their ideological convictions as both Marxists and nationalists have identified Romanian development with rapid expansion of the heavy and extractive industries. The draft Plan makes it abundantly clear that these convictions still hold sway. Agricultural improvement, then, is to be brought about by modest increases in investment, coupled with some improvement in the standard of living of the rural population., At the same time, the tendency to tinker with the system, in the form of frequent reorganizing, has not been eliminated, and it is also likely that the ideological offensive, designed to raise productivity through mobilization rather than material remuneration, will continue.

While the PCR program for the first half of the 1980s looks very much like a continuation of priorities already well established, I would suggest an alternative scenario for the 1980s, a scenario that may be brought about by the momentum of developments already underway in Romanian society.

The modernization process in Romania appears to have reached a critical level as the country heads towards the 1980s. After three decades of intensive development, emphasizing heavy and extractive industries, the modernizers of the PCR are confronted with an economic crisis of major proportions. This crisis is brought about not merely by underproduction in key economic fields, but rather by the processes of social stratification and differentiation, which have created a diversified society inhabited by increasingly well-educated and sophisticated citizens. This citizenry appears to be unwilling to accept extensive development of heavy industries, and is beginning to demand greater services, a higher standard of living, and, above all, more food for consumption. Up to the present time, the economic system of Romania has been unequal to the task of delivering the kinds of goods and services now demanded by increasing numbers of individuals, indeed by the entire social strata. It seems unlikely that the draft five-year Plan for the period 1980-85

159

can meet this level of increased demands. The regime, therefore, must decide whether or not it will meet these demands with increased ideological mobilization, perhaps even increased coercion, or, conversely, with adjustments in the political, economic, and social priorities that have been set forth in the long-range plan discussed above.

It should be emphasized here that the increasing demands for present-day payoffs after thirty years of deferred gratification are coming from all social strata, not merely a handful of individuals or a small minority of disaffected intellectuals. Indeed, the most serious expressions of rejection and dissent have in face originated in the very heart of the socialist system, the urban proletariat; it was the miners of the Jui Valley who went on strike during the summer of 1977, ultimately wresting major concessions out of the regime, at least in the short run.[42] By the same token, workers, especially young workers, in the Bucharest industrial region, struck on several occasions.[43] And the collective and state farmers, whose increased efforts during the next five to ten years are expected to provide for the enlarged demands of the expanding urban population, have openly demonstrated their disdain for some regime policies by jeering at the soldiers and school children doing their work. Given such important manifestations of dissent, the regime may be forced to make certain concessions, especially in its agricultural policies.

In practical terms, the following changes may help increase the production of agricultural commodities, thereby alleviating the economic crisis in the rural sector and also solving some of the problems of disaffection stemming from inadequate production:

1. Increase in investments in the agricultural sector;
2. A concerted effort to redirect manpower back into the countryside, thereby improving the chances for higher productivity ;
3. Expanding the educational efforts now under way to teach collective and state farmers at the mass level the improved technology now available;
4. An expansion of the irrigation system and the supply of chemical fertilizer;
5. Higher prices for agricultural commodities;
6. Improved wage and pension systems as well as fringe benefit schemes in agriculture, which can bring about greater equality in remuneration between urban and rural workers;
7. Improvements in the quality of administrative and party cadres in the countryside;
8. A toning down of the ideological offensive in the countryside as well as in the industrial sector;
9. Greater recognition of the efforts of private farmers and the private plots of individuals in socialist

agriculture, and corresponding remuneration- and pension-scheme improvements to further incentives in this field;
10. A general redirection of the outlook of regime leaders and rank and file to establish the agricultural sector as an equal partner in the modernization process by mass and elite alike.

These are certainly rather unpalatable policies for the ruling elite, and Nicolae Ceausescu clearly would like to avoid implementation of many of them, especially numbers 8 and 9, which would require considerable changes in some of the major policies implemented during the Ceausescu era. Should widespread dissent become the order of the day, the general secretary and his economic planners may nevertheless be faced with the need to change their approach even in these fields.

Barring the development of such dire events, the PCR will most likely attempt to implement half-measures from the alternatives 1 through 7 listed above; i.e., there will be some adjustments in investments designed to alleviate the problem, but the lion's share will still go to industry and fuels. In a similar vein, the pressures for skilled manpower in industry will most likely negate any regime effort to redirect manpower back into the countryside, and educational efforts among the rank and file of the peasants may founder on the current work ethic among this part of the population, which in essence appears interested in minimal, rather than maximal, efforts. It should be possible to improve the situation in irrigation and the supply of chemical fertilizers, and in these areas, upward revisions of investment and production plans appear likely during the course of the Plan. There has also been a movement in the direction of improvements in procurement prices, wages, pensions, and other benefits, and the regime may attempt to meet public demands and instances of dissent by means of upward revisions in these fields. As for drastic improvements in the quality of party and administrative personnel in the countryside, it appears unlikely that organizational measures can solve this problem during the next decade. After all, Nicolae Ceausescu has been attempting to "rotate cadres" from Bucharest to the provinces for many years now, but the results have been minimal; personnel assigned to Ilfov and Satu Mare have a tendency to drift back towards the center after a suitable period of time. The problem of personnel reassignment, in short, revolves around the very success of the PCR's indoctrination campaign, which has succeeded in instilling an urban and industrial ethos in the population, whereby everybody wants to live in the cities and eat well, but nobody wants to produce the agricultural commodities needed to realize this dream of modernity. Cadre policies in the countryside, in short, are likely to continue to founder.

In summary, then, the remedies for Romanian agriculture that are likely to be prescribed during the first half of the 1980s still represent only a partial attack on the problems of this troubled sector. The PCR and Nicolae Ceausescu are still unwilling to come to grips with the fundamental problems of socialist agriculture. They may be able to avoid such a confrontation with the basic questions of this economic sector during the period up to the mid-1980s. Whether or not difficult decisions and potentially fundamental changes in policy can be avoided past that time is another matter. In my opinion, the next decade or two will indeed be the crucial time for such reevaluations of long-standing priorities and policies. Given the nature of the Romanian "directed society," Nicolae Ceausescu and his successors will be facing a problem even more fundamental than the question of Romanian agriculture; it is indeed the question of the very nature of the societal system that is on the agenda. And Romania is not alone in this predicament. All other communist-dominated systems of Europe will face the same problem sooner or later. Therein lies the relevance of the Romanian case even beyond state borders.

NOTES

1. The best overall work on the Romanian economy is still John M. Montias, Economic Development in Communist Rumania (Cambridge, Mass.: The M.I.T. Press, 1967), especially chapter 2.
2. Poor performance in the agricultural sector certainly influenced the events of December 1970 and January 1971, which led to the demise of the Gomulka regime in Poland. For a discussion of this, see Adam Bromke, "Poland under Gierek," Problems of Communism, September-October 1972, pp. 1-20.
3. One such country is the USSR, where General Secretary Brezhnev announced recognition of the private sector in the new constitution.
4. See, for example, Montias, Economic Development, especially chapter 1.
5. I have derived the investment figures from the statistical yearbooks for this period; see Republica Socialista Romania, Directia Centrala de Statistica, Anuarul Statistic, selected years.
6. An analysis of this consolidation is provided in my Modernization in Romania since World War II, (New York: Praeger Publishers, 1975) especially chapter 2.
7. E.g., Montias, Economic Development, especially chapter 2.
8. Ceausescu himself has discussed this in numerous speeches and statements, e.g., Romania pe Drumul Desavirsirii Constructiei Socialiste (Bucharest: Editura Politica, 1968-

77, 7 vols.); a discussion of the concept is also provided in my "Ceausescu's Romania," Problems of Communism, July-August 1974, pp. 29-44.

9.   Ceausescu's report can be found in Congresul al XI-lea al Partidului Comunist Roman, (Bucharest: Editura Politica, 1974) pp. 15-87, especially 44-68 (on the 1976-80 Plan).

10.   "Catching up" usually meant increased productivity as seen from the Plans of the 1970s, e.g., the Plan for 1976, published in Scinteia, December 20, 1975.

11.   Ibid., 4 June 1977.

12.   Ibid.

13.   Ceausescu's visit to the Jui Valley was reported in Scinteia, 4 August 1977.

14.   The Jui Valley miner's strike and the problems elsewhere in the economy prompted a meeting of the Political Executive Committee of the PCR on 8 August; see ibid., 9 August 1977.

15.   Ceausescu repeatedly made this point at a congress of agricultural officials and representatives of all sectors of Romanian agriculture in April 1977; for the text of his speech, see ibid., 19 April 1977.

16.   Derived from Anuarul Statistic al Republicii Socialiste Romania, 1976, pp. 278-79 and the following issues of Scinteia: 17 December 1971; 30 November 1972; 14 February 1973, and 5 February 1974.

17.   Anuarul Statistic 1977, pp. 332-33 and the following issues of Scinteia: 20 December 1974, and 20 December 1975.

18.   Anuarul Statistic 1977, pp. 452-54; 457-60, and 470-74.

19.   "Maistri" is a term describing a degree given for work somewhat similar to that done at higher professional schools, but short of university training. Figures are derived from Anuarul Statistic 1977, pp. 452-54; 457-60, and 472-75.

20.   Anuarul Statistic 1977, pp. 476-79.

21.   For a report of the training of PCR cadres in agricultural matters, see Scinteia, 4 October 1975.

22.   The January 1971 scale was published in ibid, 25 December 1970.

23.   Radio Free Europe Research, Romanian Situation Report no. 13, 14-10 April 1977.

24.   Ibid.

25.   Ibid.

26.   Ceausescu discussed this problem in considerable detail in his address to the agricultural conference of April 1977; for the stenographic report of his speech, see Scinteia, 19 April 1977.

27.   Ibid.; for the text of the decision adopted at a conference of individual farmers, held concurrently with the agricultural conference of April 1977, see ibid., 21 April 1977.

28. This problem was discussed in great detail in an article in <u>Revista Economica</u>, 24 April 1978.

29. Ibid.

30. The most extensive discussion of this problem was furnished by Ceausescu in a speech to the agricultural conference in April 1977; see <u>Scinteia</u>, 19 April 1977.

31. Some recent personnel changes were brought about by continuing problems in agriculture. For a thorough discussion of this, see <u>Radio Free Europe Research</u>, Romanian Situation Report no. 6, 9-15 March 1978.

32. I have discussed this program in "Ceausescu's Romania," <u>Problems of Communism</u>, July-August 1974, pp. 29-44.

33. Ibid.

34. Ceausescu's speech at the celebrations of Romanian independence reflected this as well; see <u>Scinteia</u>, 10 May 1977.

35. Ibid., 6 November 1976.

36. Ibid., 5 February 1978.

37. Ibid.

38. Ibid., 26 November 1977.

39. This tendency was discussed with great indignation in <u>Scinteia Tineretului</u>, 18 July 1975.

40. <u>Scinteia</u>, 15 December 1977.

41. Ibid.

42. Changes in remuneration and other economic topics were discussed in the Political Executive Committee of the PCR on 8 August 1977; see ibid., 9 August 1978.

43. This prompted a Ceausescu "working visit" to industrial enterprises in the capital (for a report, see ibid., 18 August 1977).

8
The Hungarian Experiment in Search of Profitability

Peter S. Elek

PRECONDITIONS HERALDING ECONOMIC CHANGE IN POST-REFORM HUNGARY

Hungary, with its loyalties well ensconced in the socialist orbit, is a model of a small country on the eastern fringes of Europe, that finds itself caught in the midst of two recessive world-wide economic trends threatening its rate of development and standard of living. These are world-wide inflation and mounting energy prices. We are focusing on a nation with a GNP showing an excess of 40 percent in the foreign trade sector, that at the same time is dependent on foreign sources for over 80 percent of its energy needs.

Regardless of the degree of decentralization the Hungarian economy claims, it is for all practical purposes a planned economy seeking to achieve certain set goals. Among these goals, the operational stages are loosely planned, and within predesigned parameters a degree of freedom of enterprise prevails. The division between ownership and control typical of the western corporation has been duplicated. The role of an outside board of directors is assumed by the political leadership or central authorities. Within these limitations the markets' contributions are encouraged and exploited. Successful western production processes are encouraged, duplicated, and astutely integrated to fit the need of a socialist system.

There is a third setback threatening Hungarian goals which is domestic in nature. It is caused by low productivity in the public sector. The nature of this problem is a mix of ideology and incentive. It is caused by the living standards the public and the leadership believe should prevail, the willingness of the work force to work hard enough to achieve such goals within the limits of the wage bill, and finally the authorities' willingness and ability (within the prevailing political atmosphere) to enforce the goals.

165

The influence of international inflation is transmitted through the reappearance of the agricultural scissors, a well publicized argument of the 1920s, when either external inflation far exceeds the domestic, or primary raw material is exported at a low price while vital capital imports are furnished at a high one. Thus, the terms of trade shifted unfavorably against Hungary. Such deteriorating terms of trade in the past were overcome by foreign[1] loans, including considerable volumes from western sources.[1] But the limit of deficit in the balance of international trade is clear. The attitude of the socialist bloc to international economic treaties is a combination of reversed snobbery and neo-mercantilism. While socialist systems recognize the institution of private property in a quite limited way, they also act in the manner of neo-mercantilists and are fully aware of the advantages derived by international trade. Thus acting like neo-mercantilists they wish to and indeed do prove to the world that, although lacking the institutional private property base, they meet their obligations to the nonsocialist world without fault. Thus, the burden of international debt, specifically repayment to the West, lies heavily on the mind of Eastern European planners, who seek to limit such debts to manageable proportions.

Hungarian enterprises have the right to negotiate contracts with foreign partners. Nevertheless, a license from the central bank is required to consummate such transactions. The bank in turn guarantees payment to the foreign partners. Hence, potential losses are underwritten domestically. Any deficit developing in the balance of international payments was thus in the past renegotiated by the bank through foreign loans. According to Hungarian sources, foreign indebtedness nonetheless rapidly is approaching the upper limits of such manageable proportions.

This analysis is confined to the agricultural and the agro-industrial sector, the latter consisting of a mix of processing and complementary manufacturing and extricating operations. The objective is to review these sectors' efforts and the way they cope with adverse trends and pressures inhibiting the attainment of planned goals.

How economic policy responds to the three major pressures described in the introduction is the substantive question under review. It is clear that something has to be sacrificed, development or living standards, according to the concavity of the production possibility curve. The choices available present an open debate among the planners. They range from more centralization and tightening up, to more decentralization, liberalization, greater freedom of enterprise and markets, more inflation, less ambitious goals. The only constancy not challenged is full employment. This is a "conditio sine qua none," a basic philosophical premise which is beyond the give and take of available options.

166

The first question which arises is how does balancing economic growth fit into the profit-deepening picture. The economic reforms of the 1960s, labeled NEM (New Economic Mechanism) side-stepped the dogmatic Marxian bias against profit and, in macroeconomic terms, emancipated the viability of surplus, or profit, as a vital stimulator. Economic historians referred to these changes as moving from the "classical" Stalinist centrally planned model to a limited market orientation.

In the past ten years this experiment has become operational and vastly sophisticated. A host of market-oriented projects was introduced and, together with a new set of regulations (indicators) enacted in 1976, have now moved the Hungarian economy into a new phase.²

TRANSMITTING CHANGES WITHIN THE FRAMEWORK OF THE NATIONAL ECONOMIC PLAN

The reforms broadened immensely the decision making powers of the enterprises in all aspects of their operations. On one hand the central planners (who are synonymous with government power) disappeared from visible first-line command. On the other hand they retained concealed control over the economy by coordinating general equilibrium conditions and national priorities. Such remote controls are transmitted through centrally set prices, fiscal and monetary (credit) policies. The price policy, while freeing most prices to market forces, retained control over setting prices of certain basic raw materials and consumer goods. Then the planners let all other prices float freely around this basic core of fixed prices (i.e., coal, iron, steel, bread, transportation, etc.), which is referred to officially as "prices will fall into line." Operationally the task was carried out by a double price system of producer and consumer prices. The difference between the two was eliminated by government grants, subsidies or taxes. The policy objective was to gradually reduce the surpluses and deficits.

A second major tool of planners was exercised by setting the formulas controlling the level of enterprises' "retained profits" (or, reversing the emphasis; the rate of enterprise taxation). The tax system in the past three years was further refined and applied to that share of retained enterprise profits that enterprises could distribute as bonuses to their workers. In this manner planners sought to enforce across the board a more uniform distribution of income, by levying a 200-300 percent surcharge tax on that portion of bonus funds that exceeded set parameters. Thus, the labor force of respective plants receives its bonus shares designed by statutory formulas based on productivity only in a tapered-off manner. Planners consider this methodology as a capital intensity

167

balancer (correcting for price system malfunctions), but it obviously also contributes to adverse effects in labor productivity. On the other hand, if the enterprise does refrain from distributing to labor the excess, heavily taxed bonuses, it may retain such funds fully (excess tax exempt) for capital formation, which diverts forcefully funds into capital flows.

One may also note that enterprises' retained profit formulas were set too low to carry out major capital investments through their own savings. Thus the enterprise is forced to secure loans from the state bank to supplement its inadequate capital funds. The state bank on the other hand acts as a tool of "planners' preference" by granting or choking off the demand in line with the blueprint of national economic goals.

NEW INSTRUMENTS OF CHANGE

There is a number of new approaches in the search for increasing profitability. Some are truly new, of recent vintage; others are reorganizations under a new label. Their common goals are either cost reduction or improving the internal efficiency of the firm, by rearranging the administrative or incentive systems, and thus encouraging productivity and profitability.

The former include "joint foreign ventures" and TOPS ("technically operated production systems in agriculture") which led to successive broader horizontal integration, and successively to vertical integration. In the latter group the most significant development is the "agro-industrial combine," which joins together a horizontal-vertical non-line developed integration process. It is a socialist replica of a major Western trust, which operates its loosely knit divisions and overlapping service organizations along the concept of American corporate cost centers. Major benefits of this form derive from monopoly concentrations, that would be barred for U.S. business by prohibitive antitrusts regulations enacted through the Celler-Kefauver anti-merger act.[3]

Significant new development is attributable to fundamental structural changes affecting the character of the highly profitable private (household plot) agricultural sector. The profile of joint foreign ventures is well documented.[4] The objective in Eastern Europe is to persuade Western partners to furnish additional loans for capital equipment and new technology. Usually, the venture capital required to operate such joint ventures and the construction costs are furnished by the host country. Initially such ventures were limited to technological transfers with a 50-50 percent joint participation. Now such arrangements have been gradually extended into manufacturing, with the Western partners not infrequently assuming a larger than 50 percent share. Such arrangements are putting the socialist enterprises into minority position with regards to ownership of public goods, while the majority holdings went into foreign private hands. These were considered major ideological breakthroughs affecting the constitutional rights of public ownership, as interpreted in the past by the leading ideology. Regardless of the give and take in legal interpretation by the socialist partners, the business risk of the Western partner did not change substantially. He continues to operate in an arena external to the jurisdiction of Western international business code or political philosophy. In case of dispute redress remains fully dependent on political good will, rather than on legally enforceable statute.

Despite these uncertainties the short run success of such joint ventures, both as profitable operations and technological transfer agents, is widely acclaimed in the literature.[5] TOPS[6] were new large-scale pilot projects of successful "horizontal integration" ("combining like ventures"). The striking difference characterizing TOPS is that in contrast to the preceding Stalinist period's forced mergers, participation in TOPS is voluntary. Motivation for joining is induced by self-interest. Potential members are state farms and cooperatives that seek to improve their profitability through bolstering productivity by TOPS-generated facilities, that will ultimately contribute to excess profits and employee bonuses. Joining is a privilege, not automatically granted.[7] Eligibility is based on potential members' ability to meet certain financial obligations. TOPS transfers the latest engineering know-how and science to agribusiness and applies the newest skills and up-to-date controls by industrial engineering. Agriculture is industrialized by application of new management methods and selective investments.[8]

There is a number of different types of TOPS with different characteristics, but when classified by legal structure, most fall[9] into two major categories: first, the proprietory type, and second, the technological transfer (service) type of TOPS. The proprietory[10] type is an operational unit with a separate legal entity, formed for the exploitation of profit. It is a socialist effort duplicating corporate entrepreneurship, with stockholders replaced by state farms and cooperatives (TOPS, the Babolna model). The technological transfer type of TOPS' role approximates[11] that of a non-profit organization that through service, mass discount purchase, technological skill and credit availability, increases its members' profitability (TOPS, the Nadudvar model).

When measuring newly generated real output as a success indicator, "vertical integration" is the most controversial revitalized approach in the Hungarian economic repertoire. These types of realignments are not new. They were known since the turn of the century, when agro-industries acquired and profitably operated large agricultural holdings, or large agricultural holdings entered into the spheres of canning, sugar, or alcohol processing.

Much of vertical integration's success hinges on accounting profits created by interdepartmental transfer prices and through an exchange of byproducts, service units, and technological transfers. The processing unit benefits from a guarantee of a core volume of basic raw material supply from the primary producer. Such integration offers credit, additional venture capital that will bolster intensive cultivation, and transfer of technology. Since the price of the finished good is determined by bilateral trade negotiations, the price becomes isolated from accounting manipulations. Gain in real terms comes from technological transfer and additional venture capital and, to some limited degree, by reducing transportation costs. A similar trend was noticed in the USSR thirty years ago, when small enterprises combined into larger units to shield their cost functions against reapplication of turn-over taxes.[12]

Combining deficit and surplus units or high and low profit producers through rearranging the internal economies of enterprises contributed to a better than average profit picture, combined with a more favorable marginal tax rate.

However, statistical data on how much, if at all, such rearrangements contributed to additional real output are still inconclusive. But what is known is that many of the early ventures into vertical integration failed.[13] Blame for such failures was laid partly in the literature on the insufficient volume of business generated to make such new ventures viable, partly by the lack of "infant industry" type of protectionist subsidy. But the belated demand for such subsidies certainly speaks poorly of efficiency and new productivity-induced gains.

Agro-industrial combines (referred to as agrocombines) are the latest vintage of superstructures. They were created by multilevel horizontal and vertical integration. Such conglomerates furnish raw materials for their member firms' finished goods, or rechannel finished goods of one production cycle as intermediate goods to another member's production line. They internalize externalities, and there is a considerable urge to merge. Notwithstanding diseconomies of scale, policymakers believe that size means excess profits and prestige.

Joining the conglomerate is shrouded by ambiguity. On one hand the enterprise acts on its own initiative surrounded by an atmosphere of voluntary actions. On the other hand chartering such agrocombines requires a permit from a licensing public body. So far four charters have been granted. The act of licensing itself is an interference in the operation of free markets, which is justified by the authorities on the ground of limited supply of capital and harnessing input-output flows within the limits of national equilibrium.

Such agrocombines follow regional, rather than line development, and are financed by their members' retained profits and bank loans. Once established they assume separate legal entities and are operated by their officers with full authority, rather than by decisions approved by a council. The function of the board of directors is carried out by a production council, which is a policy making body whose membership consists of delegates of the participating enterprises and government representatives.

At present this agrocombine type of conglomerate is in the experimental stage, without adequate statistical data to measure its performance. The pilot project is the "Hajdusagi Agraripari Egyesules" (HAE: Agrocombine of Hajdusag). The other three licensed operating agrocombines are Rabakis, Kalocsa and Bekes. HAE is headquatered in Nadudvar. (For further details see table 8.1.) It is a three layer regional minitrust with five interdependent autonomous decision making authorities. Its membership consists of twelve agricultural cooperatives, one state farm, and one food processing enterprise. Each member has a spinoff of further wholly owned marketing and auxilliary outlets. The conglomerate encompasses an agricultural area of 120,000 - 130,000 hectares, for which it assumes full financial accountability.

The vital nucleus that created HAE is shown in layer II (table 8.1), the Red Star Farm Cooperative at NADUDVAR (Nadudvari Voros Csillag Termeloszovetkezet). It is the underlying legal entity, which further owns a fully independent wholly owned subsidiary known as KITE, a service TOPS (Kukorica es Iparinoveny Termelesi Egyesules).

Red Star, with its 18,000 hectares, is Hungary's largest cooperative. It primarily uses West German equipment (combines) and John Deere tractors. The tractor stock is now being replaced by Polish machines manufactured under Western subcontracts. The performance of U.S. multinationals is a mixed blessing, showing increases on the asset side of their ledger, meanwhile contributing to Western unemployment. The first 100 replacements have been received with considerable lack of enthusiasm by the local officials, who find them clumsy to operate and difficult to assemble. Local word has it that the Polish equipment has been acquired because of the Hungarian international balance of payments difficulties, shifting payments from hard currency to CMEA adjustments.[14]

Red Star's subsidiary, KITE,[14] the service type TOPS, furnishes machines and arranges for credit to acquire equipment, technical know-how, seed, technology and maintenance. It is a non-profit organization[15] that charges a fee for services rendered.[16] Its major service functions are agricultural technology, economic, and extension-maintenance services. KITE owns no equipment; all equipment is owned by the member farms, which are also the recipients of the

TABLE 8.1
Flow Chart of an Agrocombine Conglomerate: Pilot Project HAE

Layer I   HAE

Headquartered at Nadudvar, a partnership of:
    12 Cooperatives (including the leader and sponsor in II)
    1 State Farm
    2 Food Processing Enterprises
    Numerous wholly owned retail and wholesale distributive
        enterprises
Combined agricultural area = 130,000 ha (decision-making
    authority 1 and 2)

Layer II   Red Star Farm Cooperative

Headquarters at Nadudvar (but not at HAE)
Parent (sponsoring) legal enterprise also one of 12 cooper-
    atives listed in Layer I
Role in Western terms synonymous with issuer of primary
    capital stock
Red Star is the most viable (capital endowed) Hungarian
    Cooperative and the largest (farming 18,000 ha)
                        Processing and milling facilities
                        (decision-making authority 3)

Layer III   KITE

Red Star's wholly owned service TOPS

350 member farms
    (decision-making authority 4 and 5)

Source: Constructed on the basis of local information furnished by Red Star officials. Data represents conditions of Summer 1978.

172

profit. Formed in 1972 by nine cooperative and one state farm for the purpose of promoting corn and industrial crop production[17] (oil, seed, etc.), today it consists of 350 member farms operated through seven subdivisions. The member farms comprise a total of 1,200,000 hectares of land, out of which 550,000 hectares were contracted to KITE as of 1 January 1977.[18]

The size of further horizontal expansion is limited by the necessity of soil fatigue-induced crop rotation and by the need to set certain break-even points ensuring profitability. The crop rotation coordinates corn, wheat, and rice as primary products; sugar beet, sunflower, grapes, and potatoes as secondary products. The crop rotation originally applying to eighteen varieties is now simplified to 6-8. Rotation, for all practical purposes, has ceased to exist, and the system today is reduced to a loose monoculture. Soil fatigue is experienced every 4-6 years and corrected by secondary cultivation and fertilizers. The order of profitability is sunflower (9 percent of land), wheat, and corn. Due to the natural limitations applicable to horizontal integration, additional growth efforts are channelled into the vertical scale.

KITE's technical leader and pilot project is its own "holding company," the Red Star cooperative. Red Star is vertically integrated with a meat packaging plant, a broiler factory, a turkey factory, and a poultry marketing unit.

The three layers of organizations, the combine HAE, Red Star, and KITE have interlocking directorates. Through such directorships, first, they control capital flows that are channelled into areas of optimal returns; secondly they manipulate and manage production by screening it through their respective cost centers. Finally, through their interlocking directorates, inter-unit loans and subsidies are arranged.

The agrocombines' long range significance lies in assembling under one organizational structure different types of operating units: state farms, farm cooperatives, industries and marketing outlets. They improve the internal economies of the region and help to cut down the vast government machinery's bureaucratic diseconomies of scale.

They are further forerunners of the significant change of merging state farms and farm cooperatives into a single agromass producing unit, an event expected to occur around 1990. Major improvements in profitability have accrued from unplanned structural transformation occurring in the private agricultural sector. Despite the substantive achievements of the private household sector in the short run, their role in the long run is confined to a transitional state. It is estimated that no later than by the year 2000 it will be replaced by a combination of factors: the success of agromass production making the existing operation of household plots uneconomical; an age factor affecting its labor supply curve, which is becoming a serious problem. This curve represents an affluent young agro-urban population unwilling to trade leisure for labor time or private gain for service obligation.

In the past ten years substantial changes occurred in the[19] numerical volume and profile of small business ventures. Such private ventures increased to 1,681,000 units by 1977, representing a land area of over a million hectares. Their changing profiles showed withdrawal from those areas of production that overlapped and thus competed with agromass production and hence reduced the private ventures' share of comparative advantage. This advantage lies in the private sector's concealed reservoir of implicit (unpaid) labor, whose returns were rendered uneconomical in some processes by agromass production. Thus the private sector then either switched to processes offering more profitable returns or, by having accrued adequate venture capital, refrained from marketing their primary resources (e.g., corn, other feeds) and entered into a secondary household self-processing operation with the primary products produced, such as hogs, poultry, rabbits, pigeons, bees, and milk. Other shifts included turning from corn and potato production to more capital-intensive market gardening, vinticulture and fruit producing endeavors.

By regression one may measure the success of agromass production and the deficiency of labor supply with its prevailing wage structure. In the past decade the private sector's share of agricultural production declined by 7.7 percent.[20] On the other hand, when the same period is measured by constant purchasing power, the private sector's income shows a slight increase.

The data therefore provides evidence of the private sector's efficient performance having produced more constant income on a lower base of operation. Here lies the productivity which authorities have not been successful in tapping and transferring to the public domain. Collective interest here clashes with natural determinism whereby man seeks to optimize his utilities by different standards and returns when facing private gain or public wages.

In physical terms, in 1974 the private sector produced[21] the following shares of the total production: 62 percent of the potato crop, 33 percent of vegetables, 50 percent of the fruit, 59 percent of the meat and bacon, 40 percent of the poultry, 43 percent of the milk and 65 percent of the eggs, with zero cost to the public sector. If implicit labor has no other marketable outlets, the opportunity cost of such labor is also zero. If, however, the opportunity cost rises and the volume of labor time is measured by up-to-date formulas of labor productivity (man hour per output), such production processes might turn out to be expensive and wasteful.

An interesting insight into the composition of a labor force operating at zero cost to the public is shown in table

8.2 by occupational and age parameters applying to the private agricultural sectors.

A further breakdown of the age distribution of this labor force shows that 68 percent of the labor time is furnished by the age group of 45 years and older, while 37 percent falls in the sixty years and older bracket. Thus to a great extent income derived in such manner acts as supplemental income to the aging or to the green thumb and entrepreneurial type, who is willing to trade income for leisure time.

One cannot help but notice a significant policy change displayed by the authorities, who switched gear and decided: "if we can't lick them, let's join them." In the past the officialdom discussed output and productivity of the private sector with an enigmatic smile, brushing off behind the veil of insignificance the quasi-market and promiscuous profit-seeking ideology of the private sector, whose success was difficult to digest for socialist planners.

The attitude today is to assist the private sector with all possible means, as long as it remains confined to its present scope of operations. Provisions are made in the national plan to divert resources to bolster the productivity of the private sector, in the form of allocating fertilizers, mass producing garden tractors, hoses, gardening and manual farm tools.

Thus while zero labor cost may prevail, there is a mounting real capital investment in household durables in the form of garden tractors and irrigation equipment, changing the cost functions of products produced by the private plots.

Authorities developed in the field of marketing a further avenue designed to bolster the private sector. Newly formed marketing subsidiaries of state and cooperative farms, in addition to marketing their own products, distribute for a commission products of the private sector falling under their territorial jurisdiction.

Beginning with the 19th century a torrent of information was disseminated through the literature on industrial combinations, which were variously referred to as cooperations, corporations, monopoly cartel or trust agreements. They emerged in the wake of the industrial revolution and through their impact the truly competitive markets were replaced by economics of scale and monopoly like arrangements.

Startling as it is, the socialist literature recognized certain positive aspects of such changes in market structures. These were already acknowledged by Marx[22] and Lenin,[23] the ideological founders. The present attention to horizontal and vertical integration is, however, a relatively new phenomena. While there are plenty of references on the merits of integration[24] in Eastern bloc literature, full emancipation of the idea was furnished

TABLE 8.2
Percentage Distribution of Total Labor Time Furnished by the
Occupational Sources in the Private Agricultural Sector (1972)

Occupational Source of Origin	Percentage
Unskilled agrocooperative laborer	12.6
Laborers of state agro, other cooperative enterprises, or individual workers	7.5
Non agrolaborer	11.8
White-collar group	6.7
Pensioners	24.9
Household members	33.1
Students	3.4

Source: Sandor Misi and Lajos Marko, A Haztaji Kisegitogazdal-kodas (Budapest: Kossuth Konyvkiado, 1977), p. 70.

by the decree of the Central Committee of the Soviet Communist party,[25] issued in June 1976.

The decree has developed into a master plan for the entire Eastern bloc. It advocates affirmative action on four substantive issues mainly applicable to agriculture: (1) specialization (2) concentration (3) cooperation (i.e., integration among operating units) and (4) agro-industrial combinations (i.e., horizo-vertical integrations).

By definition, the term "integration" under prevailing conditions refers to a tight organizational structure that emerged among partners by recognition of some issues of mutual self-interest. To carry out the task and cater to such common interests, the partners created a new organization to act as a vehicle satisfying the following criteria: (1) to hold a separate, well defined legal entity; (2) to retain founding members' independence; (3) the new organization to coordinate economic activities of members; (4) to render uniform management of member activities; (5) to contain erosive forces endangering the accomplishment of the common objective; and (6) to be controlled by the voting power of the member organizations.

Integration can be further classified by legal structure.[26] Two basically different structures emerge in the agricultural sphere. In the first, the common endeavor is carried out among partners without being linked by a separate, joint legal entity; in the latter case a separate legal entity is introduced to carry out the derivative task.

The first group consists of (1) simple partnerships, where members engage in simple common risk-taking activities. It may do business as an unnamed partnership or assume risk taking a separate trade name (Government decree 319, 1970 bearing the power of law and decree no. 4, 1971); (2) Joint cooperative cooperation, consisting of farm cooperative partnerships (public law no. III, section no. 53, 1967); and (3) Combinations, joining state enterprises to carry out common ventures with their fellow members or other collective entities in accordance with the statutes of the civil code (public law no. 11, 1967).

The second group comprises (1) Mutuals, consisting of enterprises which carry out collectively productive activities regardless of their legal forms. Operationally they are bestowed by a separate legal entity, with by-laws governed by the contractual agreements of their members (public law no. 19, 1970 and no. 14, 1971); (2) Cooperative mutuals hold separate legal entities. They are created by farm cooperatives for common ventures. The cooperative members are subject to unlimited liability for losses of the mutuals; (3) Joint ventures, vertical integration with a separate legal entity, which are jointly owned by members, characteristic of the food processing sector (public law IV, 1971 and government decree no. 35, 1967).[27]

177

An adverse factor affecting the process of profitability derives from labor productivity.[28] Hungary fares poorly in such comparison, ranking eleventh on a list of sixteen nations (see table 8.3). Sectoral analysis shows broad cleavages between agricultural and industrial labor productivity,[29] with agricultural net labor trailing industrial productivity by 25 percent from 1956 to 1972. The farm parity program in the U.S. for the same period provides an interesting contrast. Further, in Hungary gross labor productivity is twice the size of net productivity when applied to agriculture and 3.5 times as large in the industrial sector.

Labor productivity is measured either by efficiency or by the volume intensity of labor according to the following formulae:[30] $P = T/L$ and $P = L/T$, with P = Labor Productivity, T = Output, and L = Labor Input (weighted for the degree of skill).

Labor productivity procured by efficiency shows a reciprocal relationship with the volume of labor input. The efficiency indicator focuses on output results; the intensity volume indicator measures labor saving. While a great deal of sophistication and computer time went into refining[31] these indicators, their effect was considerably neutralized by malfunctions and inflexibilities of the administered price system applicable to core inputs and wages.

POLICY IMPLICATIONS AND CONCLUSIONS

The impact of international inflation and the oil crisis turned the terms of trade against Hungary and slowed the efforts to carry out national economic goals. A senior Hungarian official claimed, "It will require more time to accomplish what we planned. For the time being something has to give. To balance our affairs either productivity or prices will have to rise or investment will slow down and living standards will have to fall."[32] The malfunctioning of economic policy is revealed through the behavior of a national income account, known as "Net Social Income" (see table 8.4). In this account the centrally controlled part of the fund, which was operated by the government, showed a steady decline in the past years[33] (from 73.6 percent in 1972 to 64.7 percent in 1975). In simple terms it meant a deficit; expenditures exceeded revenues. This unfavorable accounting balance resulted from a sudden rise in imports and other government subsidies, necessitated by balancing a deficit budget while carrying out the ambitious goals of the National Plan. part of the impact originated from the rise of Soviet oil prices in line with increases introduced by the OPEC countries to world markets.

TABLE 8.3
International Comparison of Factors Affecting Labor
Productivity

Nations (ranked by GNP per capita in US $)	Level of Development (Hungary = 100)	Agriculture's Share of GNP (percent)	Labor Productivity ($/1 ha)	Income ($/1 ha)	Rank by Labor Productivity
Denmark	230	9	5526	557	4
West Germany	230	4	2496	506	6
France	220	7	2769	278	5
Netherlands	220	7	5864	916	3
Belgium	210	5	6344	767	1
United Kingdom	200	3	6010	247	2
Austria	160	7	1756	276	9
GDR	150	13	2106	399	7
Italy	150	10	1191	271	10
Czechoslovakia	140	12	1870	287	8
Hungary	100	21	1113	237	11
Bulgaria	95	27	753	280	13
Poland	95	18	941	304	12
Romania	85	25	321	139	16
Spain	80	15	745	87	14
Yugoslavia	65	23	475	145	15

Source: Kozponti Statisztikai Hivatal 1973 (Budapest), pp. 24-39.

Hungary must import 70 percent of its demand for oil from the USSR. The Eastern Europeans, both in the past and present, have paid the USSR for oil at prices set considerably below world market prices. This "friendship price" of Soviet oil nevertheless has risen from 1974's 16 rubles per metric ton to 70 rubles by 1979.[34] Underwriting the deficit required heavy domestic and foreign debt financing. The nature of the remedial action set in force to reverse the unfavorable trend can be reviewed through a ledger of the "Net Social Income Accounts" (NSIA) in table 8.4. This account seeks to balance expansive and contractive factors. The policy adopted called for increasing the centrally (directly by the government) controlled portion of the NSIA. It was carried out operationally by reducing subsidies, rather than increasing taxes thus shifting to the enterprises many of the burdens formerly assumed by the central government.

Table 8.4 reveals that the centrally (at the discretion of the government) controlled portion of the account can be expanded by either reducing the contractive factors (i.e., subsidies) and/or increasing the expansive factors (i.e., tax burdens). The expansive factors, however, are inherently limited, since approximately only 55 percent of the profit entries are centrally controlled, while over all other factors the central authorities have 100 percent control.

Of course contracting subsidies will slow down enterprise profitability, retained profits, and investment.[35] To smooth the impact, a selective price rise is contemplated. With wages remaining constant or rising at a slower rate than prices, real income will fall. Assuming a 3 percent inflationary spiral underwritten by falling real wages, the economy's inflationary rate will still trail world-wide levels. A falling standard of living will contribute to rising public dissatisfaction that will force tighter political control and possibly introduce further limitations of political and economic freedom.

Calculations, for example, show that corn TOPS, vital tools of additional Hungarian output, with respect to international loan obligations only break even with a yield exceeding 65 quintals per hectare.[36] Out of 179 corn TOPS listed in 1975, seventy-nine fell under this benchmark. In Marxist ideology a large crop is preferable to a small one regardless of the underlying cost functions. But in Hungary this trend may be reversed, at least with respect to potential new ventures contributing to foreign currency drains. Under these conditions, a smaller total volume of output may become acceptable.

In a socialist economy, wages and pensions are virtually the sole contributors to income. Their decline is directly related to living standards that move in the same direction, except when mitigated by pseudo-market operations (i.e., household plots, repair shops, etc.). Thus wage earners'

TABLE 8.4
Components of Net Social Income

Expansive Factors	Contractive Factors
Profits	Losses
Sales Taxes	Subsidies to Productive Ventures
Interest on Capital Loans	Producer Price Subsidies
Wage Taxes	Consumer Price Subsidies
Property Taxes	Export Price Subsidies
Business and Commercial Taxes	Import Price Subsidies
Land Rental Fees	Agricultural Venture Capital Subsidies
Other Miscellaneous Minor Items	Other Miscellaneous Minor Items

Balance = Net Social Income

Source: Gado Otto, Kozgazdasi Szabalyozo Rendszerunk 1976-Ban (Budapest: Kossuth Konyvkiado, 1976), pp. 24-27.

income will fall; that of the small entrepreneurs, on the other hand, will rise or remain constant. Economic policy certainly has created a paradox for the ruling ideology.

SCENARIO ON THE CLOUDY NEW HORIZON

The corrective measures discussed above to counter the world-wide mounting inflation and energy prices I believe are inadequate to accomplish the dual task of meeting national economic goals and improving living standards. It is therefore not surprising that the Hungarian Price Bureau will introduce in 1980 a new set of price and wage guidelines. The purpose of this move is to align domestic prices better with world market realities. It is further aimed to improve labor productivity and thus maintain real wage levels. The political and economic implications of such moves are open to debate.

With harsher conditions affecting various spheres of life, national goals will be reduced or at least spread over time. Unless productivity improves, the present living standards cannot be maintained, although it is believed that they still will remain relatively higher than that of other nations sharing similar economic predicaments.

NOTES

1. Richard F. Janssen, "Debt Threat - Soviet Borrowing from the West Surge," Wall Street Journal, 22 January 1977.
2. Magyar Kozlony, "A Gazdasagi Szabalyozo Rendszerrel Kapcsolatos Jogszabalyok es Magyarazatok," A Magyar Kozlonyben Megjelent Jogszabalyok es a Tervgazdasagi Ertesitoben Kozzetett Magyarazatok Kulon-Lenyomata (Budapest, 1975), pp. 1-191.
3. This law attempted to tighten (stock) acquisition and prohibit acquisition of assets of competition, when the effect would be to lessen competition.
4. Paul Marer, "Hungary's Industrial Cooperation with the West," (Washington, D.C.: U.S. Hungarian Economic Council, Chamber of Commerce of the U.S., 1976), p. 3.
5. Bela Nagy Csikos, Growing Impact of Joint Ventures on East-West Trade, (Budapest, Hungarian Price Bureau: 1977). Report on East German economic meetings.
6. Peter S. Elek, "The Future of Agriculture in Eastern Europe--Hungary's New Agricultural Revolution as viewed through the Fifth Five Year Plan, 1976-1980," in The Future of Agriculture in the Soviet Union and Eastern Europe, eds. R. Laird, J. Hajda and B. Laird (Boulder, Colorado, Westview Press: 1977), p. 171.

7. "A Szantofoldi Novenytermelesi Rendszerek es Hatasuk a Mezogazdasagi Vallalatok Gazdalkodasara," Agrargazdasagi Kutato Intezet (Budapest, 1975).

8. Vera Tiszane-Garai es Dr. Andras Medveczky, "Tapasztalatok es Gondolatok a Szantofoldi Noveny Termelesi Rendszerekrol," Szovetkezeti Kutato Intezet (Budapest: Szovorg Nyomda, 1977), pp. 1-149.

9. Vilmos Marillai, "In 1975, 526 joint ventures operated in Hungary, 237 being separate legal entities," A Mezogazdasagi Tarsulasok Gazdalkodasa (Budapest, Akademia Kiado: 1978), p. 42.

10. Ibid.

11. Laszlo Vargha, Horizontalis Integratio a Noveny Termesztesben Kozgazdasagi Szemle (Budapest, 1975), vol. 1.

12. The author's views were gained through conferences with officials of one of the vertical showcase systems, the "Petohaza" Sugar Refinery Combine in August 1978.

13. See Joseph Benedek, "Konzervipari Tarsulasok es a Vertikalis Integratid," Gazdalkodas 10 (1974): 27-35, with respect to the failures at Bereg, Tiszamenti, and Kertunio.

14. Field Crops Produced on an Industsrial Scale by Kite (Budapest: Globus Nyomda, 1978).

15. Andras Uzsonyi, Napraforgo Termeles Technologia, 1978 (Szombathely: Sylvester Janos Nyomda).

16. Geza Buvar, Kukorica Termeles Technologiaja at Nadudvar Kite 1978 (Szombathely: Sylvester Janos Nyomda.

17. Nududvar Kite, Koposztarepce Termelesi Technologiaja (1978).

18. Interview with Istvan Suba, Deputy Director Nadudvar Kite at Nadudvar, August 1978.

19. Peter S. Elek, "The Future of Agriculture in Eastern Europe," p. 180.

20. Sandor Misi and Dr. Lajos Marko, A Haztaji Kisegitogazdalkodas (Budapest: Kossuth Konyvkiado, 1977), pp. 13-15.

21. Ibid., pp. 22-26.

22. Karl Marx, Das Kapital (Budapest: Kossuth Konyvkiado, 1973): vol. I, p. 313.

23. Lenin, Assembled Works (Budapest: Kossuth Konyvkiado, 1965), vol. 27, p. 301-302.

24. Dr. Janos Marton, Az Integralodo Mezogazdasag (Budapest: Mezogazdasagi Konykiado 1977), p. 156.

25. Decree of the Central Committee of the CPSU of June 1976. "A Mezogazdasagi Termeles Szakositasanak es Koncontralasanak Tovabbfejlesztes a Szoviet Unioban," A Vilag Mezogazdasag 25-26 (1978).

26. Buvar, Kukorica Termeles Technologiaja at Nadudvar Kite 1978, p. 157.

27. Marillai, A Mezogazdasagi Tarsulasok Gazdalkodasa, pp. 25-32.

28.   Lajos   Nagy,   <u>Munka   Termelekenyseg   es   Szemelyi</u>
<u>Jovedelmek a Mezogazdasagban</u> (Budapest: Kozgazdasagi es   Jogi
Konykiado, 1976), pp. 70-71.

29.   Ibid., pp. 70-73.

30.   Ibid., p. 33.

31.   Dr.   Otto   Pirity,   "Temelekenysegi   Tartalekok"
(Budapest: Kossutth Konyvkiado, 1978), pp. 251-177.

32.   Interviews with senior staff of the Hungarian Price
Bureau, August 1978.

33.   Gado Otto, <u>Kozgazdasagi Szabalyozo Rendszerunk 1976-</u>
<u>Ban</u> (Budapest: Kossuth Konyvkiado, 1976), pp. 7-11.

34.   David Shipler, "The Soviet Bloc," <u>The New York Times</u>,
14-15 May 1979, p. 1.

35.   Csete   Laszlo,   <u>Tervszeru   Szabalyozas   Elelmiszer</u>
<u>Gazdasagi   Tapasztalatal</u>,   (Budapest: Kozgadasagi   es   Jogi
Konyvkiado, 1974), pp. 51-74.

36.   Interviews with senior staff of the Hungarian Price
Bureau, August 1978.

9
Poland's Agricultural Policies in the 1970s: Impact on Agricultural Trade with the U.S.

Andrew A. Duymovic

Trade plays an important role in overall U.S.-Polish relations, expanding from nearly $170 million in 1970 to $940 million in 1976 according to U.S. data. After reaching this peak in 1976, U.S.-Polish trade turnover dropped in 1977 to $765 million, reflecting mostly the smaller Polish purchases of U.S. grain as well as lower grain prices.

Agricultural trade dominates U.S. exports to Poland, accounting for more than two-thirds of our total exports to Poland in both 1974 and 1975, and nearly four-fifths in 1976. Reduced Soviet grain exports to Poland combined with a poor Polish crop in 1975 resulted in large grain imports from the U.S. in 1976. Agricultural goods accounted for about three-quarters of our total exports to Poland last year.[1]

United States purchases from Poland also have been dominated by farm products, mainly ham and pork products. Although agriculture's share has been declining somewhat in recent years, it still accounted for nearly 40 percent of our total imports from Poland in 1977.

In examining U.S.-Polish trade relations, particularly the rapid expansion of U.S. agricultural exports to Poland, this paper reviews Poland's political and economic setting, and the agricultural setting in the 1970s responsible for the recent expansion. Prospects for U.S. agricultural exports to Poland over the next few years also are examined briefly.

POLAND'S POLITICAL AND ECONOMIC SETTING

The Polish Communist party chose Edward Gierek as its First Secretary in December 1970, after rioting over food-price increases forced his predecessor to resign. The change of leadership brought about essential changes in the country's strategy for economic development.[2] Instead of austerity proclaimed for 1971-75, Gierek promised the Poles prosperity.

First, incentives for increased labor productivity were introduced. The limitations on wage increases existing in production enterprises were cancelled, and wages became conditional on increased labor productivity and on economic results of the enterprise operations. In addition, economic development was stimulated by purchasing capital goods and technology from the West on credit.[3] The Poles expected that these hard-currency debts would be offset by expanded exports to the West.

Priorities in economic development were changed. The main aim was the improvement of the economic well-being of society and of satisfying, as far as possible, consumer needs. Consequently, Gierek rescinded the previously announced price increases and instituted a price freeze on consumer goods.

Poland passed from a basically agricultural country at the end of World War II to one that is now predominantly industrial. Through the 1960s, the main effort was aimed at the development of those industrial sectors which most increased the country's economic potential. This meant concentrating investments in mining, metallurgy, and machine and chemical industries. Lower priorities were established for investments in development of light industry, the food industry, and agriculture. Consequently, most of the growth during the 1970s is attributable to industrial expansion. During the 1971-75 Five-Year Plan the Polish economy grew at rates surpassing expectations. For example, national income increased by 60 percent during 1971-75 (compared with 1966-70), while the plan was for a 40 percent increase. The significance of this expansion was the steep rise in real wages. Combined with the relatively stable retail prices, the considerable increase in purchasing power was not counterbalanced with a corresponding increase in the domestic supply of consumer goods, notably food. While consumption did rise rapidly, there still existed an imbalance between demand and supply.

The change of priorities in economic development set great tasks for agriculture.[4] The government's policies that were implemented for the rural sector had the following basic aims. The major aim was to increase agricultural production to meet the increasing domestic demand. At the same time, Polish officials decided to import foods when necessary to augment domestic supplies. To sustain the growth in the livestock sector, this meant large imports of feed grains and protein supplements when domestic supplies were inadequate. Continuing exports of quality food items, particularly canned hams, were also considered important as a means of earning foreign exchange to help pay for Poland's imports. Another aim was to provide the conditions for structural changes in technical and social aspects of agriculture. It was realized that the structure of agriculture in Poland was backward and not suitable for technical advances. Provisions were, therefore, made to foster the gradual concentration of land, as well as voluntary production cooperation and increased scale of production. The third aim was to raise the standard of living in the rural sector by increasing individuals' incomes, improving working conditions, and introducing health and social insurance for individual farmers and members of their families.

THE AGRICULTURAL SETTING

Although Poland's topography is predominantly flat, except along the southern border, soil and climatic conditions only moderately favor agriculture. Soils are mostly light and sandy and the growing season is relatively short. There are no waste lands available in Poland to provide a land reserve for increased cultivation. Consequently, the only way production can be increased is to intensify the utilization of existing land. There are three forms of land ownership in Poland, individual or private, state, and cooperative.[5] In spite of far-reaching changes since World War II, private farming still predominates.

There are slightly more than three million individual farms operating in Poland, a country roughly the size of the state of New Mexico. In 1977 private farms used 77 percent of the agricultural land area and accounted for about 78 percent of the total value of gross agricultural production, and 72 percent of the commercial or marketed production. It should be noted that although the private sector is diminishing, particularly in recent years, the process has been gradual. In 1970 roughly 83 percent of the agricultural land was utilized by private individuals and accounted for 85 percent of gross agricultural production.

There are essentially three policy instruments by which the state attempts to influence individual farmers:

1. Prices of agricultural products and agricultural inputs;

2. Contract buying;

3. Investments and credits.

The influence of planners reaches producers fastest and most directly through prices. Both purchasing prices and prices for agricultural inputs are fixed by the state and reflect the preferences of the state regarding production trends. The influence of changes in prices, or lack of changes for that matter, are best illustrated in Poland's hog sector. Because of the particularly poor grain and potato harvest in 1975, many private farmers who produce about 80 percent of Poland's meat, had to buy whatever quantities of

187

livestock feed were available at relatively high prices. The rise in production costs was not matched by increase in livestock procurement prices. As profits fell, so did the incentive to raise hogs in the private sector during 1976. Hog numbers dropped from 21.6 million on January 1, 1976, to 16.8 million a year later. To remedy the situation the Polish government increased producer prices in July 1976 to stimulate Poland's recovery of hog numbers, which reached 10.6 on January 1, 1978.

Contract-buying is a system of including the production of individual farms in the socialized or planned economy. More than 80 percent of the marketed agricultural production is contracted for and bought by the state. Of the total agricultural investment outlays in Poland, farmers provide about a third, the Agricultural Development Fund 15 percent, and the state more than 50 percent.

No one denies the fact that Polish officials would like to have agriculture fully collectivized. However, this does not appear feasible in the foreseeable future. Meanwhile, the state promotes voluntary cooperation of farmers by offering economic incentives, and continues to take over land from elderly owners in exchange for pensions.[6]

Total agricultural output increased 20 percent more during the 1971-75 period than from 1966 to 70. The output of crops has shown distinctly slower rates of growth than has the livestock sector. The surge in output of livestock products was most significant after the reforms in 1971, particularly during 1972-75. Statistics show that the Poles consumed 68.9 kilograms of meat per capita in 1977, up from 53 kilograms in 1970. The peak was in 1975 when Poland averaged 70.3 kilograms of meat per person.

This substantial increase was achieved in considerable measure by resorting to sharply increased imports of feed grains, oilseed meals, and other highly concentrated protein feeds.

During 1971-77, Poland's grain output fluctuated widely, from a record of nearly 23 million tons in 1974 to only 19.4 million tons in 1977. In order to increase Poland's capacity to produce grain, official policies have promoted additional use of inputs, improved technology, and a shift from oats and rye to higher yielding varieties of wheat, barley, and corn. Recently, the government has also been promoting an increase in area sown to grains, planning to reach about 8.5 million hectares by 1980. The implementation of most of these policies has been slower than planners had anticipated because of (1) adverse weather in recent years, (2) the structure of agriculture which is characterized by many small private holdings, and (3) economic reasons such as inadequate producer price incentives.

The poor harvest of feed (grains, potatoes, and roughage) during 1975 and 1976 caused a downturn in animal numbers, especially swine. The cutback began in 1976 and continued until the spring of 1977. Meat production dropped during 1976 and 1977, resulting in severe meat shortages. In trying to satisfy consumer demand, Poland stepped up meat imports, mainly beef, and reduced its processed meat exports, namely pork.

Production shortfalls of major feeds continued in 1977. Grain output totaled 19.4 million tons, 6 percent below 1976 and 16 percent below the 1974 record output. The short potato harvest was particularly troublesome, since potatoes are an important feed ingredient in the hog sector. To avoid distress slaughter and continue its recovery of hog numbers, the Polish government had to resort to record levels of grain imports in 1977/78, about 7 million tons. Interestingly, the Polish government publicized its large outlays for grain imports to assure private farmers that adequate feed supplies would be made available.[7]

Grain output for 1978 is now expected to total about 21 million tons. Although Polish grain and potato crops were somewhat more abundant in 1978 than in 1977, they were still inadequate to meet livestock needs. The shortfall, combined with the poor quality caused by excessive moisture, forced the government to continue its substantial grain imports. Grain imports for 1978/79 are likely to be around 6 million tons.

A brief comment regarding grain use in recent years is in order. Poland's utilization of grain during the recent five-year Plan 1971-75, averaged 24.7 million tons, about three-tenths above 1966-70 levels. The rapid increase in feed use, in response to the increasing requirements of an expanding livestock sector, more than offset slight declines in food use. Livestock feed is by far the major grain use, accounting for nearly two-thirds of total use during 1971-75. Feed use has increased this past year totalling about 18 million tons, following a reduced level of 16.9 million tons in 1976/77. Actual grain consumption, totally about 27 million tons annually, obviously exceeds domestic production, leaving Poland a significant importer of grain.

In spite of the large imports of grain and recent expansion in the livestock sector, Poland continues to have serious problems in satisfying demand for meat. Consumer demand for meat has increased sharply in recent years because wage increases combined with stable retail prices at artifically low levels since 1967 has caused a considerable increase in real incomes.

To dampen meat consumption, officials attempted to raise meat prices in June 1976, but rioting in several cities caused the increase to be rescinded before it took effect. The proposed increases ranged from 30 percent for poultry to 100 percent for pork. To encourage meat production, producer prices were increased to improve the profitability of raising livestock. In addition, legislation which ties the farmers' pension to the value of commodities sold to the state was instituted to foster increased meat supplies.

The continuing retail price freeze for meat combined with rising producer prices and increased consumption resulted in increasing government subsidy costs in recent years. By 1977, food subsidies hit an estimated 15 percent of the national budget.

Following the 1976 disturbances, the government sought politically and socially acceptable remedies to restore the economy from its distorted state. Sugar rationing was introduced, which apparently resulted in orderly distribution of domestic supply. A significant development was the quiet introduction of a number of state-owned "commercial" shops that have reportedly expanded. These stores feature better meat selection, trimmed cuts, and higher quality than state stores, now referred to as "regular" shops. Prices in "commercial" shops are nearly twice those in "regular" shops. The new shops are apparently enjoying success, as some Poles prefer to pay higher prices and be assured of adequate supplies than to wait in lines for hours at less expensive shops. The new shops, and consequently the two-tier pricing scheme, seem to be gaining in popularity with tacit government approval. While these shops currently account for a small share of total meat sales, they appear to be getting people gradually accustomed to the restructuring of prices, which is essential.

To avoid making hasty decisions following the 1976 disturbances, the government appointed five commissions, one of which was to examine and recommend a retail price policy. The vacillation in formulating a firm retail price policy in 1976 resulted in hoarding of nonperishable foods, mostly processed meats, sugar, and flour. The situation improved somewhat following the rationing of sugar and appointment of the commission. Recently the commission recommended that prices be established at levels more closely related to costs of production, and be realigned in order to shift demand from food to industrial consumer goods. The Polish government, after weighing political and social consequences, opted for gradual price changes without setting a time table for increasing prices. It appears that food subsidies will continue at burdensome levels and retail meat prices will not be raised sufficiently in the near term to discourage the consumption of meat.

Recent announcements continue to show the government's desire and attempts to restructure prices. At the beginning of September 1978 the retail price for potato flour was increased 63 percent to 15 zlotys per kilogram. The increase is an attempt to obtain a more realistic relationship between production costs and retail prices. However, the price increases will not cover state costs completely, since the producer price of potatoes has quadrupled since 1960 while the price of potato flour has not changed until now, so subsidies will continue.

Modification of the 1976-80 Plan

The difficulties experienced in food marketing and general consumer discontent forced the Polish government in the fall of 1976 to modify the 1976-80 Plan. A number of concerns were considered and are reflected in the revised Plan. First, foreign borrowing, much of it short term, has reached unprecedented levels. By the end of 1977, hard-currency debt reportedly totaled an estimated $13 billion.[8] Poland's trade balance has deteriorated seriously since 1973, accumulating a deficit of nearly $10 billion during 1974-77. The imports of capital goods and grains from the West are largely responsible for the increase. The recession in the West resulted in a slowdown in Polish exports. Problems in producing adequate meat supplies also served to reduce Poland's meat exports. A second concern is the inflationary potential that has been building up domestically, particularly in regard to meat prices.[9] In spite of the measures taken by the Poles as outlined above, the imbalance of supply and demand for meat is likely to continue through 1980. The third concern is the sky-rocketing food subsidies because of stable retail prices of basic foodstuffs, increased consumption, and higher producer prices.

The modified Plan marks the transition to lower rates of economic growth in an attempt to balance internal and external accounts. Table 9.1 shows some of the principal Plan indicators. The Plan also indicates a reorientation in agricultural targets, emphasizing[10] the crop sector and curtailment of imports. Investment funds that were previously allocated to other sectors are to be shifted to agriculture and food industry. During 1976-80, 22 percent of total investment will be allocated to agriculture and the food industry. This represents a 55 percent growth for these sectors, instead of 31 percent originally planned. Despite the large increase in investments, agricultural output is expected to be close to the level achieved during 1971-75. A large part of the investment will be spent primarily for mechanization, for both small private farms and the large socialized sector.

FOREIGN AGRICULTURAL TRADE

Overall foreign trade plays an important role in Poland's economic development. While both exports and imports have expanded rapidly in recent years, Poland is disappointed in

TABLE 9.1
Selected Targets of Poland's 1976-80 Five-Year Plan
and Earlier Results (in Percent Increases)

	Planned		Actual	
	1976-80/ 1971-75/	1971-75/ 1966-70	1971-75/ 1966-70	1966-70/ 1961-65
National Income	40-42	40	60	34
Real Income	16-18	18	41	10
Industrial Output	48-50	50	64	49
Agricultural Output	16-19	19-21	20	9
Crops	20-23	17-20	12	10
Livestock	13-16	22-23	30	8
Capital Investment	43	46	132	48
Exports	75	55	142	59
Imports	26	59	189	54

efforts to export its industrial products to hard-currency markets of the West. Thus, coal, agricultural products, and other basic materials form the bulk of Polish exports to the West, while its East European trade partners import more of Poland's chemicals, machines, and other finished products. In 1977 imports were valued at $14.6 billion and exports at $12.3 billion. Poland's leading trade partner is the USSR, accounting for nearly three-tenths of Poland's imports and one-third of its exports. Until 1970, two-thirds of Polish trade was conducted with socialist countries, but this share has declined to about one-half in 1975 and 1976. This share increased in 1977 to nearly 60 percent as Poland reduced its imports from the West. The U.S. was Poland's fourth largest western trading partner in 1977, surpassed by West Germany, the United Kingdom, and France.

In recent years, the volume of U.S. trade with Poland has consistently exceeded that with any of the other East European countries. Poland is one of only four communist countries (along with Romania, Yugoslavia, and recently, Hungary), that enjoy nondiscriminatory (MFN) tariff treatment and U.S. government-backed credits.[11] While total U.S.-Polish trade increased sharply during 1975 and 1976, so did Poland's trade deficit with the U.S. To lower its trade deficit, Poland reduced its imports from the U.S. significantly in 1977.

Agricultural trade has always been of importance in Poland's overall trade. Agricultural goods accounted for nearly 13 percent of imports in 1977, virtually the same as in 1970; however, their share of exports declined from 15 percent in 1970 to 10 percent in 1977. Although the share of agricultural exports in relation to total Polish exports continues to decline, it did account for about 20 percent of total exports to nonsocialist countries in recent years. Consequently, agriculture is an important source of foreign exchange.

The policies implemented in Poland after 1970 and outlined earlier caused an increasing deficit in Polish agricultural trade for the 1973-77 period. This growing deficit was explained largely by the sharp increase in imports of feed grains and high-protein feeds necessary to insure the desired rapid expansion in Poland's livestock sector. Grain and oilseed products are the principal agricultural imports, followed by cotton and cattle hides. Large quantities of meat imports were required to meet domestic demand during 1976 and 1977. Poland's leading agricultural exports include canned hams, bacon, other canned meats, fresh meats (particularly beef), and cheese.

Although Polish imports from the U.S. dropped significantly in 1977, Poland was still by far the largest East European customer of U.S. agricultural goods, accounting for roughly one-third of our agricultural exports to the region.

The Role of Financing in Increasing U.S. Exports

The sharp increase in U.S. exports of farm products to Poland in recent years, has been facilitated in large part by financing provided under the Commodity Credit Corporation's (CCC) Export Credit Sales Program. These credits were first provided to Poland in 1962, when total U.S. farm exports to Poland totaled only about $70 million. With continued financing total agricultural purchases from the U.S. climbed rather steadily, peaking at $541 million in fiscal 1976 (October 1975 to September 1976), before dropping back to $311 million in fiscal 1977. United States farm sales to Poland rose to $523 million in fiscal 1978, mostly because of larger corn and soybean meal purchases. By October 1, 1978, total CCC financing provided to Poland since 1962 totaled about $1 billion, of which nearly $505 million was financed in 1977 /78.

Commodity Credit Corporation credits made available to Poland have not been of concessional or aid type, and all obligations have been paid in full when due. The CCC credit program is self-sustaining, and commercial interest rates are charged (currently 10.5 percent with U.S. bank and 11.5 percent with foreign bank guarantee). Payment is guaranteed by commercial bank letters of credit, and the maximum financing period is thirty-six months.

Polish officials are interested in intermediate credit financing which would be made available under the proposed Agricultural Trade Act of 1978.[12] The new program would provide financing to promote commercial export sales of U.S. farm products with repayment over a longer period than under the existing CCC program, i.e., up to ten years.

In the senate version, intermediate credit can be used to finance export sales of U.S. breeding animals. Other commodity financing would be either tied to building reserve stocks if part of an international commodity agreement; or, where determined feasible, for the establishment of facilities in the importing nation to improve handling, marketing, processing, storage, or distribution of imported agricultural commodities. Thus, proceeds from the sale of U.S. commodities to Poland could be available for construction of storage and similar facilities, if the projects were found feasible. Poland is particularly interested in obtaining financing in order to expand its port capacity and to construct storage facilities. The Poles proposed elevators in Baltic ports to provide storage for U.S. commodities moving into Poland and elsewhere in Eastern Europe.

Like the current CCC Credit Program, the new program would be commercial and not intended to be used as aid to a foreign government, or to provide balance-of-payment support for countries needing financial assistance. The program is designed to develop and expand U.S. agricultural exports.

194

Poland's Grain Imports

Total Polish grain imports averaged about 2.5 million tons annually in the 1960s and exceeded 3 million tons from 1971 to 1973, 4 million tons in 1974 and 1975, and 6 million tons in 1976 and 1977. Wheat was the principal grain imported, followed by barley, but corn imports increased significantly in 1976, accounting for about one-third of total grain imports. The Untied States' share of Poland's grain imports has fluctuated erratically since 1960. But in the last four years,the United States' share averaged nearly 50 percent of Poland's grain purchases, except in 1974 when the USSR provided the Poles with large deliveries of grain.

In November 1975, the U.S. and Poland reached an informal understanding on long-term grain sales in an exchange of letters between former[13]Secreary Butz and former Minister of Agriculture Barcikowski. Poland stated its intention to buy 2.5 million tons of grain annually until 1980, plus or minus 20 percent, depending on U.S. availability and Polish needs. In calendar 1977, the second year of the understanding, the U.S. shipped 2.3 million tons of grain worth about $216 million to Poland. That year the U.S. also exported to Poland 187,000 tons of soybean meal worth $41 million, the U.S.'s third largest agricultural export to Poland next to corn and wheat.

Following the crop failure in 1977, the Poles expressed a desire for a long-term supply agreement with the U.S., covering 3-5 million tons of grain annually through 1985. Although no supply agreement was entered into, the U.S. continued to assure the Poles that the U.S. was a reliable supplier and placed a high priority on supplying Polish needs.

From 1967 to 1974, the USSR provided one-third to two-thirds of Polish grain imports, but only one-fourth in 1975 and 4 percent in 1976. Grain imports from the USSR dropped because of the USSR's goal to expand its own livestock sector and meat consumption. Also, the USSR experienced sharp variations in grain production which greatly reduced exportable supplies.

Poland has an agreement with Canada to import 1.5 to 2.4 million tons of wheat over the three-year period beginning January 1, 1977. The Canadian agreement was amended in April 1977, to spell out the annual quantity during the three years at 500,000 to 800,000 tons of wheat, barley, and oats. Sweden signed a three-year agreement in March 1977, to supply 300,000 tons of wheat annually to Poland. The French government agreed to 600,000 tons of grain sales to Poland from August 1977 to July 1978, of which a maximum of 300,000 tons can be wheat. This agreement is renewable annually. Other grain suppliers to Poland include Argentina and Sweden.

195

Poland's Future Import Requirements

Poland's need for feed grain by 1980 and 1985 is dependent largely on whether the Poles go all out to fulfill their livestock production goals. The recent Polish proposal for a long-term grain agreement with the U.S. appears to indicate their desire to meet its planned livestock production targets. Import requirements will depend on domestic grain production, as well as supplies of forage crops and potatoes. Past performance strongly suggests that the target for grain is likely to fall short of the 1976-80 Plan. Even with the absence of severe production shortfalls, Poland's grain import requirements will be substantial for the next several years. This assumes that output of livestock products will fall slightly below planned levels.

The 3 to 5 million tons of grain imports that Poland has indicated it would need each year through 1985 appears consistent with Polish feed-livestock production objectives. Much of what the Poles actually do depends on credits made available in the near future. However, severe shortfalls of domestic feed production would likely result in some downward revision of livestock goals. The retail price policy pursued in Poland over the next few years as well as world grain prices are also factors determining the levels of Polish feed imports. Higher retail prices would indeed reduce pressures for larger meat supplies. Poland's exports to Western markets to obtain foreign exchange is another factor affecting its future feed imports. The Poles realize that they cannot continue increasing imports of feeds without end.[14]

It appears that U.S. agricultural exports to Poland should continue at significant levels for the next several years. However, increases from the volume being realized during 1977/78 are not likely, and more normal crop-production levels in Poland could result in some decline.

NOTES

1. See U.S. Department of Agriculture, Eastern Europe Agricultural Situation: Review of 1977 and Outlook for 1978, Economics, Statistics and Cooperatives Service, Supplement 3 to WAS-15, May 1978, and the earlier report FAER no. 134 April 1977 for discussion of the agricultural situation in Poland, U.S. agricultural trade with Poland, and related statistics.

2. Gierek's new economic strategy is discussed in U.S. Congress, Joint Economic Committee, "The Polish Economy in the 1970's," by Zbigniew M. Fallenbuchl in East European Economies: Post Helsinki (a compendium of papers), August 25, 1977.

3. Implications of this policy for growth are examined by Stanislaw Gomulka in "Growth and the Import of Technology: Poland 1971-1980," Cambridge Journal of Economics, March 1978.

4. These tasks for agriculture are presented in more detail in United Nations, Food and Agricultural Organization, International Agricultural Adjustment: Case Study of Poland, (C 75/LIM/3) August 1975, pp. 16-22.

5. See Jacek I. Romanowski, "Prospects for the Future of Polish Agriculture," in R. D. Laird, J. Hajda, and B. A. Laird, eds., The Future of Agriculture in the Soviet Union and Eastern Europe: The 1976-80 Five Year Plans (Boulder, Colorado: Westview Press, 1977), pp. 111-25, for further discussion of types of agricultural producers in Poland.

6. Robert Prinsky, "Poland's Tiny Frams Defy Consolidation, Forcing Dependence on Western Produce," The Wall Street Journal, November 15, 1976.

7. David A. Andelman, "Poland's Economic System, Despite Tinkering Still Drags," The New York Times, January 16, 1978.

8. See Roman Stefanowski, "Poland's Western Debt: A Progress Report," Radio Free Europe Research, Background Report no. 251, November 1978. Additional discussion of Poland's trade gap and hard-currency debt is presented in U. S. Congress, Joint Economic Committee, "Poland's Trade with the Developed West: Performance and Prospects," by Gary R. Tesbe and "Eastern Europe: The Growing Hard Currency Debt," by Joan Parpart Zoeter, East European Economies: Post Helsinki (a compendium of papers), August 25, 1977.

9. "Notes on Poland's Economic Situation: An Inside View," Radio Free Europe Research, Background Report no. 177, August 9, 1978, pp. 20-23.

10. U. S. Department of Agriculture, Thomas A. Vankai, Progress and Outlook for East European Agriculture, 1976-80, Economics, Statistics and Cooperatives Service, FAER Report no. 153, September 1978, pp. 1-7 and 30-36. This report provides the 1976-80 targets for the overall economy and details of the Plan for the agricultural sector.

11. The Agricultural Trade Act of 1978 (PL 95-501), signed by President Carter October 21, 1978, authorized Commodity Credit Corporation financing for commercial sales of agricultural commodities to the People's Republic of China.

12. The Agricultural Trade Act of 1978 was signed by the President on October 21, 1978. The uses of intermediate credit provided for in the act are the same as the senate version outlined in this paper. For a general discussion of the act see Ron Deaton, "Agricultural Trade Act Paves Way for Gains in U.S. Farm Exports," Foreign Agriculture, October 30, 1978, pp. 2-4.

13. The press release on the understanding can be found in Eastern European Agricultural Situation, FAER no. 135, April 1977 p. 18.

14.   For   example,   this was stated by the Polish Premier
Piotr Jaroszewicz in his National Harvest Festival   speech   at
Olsztyn, September 10, 1978.

10
"The Socialist Transformation of the Village": Yugoslav Agricultural Policy Since 1945

John B. Allcock

Yugoslavia, we are often told, is a remarkable country; and one of its most remarkable characteristics appears to be its success in putting into circulation a stereotypical image of itself. Just as everybody <u>knows</u> (with that special degree of certainty that characterizes our attachment to stereotypes) that the Germans are invariably efficient, and that the Chinese are inscrutable, we now all know that the Yugoslavs are "self-managing." This knowledge is not only built upon a raft of press coverage that is quite out of proportion to that country's size and economic power, but it is reinforced and elaborated by a growing superstructure of academic interpretation and analysis.

The coming into existence of a stereotype, however, is exactly the point at which a social-scientific analysis ought to begin, for the purpose of science is to probe and test the firmness and relevance of our store of common knowledge. This is precisely the intention of this essay. This is not to say that Yugoslavia's claim is fraudulent: far from it. It is not possible to argue self-management out of existence. It is nevertheless important to recognize that our preoccupation with self-management has led us to obscure a number of important aspects of the development of Yugoslav society, and caused us to overlook several factors that undoubtedly will be important for the future of the country.

An exhaustive study of this problem is clearly out of the question in an essay of this length. We will therefore confine ourselves to an examination of one aspect of the topic, namely, the appraisal of Yugoslav agriculture in the post-war period.

The general neglect of the study of Yugoslav agriculture has been, in many ways, a direct consequence of the placing of "self-management" at the center of our attention. This is quite understandable, in view of the obvious theoretical relevance of Yugoslav developments for the study of industrialization, the sociology of democracy, and socialism. Here the Yugoslav attempt to ensure decentralization has provided a lively challenge to the belief that the "logic of industrialization" necessarily involves centralization. The long-standing aspiration of socialism to develop forms that go beyond the achievements of bourgeois parliamentary democracy has found a fairly convincing candidate in the "workers' councils." These, and many related areas of interest, have drawn their energy from concerns of Western social science, located in mainly industrialized societies, and not necessarily from the objectively primary characteristcs of Yugoslav structure or experience. The Yugoslavs, however, have done nothing to challenge this assessment of theoretical priorities, since the agenda for both public and academic discussion within Yugoslavia has faithfully reflected the obsession of official ideologists with the emergence and the role of the "working class." Although several recent studies have made a brave attempt to explore Yugoslav society beyond the factory walls, the escapees have typically failed to reach open country; agrarian affairs have thus found only a peripheral place in our general picture of Yugoslavia.[1]

Although nobody would deny that Yugoslav social and economic structure has undergone very extensive change since the end of the Second World War, when more than three-quarters of the country's population lived and worked on the land, Yugoslavia is still far from being fully industrialized. In fact, with roughly 40 percent of its economically active population engaged in agriculture, only Albania and Romania, among the European countries, are "more agrarian" in structure.[2] In spite of the huge transfers of population from agriculture and the land to industry and the city, Yugoslavia is still in many ways a "rural society."[3] What is more, as the analysis that follows indicates, this is likely to remain the case for the foreseeable future. Any adequate understanding of the nature of modern Yugoslavia must take full account of these facts. Likewise, any attempt to project a course of development for the country, that fails to give proper consideration to agriculture, will be of questionable value.

A systematic consideration of the role of agriculture in the development of modern Yugoslavia is a task that clearly cannot be undertaken within the space of an essay such as this. Our aim will therefore be the more modest one of sketching the principal characteristics of Yugoslav agricultural policy during the interwar years, indicating some major problems thrown up by that policy, with respect to the overall development of Yugoslav socialism, and finally underlining the reasons for believing that the Yugoslav socialist experiment in future years will be increasingly constrained to take account of rural and agricultural matters.

THE "PRAGMATISM" OF YUGOSLAV AGRICULTURAL POLICY

It is often said that the characteristic that distinguishes Yugoslav socialism from that of many other such societies is its "pragmatism." The changeability of agricultural policy since the last war has been one of the central data on which the hypothesis of Yugoslav "pragmatism" has been built. The accuracy of this description in this context, however, depends very much upon the sense in which that word is taken.

If by "pragmatism" we mean a willingness to dispense with certain conventionally accepted methods, and to try others apparently better adapted to one's purposes, then Yugoslav agrarian policy probably can be characterized as "pragmatic." If, on the other hand, we take as the opposite of "pragmatism," not "conventionalism" of this kind, but "dogmatism," then one has great diffiuclty in finding any adequate grounds for use of the label "pragmatic."

If one takes as one's focal point the changes in the chosen instruments of agrarian policy, then the picture is one of adaptation, variation, and "pragmatism." There is no doubt, however, that these changes have not been accompanied by any major shift of the ultimate aims of agricultural policy. Neither has there been any essential change in the theoretical analysis of the rural economy and social structure on which that policy was based. Perhaps it would be useful to summarize very briefly at this stage of the argument the nature of these key aims and assumptions.

Firstly, within the overall strategy of economic development, the highest priority has been given to industrialization, and other ends have been subordinated to this. This presupposes the maximization of the productivity of agriculture, to feed the urban worker, and to provide raw materials and profitable exports. The small-scale private cultivator has typically been regarded as inherently less efficient than the large-scale, socially-owned enterprise. The long-term aim of policy therefore has been to expand constantly and consolidate the socialist sector. Although there has never been a commitment to the elimination of private property in land, it has always been expected that without the leadership of the socialist sector, the private peasant has no positive role to play in development, and that the small farmer will be pushed progressively to the margins of economy.

Thirdly and finally, the anticipated changes in the economic structure of agriculture are expected to have consequences for rural social structure, in that the increasing involvement of the agricultural worker in the socialist sector will result in the gradual approximation of his status, life-style, and culture to that of the urban industrial worker.

These aims and assumptions were epitomized in the collectivization program of 1948, and there is no evidence that they have been radically revised in the subsequent phases of Yugoslav agrarian policy. The following brief passages from a major policy document produced in 1970 will serve to highlight this continuity of belief.[4]

> The commission has reached the following basic starting position: That the development of agriculture and the village up to the present has confirmed the correctness of our specific path of the socialist reconstruction of agriculture, and the fundamental suppositions of our agrarian policy as defined in the program of the SKJ, and that it is not necessary to alter these; (page 5).
> The method of the socialist transformation of agriculture in Yugoslavia--the creation of large production units and socialization on the basis of self-managing socioeconomic relations--is supported by the teachings of the classics of Marxism concerning the socialist transformation of agriculture under those conditions in which agriculture, after the victory of a socialist revolution, is dominated by small-scale production.
> Large-scale social production in our country is accomplished by surpassing economically small-scale peasant production in faithful accordance with the principles of the socialist transformation of agriculture: gradualness, voluntarism and democracy--such as are proclaimed by the classics of Marxism.
> They (the cooperatives) have been...the most suitable instrument for the incorporation of the peasantry into the development of large-scale production, and the new contemporary social currents. (Page 7.)
> (The cooperative) is the most suitable means of binding the individual producers to the social economy. (Page 8.)

The organizational forms fostered by the policymakers have changed, and "gradualness, voluntarism and democracy" have, in varying degrees, become more fully actualized in practice. The "fundamental suppositions" of policy, however, can be traced in much the same language through the speeches and writings of Bakarić, Komar, and Kardelj, and in a host of official documents since 1945.

There is, of course, nothing inherently wrong with the consistent pursuit of policy except in those cases, like that of postwar Yugoslavia, when the policy fails. It is the question of the reasons for this failure that centrally occupies the remainder of this paper.

NOTE ON THE CONCEPT OF "FAILURE"

How do we measure the "success" or "failure" of an agricultural policy? The answer that is probably most frequently given is in terms of the rates at which productivity has grown, or improvements in crop yields. The literature, and particularly the Yugoslav literature, on the performance of Yugoslav agriculture since the war is thus replete with statistics of this kind, and especially those demonstrating the obviously superior record of the socialist sector. Thus those who are anxious to demonstrate the success of Yugoslav agriculture can cite the indices of agricultural production, which have climbed encouragingly throughout the postwar period.[5] Similarly, they can refer to yields per hectare in wheat, which have been very respectable in comparison with those of other countries in the region; in maize, which have been very good by this standard; and in some other crops such as sunflower seeds, which have been very good by anybody's standards.[6] On the other hand, those who wish to take a dim view of Yugoslav performance in the countryside can place those same production indices in their European context, revealing that this performance has been far from remarkable. Furthermore, they may choose to mention the Yugoslav results in the cultivation of some vegetables, such as potatoes, where improvements have been consistently disappointing, or Yugoslav milk production, which has one of the poorest records in Europe.[7]

The trouble with this approach is that "you pay your money and take your choice"--there are statistics for the taste of every customer. For this reason it seems more appropriate to take another approach to the assessment of success or failure, namely, measurement against the stated intentions of the policymakers. In this respect, the "socialist transformation of the village" is clearly not to be measured by statistical indices of this type, since it refers to a qualitative change in social and political relations, in fact, to criteria which are external to agriculture as such.

THE SOCIALIST TRANSFORMATION OF THE VILLAGE

Although the Yugoslav revolution was manned, if not staffed, by the peasantry, the prevailing assumption of the postrevolutionary policymakers has been that the private farmer stands outside of socialism. The task of policy is to bring him in. The starting point for the understanding of socialism, which makes this assumption necessary, is a particular analysis of the nature and function of private property. The "class enemy"--the bourgeoisie--is defined by reference to its ownership of the means of production; and it has been a consistently held belief of socialist economists and sociologists that the continuation in existence of a substantial stratum of private owners of productive resources implies the possibility that bourgeois values will continue to be generated within the system, undermining its moral and economic foundations.[8] The "socialist transformation of the village" is therefore premised upon the prizing loose of the farmer from his property.

The first attempt to tackle the problem of "transformation" (the period of "administrative measures," as it is euphemistically described by the Yugoslavs) sought to do this very directly, and in a very tough way. A fairly conventional land reform in 1945 was coupled with rigid centralist control of the market for farm produce. The famous break with the Cominform of 1948 saw the attempt to achieve the rapid socialization of agriculture through the collectivization of peasant holdings. This collapsed in 1951-2 through a combination of the effects of bad weather, inordinate haste, incompetent economic planning, and political insensitivity.

At the heart of that failure was the inability to see that collectivization involved far more than a mere transfer of property rights. The collectivization program linked together the economies of scale to be achieved through the creation of large production units, and the elimination of the chaos associated with petty private cultivation.[9] What the planners omitted from their assessment of the situation was the fact that these economies of scale could be realized only if the aggregation of production units went hand in hand with the heavy capitalization of agriculture (with investment in drainage, communications, and so forth as well as in machinery) and a total reorganization of management, the organization of work and budgeting procedures. As it turned out, the aggregation of "chaos" produced no more than larger-scale "chaos."[10]

In the years following 1955, the chosen instrument for the socialist transformation of the village was the _Opšta zemljoradnička zadruga_--General Agricultural Cooperative (OZZ). These were intended to attract the peasant into the socialist sector by offering the advantages of seed, fertilizer, machinery, credit, technical advice, and an outlet to the market for his crops. Although it was intended that "the cooperative will gradually grow into a socialist enterprise in which the private peasant's property in land is an element which must be taken into account," the resolution of the _Skupština_ which initiated this new phase of policy emphasized that "the agricultural cooperative gradually changes in a specific manner the peasant holding and its archaic economy, acting by economic means, without touching property relations and without expropriating the land and its owner."[11] Just how these two aspects of the nature of cooperation were to be reconciled was not made clear, although the fact that the OZZ were empowered to own their own estates (and in fact took over many of the holdings of the defunct SRZ) may be a relevant consideration here.

Alongside the OZZ grew the poljoprivredna dobra, or state farms, which had begun their existence immediately after the war, and which now received a new impetus to growth.

Throughout the later 1950s, progress in the socialist sector was encouraging. Targets announced for the 1957-61 five-year Plan were frequently achieved ahead of time, wheat imports were steadily reduced, and there was a steady expansion in the numbers of farmers entering into cooperative arrangements and in the area cultivated by socialist enterprises. With the turn of the decade, however, came a change in the fortunes of socialist agriculture.

The precise timing of the downturn in the cooperative movement depends upon which indicator of development one chooses, and as usual in things Yugoslav, this varies considerably from region to region. The number of members of the OZZ began to fall off around 1965, reaching a peak of around 1.3 million in that year,[12] and the area cultivated under the estates of the OZZ likewise began to decline from its high point of roughly 903,000 ha at the same time.[13] The level of employment in the cooperatives, however, began its decline in the previous year, after faltering in 1963;[14] and having dominated the market for the purchase of land from individual proprietors for many years (more than three-quarters of all purchases in 1960), the OZZ rapidly withdrew from the market, to make fewer than a third of such purchases in 1966.[15] At the same time, the participation of cooperators in the provision of a marketable surplus from individual holdings fell precipitously from around three-quarters of the total in 1960 to less than 30 percent five years later.[16]

Discussions of the reasons for these changes tend to focus on the purely economic aspects of the cooperative system, and the economic difficulties of the cooperatives have been held to be the primary cause of the switch to an emphasis on the development of Agro-Industrial Combines (AIC) in the decade since the economic reforms of 1965. In particular, the failure to create a profitable system of cooperative stock raising has been taken as a significant reason why many OZZ were disbanded during the early nineteen sixties.

There are good reasons, however, why we should be cautious of accepting too readily such explanations. Firstly, as Branko Horvat has pointed out, the level of profitability of the cooperatives was generally above that of either the poljoprivredna dobra, or of the new kombinati. Whereas there is no doubt that some cooperatives were closed through economic inefficiency, this cannot be taken as a general cause of their decline.[17]

205

Received wisdom becomes especially questionable in connection with the alleged problems of stock raising as a leading factor in the decline of cooperation. Again, there is no reason to doubt that this branch of agriculture has presented peculiar problems in all attempts to advance the socialist sector. It is necessary to bear in mind, however, that the "retreat" from cooperation has been observed not only in stock farming. If we look at the years following 1965, when cooperative membership reached its peak, the number of cooperants in stock raising had fallen by 1969 by 25 percent, but also the number of cooperants in arable farming fell by 15 percent in the same period.[18]

From these indications one can surmise, not unreasonably, that at least as important in guiding us to an understanding of the weakening of the cooperatives during the nineteen sixties, are social and political factors, which are needed to supplement purely economic explanations. The most important changes in this respect seem to be associated with the attempt to spread workers' self-management to the cooperatives during this period. Under legislation of the early postwar years, the cooperatives had been governed by a managing board which was responsible to an assembly of shareholding members, whose interests had been guarded by a watchdog body called the supervisory board. Legislation enacted in 1958, and supplemented in 1961, replaced this structure with a council (analogous to the Workers' Council of Industrial Enterprises)[19] and a managing board. The significant difference between the assembly and the council is that the latter included representation from all those associated with the organization, on an equal footing with the cooperants. Process and maintenance workers, clerks and administrators, agronomists and veterinarians, now all had a voice in cooperative government, and access to the direction of policy. Changes in the composition of these bodies during the period in question are instructive. (See table 10.1.)

It is necessary to consider the councils and the managing boards separately. In the former, the major forum for the democratic participation of the membership, the representation of peasants slipped from more than 70 percent to less than a half within five years. A similar tendency with respect to the boards was also under way in the early years, but this was, in fact, checked by legislation which specified the proportions of the representation on these bodies of different interest groups. Our hypothesis, which in the absence of more systematic information cannot at present be carefully tested, is that the withdrawal of the peasants from the cooperatives during the sixties, and their more general enfeeblement, are consequences of the loss of confidence on the part of the

TABLE 10.1

Composition of Councils and Managing Boards of
General Agricultural Cooperatives

Year	Level of Control	Peasants (%)	Employees (%)
1958-59	Council	71.6	28.4
	Managing Board	55.8	44.2
1961	Council	53.0	47.0
	Managing Board	46.6	53.3
1964	Council	48.7	51.3
	Managing Board	60.1	39.9

Source: Adapted from Čukanović, Zemljoradiničko
zadrugarstvo, p. 82 and Vučković, "Peasant
Cooperative," pp. 21-2.

peasant cultivator in an institution which was increasingly
alien to him, and less and less responsive to his interests.

This interpretation can be tentatively supported by a
number of other observations. Vučković has clearly indicated
the centrality of political considerations to these changes in
cooperative organization.[20]

The principle of workers' management, if rightly applied,
can solve many other problems associated with the
transformation of the structure of agricultural production
in Yugoslavia, i.e., with the process of detaching the
peasant from his land. Under the socio-economic
conditions of the socialist reconstruction of agriculture
in Yugoslavia, the peasant....is gradually being converted
into a social producer entrusted with the management of
social means of production.

Finally, the implementation of the principle of workers'
self-management in peasant cooperatives has greatly
contributed to supplanting old ideas of the role and
character of the peasant cooperative, ideas that were

still to be found in the village, particularly among old members of cooperatives; for instance, the mistaken idea that cooperatives were a kind of organization providing service facilities for peasant small-holders contributed to the conservation of the old type of backward peasant holding.

It could hardly be more clearly indicated that the cooperatives were not intended to serve the interests of the peasant, but to hasten his abolition. To ensure that the cooperative movement conformed to this purpose, a good representation of nonpeasant employees on the governing bodies of the OZZ has been considered necessary in order to prevent "seljakovanje,"[21] or the "peasantising" of these organizations and their aims.

Finally, the political role of cooperatives in the "socialist transformation of the village" is illustrated by official opposition to "wild" or spontaneous cooperatives, which sprang up particularly in the grain growing areas during the early nineteen sixties.[22] Taken together with the falling rate of investment in agriculture after 1959,[23] these indications suggest that the decline of cooperation at that timne may have to do with the awareness of the private farmer that cooperation did not any longer hold out the prospect for independent self-improvement and security which the concept of cooperation had hitherto represented.

Since the economic reforms of 1965, the only major policy development in agriculture has been the advancement of the Agro-Industrial Combines. These enterprises involve the vertical integration of the cultivation, processing, and marketing of a variety of types of agricultural produce; and they have been formed in a variety of ways, sometimes from the extension of the activities of state farms into manufacturing, sometimes from the reorganization of existing cooperative ventures, and sometimes as entirely new enterprises. From the farmer's point of view, their chief novelty lies in the fact that they offer contractual assurances of purchase for a stipulated crop, along with the provision of the appropriate materials, seed, fertilizers, and so on. Sometimes these arrangements include the availability of credit to the private cultivator, for the purchase of machinery or other capital investment, and more frequently in recent years they have included access to social security and other benefits, in which the private farmer has been seriously disadvantaged in earlier years.

It is difficult to say with any confidence exactly how much these new ventures have grown over the past decade, since official statistics for agriculture do not usually separately identify them or their product in reporting the performance of the social sector. Such partial information as we have at present does suggest that they do have a significant impact on levels of market involvement of farmers in their vicinity, and upon the more general level of economic development.[24] It is entirely unclear, however, to what extent their operation and consequences relate to the frequently enunciated goal of the "socialist transformation of the village." R. F. Miller suggests that they have been no more successful in this respect than their predecessors, the General Agricultural Cooperatives (OZZ), and for largely the same reasons. For any "group of cooperatives to pool their resources for the establishment of secondary production-type associations means inevitably to lose control over them."[25] One surmises that the peasants will be prepared to accept the AICs as trading partners, while endeavouring to hold the "socialization" of their farms at arm's length.

Whatever the precise impact of the Agro-Industrial Combines, one thing is certain, namely, that the "private sector is the dominant sector in agriculture, and will remain so for a long time."[26] The individual small holder in Yugoslavia still owns roughly 85 percent of the cultivated land, rears about 90 percent of the livestock, and provides more than half of the "authorized purchases" from agriculture.[27]

SOCIALISM AND AGRICULTURE: THE CHOICES FACING YUGOSLAVIA

It is now necessary for us to place this brief review of the development of Yugoslav agricultural policy in its context. In this respect, the major feature of postwar Yugoslav rural society can be said to be the "exodus from agriculture." There is no way of calculating accurately the numbers of people who have been lost to agriculture in Yugoslavia since 1945, but Vlado Puljiz has estimated that between 1948 and 1971 the rate of mobility was something like 240,000-255,000 persons per annum.[28] This has meant that in the space of thirty years the agricultural labor force of this country has slumped from more than three quarters to less than 40 percent of the total economically active population.

These events have been in line with both the intentions and the expectations of those in charge of Yugoslavia's economic policy, and a part of the basis of the plan to modernize agriculture. It is evident, however, that these changes have not been an unmixed blessing, and it is unlikely that such a rate of change either can or should continue into the future. Already, during the past ten years, there has been a regular growth in the rate of unemployment in the country, and although there is no reason to doubt that considerable further industrial expansion is possible, this is unlikely to continue to absorb labor at the rate at which it has done in the past. The type of industrial development that is at present being both planned and implemented (for example, in petrochemicals) is far from being labor intensive. Furthermore, the "industrialization" of agriculture, which currently dominates official thinking, led over the years between 1965 and 1971 to a steady decline in the numbers actually employed, and although there has been some recovery since, the total still has not reached the 1965 level.[29]

Since plainly it would be undesirable for this "rural exodus" to continue without the means of either employing or housing the migrants, in future years it will be necessary for the Yugoslav government to give thought to ways in which this flow can be slowed down. An obvious part of the solution to this problem seems to lie in making agriculture more attractive as an occupation, and the village more acceptable as an environment for the modern worker. It seems unlikely that this can be achieved within the present framework of policy.

Two major obstacles to such a development have been created by previous policy. Firstly, the level of remuneration to the farmer has been kept much lower than that of the industrial worker. Prices of agricultural goods were kept artificially low in comparison with the prices of manufactured goods up until 1961, when they were allowed to move towards freely competitive levels. Although the price of food has thus risen over the past eight years more rapidly than any other costs in Yugoslavia, this has not corrected the disparity. In fact, the incomes of families living exclusively from farming have fallen relatively further behind. In 1963 the incomes of such families were 25 percent below the national average; but by 1973 this gap had widened to 27.5 percent. The incomes of nonagricultural workers in 1963 were 42.7 percent above those of those living solely from farming, and a decade later this had risen to 50 percent.[30]

Hand in hand with the economic neglect of the rural worker has gone the demoralization of agriculture. This has been commented upon widely in the Yugoslav literature. A single quotation will suffice to make the point in a brief essay of this character.

> The immobility of young men left behind in the villages who have followed in their fathers' footsteps, becomes prima facie evidence of their incapability and inferiority. This norm has become accepted not only by the young but, it seems also, by their parents. Their foremost worry is how to educate their children rather than to settle the inheritance of the family estate.[31]

Under these conditions, the most energetic, able, and vigorous leave for industrial or administrative appointments, thus reducing the supply of able managerial talent available to agriculture. This unwillingness to remain in the village is, of course, not only a consequence of levels of earnings. It reflects also the disparities between town and country in physical, social, and cultural services of all kinds.

The socialist sector of agriculture has shown itself so far to be quite incapable of responding to these developments, and not only because of its inability to provide employment in the village at a sufficiently high rate. The expectation repeatedly enunciated since the war, that as the peasantry deserted the land for the towns, the public sector would take over the cultivation of their holdings, has been discovered to be largely utopian.

In the first place, notwithstanding the remarks made above about the "rural exodus," the private cultivator has been remarkably reluctant to relinquish his land. (The number of holdings has held steady at around 2.6 million for some time now). In spite of the low earnings of agriculture, he has been able to retain his land by dint of taking other kinds of employment to supplement his income from the farm. This has been aided by the Yugoslav policy of dispersing industrial development widely. Consequently the "peasant-worker" has become a notable, and possibly permanent, feature of Yugoslav social structure.

Secondly, as a consequence of this continuing demand for land, (and in spite of the "senilization" of the village) the price of land has generally remained high, so that where additional land has become available, the socialist sector has not always had the resources to take it into cultivation.[32] In any case, the integration of the estates of small holders is a more complex and costly process than simply purchasing land. Its incorporation into large-scale and mechanized agriculture assumes that this land is contiguous with the existing estates of the purchaser. Where this is not the case, legal facilities exist in Yugoslavia for the arondacija, or comassation, of fields, by exchange with other landholders. This, however, is an expensive and protracted process requiring legal arbitration. To these costs also must be added those incurred in the drainage of land and the extension of communications facilities and so forth. Bearing in mind also the relatively low levels of investment in agriculture during the postwar period, it is not altogether surprising that the expansion of the socialist sector by these means has been so slow.

Finally, in spite of the flight from the land, to which we have already alluded, projections from current demographic patterns, taken together with surveys of the attitudes and intentions of farming families, indicate that there is likely to be a substantial private sector in agriculture in the foreseeable future. A study by the Institut za Ekonomiku Poljoprivrede in Belgrade forecast in 1970 that, although the agricultural population was expected to continue to decline to around 30 percent of the total by 1985, this would still leave an economically active agricultural labor force of around three and one-third million. Within this category, the private sector would still control roughly two-thirds of the agricultural area of the country, and three-quarters of its arable surface.[33]

The primary and continuing aim of Yugoslav agricultural policy since the war has been the "socialist transformation of the village." As this paper has attempted to show, this policy has not been realized and seems unlikely to be realized in the future by the means chosen. Yugoslav theorists of socialism have constantly and emphatically rejected, however, the farmerski put (farmers' path) to development, in the belief that the building up of private holdings would lead inevitably to the restoration of capitalism.[34] However, these theorists have never successfully demonstrated the case for considering that this danger necessarily accompanies the perpetuation of private landholding, or even that the private farm is inherently antisocialist. What is more serious is the fact that it has not been shown that this danger is a greater threat to the future of socialism than the continuation of present policies.

All observers of Yugoslavia seem to agree that the country will face in the relatively near future some fairly serious tests of its stability and integrity. The legitimacy accorded to any socialist regime will depend in good measure upon its ability to provide a more just and egalitarian order of society than would be offered by any immediately available alternative. Yet a direct consequence of the agricultural policy of the postwar years has been the creation of "two nations," where the backwardness and relative poverty of the villager still compare very unfavorably with the relative affluence of the industrial worker and urban citizen. The pressing problems of equality in Yugoslavia do not relate solely to the rural/urban division, (and within that, not only to the division between social and individual ownership) but also involve the differences between regions, nationalities, and classes more generally. The position of the individual peasant farmer stands out, however, as being among the most pressing of the issues in this area.

Socialist theory has always denied to the peasant a "progressive" role in history, and this is in accordance with the more generally held view in sociology and anthropology that the peasant mode of production can never develop into an independent social system, but always exists in a "part-society" relationship to some other system, be it socialist, capitalist, or whatever. This may be true; but if the Yugoslavs do not succeed in raising the general level of development of the private sector of agriculture fairly rapidly (by the farmerski put or any other way), the peasantry may well serve to pull the country backwards, and away from any prospect of a genuine advance towards a socialist society.

NOTES

1. Two recent studies may be cited that exemplify advances in this direction. Peter Jambrek's <u>Development and Social Change in Yugoslavia</u> (Saxon House, 1975) adds a good deal to our awareness of the importance of local government and the real interest of Yugoslav experiments at this level. In her <u>Beyond Marx and Tito</u> (Cambridge University Press, 1975) Sharon Zukin reinforces this emphasis, adding to it particularly an awareness of the wider aspects of Yugoslav political culture. Both of these books, however, confine themselves largely to material relating to urban milieu.

2. In 1976 Albania employed 62.7 percent of its economically active population in agriculture, and Romania 50.7 percent which Yugoslavia followed with 42.3 percent. Greece and Bulgaria followed closely with 40.5 percent and 38.2 percent respectively. See, United Nations, Food and Agricultural Organization (FAO) <u>Production Yearbook</u>, Vol. 30, 1976, table 3, pp. 66-68.

3. The figures for employment in agriculture disguise this more general feature to some extent, since they do not take account of rural residence, which in Yugoslavia is very widespread among industrial workers, nor do they reflect the continuing cultural heritage of the recently industrialized worker.

4. <u>Agrarna politika i zadaci Saveza Komunista Jugoslavije</u> <u>(Nacrt teza za pripremu Konferencije SKJ)</u>, Predsedništvo SKJ, Komisija za agrarnu politiku, Beograd, March 1970, pp. 5-8.

5. See, for example, Organization for Economic Cooperation and Development (OECD), Agricultural Policy Reports, <u>Agricultural Policy in Yugoslavia</u>, OECD, Paris, 1973, p. 11.

6. See, for example, United Nations, FAO, <u>Production Yearbook</u>, Vol. 29, 1976, tables 13, 16, and 45, pp. 60-61, 67, and 109.

7. See, for example, ibid. tables 25 and 114, pp. 81 and 262-63.

8. This approach goes back at least to Lenin's study of <u>The Development of Capitalism in Russia</u>. It has been a persisting error of Yugoslav social science that Lenin's insights into the economic history of Russia have been taken as authoritative pronouncements rather than as hypotheses. Hence the entire corpus of the literature on agriculture in the prewar period is premised upon the belief that Yugoslav rural social structure was undergoing a rapid process of polarization into a rural bourgeoisie and a proletariat at that time. In a manuscript not yet published I have attempted systematically to refute this hypothesis.

9. Some of the most instructive critical discussion of policy in this period is found in the speeches and articles of Dr. Slavko Komar. See his <u>Poljoprivreda u izgradnji</u>

socijalizma: izabrani govori i članci (Zagreb: Agrarno-politicka biblioteka, 1967). I have attempted a review of the literature on this period in a paper shortly to be published, entitled, "The Collectivisation of Yugoslav Agriculture and the Myth of Peasant Resistance."

10. An adjective conventionally used to describe private, small-scale agriculture in Yugoslav sources is stihijski, meaning chaotic, randomized, wild, and untamed. See for example, Edvard Kardelj, Problemi socijalističke politike na selu (Beograd: Kultura 1959), p. 111.

11. Quoted in S. Čukanović, Zemljoradiničko zadrugarstvo u agrarnoj politici Jugoslavije, (Beograd: NIP Mala poljoprivredna biblioteka, 1971), p. 63.

12. Ibid., p. 143.

13. Ibid., p. 108.

14. Ibid., p. 102.

15. Ibid., p. 95.

16. See Čukanović, Zemljoradiničko zadrugarstvo, p. 106.

17. See Branko Horvat, The Yugoslav Economic System (New York: International Arts & Sciences Press, 1976), p. 141. He quotes estimates of the profitability of these various types of enterprise by Pjanić for the period 1964-68, as follows: Agro-industrial combines, 6.4 percent, Agricultural estates, 6.8 percent, General Agricultural Cooperatives, 8.0 percent; Peasant Work Cooperaties, 9.6 percent; Industry and mining, 9.6 percent. He also remarks, "It is symptomatic that this phenomenon has not been subjected to scholarly analysis and that there has been no expert and political discussion of it." This tends to reinforce my own inclination to believe that the major reasons for the change of direction have been political and ideological rather than purely economic.

18. See Čukanović, Zemljoradinicko zadrugarstvo, p. 143. It should be pointed out, of course, that the numerical decline of cooperants engaged in stock-raising was far smaller than the decline experienced in other branches of agriculture, about one-third of that recorded for arable farming.

19. Changes in the legal position of the cooperatives in the postwar years are reviewed in M. Vučković, "The Transformation of the Peasant Cooperative," in R. Stojanović, ed., Yugoslav Economists on Problems of a Socialist Economy (New York: International Arts & Sciences Press, 1964). See especially pp. 18-20.

20. Ibid., p. 21. His discussion of developments is particularly misleading, however, since he uses figures for the growth of cooperative membership before 1959 to illustrate the consequence of structural changes that came into effect largely after that date.

21. See Horvat, Economic System, p. 138. The response of villagers to cooperatives, and in particular their tendency to treat them as an alien imposition, is illustrated very well in Irene Winner's study of a Slovenian village. See her

Slovenian Village: Žerovnica (Providence: Brown University Press, 1971), pp. 99-110.

22. See ibid., pp. 146 and 149 ff. These often involved the cooperative purchase of large items of farm machinery, and were suspect as possible points at which capitalistic labor relations might develop.

23. See Čukanović, Zemljoradiničko zadrugarstvo, pp. 65-66.

24. One such investigation has come my way to date, in the form of an unpublished essay by P. Gaži et al., "Influence of the Agro-Industrial Complex on Income and Employment of Agricultural Population: A Case Study of 'Podravka,' Koprivnica." I am indebted to Dr. Zvonimir Baletić for making this information available to me.

25. See R. F. Miller, Socialism and Agricultural Cooperation: the Soviet and Yugoslav Cases, Department of Political Science; Research School of Social Science; Australian National University, Occasional Papers, No. 9, Canberra, 1974, p. 55.

26. The quotation is from Z. Baletić, "Mjesto poljoprivrede u ekonomskom razvoju Jugoslavije," MS in the files of the Ekonomski Institut Sveučilišta, Zagreb, 1967, Chap. III, p. 6.

27. OECD, Agricultural Policy in Yugoslavia, p. 8; Statistički Godišnjak SFRJ, 1975, (Beograd, SZS) table 108-2, p. 154. It has been estimated that because the figures for "authorized purchase" do not include transactions in peasant markets, the real contribution of the private sector is probably at least two-thirds of Yugoslavia's requirements for food.

28. See Vlado Puljiz, Eksodus poljoprivrednika (Zagreb: Biblioteka sociologija sela, 1977), especially pp. 118-19.

29. See OECD, Economic Surveys, Yugoslavia, OECD, Paris, April 1976, p. 43.

30. Figures adapted from Statistički Bilten, nos. 314 and 876, by Prof. Gorazd Nikić, of Zagreb, (from an unpublished MS). This picture is, of course, complicated by two factors which are not analyzed here. Firstly, incomes in the socialist sector are rather larger than those in the private sector, other things being equal. Secondly, I have left out of the comparison the complex category of "mixed" households.

31. Quoted from Josip Županov, "Non-economic Factors in the Transfer of Rural Population to Non-agricultural Activities in the Period of Accelerated Industrialisation--the Example of Yugoslavia," pp. 16-17. This is an unpublished MS made available to me privately.

32. There seem to be no systematic investigations into the price of land in Yugoslavia. I owe the majority of this paragraph, therefore, to conversations with informed individuals. I am particularly grateful to Dr. Zvonimir

Baletić, of the Ekonomski Institut Sveučilišta in Zagreb for his help in this regard.

33. See Institut za Ekonomiku Poljoprivrede, <u>Osnove politike dugogodišnjeg razvoja poljoprovrede Jugoslavije: prethodni rezultati istraživanja</u>, Beograd, May 1970, especially p. 6.

34. See, for example, <u>Agrarna politika i zadaci SKJ</u>, p. 45. Here the aim of raising productivity is expressly subordinated to the need to persist in the long-term aim of the socialization of the land. The problem is also discussed very well by Horvat, <u>Economic System</u>, pp. 149 ff.

Part 3

Cross-National Analysis

Introduction

Ronald A. Francisco

The Council for Mutual Economic Assistance (CMEA) celebrated in 1979 its thirtieth anniversary, its twentieth since the ratification of a new charter giving it the same status as the West European EEC. The public political euphoria must have been muted, however, by private misgivings, for it is remarkable how poorly integrated and coordinated Eastern Europe remains. That this is true for a system devoted to hierarchical coordination and control is still more surprising, and nowhere is this more the case than in agriculture.

The classic law of comparative advantage in international economics posits a strong motivation in any trading system for specialization and division of labor. Yet we confront in the CMEA an economic alliance that is much less than the sum of its parts, and one that shows few signs of recognition of comparative advantage. Eastern European agricultural policies are, of course, similar. That is evident in section two. Yet these policies are not closely coordinated by the CMEA. Every nation independently continues to attempt to do virtually everything in agriculture, as if it were in a kind of economic vacuum.

Cross-national analysis in this section shows that East European agricultural programs are still very country-specific and are driven more by national than by supranational forces. Nearly everywhere there is emphasis upon mechanization and agro-industrial integration, but just as there is a Yugoslav road to socialism, so too is there an Hungarian road to agro-industrial integration. Many of these policies have already borne fruit. Growth rates in several countries have been impressive. Yet the stark fact remains that Eastern Europe fails regularly to meet production targets, imports increasing quantities of basic foodstuffs, and lags far behind even mediocre producers in Western Europe.

11
Problems of Agricultural Integration within the CMEA

Günter Jaehne

INTRODUCTION

The cooperation of the member countries of the Council for Mutual Economic Assistance (CMEA) in the field of agriculture has obviously entered a new phase. At the thirty-second council meeting of the CMEA in Bucharest in June 1978, the heads of the states of this economic community decided on so-called "long-term specific programs" for important branches of trade, including agriculture and the food-processing industry. For the agriculture within the CMEA this means a considerable political-economic revaluation. It is, however, at the same time a reference to the urgency of the existing problems that must be solved in the years to come. It is the aim of the program to bring farm production within the CMEA by 1990 to such a level that the supply of the principal food and agricultural raw products can be satisfied entirely and on a high standard by the production of the member countries of the CMEA alone.

Today the CMEA is still far away from the realization of this aim. It is true that the increase of farm production has been considerable in the last ten to fifteen years--indeed, it has been greater than the average increase in the world, including the Western countries. Yet, although the growth has been faster than the increase in population within the CMEA, it is not sufficient to satisfy completely and constantly the rapidly increasing demands of the customers in terms of assortment, structure, and quality, especially among important products like animal products, fruits, and vegetables.

The Romanian head of the state and party secretary, N. Ceausescu, recently confirmed with his statement that the socialist countries could not satisfy the desires of their consumers--especially for food--that the CMEA countries still would have shortages in their food supply.[1] The Communist party chiefs of these countries cannot be unconcerned about this problem, since they promised their people at the last party assembly a rapid increase in the standard of living. An improvement of their living standard still means for most CMEA countries an improvement of their nutrition level. Thus the fulfillment of one of the most important aims of communist welfare policy is decided in the field of agriculture.[2]

The countries of the CMEA[2] try to solve permanently the "food problem" in two ways: (1) higher agricultural investments, more and better means of production, and greater material incentives for agricultural producers as a national effort to increase production, and (2) international cooperation in all fields of agriculture, agricultural science, agricultural engineering, and especially in those branches that produce agricultural means of production. Successes could be cited, but they were obviously less spectacular than in other fields of economic cooperation in the CMEA.

THE POTENTIAL OF THE CMEA AGRICULTURE

Let us first consider the economic potential of CMEA agriculture.[3]

Position in World Agriculture

Put together and calculated in absolute quantities, CMEA countries are the most important producers of agricultural products in the world, especially with reference to grain, root crops, and technical crops. According to Soviet figures, the USSR produces on 15 percent of farmland and about 20 percent of arable lands in the world one-third of the world's agricultural production.[4] Figures of the German Democratic Republic speak of 25 to 28 percent of the CMEA share in the gross produce output of the world, which seems more likely than the Soviet claim.

The member countries of the CMEA today comprise about 374 million people. This is 9.3 percent of the world population. It is relevant with reference to the situation of world nutrition that the CMEA, in spite of its disproportionately high share of the farm production of the world still needs the world market for the nourishment of its population--and this in an apparently increasing quantity. The CMEA countries are net importers of agricultural products. In terms of the principal agricultural products, the CMEA share of world production corresponds to its share of the world's arable lands (for example, grain and meat constitute about 20 percent of world production).

It is however insufficient to refer to these figures alone, as is shown with the example of meat: The USA produced 25.38 million tons of meat (FAO figure) in 1976, thus producing more than 2.4 million tons of meat more than all the countries in the CMEA (which produced about 23 million tons according to national and CMEA statistics). And one has to keep in mind that in the countries of the CMEA there are over 150 million more people than in the USA.

The added potential of production in the CMEA countries is based on extremely different national contributions. Without giving a detailed account of area per head, harvest, and livestock production, we have to realize that the Soviet Union has 70 percent of the total population of the CMEA and produces almost two-thirds of the CMEA agricultural output.[5] Poland is second with about 10 percent of the CMEA population and 10 percent of its total agricultural production. The shares of the other members rank far below these. These figures are naturally not only of statistical importance in the economy. They represent, moreover,--also in the socialist countries--power and interest in a certain policy in an economic community.

THE POSITION OF AGRICULTURE IN THE CMEA

The position and importance of agriculture within the economy and society of Eastern Europe is considerably higher than in the industrialized West--e.g., in the European Economic Community (EEC). In most of the CMEA countries, agriculture ranks behind industry as the second biggest sector, in others it forms the foundation of the economy.

In spite of the decline of the agricultural sector in the CMEA in terms of national income and employment, as the consequence of industrialization, it is still remarkably greater than in Western countries. For instance, the share of agriculture in the national income (according to Soviet calculations) is higher than 20 percent in the CMEA, whereas it was only 5 percent in the EEC in 1976.[6]

These comparisons may be questionable, yet they at least give evidence of great differences. The same applies to the proportion of the people working in agriculture compared with the total number of employees. According to estimates of the FAO, about 24 percent have agricultural jobs in the CMEA compared to about 8 percent in the EEC. In addition it must be realized that the social and economic position of agriculture is very important in the CMEA, since some of the member countries (Cuba, the Mongolian People's Republic, and Vietnam) are definitely agriculturally undeveloped countries with all the resulting consequences for the economic growth, the standard of living, and the social structure. Other CMEA states (Romania and Bulgaria) have passed the take-off phase successfully, yet they are still in the initial stage of industrial development. These differences in structure consequently lead to tension and conflicts of interest in all communities. One more reason that farming and agricultural production have such a great influence on politics and public consciousness is rooted in the fact that in the CMEA countries almost one-half of the population (44 percent) lives in the country.[7]

The great socioeconomic significance of agriculture in the CMEA countries, however, is based on its ability to supply raw food and agricultural produce and in its resulting effect on the market balance. Since the supply of quality industrial articles of consumption is very poor, agricultural products are the raw produce basis for approximately one-half (GDR) to three-quarters (USSR) of all articles of consumption. Ignoring the service sector, which in most of the countries is not highly developed anyway, the CMEA consumers spend about 50 percent of their income on food and heavily taxed semiluxuries. Agricultural products also are important sources of export goods for quite a few Eastern European countries[8] as well as Cuba and the Mongolian People's Republic. In spite of its importance in the general economy, CMEA agriculture has never played such an important part in the international economic political discussion as agriculture in the EEC. One of the main reasons for this might be the strongly marked national competence of the CMEA countries for planning and developing their agricultural economy.

Integration of Economy in the CMEA

The influence of the CMEA and its special organs on the development and structure of the agricultural production in its member countries could increase in importance if their "long-term specific programs" would not remain new verbal phrases of intention, but would become a real program of action. There are quite a few indications--among others the more scientific approach and the apparently better material and technical basis of the project--that this new attempt to solve the key problems in the CMEA, including agricultural production, has a more solid basis than previous projects. TASS complains, for example: "Up to now in the history of the CMEA those complicated and large-scale tasks have not yet been solved."[9]

The delegations of the CMEA member countries furthermore reported at the thirty-second council meeting in Bucharest in 1978 in a special statement that the "long-term specific programs" are a "concretization and extension of the comprehensive program of socialist economic integration" of the CMEA.[10]

Yet what is the meaning of "socialist economic integration"? After long avoiding this topic, the representatives of Marxist political economy started to discuss idea, content, and aim of economic integration at the end of the 1960s. Not integration as such, but socialist integration is discussed, to be precise, economic integration in the CMEA. Although the number of scientific papers about this topic is constantly increasing in Eastern Europe, there is no sound theory of socialist economic integration in the CMEA. Even in the most important economic and political basic document of the CMEA, the so-called "comprehensive program," there is no explicit explanation of socialist economic integration. The lack of theory is said to be caused by the fact that integration is a "relatively new and not yet sufficiently investigated phenomenon."[11]

It is not possible to describe the problems of the integration in the CMEA in detail. Therefore, only a few relevant aspects will be mentioned and analyzed which might help us to see this problem more clearly.[12] In Marxist political economy "integration" is generally defined as a special form of internationalization of the economic life of two or more countries. According to this theory socialist economic integration means "the convergence of the socialist countries, the development of their mutual economic relations, and the gradual interlocking of their economies to an uniform community."[13]

This development is carried through as a "systematically planned socialist division of labor." It is not quite clear, and there is no indication in the "comprehensive program," whether Lenin's prophecy of a "socialist world-cooperative association" or a "common market" of the socialist world economy shall be reached by the process that has been defined as complicated and long-range.

Interim aims for the period of fifteen to twenty years covered by the "comprehensive program" are among others:[14]

- accelerated economic growth
- development of modern structures of production
   in the countries
- a better supply of domestic markets - among
   other things, with raw material, energy,
   investment goods, food and other consumer
   goods predominantly from CMEA resources
- increase of living standards
- convergence and assimilation of the economic
   standards of the countries
- accelerated and stable growth of the CMEA trade
- strengthening of the CMEA position in the
   world economy and a victory in the economic
   competition with capitalism
- strengthening of the defense economy of the
   CMEA countries

CMEA Agriculture and Integration

From these demands one can derive branch-specific aims for agriculture like growth of production, modern structures of production, reduction of the great differences in the standards of agricultural production (a striking example for this is the comparison between the GDR and the Mongolian People's Republic), a greater efficiency of output, etc. These aims will be realized with an increasing intensity through cooperation in the CMEA in the creation of an international division of labor in agriculture.

In the voluminous catalog of measures that the "comprehensive program" demands, the following items are of interest:

- setting up long-term prognoses for the develop
  ment of the needs, the production and the
  marketing of individual products and
  branches of agriculture and food-processing
  industry
- coordination of long-term plans of perspective
  with the help of these prognoses
- integrated, planned activities of production
  and marketing of individual products
- promoting farm production and agricultural
  exports (in the CMEA) by means of price
  policy and other economical instruments
- increase of the agricultural foreign trade
  with the aim to cover the import need
  gradually within the CMEA
- specialization and division of labor in certain
  branches and sectors of agriculture within the
  CMEA

The measures suggested in the "comprehensive program" are elements in the direction of an increasing interlocking of agriculture within the CMEA. Seven years have passed since then. Only a few projects have been successfully carried through according to information from Eastern European literature. Among them are the detailed planning of prognoses of future needs, production, and marketing certain agricultural products. Based predominantly on national estimates, they have been transferred into jointly planned prognoses of the CMEA, so that today the council organs have precise ideas about the future development of those products up to 1985, and in some cases up to 1990.[15]

There are also numerous forecasts about the need for and the production of agricultural means of production, about certain scientific agricultural branches of research, and scientific technical conceptions, which partly reach up to the year 2000 (here, however, not to be dealt with). The most important thing about the long-term prognoses is--apart from their improved quality and the greater number of products[16]-- that they also contain dates about structure and possible development of the need for agricultural products. Up to now it has been easier for agricultural exporters among the CMEA countries to analyze the development of agricultural production and consumption in Western markets in order to form their foreign trade strategy than gaining information about the CMEA. Yet it remains uncertain how intensively individual CMEA countries will develop their policy of self-support with agricultural products.

The agricultural prognoses have at least theoretically improved the preconditions for an international product specialization in agriculture. They are also a necessary guide for long-term, multilateral Plan coordination of the development of farm production, as well as for the conclusion of multilateral long-term arrangements about agricultural foreign trade (that has been up to now short-term and bilateral). The "long-term specific program for agriculture and the food industry" has most likely been realized on this basis.

While the competence of the individual state for its agriculture is fully preserved in the Plan coordination, it is at least uncertain in the common planning of producing and selling agricultural products, as it is recommended in the "comprehensive program" in order to intensify the division of labor. It seems as if the proposal has not got on well so far. CMEA countries apparently have not begun with joint planning for farm production.[17]

Problems of Prices and Foreign Trade

Foreign trade of agricultural products belongs to one of the branches with "special significance" in CMEA cooperation. The reason is that agricultural products play an important part in the foreign trade of the member countries. For, apart from the fact that agricultural products (1) because of their limited transportability and (2) because of the unsatisfied demand on the home markets of the CMEA countries serve above all the national domestic supply, an increasing quantity of agricultural products goes into foreign trade as production grows.[18] They are exported to socialist countries as well as to states outside the CMEA.

A more efficient interlocking in foreign trade in the CMEA is prevented by the fact that price regulations for agricultural products are not satisfactory and cause clashes of interest between exporting and importing countries. Without dealing with the complicated price problem in the intra-CMEA trade we can come to the following conclusions: The mutual exchange of goods among CMEA countries is not based on an original price system of their own. For want of this the CMEA states orient themselves in their trade to the prices of the capitalist world market. The world prices, no matter how they are determined and defined by the price and foreign-

227

trade offices of the CMEA countries, are transformed into so-called contract prices for groups of merchandise or single products in a circumstantial process that is not free from arbitrariness. These prices are used in the bilateral foreign trade.

Normally the CMEA contract prices for agricultural products do not cover the costs of production of the exporting countries, because their agricultural structure of costs and their costs as such are different from those on which the world market prices are based. This applies especially to agricultural raw products and little processed agricultural products, but not for other food. The consequence of too low contract prices for agricultural products in CMEA trade is that the exporting countries subsidize their agricultural exports. In principle this means the more agricultural exports that go into CMEA trade, the higher are the subventions. For countries with a very high share in the agricultural products in CMEA trade like Bulgaria, Hungary, Romania, and the Mongolian People's Republic, this price arrangement leads to considerable financial burdens for their national budgets. For the net importing countries in agricultural products, like the GDR, Czechoslovakia and, to a certain extent Poland, and the USSR, this system grants--at least by way of calculation--advantages. This becomes more relevant through the fact that the contract prices for important manufactured goods in CMEA trade are sometimes much higher than comparable prices in the world market. From the fact that agricultural exporting countries in CMEA foreign trade and in relation to the goods groups mentioned above (agricultural products versus industrial finished products) have to accept unfavorable terms, one cannot necessarily conclude that there is price discrimination by the industrially developed CMEA states.

The fact that contract prices for agricultural products in CMEA trade in comparison to their production costs are too low has various negative consequences for the process of integration. It might have, for example, the effect that those CMEA countries, where agricultural products play an important part in the economy and foreign trade, are not motivated to orient their potential of agriculture and food towards the needs of those CMEA countries dependent on imports.

Another consequence is that agricultural exports from the CMEA community are directed towards markets offering better profits and additional hard currency. In fact, such a foreign-trade policy is practiced in the CMEA, giving special advantage to those countries that can offer agricultural specialities and quality products. Seventy percent of Czechoslovakia's agricultural exports go to the West,[19] expecially to the zone with convertible currency, whereas it receives two-thirds of its agricultural imports from socialist countries.[20] The GDR pursues a similar policy in exporting to the Federal Republic of Germany a large quantity of animal products, while at the same time trying to cover the greatest part of its import needs by buying agricultural products from the CMEA. The consequence is a strong clash of interests and negative effects on integration. Attempts to coordinate "the disharmonious behavior of some brother countries," with regard to their agricultural exports to the West, by a joint foreign-trade policy with third countries, have not yet brought any positive results. The negative consequences of CMEA contract prices for agricultural products in the intracommunity trade, which do not cover the costs of production, have long been the target of criticism. in the "comprehensive program" the members had agreed to work out methods and possibilities up to the year 1973 to stimulate by means of "prices and other economical instruments" agricultural production and the export of agricultural products in the member countries of the CMEA. The solution of this problem, which is an important precondition for progress in the international agricultural specialization of production, has not yet been achieved, because of "the complexity of the matter." In any case, this conclusion can be drawn from a statement of the Romanian prime minister Manescu at a CMEA council meeting in 1977, when he criticized, with reference to the task in the "comprehensive program," that no practical result had been achieved in stimulating agricultural export prices.[21]

Apart from the politically different case of the Cuban sugar price, the Soviet Union and some other CMEA countries have only once conceded financial aid on contract prices for agricultural products. This was in the case of the Mongolian People's Republic's meat exports into CMEA countries. Aside from this common action in the period between 1971 and 1975, the Soviet Union, as the biggest importer of slaughter cattle and animal products from the Mongolian People's Republic, paid its Asian neighbor higher export prices for these goods in some years.[22] The USSR thus contributed, so to speak, to the stabilization of Mongolian cattle farming, the development of which must suffer especially hard under the consequences of the "price scissors" between costs of production and export income in the CMEA.

If up to now a basic agreement about more realistic export prices for agricultural products among CMEA countries has not been realized, this is not only because of the typical difficulties of planned economies in this field, but moreover because of the different interests of the member countries. For Bulgaria, Hungary, Romania, the Mongolian People's Republic, Cuba, and Vietnam, the export of agricultural products is of much greater importance in their foreign trade than agricultural imports, whereas the opposite is true in the GDR, Czechoslovakia, the Soviet Union, and Poland.

I am not familiar with the individual attitudes of all the countries towards this problem, but it is most likely that the countries exporting agricultural goods share Bulgaria's opinion, which pleads for a turning away from the world market prices of the West as a basis for agricultural contract prices in CMEA trade. Instead, it supports an introduction of foreign-trade prices that stimulate production. The Soviet Union is of the opinion that the foreign-trade prices should include the specific, and in the CMEA generally unfavorable, natural conditions of production and transport. It also takes the view that the additional investment costs should be shared by the countries interested in imports. This point of view has always been held by the Soviet Union with reference to raw-material trade within the CMEA.

The most important countries importing agricultural goods in the CMEA--especially the GDR--are obviously afraid that abandoning the present principle could lead to a general price jump in the "socialist market," which could cause difficulties in the balance of payments. As an industrialized country, the GDR takes in this connection the view that the production of new techniques does not result in lower costs than the agricultural production of raw materials. It is very instructive to see in this discussion that the CMEA countries exporting agricultural goods expect to cover of their costs only by means of higher sales, yet do not consider a cost reduction in their agricultural production as a very successful means.

The foreign-trade and price experts in the CMEA countries may look at the problem from whatever angle they like, but they cannot ignore the necessity of establishing foreign-trade prices that can set the standard for the calculation of the absolute and comparative advantages of costs. This is a precondition for a rational international division of labor in the CMEA as a whole and in agriculture.

No Integration of Agricultural Production

It cannot be estimated exactly if the absence of this precondition--among others--is the reason for a lack of integration in the agriculture of the CMEA. After all, in other economic branches of this group, a process of integration is being carried through, although the same restrictions are relevant there as well. In the field of international specialization and cooperation in agricultural production, however, we can only trace very marginal beginnings in this direction. Apart from the few CMEA activities, such as common cultivation of new sorts of plants and efficient species of animals, and the exchange of breeding cattle and seeds, which are all very important, but do not reflect the integration of an economic branch, there is no international division of labor in agricultural production. For example, neither does the Soviet Union, as an agricultural giant, produce soybeans for member countries (although they urgently need them, or at least enough fodder cereals), nor are Poland, Czechoslovakia, or the GDR interested in decreasing the Soviet deficit in barley for brewing by increasing their own production. And none of the CMEA countries does anything to lessen the Soviet Union's meat shortage.

The natural preconditions for such an international division of labor (soil, climate) are there. In fact, concrete plans exist, which stipulate agricultural goods could be best produced in specific CMEA areas. Yet this potential has not been utilized, if we exclude the extension of traditional centers of production, like fruit, vegetables, and tobacco in the south-eastern CMEA countries, sugar-cane in Cuba, cattle production in the Mongolian People's Republic, and cotton in the Soviet Union.

International specialization in agriculture, as the result of a deepening process of integration, is reflected in changing national cultivation structures. The reason for this is that the cultivation of one product (or a group of products) is limited, or entirely stopped for the sake of the extension of the cultivation of another. If one examines the agricultural cultivation structures of the CMEA countries for the last twenty years one cannot detect any fundamental changes as the consequence of measures of specialization.

Every CMEA country is more interested in its own national aims in animal production than in crops. The CMEA policy is to produce the products of stock-farming where they are consumed. Only the Mongolian People's Republic is an exception. With a relatively high consumption of meat per head and as the result of the dominating position of animal production, the country increasingly exports slaughter cattle, meat, and other animal products. An international specialization of animal production on a larger scale in the CMEA is still hindered by the absence or inefficient capacities of processing, transporting, and cooling.

The marginal agricultural specialization of production among the CMEA countries corresponds on the other hand, to widespread national drives for independence. Similar to attempts in Western Europe, the CMEA countries try to restrict their dependence on agricultural imports by enlarging their national productive capacity. In doing so the economic leaders have adhered to the principle that it is economically more advantageous to supply agriculture better with means of production, rather than importing what can be produced domestically. This refers above all to agricultural imports from Western countries, which must be minimized for economic, ideological and strategic reasons. Yet also within the CMEA every country pursues a policy of self-support with important groups of production. This does not apply only to the Soviet Union with its physical advantages, but also to countries like the GDR and Czechoslovakia, that have very unfavorable preconditions to be self-supporting because of the barely sufficient agricultural resources per inhabitant.

It cannot be said that these countries' policies are inconsistent with the principles of the CMEA. On the contrary, they can appeal to the aim of the CMEA, which maintains that one of the main goals of agricultural cooperation is to help the member countries gain a maximum of agricultural self-support.

Whereas for EEC countries the high degree of self-support (apart from protein fodder) has to be seen in connection with production surplus, the determined policy of autarchy in the CMEA results from short supplies and from the realization that a stable national food supply must be based on a solid domestic basis of production. Moreover, the USSR is no longer reliable to deliver enough, and there are no agricultural reserves in the CMEA for crises situations or to balance fluctuations in harvests. The discussion, begun in Eastern Europe in the early 1970s, to build stores of natural resources for important kinds of agricultural raw produce-- among them a grain fund--have not led to any positive results.[23] Recently the problem surfaced again, in connection with the long-term specific program for agriculture, which-- without giving detailed information--plans the installation of agricultural reserves.

In this connection the question arises whether the agricultural policy of the CMEA countries directed towards national self-support facilitates the development of an international agricultural division of labor. Apart from the fact that the CMEA lacks economic criteria to find optimal places for production, the future tasks of the "long-term specific program for agriculture" can hardly be realized by intensifying the cooperation in the areas of agricultural means of production, agricultural science, and so forth. This can be achieved only "by deepening and using other forms of international socialist division of labor in harmonized branches and fields of agriculture," as was recommended in the "comprehensive program" of 1971.

There has been no information about the aims of production in the "long-term specific program" for agriculture mentioned at the outset of this chapter. Nor is it likely that any will be released. However, in connection with this program a full self-sufficiency in food is proposed. According to a calculation of the Moscow "Institute for Socialist World Economy"[24]--although in another connection--this goal requires a considerable increase in CMEA agricultural production, especially meat (40 to 42 percent), milk (28 to 30 percent), eggs (45 to 47 percent), vegetables (40 to 45 percent), and fruit (60 to 65 percent).

As a whole CMEA agriculture is still in a developing phase in which the greatest cooperation is in those sectors directly related to agricultural production. The "long-term specific program" for agriculture's goal of guaranteeing self-sufficiency in agriculture in the CMEA by the year 1990 can be attained only by intensifying specialization and cooperation in agricultural production.

NOTES

1. N. Ceausescu at a party assembly in Bucharest on 3 August 1978. Agerpress (Bucharest) (3 August 1978); quoted in Ostinformationen des Bundespresseamtes (Bonn) no. 148 (4 August 1978).
2. Today the CMEA has member countries on three continents. In addition to the Soviet Union, member states include Poland, Romania, the German Democratic Republic, Czechoslovakia, Hungary, Bulgaria, the Mongolian People's Republic, Cuba, and since June 1978, Vietnam. Yugoslavia is an associate member; for example, it cooperates with the CMEA in the field of agriculture. Alabania no longer participates.
3. Both here and in later references, "CMEA agriculture" is simply a shortened expression for the concept of agriculture in the member states of the CMEA
4. See Mir sotsializma v tsifrakh i faktakh 1976 (Moscow, 1977), p. 46. It is not known how the Soviets calculate this proportion. It has remained the same size in Soviet reports since about 1973; see Sel'skaya zhizn', no. 80 (7 April 1978).
5. See M. Rajchart, Problémy rozvoje a prolubovani spolupráce členských statu RVHP v zemědělstvi (Prague, 1973), p. 20. This source quotes a proportion of 58 percent.
6. Figures for the CMEA are in Sel'skaya zhizn, no. 129 (3 June 1977). Figures for the EEC are in Bundesernährungsministerium Bonn, BMELF-Mitteilungen, no. 11 (13 March 1978).
7. See Sel'skaya zhizn, no. 129 (3 June 1978).
8. Bulgaria, for example, has long used its agricultural exports to subsidize importation of fuel, minerals, metals, and machines.
9. Tass, 6 July 1978. Tass comments on a meeting of the executive committee of the CMEA, which dealt with this complex of questions before the thirty-second council meeting.
10. This statement was also published in Neues Deutschland, no. 152 (30 June 1978). The complete name of the "Comprehensive Program" of the year 1971 is: "Comprehensive Program for the Further Extension and Improvement of Cooperation and the Development of Socialist Economic Integration of the CMEA Member Countries." It was published, for example, in International Zeitschrift der Landwirtschaft (June 1971): 609-650. Pages 641-44 discuss main directions and aims of the development of cooperation in agriculture and the food-processing industry.

11. See, for example, J. Schischkow, Two Worlds--Two Types of Integration (Moscow, 1974), p. 5. Author's translation.

12. This discussion is based on material in J. Bethkenhagen and H. Machowski, Integration im Rat für gegenseitige Wirtschaftshilfe (Berlin, 1976); H. Winter, Institutionalisierung, Methoden und Umfang der Integration im RGW (Stuttgart, 1976); Handbuch der DDR-Wirtschaft (Hamburg, 1977), pp. 272-88; P. M. Alampijew, O. T. Bogomolow, J. S. Schirjajew, Ökonomische Integration--objektives Erfordernis der Entwicklung des Weltsozialismus (East Berlin, 1973), translated from Russian; W. Bröll, Comecon (Munich, 1975); Sozialistische ökonomische Integration (East Berlin, 1977); Wörterbuch der Okonomie--Sozialismus (East Berlin, 1973); Wörterbuch zum sozialistischen Staat (East Berlin, 1974); and Bol'shaya sovetskaya entsiklopediya (Moscow, 1972), volume 10.

13. Alampijew, Ökonomische Integration, p. 42.

14. Bethkenhagen and Machowski, Integration im Rat für gegenseitige Wirtschaftshilfe, p. 23.

15. Among them are grain, meat, milk, eggs, wool, oil plants, cotton, vegetables, fruit, grapes, and presumably processed products.

16. Forecasts have been made for approximately thirty-five products, including grain, oil plants, cotton, vegetables, fruit, grapes, meat, milk, eggs, and wool.

17. A Bulgarian statement notes that "the new perspective forms of cooperation...joint planning, have not yet been realized." See Internationale Zeitschrift der Landwirtschaft, no. 2 (1978).

18. CMEA trade in agricultural products increased more than twofold between 1971 and 1975 over previous levels. Approximately 55 percent of these exports and more than 40 percent of the imports are part of the intra-CMEA trade. See ibid.

19. Most of this trade is in slaughter cattle, animals, meat specialties, and draught beer.

20. See I. Kravoca, "Domestic and International Integration in the Agriculture of the CMEA countries (in Russian)," Nauchnye trudy Moskovskogo instituta inzhenerov zemloistroistva, Vyp. 66 (Moscow, 1973), pp. 179-88.

21. Neuer Weg (Bucharest) no. 8742 (24 June 1977).

22. Ekonomika sel'skogo khozyaistva, no. 5 (1974) pp. 112-15. See also the explanation of the Mongolian People's Republic's head of government, Zh. Batmunch, at the thirtieth council meeting of the CMEA in 1976, in Ekonomicheskoe sotrudnichestvo stran-chlenov SEV, no. 4 (1976) p. 25.

23. See, for example, Problemy razitiya sel'skogo khozyaistva sotsialitsenkik stran Evropy (Moscow, 1973), p. 195, and Nauchnye trudy Moskovskogo instituta inzhenerov zemloistroistva, Vyp. 66, p. 187.

24. *Otraslevaya sotsialisticheskaya integratsia* (Moscow, 1976), p. 266. Self-sufficiency refers to full provision of the "so called scientifically substantiated norms of consumption for food." The percentages refer to the CMEA level of production in the mid-1970s.

12
The Impact of Agro-Industrial Programs on East European Agriculture

Everett M. Jacobs

Attempts to achieve the concentration and specialization of agricultural production in Eastern Europe have been hindered by a number of factors. Even though amalgamations created cooperative and state farms that were large by West European standards, these farms often lacked the capital, material resources, and labor resources to make large-scale agricultural production projects feasible. Moreover, most farms were prevented from specializing because of their more or less compulsory contractual obligation to deliver a wide range of products to procurement agencies. For example, until the full-scale introduction of agro-industrial complexes (APKs), most Bulgarian cooperative farms were producing between fifty and sixty different crops and several different kinds of farm animals. The most typical attempts to solve these problems involved the merger of farms into larger production units, increases in prices paid to farms (in the hope that they would then operate profitably and be able to accumulate investment capital), and offers of certain credits for the construction of new facilities. However, these efforts usually did not encourage specialization, nor did they lead to the desired concentration of production, since financial, technical, and labor resources and management techniques were still inadequate. The different forms of agricultural integration introduced in Bulgaria, Czechoslovakia, East Germany, Hungary, and Romania in recent years have been designed to circumvent these problems.

In general terms, horizontal integration implies greater financial and economic cooperation and coordination between farms in production work and product specialization. Farms operating under similar conditions are brought together in some form of association or complex, which then becomes integrated within itself. Some types of association or complex will process, as well as produce, a given agricultural product, but in horizontal integration schemes, there is no integration between the association or complex and related industrial processing enterprises or sales organizations. By contrast, in vertical integration schemes, the already integrated agricultural sector becomes fully integrated with the industrial sector relating to it so that the whole economic process, from producing the primary product to selling the final product, is the responsibility of a single corporate unit. The eventual goal of vertical integration is to make agriculture into a branch of the food industry and light industry.[3]

HORIZONTAL INTEGRATION

Horizontal integration of agriculture has proceeded farthest in Bulgaria, through the institution of the agro-industrial complex (APK), which is supposed to introduce industrial methods and technology to farming. Bulgaria is the only communist country to have introduced horizontal integration on a national scale. The decision in April 1970 to make APK into the basic economic and social unit in the countryside[4] all but negated the significance of individual cooperative and state farms. APKs unite neighboring cooperative farms, state farms, or both kinds of farms. In the first stage, the constituent farms retain much of their former independence. However, as production specialization in the APK develops, responsibilities are transferred to the APK management, which eventually assumes full legal and economic control over all member farms of the complex.[5] When an APK becomes "unified" in this way, the component farms lose their autonomy and become branch or subfarms of the APK with their own production specialization. Production management changes from a territorial to a specialized branch basis, and a number of directorates (e.g. for livestock, crops, mechanization, agrochemical matters, and economic affairs) are established to oversee things. Under each directorate are a number of specialized branches in charge of one line of production, such as grain, vegetables, fruits, different types or groups of livestock products, and so forth. Unification of an APK is not supposed to occur until a certain level of concentration and specialization of production has been attained, and the level of labor remuneration among the member farms has been equalized.[6] Some opposition has been expressed against the abolition of independent farms in APK unification schemes, on the grounds that the preconditions for unification have not been fulfilled.[7] Nevertheless, by the end of 1975, eighty-three APKs, or more than half the total, had become unified.[8] It was planned to unify the remaining APKs by 1980,[9] but this task seems to have been accomplished for the most part by mid-1978,[10] by which time a reorganization of APKs had begun (see below).

238

Before the reorganization, each APK was composed on average of five or six formerly independent cooperative and/or state farms, and had more than 24,000 ha of cultivated land, around 5,835 permanent workers, more than 660 15-h.p. tractor units, and basic funds totalling around 28.5 million leva (all data for the end of 1976).[11] Some complexes were much larger than average (with up to 100,000 ha and more of cultivated land), but some were considerably smaller than average (at the end of 1976, twenty-four of the then 146 APKs had less than 12,000 ha of cultivated land, and thirty-three had between 12,000 and 20,000 ha).[12] It is interesting to note that although the average size of APKs increased somewhat between 1975 and 1976 through mergers of APKs and the redistribution of land, there was a noticeable decrease in the number of the largest APKs with over 36,000 ha of cultivated land (from twenty-five, to nineteen),[13] apparently reflecting a desire to operate APKs of more manageable sizes. By mid-1977, the number of APKs had fallen further to 144,[14] from a high point of 170 in 1972. Each district originally had between five and seven APKs within its borders,[15] but by mid-1977, the range had dropped to between four and six.

Under the APK system, the emphasis has been on creating relatively large production units within the complexes. In an APK, the broundaries separating individual farms and fields sown with different crops are abolished, and very large fields, called "massives," sown to a single crop are created. The complexes concentrate production on four of five main crops, plus several additional crops,[16] and usually limit themselves to only one branch of livestock production.[17] Before the establishment of APKs, grain was grown in Bulgaria in more than 45,000 fields, each with an average area of 40 ha. In 1976 the size of grain fields ranged from 200 to 1,000 ha. Up to 1970, vegetable crops were grown in 17,000 fields, but in 1976, production in the socialist sector of the APKs was concentrated on basically 260 fields, averaging 315 ha each.[18] Fruit and grape plantations now have from 1,000 to 2,500 ha, and concentration is evident also in the production of sugar beets, rice, cotton,[19] maize, sunflower seed, tobacco, and other crops.[20]

In connection with production specialization, plans for 1980 called for 60 percent of Bulgaria's wheat to be produced in ten out of the country's twenty-seven districts; 56 percent of the sunflowers in eight districts; 65 percent of the pigs in ten districts; and 80 percent of the chickens in thirteen. Maize production on nonirrigated land was to be concentrated in northern Bulgaria, and on irrigated land, in southern Bulgaria.[21] Under plans for regional specialization in livestock production, only cattle were to be raised throughout the country, although production methods were supposed to be geared to local conditions. Other livestock enterprises were to be limited to the best-suited areas, where needed grains and oilseeds could be produced also.[22] Livestock enterprises

were supposed to be located to minimize transport costs either
from the source of fodder supplies or to the market. In
particular, milk production was to be concentrated around
large cities.[23] Under this program, by 1978 some fourteen
APKs concentrating on poultry production put through an
average of three million broilers each, eleven APKs
concentrating on egg production had an average of 160,000 hens
each, twenty-four hog-fattening APKs put through an average of
44,000 animals each, forty-eight milk APKs had an average or
more than 500 cows each, and there were sixteen APKs
specializing in calf fattening.[24]

For a long time such large-scale enterprises reflected the
dominant trend in APK development. For example, the huge
Silistra APK, established in February 1976 for grain and
livestock production and the production and processing of
fruit and vegetables, covered almost all the land of the
district (153,000 ha out of 173,000).[25] However, as noted, a
contrary trend involving the splitting of the largest APKs
became apparent in 1976, and this trend eventually culminated
in a reorganization of APKs beginning in early 1978. At that
time, the country's 27 districts were subdivided into "systems
of inhabited places," which totalled 283 by the end of the
year. These systems became responsible for socioeconomic and
administrative matters, and the territories of the APKs were
to be changed, through splitting, to coincide with system
boundaries.[26] By May 1978, 23 new APKs had been created in
this way, and the total reached 170,[27] leaving a further 113
APKs still to be organized. At the end of the reorganization,
the average size of an APK will probably have fallen by almost
50 percent from the level at the end of 1976 to about 12,500
ha of cultivated land. Even at that size, they will still
probably be among the largest farms in the communist world.

Before the reorganization, the system suffered from
current planning inflexibility at the level of the APK, a
relatively low level of labor productivity as compared with
other communist countries, high production costs (caused by
high transport costs and the necessity of equalizing labor
remuneration among the member farms), the wide range of
natural conditions encountered in one APK, and the general
disadvantages of bigness.[28] On one hand, at times there were
problems of overspecialization, making it difficult for some
APKs to react efficiently to climate and market variations,
while on the other hand, most APKs were criticized for failing
to stress sufficiently the specialization and concentration of
production and the introduction of industrial technologies
when switching to the specialized branch structure of
farming.[29]

The new system, by reducing the size of individual APKs,
was designed to strengthen direct management of the production
units within the APK through so-called "two-level management."
Under this, brigades, breeding farms, and shops are in most
cases supposed to be supervised directly by the complex.

240

"Three-level management," in which productional sectors or branch farms (both of which are subdivisions of the complex) supervise brigades, breeding farms, and shops, is to be allowed only in exceptional cases.[30] However, reports indicate that local leaders have been reluctant to change to the new organization of production, and this has elicited threats to impose the system on them if they persist in noncompliance.[31] To introduce more flexibility in planning by the complexes, control figures have been reduced to four main items: obligatory sales (limited to no more than eight products) at fixed prices to procurement bodies; payment into the state budget, in the form of taxes based on total agricultural land, excluding personal plots; currency income from exports, and currency limits for imports; and limits for the supply of the basic kinds of machinery and equipment, raw materials, fuel, and power. Moreover, APKs now have the opportunity to negotiate prices with procurement bodies for sales outside or above the Plan.[32] APKs are free now to develop their own Plans from the control figures, determining the crop structure, number of livestock, average yields, average wages, and so forth. In keeping with the changes, the Ministry of Agriculture and the Food Industry has been abolished because of its "excessive interference" in the work of the APKs, but its functions have been taken over by a National Agro-Industrial Union.[33]

Even though the decision-making powers of the APKs seem to have increased as a result of the reform, it is apparent that a considerable amount of central control is still exerted over the complexes. The role of the "systems of inhabited places" in overseeing the operations of the APKs is not yet clear, but it is quite possible that in practice they will limit what planning flexibility has been granted to APKs. Although the size of the APKs is being reduced, the complexes are still very large, and undoubtedly will continue to suffer from many of the problems of scale obvious before the reform. At the same time, the reform appears to do little to foster the specialization and concentration of production, which was one of the original tasks of the APKs. Last, it is by no means certain that the Bulgarian system of horizontal integration will accomplish one of its main aims, that of improving relations between the farm, the suppliers of its inputs, and the processors of its outputs. All the same, the Bulgarian experiment is of obvious interest to the other communist countries.

Next to Bulgaria, horizontal integration of agriculture is now farthest advanced in East Germany, which recently overtook Romania in this respect.[34] East Germany had made considerable progress in the concentration and specialization of agricultural production in the period up to the end of 1975 on the basis of cooperative farms (LPGs) and state farms (VEGs) which were relatively small by communist standards. For instance, at the end of 1975, Type III LPGs (similar to Soviet

241

kolkhozes) averaged 1,180 ha of agricultural land, and VEGs were even smaller, covering on average 1,023 ha. However, since 1971 the development of interfarm cooperation associations (KAPs) for both crop and livestock production had helped to foster large-scale specialized farming. In KAPs, the member LPGs and VEGs retained their economic independence but pooled their land and financial, material, and labor resources. By the end of 1975, some 1,210 KAPs for crop production covered more than 84 percent of the country's agricultural land, and averaged 4,130 ha each.[35] The creation of KAPs made it profitable to purchase modern technology and systems of machines for crop production, which the KAP's members could share.

By the end of 1977, East Germany also had 334 interfarm cooperation associations (ZBEs) for livestock production (against 394 at the end of 1975), concentrating on milk production, hog and cattle fattening, heifer rearing, and poultry and egg production.[36] The state gave substantial financial incentives to encourage the construction of large-scale livestock complexes operating on an industrial basis.[37]

Moves to foster horizontal integration of agriculture greatly accelerated in East Germany after mid-1975. Upgrading the remaining Type I and II LPGs into Type III LPGs was completed in 1976, and the organization of Type III LPGs themselves was affected by major changes in that year. In increasing numbers, new specialized crop-growing LPGs were created on the basis of crop-farming KAPs, leading to the demise of those KAPs and their constituent VEGs and old-stype LPGs. The specialized crop-growing LPGs concentrate mainly on grain, sugar beet, and potato production, and emphasize the use of advanced technology. Also, new livestock LPGs, usually with "broad" or "multi-branch" (in contrast to "narrow") specialization were set up, mainly on the basis of the livestock sector of the old LPGs. Development of narrowly specialized livestock LPGs and VEGs has been held back by insufficient capital investment (there were only seven such LPGs and twenty-nine such VEGs in 1977),[38] but the intention is to establish these universally by 1990.

The number of specialized crop-farming LPGs rose from 47 at the end of 1975 to 161 in 1976 and 329 in 1977. They covered about 1,700,000 ha of agricultural land in 1977, for an average of 5,178 ha per LPG. As a result of the creation of specialized crop-growing LPGs and also the effects of KAP amalgamations, the number of crop-growing KAPs fell to 833 at the end of 1977, averaging 4,667 ha of agricultural land each (which was somewhat larger than two years earlier). Also, the conversion of crop-growing KAPs into specialized crop-growing LPGs has resulted in a considerable loss of agricultural land from the state farm sector (down from about 474,000 ha at the end of 1975, to about 187,500 ha at the end of 1977). Such a transfer of land from the state to the cooperative sector is extremely rare in communist agriculture, but it is in keeping with the increasing livestock specialization of East Germany's VEGs. Only about one-quarter of the VEGs now concentrate on crop production, and they are being enlarged to some extent by the transfer of land from the KAPs. The other 330 or so VEGs concentrate on livestock production, and this is reflected in the average size of East Germany's VEGs (446 ha of agricultural land at the end of 1977), which are by far the smallest state farms in the communist world.

The number of livestock LPGs stood at 3,421 at the end of 1976, but through amalgamations fell to 3,165 a year later. These livestock LPGs have very little land, totalling about 112,000 ha at the end of 1977, or about 35 ha per LPG.[39] Specialized livestock LPGs and VEGs are now developing poultry, pork, and beef production on an industrial basis, but they have as yet had little impact on livestock marketings.[40]

It can be expected that the number of specialized crop LPGs will continue to grow at the expense of KAPs as specialization progresses. It also appears that the development of livestock LPGs is receiving more emphasis than the expansion of ZBEs for livestock production. It is unclear what effect the above changes will have on future East German developments in agricultural integration. Certainly, the KAPs and ZBEs succeeded in fostering considerable concentration and specialization of agriculture before the reorganization. For example, in the socialist sector in 1976, some 39 KAPs produced 44 percent of the grain, and 27 produced 88 percent of the sugar beets. Among ZBEs, 108 specializing in meat production accounted for 60 percent of the pork and 15 percent of the beef, and 90 produced 56 percent of the milk.[41] However, the new arrangements for LPGs seem to have made the old-style KAPs and ZBEs largely redundant.

Because most livestock LPGs have little or no farm land, there is an obvious need to ensure the efficient integration of the crop and livestock sectors. Two solutions to this task have merged. The first is the creation of a very large agricultural association, such as the one operating in Neubrandenburg county. The association has been set up by two LPGs, one concentrating in crop production, and the other in livestock production. These LPGs themselves were created through the amalgamation of ten multi-branch and two old-style specialized LPGs. The new specialized crop-growing LPG has about 5,000 ha of land, of which about 4,000 ha are arable. It produces seed potatoes (550 ha), grasses for seed (200 ha), sugar beets (350 ha), rape (300 ha), and grain (1,000 ha), with the rest of the land devoted to fodder crops. This LPG is a member of the district's agrochemical center (there were 372 in East Germany in 1976), from which it receives its mineral fertilizer, plant protection agents, machinery for mixing and spreading fertilizers, and so forth. The livestock LPG has 2,500 head of cattle (including 1,200 cows) and 4,500 pigs, and appears to have little or no land attached to it. The crop LPG's output of fodder crops is processed in a joint

enterprise, for use by the livestock LPG.   The latter rears
suckling pigs for fattening in an interfarm enterprise, and
the LPGs have also established interfarm enterprises for the
fattening of beef animals and for rearing pedigree pigs.[42]

The   second   new   solution   to   integrate   the   crop   and
livestock sectors in East Germany has been the creation of
agro-industrial   complexes,   along   the lines of the Bulgarian
model.   These   complexes   unite   specialized   KAPs   and   ZBEs,
rather   than   individual   farms,   and   thus   the scale of their
operations   is   exceptionally   large.   For   example,   the
"Fehrbellin"   agro-industrial   complex   in Potsdam county is
composed of one KAP and one ZBE.   The KAP for crop production
encompasses three LPGs and one VEG, and covers about 25,000 ha
of land.   The livestock ZBE is composed of three livestock
LPGs   and   two   livestock VEGs, and has 29,000 head of cattle.
The agro-industrial complex also has an interfarm enterprise
for fattening cattle, a milk complex with 2,000 cows under one
roof,   an   agrochemical   center,   and   a modern factory for
producing   fodder   granules   (pellets).[43]   There is as yet no
clear indication whether the trend in East Germany will be to
develop   large   agricultural   associations   or agro-industrial
complexes to achieve integration of the crop and livestock
sectors.   However,   if   the   agro-industrial   complexes prove
successful, it is likely that they will be adopted, as in
Bulgaria,   in   preference   to   the   smaller   agricultural
associations.

In   the   past, the relatively small size of East German
farms   and   interfarm   cooperation   associations   helped   to
maintain a degree of flexibility in the system.   However, the
new developments have given increased importance to contract
relations between farms and to the role of government agencies
in coordinating and confirming the Plans of the farms, the
various types of cooperation associations, and agro-industrial
complexes.   As a result, it appears that the autonomy of these
units,   and   the   flexibility   of   the   system,   have   been
significantly reduced by the recent changes.

In   Romania,   horizontal   integration   of   agriculture
proceeded mainly through Inter-Cooperative Associations until
the   introduction   of   changes   at the beginning of 1979.   The
Inter-Cooperative   Associations   engaged   in   specialized
production   activities,   and fell into three basic types.   One
type was devoted to the production of agricultural products
including,   among   other   things,   livestock   breeding   and
fattening; milk production; egg and poultry production; fish
farming;   and   the hothouse production of vegetables.   Another
type concentrated on the processing, storage, and sale of
agricultural produce.   The last type dealt with the provision
of joint production services, including the production of
construction   materials.[44]   The   number   of associations grew
continually, despite the dissolution of a certain number over
the years.[45]   There were 254 Inter-Cooperative Associations in
Romania at the start of 1971,[46] and 412 at the beginning of

February 1973.[47] At the end of 1973, there were 463 Associations, of which (with some duplication) 70 were for crop production, 335 were for animal breeding, 66 produced some type of fodder, and 56 had other specializations. Some of these undertakings have been very large, as seen from the "optimum" sizes specified in 1974 for Inter-Cooperative Associations specializing in livestock production: for hog-fattening, 15,000-30,000 hogs; cattle fattening, 2,700 head (maximum); sheep fattening, 15,000 head; poultry, 600,000 broilers; and eggs, 36,000 hens.[48] In 1973, the agricultural production of Inter-Cooperative Associations represented about 10 to 12 percent of the value from the cooperative sector.[49]

An Inter-Cooperative Association usually has had four or five cooperative farms as members, but some, depending on the character of the activities, have involved fifty or sixty, or even a hundred farms, sometimes 100 to 150 km or more apart.[50] The larger associations have been set up usually to create poultry-breeding or pig-breeding enterprises, calf-fattening combines, or mixed-fodder factories.[51] Some cooperative farms are members of five or six associations.[52] Members of an association retain their formal economic and legal independence, but must contribute cash and equipment to the association's enterprise fund to ensure fixed assets and necessary operating capital. The associations receive fixed prices for agricultural sales to the state in accordance with their production Plans, but they can sell above-Plan produce directly on the open market. Up to 70 percent of any profit made by the association is distributed among the members according to their contribution to the association's activities, while the remaining profit goes into various funds. Inter-Cooperative Councils, covering the territory of one or more communes, have been responsible for drawing up and ensuring the fulfillment of production and financial plans of associations and cooperative farms in their area,[53] and this practice has severely curtailed the autonomy of the Inter-Cooperative Associations, their member farms, and other cooperatives in the area.

Horizontal integration of agriculture in Romania has developed also through mixed cooperation associations of cooperative farms and either state farms, state industrial enterprises, or consumer cooperatives within the area covered by one Inter-Cooperative Council. Objects of cooperation include the creation of new production facilities, storehouses, and processing and servicing facilities. Members of mixed cooperation associations retain their formal economic and legal independence, and cooperation is organized on the basis of the production and financial Plans of member units. The actual autonomy of the mixed cooperation association or its members (as in the case of the Inter-Cooperative Associations) has been strictly limited by the overseeing role of the Inter-Cooperative Council, in addition to supervision by state farm bodies (if the mixed association includes a state farm), industrial ministries (if the association includes a state industrial enterprise), or consumer cooperative bodies (if it includes a consumer cooperative). After deductions for the bonus fund and the payment of income tax, 55 percent of the profit is distributed to the association's members, and the rest goes into various funds.[54] It seems that the incentive for cooperative farms to join mixed cooperation associations has been blunted by the less favorable distribution of profits and greater degree of administrative interference when compared with membership in Inter-Cooperative Associations.

Although horizontal integration schemes have been introduced fairly extensively in Romanian agriculture, their operation has been somewhat unsatisfactory. The trend for Inter-Cooperative Associations to involve more and more farms quite distant from each other, and for farms to be members of several associations, apparently has weakened the objects of deep concentration and specialization. Romanian planners have been concerned that farms have not taken much interest in joint enterprises located far away, that their production interests have been diverted in too many directions at once, and that their investments have not been used to best advantage.[55] Also, doubts have been expressed about the large size of some of the associations, especially since it appears that farms join the associations less because of economic interests than because of pressure from above. Cooperatives are said to have reservations about the associations because they have tended to lose money. Since the associations are not legal persons, member cooperatives have been required to cover the losses instead of receiving additional income from the new activity.[56] Another problem has been that the large Inter-Cooperative Associations cut across the boundaries of several local Inter-Cooperative Councils, that have been responsible for overseeing the activities and development of the associations. In such cases, county Inter-Cooperative Councils, charged with working out, supervising, and checking the fulfillment of the county's overall agricultural Plan, have been responsible for coordinating the work of the local councils and exercising supervision over the activities of the Inter-Cooperative Associations.

The failure of Romanian agriculture to fulfill production Plans in recent years has brought increasing direct and indirect criticism of the integration schemes on the grounds that specialization and concentration of production have proceeded neither far enough nor fast enough. In an effort to improve the performance and integration of agriculture, in February 1979 the party's Central Committee approved the creation of 709 "unitary state and cooperative agro-industrial councils," covering on average from 15,000 to 20,000 ha of agricultural land. The councils now have responsibility for overall planning and production management of state and cooperative farms, stations for agricultural mechanization,

Inter-Cooperative Associations, mixed cooperation associations, and so on in their area. The councils are charged with establishing unitary management and "ever fuller integration" in the production activities of the subordinate agricultural units (which retain formal administrative autonomy over their own revenue and expenditure budgets, and are responsible for fulfilling their planned tasks). Among their duties, the new councils must secure fulfillment of the Plan it receives from the county general directorate of agriculture; ensure efficient use of land (regardless of whether it is in the cooperative or state sector), fertilizers, manpower, and material and financial resources; and also achieve the economic consolidation of each agricultural unit.[57]

It is not yet clear how the integration of production and economic activities of cooperative and state units is to be achieved, or how joint actions for the use of financial means and manpower will be carried out. The number of cooperative farms has been relatively stable in recent years (there were 4,418 at the end of 1976), but a sharp decrease in numbers through mergers is likely in order to create supposedly more-efficient farming units. The merger of cooperative and state farms into a new kind of unit appears not to have begun yet, but this development seems likely, perhaps following the example of the Bulgarian APKs. The creation of unitary agro-industrial councils in Romania seems to make the Inter-Cooperative Councils largely superfluous, and leaves the continued existence of the Inter-Cooperative Associations in their present form very much in doubt. It appears that the February 1979 reforms are only part of an ongoing program to try to increase the efficiency and integration of Romanian agriculture, and further changes can be expected in the near future.

The Hungarians have tried to use the amalgamation of farms as one method to achieve the concentration and specialization of production. A vigorous campaign from 1972 through 1975 reduced the number of cooperative farms from 2,321 to 1,599 at the end of 1975. The number fell further to 1,425 at the end of 1977, at which time each farm averaged 3,624 ha of agricultural land.[58] However, it has been found in Hungarian conditions that the value of output per hectare does not grow with farm size, and production cost per unit does not decline accordingly. The enlargement of farm enterprises has not led to improved efficiency,[59] nor on its own has it benefited production concentration or specialization. For those reasons, and because of problems in the coordination of activities and the excessive size of some farms, criticism of further mergers began to appear in 1975.[60] The approval of the Ministry of Agriculture and Food has been necessary for new mergers to proceed since October 1975, and a further order in March 1978 established that new mergers should be implemented only in "exceptional cases."[61] However, these obstacles apparently have not curbed the mergers, since middle-level party and administrative officials desire them as a means of "eliminating" weak farms and also gaining prestige for themselves.[62]

Where Hungary has been able to move forward in the concentration and specialization of production has been with the introduction of the Closed Production System(CPS). The CPS is a form of horizontal integration designed to apply comprehensively in Hungary advanced techniques and industrial methods (encompassing, for example, seeds, fertilizers, plant protection agents, breeding stock, machinery, and technology) to the production, and sometimes also the processing, of certain agricultural products. In 1974, there were sixty-one such production systems in operation in Hungary, fifteen for crops (particularly maize, wheat, sugar beets[63] and sunflowers), and forty-six for livestock production. In 1977 some 67 systems operated, involving 117 out of a total of 141 state farms, and 1,116 out of a total of 1,425 cooperative farms. The CPS was used on one-third of Hungary's arable land, and 40 percent of all dairy farms were operating under one system or other.[64] It is reported that in 1977, average crop yields on farms using the CPS exceeded those on non-CPS farms by 67 percent for potatoes, 56 percent for maize, 49 percent for sunflower seeds, and 16 percent for wheat[65] and were also considerably above average for sugar beets. In contrast to these achievements, results have been variable in the livestock sector. Poultry and egg production, particularly in the system employed by the Babolna Agricultural Combine, have usually benefited from the CPS, but the raising and fattening of hogs has met only a qualified success.[66] The introduction of new production systems is to be more gradual than in the past because many farms lack the necessary prerequisites (skilled workers, efficient management, and adequate financial reserves) to make the systems run optimally. Also, although yields and total output have improved through introducing the CPS, production costs have been high, leading to the call to use more rigorous standards in the creation and operation of the CPS.[67]

The organizer of the CPS is as a rule a large leading enterprise which through contracts unites a number of farms providing land area, production facilities, and labor force. The member farms retain their basic independence, but agree to follow the instructions of the chief enterprise regarding the CPS. It is clear that the degree of central control here is far less than in other schemes for horizontal integration. The chief enterprise provides participating farms with equipment, machinery, spare parts, seeds, fertilizers, and herbicides. The organizing farm also works out the technology of production, organizes the training of personnel, sees to technical services, and so forth. In return for this help, the beneficiary farms pay the chief enterprise a defined percentage commission from the additional harvest received by the farms after the introduction of the system. A CPS for maize production on the base of Nadudvar cooperative began in 1973, uniting 10 cooperatives with 10,500 ha of maize. In 1975 it had 234 members, and CPSs had also been introduced for sunflowers (25,000 ha), sugar beets (26,000 ha), and soya (3,000 ha), in addition to maize (125,000 ha). In 1977, the Nadudvar scheme had almost 300 members.[68] The Babolna Joint Enterprise for the Industrial Production of Maize, with 200 member farms in 1977, has a similar history.[69]

A great problem in the introduction of the CPS has been the shortage of hard currency to buy the required machinery, equipment, and other inputs from Western suppliers. Hungary has been uanble to depend on its CMEA partners, and does not produce most of the necessary machinery, or enough chemicals and fertilizers, itself. Moreover, the drain on resources caused by the recent amalgamation campaign has slowed development of CPSs. Last, the government's recent attempt to transfer an additional part of the cost of the CPSs to the farms through increased charges for fertilizers and chemical agents has inhibited the expansion, and full efficiency, of the system. Although net income tends to remain stagnant using the CPS, the great benefit is that it helps yields to increase,[70] which has enabled Hungary once again to become a net exporter of grain, particularly maize, thereby earning needed foreign currency. The American-Hungarian system used in maize production is now being marketed to other communist countries (Czechoslovakia and the USSR have recently concluded deals),[71] and so the use of this system should soon become more widespread in the communist world.

The progress of horizontal integration in East European agriculture has been slowest in Czechoslovakia. A very vigorous campaign to merge cooperative farms has occurred in recent years, and this seems to have taken some of the drive out of plans to introduce horizontal integration. The number of cooperative farms in Czechoslovakia fell from 3,619 in 1974 to 1,813 at the end of 1977, while the average size rose from 1,210 ha of agricultural land to 2,447 ha. So far, the practical results have not matched expectations. In the large merged cooperatives, control has become more difficult and there has been a trend to a relatively fast increase in production costs without a corresponding growth in efficiency.[72] Thus, the farms have received little or no benefit from the attempt to concentrate and specialize agricultural production. In November 1977, the government was forced to announce that future mergers would be carried out only after careful consideration of all circumstances,[73] indicating that the campaign may now be abating.

There are two basic forms of agricultural cooperation in Czechoslovakia: the cooperation group, where no new organization is created, and the tasks cannot be separated from the agricultural work of the farms involved; and the joint agricultural enterprise (JAE) where a new legal entity is created (although the member farms retain their economic and legal independence) to carry out an agricultural or nonagricultural activity. On 1 January 1978, there were 453 cooperation groups, each usually uniting two to four socialist farms (mainly cooperatives). As in the past, most cooperation groups deal with the joint use of machinery or with joint activities in land-dependent branches of animal husbandry. Only very rarely have [74]cooperation groups coordinated activities among themselves.[74] Moreover, very few of the groups are yet involved in much favored so-called complex cooperation in crop farming, which entails the common cultivation of fields in interconnected crop rotation schemes without respect of farm boundaries.[75] The recent wave of mergers, creating relatively large cooperative and state farms, seems to reflect the desire of farm managers to avoid the numerous complications of complex cooperation by improving conditions for narrow cooperation, for example, the joint purchase and use of machinery.

Czechoslovakia's JAEs represent a more-developed form of horizontal cooperation, and have received much more emphasis than the cooperation groups. By January 1978 cooperative or state farms, or a combination, had set up 357 active JAEs in Czechoslovakia: perhaps with some double-counting, forty-seven JAEs were involved in egg production, twenty-six in poultry production, thirty-six in suckling pig rearing, seventy in hog fattening, and forty-three in the drying and production of fodder. The remaining JAEs (136 according to these figures) dealt with construction, land improvement, and agrochemical services, but this total appears to be too low.[76] In the sphere of agricultural production, the impact of JAEs has been greatest in the livestock sector, where an extremely high proportion of their output is marketed. For example, it is reported that already in 1975, marketings accounted for 100 percent of the poultry and pork, and 98.2 percent of the eggs produced by JAEs.[77] In 1976 JAEs were responsible for 42.3 percent of the eggs, 16.7 percent of the fattened hogs, and 7.7 percent of the poultry marketed in Czechoslovakia.[78] However, farms are reluctant to join JAEs, especially where the aim is to specialize in crop farming or in land-dependent branches of animal husbandry, preferring instead to merge with another farm.[79] As a result, most of such schemes are imposed on the farms.

One of the great disincentives for farms to join JAEs was that the tax laws seemed to penalize such participation. Until the start of January 1975, taxation was based on a cooperative farm's gross income, without reference to profits, thus giving a great advantage to profitable farms. On the other hand, taxes for JAEs were based on profits. Cooperatives were faced therefore with the possibility of having to give up profitable lines to JAEs, thereby reducing the coopeative's profitability, while at the same time making it liable to higher taxes on profits for the JAE's operations.

On 1 January 1975, a new agricultural tax law was introduced, basing taxes on land values and the profit of the farm or enterprise, eliminating the previous anomaly. Moreover, in order to promote concentration and specialization, newly established JAEs, such as those breeding pigs, producing eggs, fattening cattle, and so forth, were exempted from taxes on profits for the first five years.[80] It is expected that these changes will now encourage farms to participate more readily in JAEs.

VERTICAL INTEGRATION

In terms of vertical integration of agricultural production, the East Germans appear to have progressed farther than the other East European communist countries. The East German methods for the most part entailed the establishment of so-called cooperation unions (KOVs). A KOV's membership may include LPGs, VEGs, interfarm enterprises and associations of different specializations, industrial processing enterprises, trade organizations, transport and other service enterprises, and so on. KOVs specializing in the milk and meat sector have an average of thirty participating members; in other sectors, the average membership usually ranges from fifteen to twenty.[81] The member bodies are all supposed to be equal, but in practice, the processing enterprises predominate. All the enterprises and organizations in a KOV keep their economic and juridical independence, although the combine itself is a legal entity and operates under the system of economic accountability.

All KOV members enter into contracts with each other, basing these on their centrally approved overall production Plans. The contracts generally run for two to three years, after which they are revised, and nonfulfillment imposes financial penalties and legal responsibilities on the defaulter. A joint material and financial fund is maintained by the KOV to finance joint projects.[82] KOVs have been formed for meat, milk, vegetable, fruit, and jam production and processing. There were more than 380 KOVs in East Germany in 1975, of which more than 220 were for the production and processing of livestock products and poultry, and more than 160 were for the production and processing of vegetables, potatoes, and other crops.[83]

Another form of vertical integration developed in East Germany is the agro-industrial association (AIV) for crop production. At the start of 1978, there were fourteen AIVs for crop production, each having from eight to eleven members, including usually from four to six specialized crop-growing LPGs or crop-growing VEGs, plus an agrochemical center, machine repair workshop, processing enterprises, and so on. AIVs for crop production cover up to 35,000 ha of agricultural land. The members officially retain their economic and

251

juridical independence, although the AIV has a central administrative body to implement complex planning and direct the allocation of financial and material resources.[84] It appears that the member farms have less say in their own affairs than those in KOVs, and that the degree of vertical integration is greater in AIVs than in KOVs. All the same, development of AIVs for crop production has proceeded slowly, and it is not likely that they will supplant the KOVs in plans for vertical integration in the near future.

Bulgaria now has three organizations involving vertical integration in agriculture: the Industrial-Agricultural Complex (PAK), the Scientific-Productional Association (NPO), and the Scientific-Productional Complex (NPK). PAKs, in contrast with APKs, NPOs, and NPKs, are distinguished by the predominance of an industrial enterprise in their organizational structure. Compared with APKs, the PAKs now appear to be under closer central supervision of planning and management, but this may change if and when the reform affecting the APKs is extended to them. PAKs have more concentrated capital investments than do the APKs,[85] and also they are considerably larger, having on average around 46,000 ha of cultivated land, against 24,000 for APKs at the end of 1976. The first PAKs were set up at the end of 1972 as constituents of the Bulgarian Sugar Industrial-Agricultural Association. At the end of 1976, this association encompassed eight PAKs, including seven sugar refineries and one seed farm, three enterprises for producing alcohol and yeast, twelve APKs, and several cooperative farms having significant areas of sugar beets.[86] The beets are grown in rotation with fodder crops which, together with by-products from the sugar industry, form the basis of cattle breeding on the complexes.[87] The association's land area extends over 370,600 ha, and in its integrated economy, it produces and processes the beets and packs them ready for sale (it does not market them itself).[88] Regardless of the type of farms in a PAK, the farms lose their independence to the PAK, which is classified as state property.[89]

The first NPOs were established in 1974 with the purpose of rapidly introducing industrial methods and advanced science and technology into those branches of agriculture which have a high degree of specialization and are engaged in mass production, and where international standards can be, or have been, reached[90] In September 1976, there were five NPOs in operation (for poultry production, pork production, cattle and sheep production, veterinary services, and seed and plant breeding).[91] The poultry NPO was composed of a research institute, a poultry APK, and also a poultry processing factory. This NPO not only produces and processes, but also markets its products.[92] Most NPOs deal with livestock production, while NPKs deal with crop production. It appears from reports that the NPOs have less land attached to them than the NPKs, reflecting the difference in specialization.

252

NPOs are apparently dependent to some extent on outside sources for fodder.

The emphasis in an NPK, as in an NPO, is on integrating science with industrialized production methods. The chief enterprise in both is the scientific institute, whereas it is the processing plant in the PAK. The first NPK was created for viticulture and wine production in March 1974 out of one research station, part of an existing APK (the remaining part was reorganized into a new APK), and sections of both a nearby[93] cooperative farm and a state farm. The main purpose of the NPK was supposed to be the introduction of innovations and technical improvements, with other aspects of viticulture and winemaking taking second place. A more ambitious NPK was set up at the end of 1976 for fruit and vegetable production and processing in Plovdiv. It had 37,000 ha of arable land, making it much larger than the average APK, two scientific research institutes, an institute on the canning industry, two entire APKs and part of another, a number of hothouses, and other holdings.[94] As previously, the land area of the NPK (unlike that of a PAK) did not form a contiguous unit. The application of science to production and processing was obviously important in the Plovdiv NPK, but its scale of operation indicates that it was set up not only for the experimental purposes but also as a serious economic venture. Additional NPKs now operate for maize production, viticulture, fruit and vegetables raising, and the production of attar of roses and other[95] essential oils, making six NPKs in all at the start of 1977. Plans call for the creation[96] of other NPKs for wheat, soybeans, barley, and other crops.

It is interesting to note that the development of the NPOs and NPKs has taken place at a time when production results[97] from the sugar industry PAKs have been disappointing. Moreover, NPOs and NPKs are being introduced into a number of different production spheres, unlike the PAKs. NPOs and NPKs already outnumber the PAKs, and might eventually form the basis for the further development of vertical integration in Bulgarian agriculture. However, the recent moves to reduce the average size and increase the planning autonomy of Bulgaria's APKs raise the question of whether the PAKs, NPOs, and NPKs will continue to exist as such large-scale enterprises, or whether they too will be split up or otherwise reorganized. Each PAK and NPK now extends over several "systems of inhabited places," and this may lead to planning and administrative problems. It seems certain that the problems of scale are adversely affecting Bulgaria's vertically integrated enterprises, and it is likely that changes will be introduced in the near future in an attempt to remedy this.

Vertical integration in Hungary has progressed by means of the expansion of ancillary activities of farms (often through the creation of joint or intersectoral enterprises), and through the formation of agricultural combines and agro-industrial associations. The introduction of the New Economic Mechanism to agriculture in 1968 encouraged farms to develop ancillary enterprises. In 1973 nonagricultural activity contributed 21.2 percent of cooperative farm income, almost half of which (9.8 percent) was from industrial activity. In 1976, 22.7 percent of the income of Hungary's agricultural sector was derived from nonagricultural activity.[98] However, the practice of cooperative farms engaging in purely industrial activity has been greatly curtailed, after it was found that some cooperatives had constructed airfields, operated printing works, and carried out[99] other projects unconnected with agricultural activities. Nevertheless, some complaints have been quite unfounded, as when one industrial producer tried to stop cooperatives from fermenting their own cabbage crops.[100]

In an effort to maximize resources to achieve vertical integration, joint or intersectoral enterprises have been set up. These combine cooperative farms, and sometimes cooperative farms and state enterprises, under the rules relating to economic associations. In 1974 Hungary had 515 joint enterprises involving cooperative farms, of which 265 were independent enterprises.[101] However, about 80 percent of these enterprises involved only cooperative farms, and were not truly speaking intersectoral enterprises.[102] Most of the associations dealt with construction and marketing, and only 15 percent were in any way agricultural.[103] In 1977 there were approximately 300 independent joint enterprises, with an average of twelve members each, concentrating mainly on construction work, agricultural services, and also wine production and milk and meat processing.[104]

A number of problems have hindered the development of joint enterprises. First, many Hungarian cooperatives lack sufficient capital to participate in such schemes. Second, state industrial enterprises and agricultural processing enterprises have fought to maintain their monopolistic position by opposing the too-rapid expansion of joint or intersectoral enterprises. For example, the Milk Industry Trust tried unsuccessfully, to prohibit the marketing of dairy products produced by intersectoral cooperative-state associations.[105] Last, cooperatives are disinclined to enter into intersectoral enterprises because such bodies come under tax laws, and also requirements for the creation of enterprise funds, which relate to state enterprises and these regulations are disadvantageous to cooperatives.[106] For their part, some directors of state enterprises fear that state funds will be dissipated in enterprises involving cooperatives. Faced with these obstacles, cooperative farms have tended to establish their own processing plants and other ancillary industrial activities,[107] thus hindering progress in what appears to be a more-efficient method of vertical integration.

Agricultural combines have been formed in Hungary by the merger of large, previously independent, vertically integrated units (such as state farms already performing many ancillary activities) under a single management.[108] An interesting feature of combines is that they usually have some degree of export orientation. For example, the Tokaj Wine Combine operates as an independent enterprise, subject only to the direct supervision of the Ministry of Agriculture and Food.[109] It processes its own grapes (about 40 percent of the total it processes) and purchases the production of nearby cooperative farms and cooperative farm members. The Tokaj Combine sells its wine through the usual wholesale, retail, and export channels, but also has its own network of shops for the sale of wine and grapes.[110] The Babolna state farm has developed into the Babolna Agricultural Combine, specializing in maize production through the CPS method, and the production and sale, including export, of poultry and eggs. Recent speeches and articles indicate that the likely future trend in production systems is in the direction of vertical integration, in which farms, processing enterprises, and marketing organizations participate.[111]

The most recent, and as yet not widespread, form of vertical integration in Hungary is the agro-industrial association. This is a large-scale enterprise in which cooperative and state farms and state food-industry enterprises retain their formal independence (in contrast to members of agricultural combines), but, through contracts and agreements, coordinate their development plans and concentrate their investments and fixed assets on particular activities. Under the regulations governing such associations, the cooperative and state enterprises contribute to the association from their development funds, and share in the profits in accordance with their investments. The association's operating costs are supposed to be covered by income, and part of the association's profits goes towards a social and cultural fund. Should a member decide to leave the association, the regulations provide that only the financial equivalent of the property and funds contributed at the start will be returned.[112] A chief virtue of this form of enterprise is that it allows the selective enlargement, or reduction, in the scale of activities, with consequent opportunities to improve efficiency.

The first Hungarian agro-industrial association was organized in Nadudvar in April 1976. The association, which showed similarities to the East German KOV, combined on a contractual basis fourteen cooperative farms, one state farm, and the Debrecen Poultry Processing Enterprise.[113] The Sziegetkoz Agro-Industrial Association links ten cooperative farms, one state farm, and six state food-processing enterprises, and covers 48,000 ha of land. Its main purpose is to expand the county's cattle breeding and vegetable

255

production.[114] Some associations appear to market, as well as process, what they produce. It is likely that increasing emphasis will be placed on building up agro-industrial associations in Hungary in the next few years, especially since they appear to bypass so many of the problems found in the old form of intersectoral enterprise.

In Romania, the Inter-Cooperative Councils received new powers at the end of 1976 to encourage the vertical integration of agriculture. The local councils were to stimulate the development of a wide range of industrial and processing activities linking farms closely with industrial enterprises and processing units run by consumer cooperatives in the area. The councils also were called upon to set up units for storing and partially processing vegetables, fruits, and other products. Where conditions were suitable, bakeries, butcher shops, milk and meat processing units, and so forth were to be established under local Inter-Cooperative Council auspices.[115] However, the organizational changes introduced in Romanian agriculture in February 1979 seem to remove responsibility for developing vertical integration from the Inter-Cooperative Councils, putting it into the hands of the newly organized "unitary state and cooperative agro-industrial councils." The February 1979 Central Committee Plenum decided to make the centrals for the industrialization of meat, for milk industrialization, for the production and industrialization of sugar beets, for edible oil, etc. subordinate to a new Department for the Industrialization of Farm Products within the Ministry of Agriculture and the Food Industry. Among other things, the department has responsibility for developing new industrial units for processing agricultural raw materials within the framework of the unitary state and cooperative agro-industrial councils,[116] which seems to be the future method for proceeding with vertical integration in Romanian agriculture. However, given the problems the Romanians have had with introducing horizontal integration, it is unlikely that much progress will be made with vertical integration for several years to come. The same is true in Czechoslovakia, where vertical integration of agriculture has made no progress to date.[117]

CONCLUSIONS

It is clear that the organizational frameworks for agricultural integration in Eastern Europe are now undergoing a number of far-reaching changes, motivated to a great extent by the past failure of the integration schemes to produce the expected results. It seems from the direction of the changes that the "lessons" learned by the planners in the various countries have been somewhat contradictory. For example, in Bulgaria, there is now an obvious attempt to bring the APKs down to more manageable sizes (although they remain quite large) and to introduce a noticeable degree of decentralized planning and decision making. By contrast, East Germany and Romania seem to be moving closer to the unrevised Bulgarian model of horizontal integration, creating ever-larger production complexes, with extremely limited planning and economic autonomy.

The Hungarian approach to horizontal integration, through the CPS, seems to be the most successful to date in creating large production units while maintaining a degree of flexibility and autonomy in the operation of the unit's members. However, Hungary's improved yields and output results have been achieved at the expense of significant costly imports of technology from the West and generally high production costs, conditions which the other communist countries are trying hard to avoid. Czechoslovakia has proceeded the most slowly in horizontal integration of agriculture, and has made no headway with vertical integration, seemingly because, as in Bulgaria and Hungary, it was found that production costs in these schemes were increasing quickly, without a corresponding growth in efficiency.

Experience has shown that large production units in communist agriculture cannot on their own guarantee successful concentration and specialization of production. It appears that in many East European schemes, the prospects of the economies of scale and the benefits of integration have caused some disregard for the visible diseconomies of scale and the uneven production results of integration schemes. To be effective, integration plans must be accompanied by other measures, particularly by adequate investments in new machinery and technology, and in fertilizers, plant protection agents, breeding stock, veterinary services, storage facilities, and so forth. Also, sufficient numbers of trained personnel must be available. There must be adequate financial incentives (to production units and farmers) to favor integration and, especially for vertical integration, industrial enterprises must be willing to participate in the schemes. The links between the crop and livestock sectors must be reliable, and even specialized farms should have some flexibility in responding to changes in climatic or market conditions. Many of these conditions are at present absent from the East European integration schemes, and to that extent, we can expect that the overall results from the schemes will continue to fall below the originators' anticipations and the economic requirements of the East European countries.

It is of course possible to impose integration plans on farms and enterprises before conditions are suitable, as is being done in some of the countries under discussion. However, this is likely to lead to a waste of resources without achieving the expected benefits. The task then for the East European countries implementing agricultural

257

integration is not only to choose systems most suitable for their conditions, but also to improve the overall efficiency of agricultural production within the organizational framework chosen. The latter task undoubtedly will prove more difficult to accomplish in the foreseeable future.

NOTES

The author gratefully acknowledges the financial support received from the Knoop Economics Research Fund of the University of Sheffield in this research.
1. Voprosy ekonomiki, no. 5, (1972), p. 148.
2. Poland and Yugoslavia have been omitted from this study because of the relatively minor role of the socialist sector of agriculture in these countries; Albania, because of lack of information.
3. Ekonomika sel'skogo khozyaistva, no. 3, (1973), p. 116.
4. U. S., Congress, Joint Economic Committee, "The Bulgarian Economy in the 1970s" by Mark Allen in East European Economies Post-Helsinki (Washington, D.C.; Government Printing Office, 1977), p. 676.
5. Paul Wiedemann, "The Organisation of Bulgarian Agriculture," a study forming part of the Ford Foundation Research Project on "The Organization and Comparative Efficiency of Soviet and East European Agriculture," Glasgow, 1976, (mimeographed), p. 19.
6. V. Araf'ev and I. Karpenko, "Spetsializatsia v ramkakh sotsialisticheskoe integratsii," Ekonomika sel'skogo khozyaistva, no. 3 (1977), p. 109.
7. See Allen, "Bulgarian Economy," p. 677.
8. Novo Vreme, no. 2 (1976), p. 48.
9. Allen, "Bulgarian Economy," p. 677.
10. In May 1978, only 22 out of the total of 170 APKs were not yet "unified" (Rabotnichesko Delo, 5 May 1978).
11. Statistichiski godishnik na narodna republika Bulgaria, 1977 (Sofia, 1977), p. 268.
12. Ibid.
13. Ibid.
14. Ekonomika sel'skogo khozyaistva, no. 6 (1977), p. 113.
15. Rabotnichesko Delo, 22 September 1970.
16. Ekonomika sel'skogo khozyaistva, no. 2 (1978), p. 111.
17. Voprosy ekonomiki, no. 5 (1972), p. 148.
18. Aref'ev and Karpenko, "Spetsializatsia," p. 109.
19. Ibid.
20. Ikonomicheski Zhivot, 24 March 1976.
21. Rabotnichesko Delo, 23 September 1976, and Ekonomika sel'skogo khozyaistva, no. 2 (1978), p. 111.

22. Miles J. Lambert, "Bulgaria Seeks Western Know-How to Spur Farming," Foreign Agriculture, 9 February 1976, p. 11.

23. Ekonomika sel'skogo khozyaistva, no. 2 (1978), p. 111.

24. A. Ganev, "Sotsialisticheskoe pereustroistvo i razvitie sel'skogo khozyaistva Bolgarii," ibid., no. 9, p. 103.

25. See Everett M. Jacobs, "Recent Developments in Organization and Management of Agriculture in Eastern Europe," in East European Economies Post-Helsinki, p. 344.

26. Kooperativno Selo, 21 December 1978.

27. Rabotnichesko Delo, 5 May 1978.

28. Jacobs, "Recent Developments," pp. 340-42, 344-45, and Allen, "Bulgarian Economy," p. 678.

29. Rabotnichesko Delo, 5 May 1978.

30. Kooperativno Selo, 21 December 1978.

31. Rabotnichesko Delo, 6 and 7 March 1979.

32. Darzhaven Vestnik, 23 January 1979.

33. Ibid., and Rabotnichesko Delo, 30 March 1979.

34. For the position as it existed in early 1977, see Jacobs, "Recent Developments," pp. 345-49.

35. Statistisches Jahrbuch der Deutschen Demokratischen Republik, 1978 (Berlin, 1978), p. 157.

36. Aref'ev and Karpenko, "Spetsiatizatsia," p. 111, and Kh. Nau and S. Gryadov, "Tendentsia razvitia zhivotnovodchiskikh predpriatii v GDR," Ekonomika sel'skogo khozyaistva, no. 1 (1979), p. 82.

37. See Jacobs, "Recent Developments," p. 348.

38. See D. Rezhets, "Osnovnoe napravlenie spetsializatsii i tipy predpriatii v sel'skom khozyaistve GDR," Ekonomika sel'skogo khozyaistva, no. 10 (1978), pp. 106-108, and Nau and Gryadov, "Tendentsia," p. 84.

39. See Statistisches Jahrbuch der DDR, 1978, pp. 156-57.

40. Nau and Gryadov, "Tendentsia" p. 83, and Ekonomika sel'skogo khozyaistva, no. 4 (1979), p. 89.

41. K. Epifanov and A. Shkilev, "Mezhkhozyaistvennaya kooperatsia v GDR," Ekonomika sel'skogo khozyaistva, no. 10 (1977), p. 115.

42. Ibid., pp. 114-16.

43. Ibid., p. 115.

44. L. Popova, "Mezhkooperativnye odedinenia v Rumynii," Ekonomika sel'skogo khozyaistva, no. 8 (1978), p. 99.

45. Michael Cernea, "Organizational Build-up and Reintegrative Regional Development in Planned Agriculture," Sociologia Ruralis, no. 1/2 (1974), p. 35.

46. Voprosy ekonomiki, no. 4 (1972), p. 110.

47. Cernea, "Organizational Buildup," p. 35.

48. Romania Libera, 7 May 1974.

49. See the discussion of these associations in Probleme Economice, no. 3 (1974).

50. See ibid., no. 1, and Popova, "Mezhkooperativnye," p. 99.

51. Popova, ibid.
52. Probleme Economice, no. 1 (1974).
53. Buletinul Oficial, 4 October 1977, and Popova, "Mezhkooperativnye," pp. 99-100.
54. Buletinul Oficial, 4 October 1977.
55. See Probleme Economice, no. 1 (1974).
56. See the discussion in ibid., no. 2.
57. Romania Libera, 3, 5, 6, and 14 February 1979, and Scinteia, 20 February 1979.
58. Statistical Pocket Book of Hungary, 1976 (Budapest, 1976), p. 99, and Statistical Pocket Book of Hungary, 1978, (Budapest, 1978), p. 104.
59. Lewis A. Fischer, "The Organization of Hungarian Agriculture," a study forming part of the Ford Foundation Research Project on "The Organization and Comparative Efficiency of Soviet and East European Agriculture" Glasgow, 1978, (mimeographed), pp. 38-39.
60. See U.S., Congress, Joint Economic Committee, "Hungarian Agricultural Performance and Policy during the NEM," by Z. Edward O'Relley, in East European Economies Post-Helsinki (Washington, D.C.; 1977), p. 370.
61. Magyar Mezogazdasag, 1 October 1975, and Nepszabadsag, 18 March 1978.
62. See Figyelo, 26 July 1978.
63. O'Relley, "Hungarian Agriculture," p. 372.
64. Magyar Hirlap, 30 March 1978, and Nepszabadsag, 24 December 1978.
65. Magyar Mezogazdasag, 2 March 1978, and Nepszabadsag, 25 February 1978.
66. O'Relley, "Hungarian Agriculture," p. 371. Poultry farming has been given up on sixteen cooperatives under the Babolna CPS because it proved to be unprofitable (Magyar Mezogazdasag, 20 December 1978).
67. Nepszabadsag, 18 March 1978. See also O'Relley, "Hungarian Agriculture," p. 372.
68. Aref'ev and Karpenko, "Spetsializatsia," p. 110, and Magyar Hirlap, 21 June 1977. See also Peter S. Elek, "Hungary's New Agricultural Revolution and Its Promise for the Fifth Five-Year Plan," in Roy D. Laird, Joseph Hajda, and Betty A. Laird, eds., The Future of Agriculture in the Soviet Union and Eastern Europe: The 1976-80 Five-Year Plans (Boulder: Westview Press, 1977), pp. 174-80.
69. Nepszabadsag, 23 February 1977.
70. Fischer, "Organization," p. 42.
71. Magyar Nemzet, 21 September 1977.
72. Zemedelske Noviny, 8 September 1977, and Rude Pravo, 13 May 1978.
73. Prace, 17 November 1977.
74. Ya. Dostalova and L. Shpirk, "Glavnye puti mezhkhozyaistvennogo kooperirovania v ChSSR," Ekonomika sel'skogo khozyaistva, no. 5 (1979), p. 68.

75. Ibid., pp. 68-69. In mid-1973, less than 6 percent of the then 387 cooperation groups were involved in complex cooperation (Vladislav Bajaja, "The Organization of Czechoslovak Agriculture," a study forming part of the Ford Foundation Research Project on "The Organization and Comparative Efficiency of Soviet and East European Agriculture" Glasgow, 1976, [mimeographed], pp. 69-70).

76. Dostalova and Shpirk, "Glavnye puti," p. 68. The figures for nonagricultural JAEs in 1978 seem too low, since in 1977, 110 of the then 345 JAEs were purely construction or land-improvement firms, and 79 were agrochemical enterprises (see Dr. Bajaja's contribution to this volume, chapter 13).

77. Ekonomika sel'skogo khozyaistva, no. 6 (1978), p. 114.

78. See Dr. Bajaja's contribution to this volume.

79. Bajaja, "The Organization of Czechoslovak Agriculture," pp. 50, and 71, and see also Joseph Hajda, "Principal Characteristics of Agricultural Policy Trends in Czechoslovakia," in Laird, Hajda, and Laird, eds., Future of Agriculture, pp. 163-64, and 167.

80. See Rolnicke Noviny, 26 October 1974, and Zemedelske Noviny, 25 October 1974.

81. Aref'ev and Karpenko, "Spetsializatsia," p. 112, and Rezhets, "Osnovnoe napravlenie," p. 113.

82. Ekonomika sel'skogo khozyaistva, no. 5 (1970), pp. 115-117.

83. Aref'ev and Karpenko, "Spetsializatsia," p. 112.

84. M. Bukh, "Ustavy rastenievodcheskikh i zhivotnovodcheskikh proizvodstvennykh kooperatov v GDR," Ekonomika sel'skogo khozyaistva, no. 10 (1978), p. 112.

85. See Lambert, "Bulgaria Seeks," p. 11.

86. Aref'ev and Karpenko, "Spetsializatsia," p. 109. By mid-1978, the number of PAKs reportedly fell to seven (Rabotnichesko Delo, 5 May 1978).

87. Allen, "Bulgarian Economy," p.680.

88. Aref'ev and Karpenko, "Spetsializatsia," p. 109.

89. Rabotnichesko Delo, 17 January 1974.

90. Allen, "Bulgarian Economy," p. 680.

91. Ekonomika sel'skogo khozyaistva, no. 6 (1977), pp. 112-13.

92. Aref'ev and Karpenko, "Spetsializatsia, p. 110.

93. Darzhaven Vestnik, 29 March 1974.

94. Otechestven Glas, 22 December 1976.

95. Allen, "Bulgarian Economy," p. 680.

96. Rabotnichesko Delo, 12 June 1976.

97. After years of operation, there are still major problems in coordinating the activities of the processing factories with the farms and in efficiently determining the crop structure of the PAKs' farms (see Allen, "Bulgarian Economy," p. 680).

98. Statistical Pocket Book of Hungary, 1975 (Budapest, 1975), p. 159, and Statistical Pocket Book of Hungary, 1978, p. 105.

99. Jacobs, "Recent Developments," p. 353.

100. See Magyar Hirlap, 3 December 1971.

101. Aref'ev and Karpenko, "Spetsializatsia," p. 110.

102. Fischer, "Organization," p. 41.

103. Nepszabadsag, 10 April 1975.

104. V. Marilai, "Mezhkhozyaistvennaya kooperatsia v Vengrii," Ekonomika sel'skogo khozyaistva, no. 4 (1978), pp. 115-16.

105. Magyar Hirlap, 27 April 1973.

106. Ibid., and Marilai, "Mezhkhozyaistvennaya," p. 116.

107. Fischer, "Organization," p. 41.

108. O'Relley, "Hungarian Agriculture," p. 372.

109. Figyelo, 10 February 1971.

110. Aref'ev and Karpenko, "Spetsializatsia," p. 110.

111. O'Relley, "Hungarian Agriculture," p. 372.

112. Magyar Kozlony, 19 June 1976.

113. Nepszabadsag, 27 April 1976.

114. O'Relley, "Hungarian Agriculture," p. 373.

115. Agricultura Socialiste, 26 February 1977.

116. Romania Libera, 5 and 6 February 1979.

117. See Dostalova and Shpirk, "Glavnye puti," p. 68.

13
Concentration and Specialization in Czechoslovak and East German Farming

Vladislav Bajaja

INTRODUCTION

The agricultural sectors of Czechoslovakia and East Germany (GDR) bear a generally strong analogy in organizational framework, intensity of farming, and output performance. Their overall level of development is doubtlessly the highest among all CMEA countries, depending on tradition, industrial capacities, and the skills of farm managers and workers. Whereas natural conditions for farming are more favorable on average in Czechoslovakia, East German agriculture has achieved so far a slight edge in the level of organization. As far as technology and mechanization are concerned, there is hardly any significant difference between the two neighboring countries, but larger quantities of fertilizers are applied in the GDR. As a further indicator, the land area available for farming per head of population in 1976 was 25 percent greater in Czechoslovakia than in East Germany in the case of agricultural land, and 16 percent in the case of arable land. Currently, population is growing notably in Czechoslovakia, whereas it is stagnating in the GDR. Although the difference has diminished a little in recent time, the still significantly greater endowment of land in Czechoslovakia might constitute a factor of some importance for an assessment of the future prospects of agricultural production. In both countries, agricultural policies are in the main designed to achieve a high degree of self-sufficiency in agricultural products of a given climatic zone, especially in grain and basic livestock commodities.[1]

In the command-type, centrally planned economies of Czechoslovakia and East Germany, the most important decision-making powers are concentrated in the hands of top Communist party and government authorities. In the past, long-term strategies of Soviet descent were employed by the Communist Party of Czechoslovakia (KSČ) and the ruling GDR

Sozialistische Einheitspartei Deutschlands (SED) in order to transform the formerly small-scale, privately operated farming sectors in their countries along socialist principles. The respective policies of collectivization and socialization were neither fully identical in methods and measures nor exactly coincidental in timing, but the ultimate goals were to create farm structures of distinctly large-scale character, which would make it easier to manage and control agriculture from the center.

In both countries, the structures that emerged from the collectivization drive were still overwhelmingly represented by one-village collective farms. They were not yet entirely suited to the idea of large-scale socialist agriculture, mainly because of their rather modest levels of mechanization and relatively low efficiency. In spite of the first amalgamation waves in the early 1960s, this characteristic remained basically true until the end of the decade, which can be retrospectively viewed as a period of consolidation.

However, in this period first steps were already undertaken towards a further transformation of the structural and organizational framework of agriculture. This applies more pronouncedly to the GDR, where a comprehensive scheme of interlocked measures was elaborated in 1967 for further concentration and specialization in agricultural production, horizontal cooperation between specialized farming units and, last but not least, their vertical cooperation with related industrial branches and commercial organizations. Later, the SED introduced some substantial changes to the original scheme and, quite recently, further modifications to it, which might possibly announce the final stage in the search for new structures, especially in the crop-growing branches of agriculture.

After the termination of the reform rule, Czechoslovak agriculture soon adopted some of the elements of the East German model. In February/March 1971, a scheme for concentration, specialization, and inter-enterprise cooperation was approved by the highest authorities of the ČSSR. However, as far as certain subtle details were concerned, the scheme built upon already developed structures, and specific Czechoslovak conditions were taken into consideration.

The aim of this paper is to analyze and to compare the more recent trends in concentration, specialization, and, as it is a related phenomenon, cooperation in Czechoslovak and East German farming. It seems that a consequently simultaneous treatment of the two countries would be rather confusing. Therefore, a more detailed description and evaluation of the structural development with special emphasis on the 1970s will be presented separately for each country.

RECENT STRUCTURAL CHANGES IN CZECHOSLOVAK AGRICULTURE

Czechoslovak policymakers and agricultural economists usually argue that the high level of concentration achieved in their country's farming is necessary for rational specialization and full utilization of modern technologies and powerful machinery. In their view, as the process of specialization goes on, production structures on farms are becoming simplified, and ultimately a combination of sufficiently large branches is achieved, which is in accordance with both natural and economic conditions of the given enterprise.[2] However, it should be born in mind that there can be no linear dependence between concentration and specialization in the sense of degree of specialization increasing with greater concentration. Especially in Central European agriculture, large enterprises such as the existing socialist farms cannot be very narrowly specialized because of the necessity to maintain one or more crop rotation schemes adapted to variable climatic and soil conditions and to balance for considerable production risks. This applies not only to Czechoslovakia but also to East Germany, where so-called specialized crop-growing collective and state farms have to operate quite a number of production branches and, secondly, to cooperate very closely with the animal-producing enterprises, especially with those keeping cattle.

The development of farm sizes in Czechoslovakia has been influenced by the idea that it should be possible to employ in every farm the biggest machine or complex of machines delivered by the socialist industry, or the largest barn designed and built by construction organizations.[3] The first campaign for mergers of the collective farms was started soon after the virtual completion of the socialist transformation of Czechoslovak agriculture. However, it came to an end in 1961 as a result of a serious economic setback. Only since 1971, substantial steps towards further concentration of land, capital, and labor in both collective and state sectors have been undertaken in accordance with the aforementioned scheme. Officially, farm amalgamations were not considered as a universal means to achieve larger production capacities and a higher degree of specialization. Only in the case of relatively small Uniform Agricultural Cooperatives (UAC), with agricultural land of less than 500 hectares (later less than 1,000 hectares), further mergers were recommended and, in fact, had to be carried through. As will be discussed below in more detail, the new policy provided for priority of cooperation between relatively independent agricultural enterprises. The reasons were supposedly greater organizational flexibility and lesser social implications of the cooperative solution of the concentration problem. Until 1972, the practice seemed to correspond with this conception. Later, however, many UACs,

TABLE 13.1
Distribution of Agricultural and Arable Land in the ČSSR
by Sectors, 1960, 1970 and 1976 (End of Year)

	Agricultural Land			Arable Land		
	1960	1970	1976	1960	1970	1976
Total agricultural/arable land (1,000 ha)	7,327	7,093	6,990	5,131	4,998	4,907
Shares of sectors in percent[a]:						
Socialist sector	82.4	85.1	91.7	85.7	88.9	95.4
State sector	20.3	29.4	30.5	19.4	28.5	29.6
State farms[b]	15.5	20.2	19.9	16.4	20.3	19.9
Collective farms	62.1	55.7	61.2	66.3	60.5	65.8
Private sector, total	16.6	14.0	7.3	14.1	10.9	4.3
Subsidiary holdings of collective farms members	4.8	4.1	2.1	5.0	4.1	1.3
Private peasants[c]	11.7	10.0	5.2	9.0	6.7	3.0

Sources: For 1960 and 1970: Vladislav Bajaja, "The Organization of Czechoslovak Agriculture" (Glasgow, 1976), pp. 23-23, Tables 2 and 3; for 1976: Statistická ročenka ČSSR 1977, pp. 33, 268, 271, and 294.

a The percentages do not add up to 100 percent because of some land "not belonging to agricultural enterprises" (1.0 percent with agricultural land, 0.2 - 0.3 percent with arable land).

b Excluding joint agricultural enterprises.

c Including private grazing corporations in Slovakia.

and not only those with less than 500 ha of agricultural land, have given preference to merging with neighboring collective farms, as their managers became aware of certain complications, inefficiencies, and even dangers connected with the cooperation scheme.[4] Although in 1970 6,270 UACs existed, their number declined to 4,449 by the end of 1973. Even then the amalgamations continued to be arranged with surprising speed. It is reported that there were just 1,792 independent UACs in the whole ČSSR as of 1 January 1978, with an average size of 2,373 ha of agricultural land.[5] Quite probably, the amalgamations in the collective sector have not yet come to their ultimate end, but the space for them seems to be already limited.

The wave of mergers among the UACs has until now been accompanied by some other, in this case deliberate and preplanned, measures by the state agricultural administration to push forward production concentration and centralization of the decision making. The area of small-scale private farming has been further reduced through collectivization in the foothill and upland regions of Slovakia as well as through restrictions on (and more or less voluntary) abandonment of subsidiary land holdings of collective farm members. In the state sector of agriculture, the number of state farms proper[6] fell from 336 in 1970 to 213 in 1976, with a jump in the average size of an enterprise from 4,264 ha of agricultural land to 6,546 ha.[7] Besides this, eight extremely large enterprises, with 47,820 ha of agricultural land and 31,000 ha of arable land on average, have been created out of smaller state farms. All of them are located in the formerly German-populated border regions of the Czech lands (ČSR), where serious organizational problems remain a limiting factor to performance. These enterprises are directed by their regional agricultural boards or by the Ministry of Agriculture and Food of the ČSR. Some of them are the sole organizational units of socialist agriculture in their respective administrative districts. It is expected that more such "district farms" will be constituted in the regions bordering the Federal Republic of Germany and Austria.[8]

Data in table 13.1 show the changes in the use of agricultural and arable land by sectors from 1960 to 1976 as indicated by official statistics.[9] Obviously, the private sector plays only a minor role in Czechoslovak agriculture today. Even its contribution to the food supplies of the rural population is continuously shrinking, as more and more young people decline to till their own vegetable garden and to hold one single cow allowed them by law. Hence, the two sectors of socialist agriculture are not almost solely responsible for the satisfaction of the growing food demand in terms of quantity and, far more strikingly, quality. With some very regrettable exceptions (such as periodic shortages of fruits and vegetables, for which excessive specialization and faults in agricultural policy must be blamed) the quantitative side of the Czechoslovak diet is no longer a serious problem. But high-quality foods are rather scarce, if contemporary standards of the prosperous Western countries are taken as a yardstick for comparison. In this respect socialist agriculture bears responsibility for some of the present failures, e.g., for the lack of whole milk on the market. However, a great part of the fault is to be attributed to the technological gap in the socialist food industry, which organizations suffered from a lack of appropriate innovations, as well as from restrictions on imports and rather unfortunate export policies of the foreign trade organizations.

The development of concentration on Czechoslovak collective and state farms in terms of average land area (private holdings of collective farm members not included), average number of cattle, pigs and poultry, average size of equipment park and average size of labor force (permanently employed persons) per farm between 1970 and 1976 is shown in table 13.2 Another approach to the question of farm sizes in Czechoslovakia is shown in tables 13.3 and 13.4 where the grouping of collective and state farms according to their agricultural area is illustrated for 1970 and 1976 (1975).

It may be pointed out that the once characeristic, relatively small one-village UACs are not only a small minority and will doubtlessly be merged with other collective farms in the near future. The new pattern of Czechoslovak UACs are large, multibranch farms with 1,500 - 3,000 or more ha of agricultural land, with considerable animal stocks (especially cattle) and other resources, but still partly undermechanized in comparison with modern Western farms. The UACs comprise several hundred workers and teams of well-educated managers. For their office and worker staff, the UACs maintain various social and cultural facilities.

The majority of large UACs and practically all state farms in Czechoslovakia have developed an area-oriented organization.[10] This means that there are several divisions (sub-farms) with their own area and relatively closed production programs. As a rule, the divisions are more specialized than the farm as a whole (intrafarm specialization), but they lack genuine managerial independence. All important decisions beyond the operative sphere are taken by the management board of the farm. However, most divisions have a material interest in their economic results and for this purpose systems of "intrafarm khozraschet" were developed, for which the balance of internal farm prices is of crucial importance.[11] Smaller UACs and those larger farms that have greatly simplified their production programs through specialization have branch-oriented organization structures. In this case there are no area-closed divisions, but the branches (or groups of

TABLE 13.2

Development of Collective and State Farms in the ČSSR, 1970 and 1976 (end of year)

	Collective farms 1970	Collective farms 1976	State farms 1970	State farms 1976
Number of farms	6,270	2,097	336	213
Average area per farm (in ha)				
agricultural land	630	2,040	4,264	6,546
arable land	482	1,539	3,023	4,577
Average number of live-stock per farm[a]				
cattle	401	1,456	2,564	4,366
cows	165	579	1,083	1,756
hogs	485	1,899	2,332	4,000
poultry	1,497	n.a.	14,224	30,343
Average equipment per farm				
tractors (physical units)	14.3	44.2	83.2	125.6
grain combine harvesters	1.46	6.08	10.35	16.98
trucks	1.53	6.87	7.33	17.85
Average labor force per farm (number of perma-nently employed persons)[b]	114	302	589	795

Sources: For collective farms – number of farms, agricultural and arable land 1970 and 1976: Statistická ročenka ČSSR 1977, pp. 32–33; livestock numbers 1970: Statistická ročenka MZVž 1970, p. 524; 1976: computed from Statistická ročenka ČSSR 1977, pp. 33, 288, 296 (in order to obtain figures not including livestock in joint agricultural enterprises); for tractors, grain combine harvesters and trucks 1970: Alois Vojáček,Vývoj socialistického polnohospodarstva na Slovensku (Bratislava, 1973), p. 926, Table P 220; 1976: Statistická ročenka ČSSR 1977, p. 304; for labor force 1970 and 1976: Statistické přehledy/Zemědělská ekonomika, no. 7 (1977), p. V.
For state farms 1970: Statistická ročenka ČSSR 1971, pp. 313, 337; Statistická ročenka MZVž 1970, pp. 519, 524, 539; 1976: Statistická ročenka ČSSR 1977, pp. 271, 288, 294, 304.

a   In the case of collective farms, livestock of the Joint Agricultural Enterprises is not included.

b   In the case of collective farms, the figures are based on employment on an unspecified date (possibly as of 30 June of the given year). For state farms, the figures give the average labor force of the year (in man-years).

270

TABLE 13.3
Distribution of Czechoslovak Collective Farms According to Size of Agricultural Land, 1970 and 1976

Size Group (hectares of agricultural land)	Number of Collective Farms in (January 1) 1970	Size Group (hectares of agricultural land)	Number of Collective Farms in (December 31) 1976
Up to 100 ha	35	Up to 500 ha	36
100 – 200 ha	422	501 – 1,000 ha	257
200 – 500 ha	2,394	1,001 – 1,500 ha	475
500 – 1,000 ha	2,545	1,501 – 2,000 ha	455
1,000 – 2,500 ha	917	2,001 – 2,500 ha	327
2,500 – 4,000 ha	23	2,501 – 3,000 ha	208
Above 4,000 ha	3	3,001 – 3,500 ha	123
		3,501 – 4,500 ha	127
		Above 4,500 ha	89
Total number of collective farms	6,339	Total number of collective farms	2,097

Sources: For 1970: Statistická ročenka ČSSR 1972, p. 314; for 1976: J. Matouškavá, "Problémy dalšiho rozvoje mezipodnikové kooperace v zemědělství", Zemědělská ekonomika, no. 2 (1978): 86.

TABLE 13.4
Distribution of Czechoslovak State Farms According to Size of Agricultural Land, 1970 and 1975

Size Group (hectares of agricultural land)	Number of State Farms in 1970 (January 1)	Size Group (hectares of agricultural land)	Number of State Farms in 1975
1,000 – 2,500 ha	22	Up to 4,000 ha	47
2,500 – 4,000 ha	138	4,000 – 10,000 ha	149
4,000 – 6,000 ha	147	10,001 – 30,000 ha	13
Above 6,000 ha	32	...	...
Total number of state farms	339	Total number of state farms	209[a]

Sources: For 1970: Statistická ročenka ČSSR 1972, p1 314; for 1975: J. Matoušková, "Problémy," p. 86.

There is some evidence that this was not the total number of state farms really existing at that time.

272

branches) exercise approximately the same degree of independence as the divisions with area-oriented organization. As so-called coat-bearing sections (nákladová střediska), they are also similarly interested in economic results.

In larger UACs or state farms with consolidated holdings (which is not always the case, since as state-farm holdings are often interspersed with other enterprises), the transition to branch-oriented organization is only possible if intrafarm specialization has reached a high level. This applies especially to animal husbandry, where existing area-oriented divisions should be, as the first step, specialized in only one branch. In crop production, rotations should be unified without respect to the borders of previous state farm divisions or former small UACs in merged collective farms. The traditional field brigades, i.e., groups of manual workers (mostly composed of elderly women), that still do an important part of the field work, should be gradually replaced by fully mechanized brigades or by mixed brigades for specialized tasks such as the production of fruit, vegetables, or wine grapes.[12]

The organization of the tractor and machine park is, however, often solved by creating one centralized brigade for heavy machinery, whereas smaller tractors and machines (as well as machines destined for only one purpose) are assigned to field or mixed brigades.

The management systems of most Czechoslovak socialist farms have three levels. On the top management level (board of management) of a state farm, a staff of specialists works under the director of the farm. The board of management (ředitelství) is the chief executive body of the state farm. It is here that the planning, bookkeeping and financing of all activities of the farm take place. Only limited spheres of administration are delegated to the divisions. The director of the state farm is the superior for all heads of divisions, who are the only immediate superiors for their staff. However, it is quite common for the chief agronomist or the animal specialist of the enterprise to give orders to the agronomists or the animal specialists of the divisions. The lowest management level is represented by field brigades or groups, which also have their responsible heads.

Recently, many uniform agricultural cooperatives have taken over some of the main features of the management system used in the state sector. According to the law on agricultural cooperative system (no. 122/1975)[13] and to the model statutes of the UACs in the wording of the decree of the government of the ČSSR of 4 December 1975[14], both in effect since 1 January 1976, the top management body of a collective farm is the general assembly of members, meeting at least twice a year. However, the UACs with a large number of members have the right to summon the general assembly only once a year, if there is an elected "assembly of representatives" that must meet more frequently, and exercise some of the rights and the responsibilities of the general assembly. Between general assemblies an elected committee (představenstvo), headed by the chairman of the UAC, officially has all substantial decision-making powers. The real situation in the majority of collective farms, especially the larger ones, has, however, retreated from these principles. In fact, the authority of the general assembly to manage the UAC has been always very limited. The Communist party and the government would have suffered a serious challenge to their claim to leadership of the whole national economy, if they had allowed the UACs to be masters of their own fate. As the management processes on collective farms have become ever more complicated in the logical sequence of concentration, the authority of the general assembly has been declining further. Meanwhile, the elected committees, too, have lost most of their powers in favor of--for some time unofficial--executive bodies, consisting of the leading specialists with the chairman of the UAC acting as the supreme executive. Aiming at a further improvement of the level of management on the UACs, party and government awarded full legality to these bodies through the new legal regulations cited above. As "boards of economic management" (hospodářské vedení), they are to be formally established by the general assembly. The assembly itself is, however, the place where decisions made by the chairman and the board of economic management are simply ratified. Also, in larger UACs, the system of management consists of three levels as in the case of state farms, and managers appointed by the chairman are the superiors for common members of the UAC working in their respective divisions or brigades.

Data on average farm sizes or on size structure as depicted above do not provide a full portrait of the real production concentration in Czechoslovak agriculture, i.e., of the concentration of technological processes in crop sectors or of the size of technological units in livestock branches. According to J. Matoušková, large collective and state farms maintain notable internal reserves to increase concentration without further merging. However, even farms that have generally reached an expedient size should consider pooling financial resources, technological capacities and labor force as a means of inter-enterprise cooperation [15].

This advice is very similar to that given to the then far smaller UACs at the beginning of the 1970s. The agricultural policy programing of 1971, which is basically still valid, aimed generally at further intensification of agricultural production and higher labor productivity. It emphasized cooperation rather than farm amalgamations. According to this scheme, the following organizational forms of inter-enterprise cooperation are envisaged: [16]

1. Joint enterprises for specialized services in field work, e.g., agrochemical enterprises (for each of the cooperation districts--see below) and repair stations for tractors and other heavy machinery.[17]

2. So-called narrow cooperation in crop farming, especially for joint purchase and use of expensive high-performance machinery.

3. So-called broad or, in its highest form, complex cooperation in crop production and, to a certain extent, also in animal husbandry, organized in cooperation groups (lower level) and cooperation districts (higher level).

4. Jointly financed large-capacity livestock housing for land-dependent branches of animal husbandry, above all for cattle-rearing, milk production, bullock fattening, etc. No new legal entity would be created here, since the housing would be a division of one of the cooperating farms.

5. Joint agricultural enterprises, especially for branches of animal husbandry not highly dependent on land, such as hog fattening, or egg and broiler production, as well as for other activities (including some nonagricultural ones), that can be separated from traditional agricultural enterprise. Here, a new legal entity comes into existence.

Of these organizational forms of cooperation, only joint agricultural enterprises (JAE) had existed before 1971, and were in fact a widespread phenomenon. With the advent of economic reform and the revival of entrepreneurial atmosphere in the Czechoslovak economy, free cooperation between socialist farms in agricultural and nonagricultural activities grew rapidly in importance in the late 1960s. In addition to many forms of noninstitutional, often short-term cooperation (such as mutual aid with machinery), collective and state farms began creating joint enterprises for the land-independent branches of animal husbandry and for other agricultural activities, such as potato or feed drying. Construction firms and organizations for marketing of some freely marketed goods (such as fruits and vegetables) were founded. By the end of 1968, there were 174 JAEs in the whole country, of which 130 were in the ČSR and 44 in the SSR.[18]

The JAEs are similar to stock companies, but there have been many quite curious models of profit distribution among the capital investors. In order to avoid taxes, prices for intermediate products paid to member farms are deliberately high in some JAEs, so that there is little or no profit in the joint enterprise itself. Surprisingly enough, in spite of the political support for joint ventures in agriculture during the reform period, a tax regulation that was very discriminatory (in contrast to regulations for other agricultural enterprises) applied to all business activities of the JAEs until 1970. For this reason, inter-enterprise cooperation remained at that time limited to some highly profitable activities and was concentrated in regions with good natural conditions, such as East Bohemia, South Moravia, and West Slovakia. Since January 1971, taxation of the JAEs has been greatly reduced, but the freedom enjoyed during the reform period to create joint enterprises in accordance with the economic interests of farms has been restricted.

The agricultural policy program approved by the new Communist party leadership in 1971 sought, above all, to strengthen the control of agriculture from the center. The intention was to redefine the set of relationships and interactions in the agricultural sphere and to restructure the existing enterprises through further centralization of the decision-making processes[19] concentration of resources, and production specialization. One of the aims of this program, specialization on the regional level, is a strategic goal continually pursued with the help of five-year and current year plans of production, that are specified down to the level of district agricultural administration and to every socialist farm.[20] Efforts are also made to establish long-term planning for agriculture, for ten to fifteen years ahead, which should be based on scientific prognostication and computerized allocation models (linear programming models). As a part of this long-term planning, district studies of specialization, concentration and cooperation for the period up to 1985 were organized in the early 1970s.[21] Currently, new regional and district projects of "rational allocation of agricultural production" are to be worked out, which have to cover the period up to 1990.[22] In the final stage of the implementation of regional and district studies, socialist farms are expected to achieve a high level of specialization in accordance with their natural conditions and the output requirements of the state Plan.

As indicated above, it was the strategy of inter-enterprise cooperation rather than farm amalgamations which, according to the new policy, should lead to larger production capacities and a higher degree of farm specialization. In order to obtain a fixed organizational framework for the proposed broad or even complex cooperation between socialist farms of both sectors, the cooperation scheme within the agricultural policy program called for the creation of territorially demarcated cooperation groups[23] and cooperation districts. The above-mentioned district studies envisaged that a total of 681 cooperation groups with an average 5,850 ha of agricultural land should be established in the whole ČSSR. Socialist farms were expected to switch gradually from some initial stages of socalled narrow cooperation (such as grouping of grain combine harvesters for joint work on their huge fields), which many of them had already practiced for years, to ever broader forms of mutual assistance within the

276

framework of their respective cooperation group. The next step would be the financing and purchase of joint fleets of heavy tractors and high-performance machinery. Later, cooperating farms should adopt joint planning of the whole crop production and cultivate fields on the basis of interconnected or completely unified rotation, without respect to former farm boundaries. The original enterprises would keep only some of their livestock-producing branches (branches not dependent on land would be abandoned in favor of the JAEs) and nonagricultural activities. Even for their remaining branches of animal husbandry, mainly dairy cows and young cattle, plans for specialization and concentration would be elaborated and gradually put into operation.

The unexpected avalanche of farm amalgamations between 1972 and 1978 has quite substantially affected the preconditions on which the original cooperation scheme had been based. Many of the collective farms of second (or even third) generation are so large that there might be, at least for some time to come, relatively little need for any broader cooperation in crop farming beyond some joint use of machinery. In comparison with contemporary East German agriculture, a significant feature of the structure created in Czechoslovakia is the emergence of very large farms with combined crop and livestock production.

An example of the magnitude of resources concentrated under the roof of one of the most successful agricultural enterprises in Czechoslovakia is the UAC Slušovice, located near the town of Gottwaldov.[24] Since 1976, the UAC Slušovice cultivates 6,130 ha of agricultural land in 17 villages.[25] It has a labor force of 1,480 workers and managers (among them, fifty-seven university graduates). There is an adequate animal stock, with dairy cows giving 5,005 liters of milk a year on average. In spite of such considerable farming capacity, this UAC derives only 18.5 percent of its income from agriculture proper; 17.2 percent comes from activities connected with agriculture, and 64.3 percent of total income are derived from various other activities including forestry, woodworking, construction, transportation, and industrial production. Since 1977, the UAC Slušovice operates a large supermarket in Gottwaldov, where fruits, vegetables, and flowers from their own as well as from contractual production are sold.[26]

The reactions among Czechoslovak agricultural policymakers and economists to the situation created by the great wave of farm mergers seem quite ambivalent. On the one hand, many state agricultural administrators might feel rather happy over the fact that the average number of collective farms per district decreased from fifty-five in 1970 to seventeen in 1977. On the other hand, it is actually feared that members of a large collective farm would not be as immediately interested in the farm's economic results as they were when the farm was smaller. Suchý goes as far as to say: "As long as the members of a collective farm work in an enterprise where they alone decide all problems, have knowledge of all facts and can see how their working efforts affect the economic results of the farm, they realize that this enterprise is their property and they have a positive attitude about this common property. In an amalgamated, overlarge enterprise the members lose their sense of ownershp. Decision making in a large collective is not the same as in a smaller collective. In a very large enterprise facts are difficult to ascertain. At the same time, the correlation between the performance and remuneration can also become distorted."[27]

These words express the real dilemma of the present and possible future enlargement of collective farms in Czechoslovakia. The lack of individual initiative of rural managers and workers on the one side and the problems of supervision on exceedingly huge farms are and will probably remain the most serious handicap in the performance of socialist agriculture in comparison with the flexibly operated private Western farming.

In November 1978, Jan Zavíral from the Prague School of Economics presented an interesting analysis of some recent problems of concentration and specialization in Czechoslovak agriculture.[28] His main conclusion is that, in terms of acreage, animal stocks, labor force, etc., all state-owned agricultural enterprises and the overwhelming majority of the UACs have already acquired sufficient size for rational concentration from a technological viewpoint. The author argues, however, that farm specialization as a factor with the greatest influence on the potential for technological concentration has been almost completely neglected during the 1970s.

With special regard to milk production in Czechoslovakia, Zavíral's investigation shows that productivity is still quite low, in spite of the rather high degree of concentration (ninety-six milk cows per barn on average). The main reason for this unfavorable situation is the insufficient standard of technology. At the same time, however, Zavíral does not conceal his skepticism about the prospects for better efficiency in newly built large barns. He makes a strong point about the problem of rising transportation costs: For a dairy cow barn with a capacity for 1,000 animals, the average distance for fodder and manure transportation is ten kilometers longer than in the case of a barn for ninety-six cows. The Prague expert maintains that such a rise in transportation costs may be compensated through higher labor productivity if the average milk performance were 4,000 liters per cow, but it is impossible to compensate for such costs with a performance of 2,000 liters per cow per year.[29]

The future development of Czechoslovak agriculture may be, to a certain degree, influenced by the experience gained in the GDR with the organizational separation of crop farming from animal husbandry (and vice versa). There is some indication that in most parts of Czechoslovakia large collective and state farms with combined production will remain the prevailing mode of agricultural structure. Nevertheless, efforts to pursue the idea of complex cooperation in field work, with subsequent formation of one single, specialized crop-growing UAC and several animal-producing UACs from traditional farms with mixed production, might be intensified in some selected regions.

Only eight cooperative associations for joint crop production existed as of January 1977, out of a total number of 489 cooperative structures engaged in crop farming (mostly so-called narrow cooperation), animal husbandry, and other activities, for which no juridically independent units were founded.[30] The associations for joint crop production in Czechoslovakia are direct counterparts to the "cooperative crop-growing farms" (KAP) in the GDR. Some deviations from the East German pattern can, however, be detected. Four of these eight associations are located in the district of Ústí nad Orlicí (East Bohemian region). According to a detailed account,[31] there were three different types of economic relationships within three of the above associations in 1974, deviating especially in details concerning capital investment through member enterprises.

Relatively little information is available about the constitution and activities of the cooperation districts, which are planned as the territorially larger and organizationally higher level of broad or complex cooperation in Czechoslovak agriculture. The cooperation district is expected to be the territorial unit, in which the turnover of the cattle herd is in most cases closed, in contrast to single farms and even to cooperation groups, where under certain circumstances open herd turnover could be practiced. The most important purpose for forming cooperation districts is, however, the common financing and building of agrochemical enterprises, through which concentration and rationalization of all chemical services to agriculture should be accomplished. At present, facilities for the storage and application of fertilizers are grossly insufficient.

The policy changes affected neither the status nor the importance of the joint agricultural enterprises, but they aimed at a further concentration of their resources, often through amalgamation. There were 247 "economically active" JAEs as of July 1973, including 17 district JAEs, which are something like uniform common enterprises for the whole administrative district, with several agricultural, nonagricultural, and service branches. In addition, another 324 JAEs were "in construction."[32] By January 1977, the

279

number of active JAEs reached 345, but their structure had
significantly changed since 1968. Of this number, 21 were
district joint enterprises, 21 specialized in hog fattening, 6
in fattening calves and cattle, 10 in egg production, and 24
in feed drying as well as production of feed mixtures.
Another 110 JAEs were construction or land-improvement firms,
and 79 JAEs offered agrochemical services. Just two JAEs were
organizations for sale of agricultural products. Seventy
Joint Enterprises were engaged in multiple unspecified
activities.[33] The JAEs have acquired an important position as
producers of pork, eggs and poultry. In 1976, the share of
the JAEs in total marketing in the ČSSR reached 16.7 percent
for fattened hogs, 42.3 percent for eggs, and 7.7 percent for
poultry.[34] Their production facilities are mostly new, very
large, and highly mechanized. There were 357 JAEs in January
1978, of which 240 were in Czech lands and 117 in Slovakia.[35]

DEVELOPMENT OF AGRICULTURAL STRUCTURE IN EAST GERMANY

Agriculture in the German Democratic Republic during the
early 1960s was structually transformed into three types of
agricultural production cooperatives (LPG), each type
representing a greater degree of collectivization (and
conversely less private ownership).[36] In contrast to the USSR
and Czechoslovakia, state farms (VEG) have always been less
significant in the GDR. Table 13.5 indicates the relative
weight of various sectors according to their pattern of land
ownership from 1960 to 1975. Clearly, type I collectives,
with private animal husbandry and feed production and long
important in the southern regions of the GDR, were gradually
transformed to the highest, most socialized type III LPGs.
Simultaneously, amalgamations of collective farms contributed
to a further centralization of command and concentration of
resources (Tables 13.6 and 13.7).
Since 1967 (the year of the seventh congresss of the SED),
a comprehensive agricultural policy program has been pursued
in the GDR, through which a complex transformation of the
farming structure has taken place that is, in a world-wide
sense, unique. The basic idea of the East German plan is the
shaping of an industrially organized and producing agriculture
with close vertical ties to the subsequent food processing and
marketing sectors (so-called "Stufenplan"). In agriculture
proper, not only should a high degree of concentration be
achieved through farm mergers, but also a radical
specialization by organizational separation of crop farming
from animal production and through formation of specialized
large-scale enterprises for such tasks as chemical services,

TABLE 13.5
Shares of Sectors in Total Agricultural Land in the GDR, 1960, 1970 and 1975

	1960	1970	1975
Total agricultural area (1,000 ha)	6,420	6,286	6,295
of which (in percent):			
State farms (VEGs)	6.2	7.0	7.5
Collective farms (LPGs)[a]	73.4	78.2	82.0[b]
Collective farms (LPGs)[c]	84.2	85.8	85.7[b]
LPGs Type I/II	31.5	13.8	1.5
LPGs Type III	52.7	72.0	79.9[d]
Horticultural cooperatives (GPGs)	0.2	0.3	0.4
Private farms and small holdings[e]	7.6	5.8	5.5

Sources: Horst Lambrecht, Die Landwirtschaft der DDR (Wiesbaden: Hessische Landeszentrale fur politische Bildung 1978), Part I; for collective farms (data not including private holdings of members): Statistical Yearbooks of the GDR, various years.

[a] Private holdings of collective farm members not included.

[b] Including 47 crop-growing LPGs.

[c] Private holdings of collective farm members included.

[d] Most of the land was cultivated by Cooperative crop-growing farms (KAPs), see table 8.

[e] Estimates; including church properties.

281

TABLE 13.6
Number of Enterprises in East German Agriculture, 1960 to 1978

Form of Enterprise	1960	1970	1975	1976	1977	1978
State farms (VEGs)	669	511	463	424	420	443
Collective farms (LPGs)	19,313	9,009	4,621[a]	3,562[b]	3,494[b]	3,681[b]
LPGs Type I/II	12,976	3,485	306	...	...	...
LPGs Type III	6,337	5,524	4,260	...	...	...
Horticultural cooperatives (GPGs)	298	346	287	241	229	218

Sources: Statistisches Jahrbuch der DDR 1976, pp. 176-177; Statistisches Taschenbuch der DDR 1977, pp. 72-73; Statistisches Taschenbuch der DDR 1978, p. 60; Presse-Information der DDR, 13 June 1978.

[a] Including 47 crop-growing LPGs and 9 specialized animal-breeding LPGs.
[b] Only crop-growing and animal breeding LPGs; see also table 8.

282

TABLE 13.7
Average Sizes of Socialist Farms in East Germany, 1960, 1970 and 1975 (hectares of agricultural land)

	1960	1970	1975[a]
State farms (VEGs)	591	866	1,023
Collective farms (LPGs)[b]	281	599	1,172
LPGs Type I/II	156	249	309
LPGs Type III	534	819	1,180[c]
Horticultural cooperatives (GPGs)	46	60	86

Source: Lambrecht, Die Landwirtschaft der DDR.

[a] Average sizes of land property. The land was however mostly cultivated by the Cooperative Crop-growing Farms.

[b] Including private holdings of collective farm members.

[c] Including 47 Crop-growing LPGs.

283

feed drying, etc. At the same time, however, intensive horizontal and vertical cooperation is needed in order to master all the problems of mutually interconnected farming activities.

Intensive merging of collective farms was regarded as the correct road towards higher concentration in East German agriculture in the early 1960s. Since 1965, cooperation associations (Kooperationsgemeinschaften--KOG), i.e., territorially demarcated groups of enterprises of both sectors, have been assembled in order to cooperate, at first mainly in joint use and purchase of expensive machinery. However, party and state authorities later came to the conclusion that the KOGs would only lead to "large LPGs" (Gross-LPG) with combined, multibranch crop and livestock production. As they now wished to realize a plan for an industrially organized agriculture with very large, but specialized production units[37] and with strong vertical ties to the food industry and the marketing organizations, the leaders ultimately took a resolute position against the KOGs and "large LPGs." Gerhard Grüneberg, the party secretary for agriculture and member of the politburo, later declared that the conception of "large LPGs" had been a complete failure. Interestingly enough, similarly large collective farms with mixed production have become the pattern of organization in neighboring Czechoslovakia, the other socialist country with relatively highly developed agriculture. Yet unlike their Czechoslovak counterparts, collective farms were not of the old, "traditional" type III in the GDR were not able to resist successfully the plans pursued by the SED and the agricultural administration.

The new agricultural policy program encompassed the gradual dismemberment of the nonspecialized collective and state farms and their restructuring along horizontal and vertical lines, as well as the foundation of specialized enterprises for crop farming, various livestock branches, and agricultural services. For this purpose, the following cooperative farm units or forms of association were created throughout the whole GDR.[38]

1. Cooperative crop-growing farms (Kooperative Abteilungen Pflanzenproduktion--KAP), cultivating land belonging to several old (basic) collective and state farms.

The cooperative crop-growing farms were the most prominent element of the agricultural structure in the GDR between 1972 and 1977. Through the formation of the KAPs, magnitudes of 3,000 - 5,000 ha of agricultural land were reached. Nominally, the cooperative crop-growing farms were not designed to become legally and economically independent from the LPGs and VEGs that founded them. The basic LPGs and VEGs had, at least at the outset, some decision-making powers in the KAPs. They retained only livestock production, but even here they often abandoned certain branches in favor of

284

specialized cooperative enterprises. Nevertheless, as their internal organization grew more stable, the KAPs actually became rather independent operational units. Separate Plans were imposed upon them by the district agricultrural administration, and they developed their own funds. However, the KAPs on the one side and the basic LPGs and VEGs on the other side must cooperate very closely because of their integrated production program. They have to work out a more or less balanced system of prices for the intermediate products that they deliver to each other according to long-term mutual agreements. In cases of economic disequilibrium caused by unpredictable events or by errors in determining internal prices, the[39]cooperation partners must arrange for income redistribution.

2. Inter-enterprise establishments for crop production (Zwischenbetriebliche Einrichtungen Pflanzenproduktion), founded for cultivation of land belonging formerly to state and collective farms.

Only ten inter-enterprise establishments for crop production came into existence throughout the GDR. Their organizational structure was (still is) quite similar to that of the KAPs, but they were constituted as legally and economically independent cooperative units, in which a state farm usually is the strongest partner.

3. Cooperative establishments (Zwischenbetriebliche Einrichtungen--ZBE, or Zwischengenossenschaftliche Einrichtungen--ZGE), founded mostly for branches of livestock production not dependent on land, such as hog fattening, egg and poultry production.

The ZBEs/ZGEs are very similar to joint agricultural enterprises in Czechoslovakia, but they have attained[40] a greater importance. Their number in mid-1978 was 328. In 1977, they accounted for a share in total livestock herds of the GDR of 7.4 percent for cattle (of which 6.2 percent for cows), 9.4 percent for hogs, 9.6 percent for sheep, and 8.6[41] percent for poultry (of which 9.5 percent for laying hens).

4. Centers for agrochemical services (Agrochemische Zentren--ACZ), constituted as cooperative establishments.

Substantial joint capital investment by agricultural enterprises and the state was needed to build up the present network of 263 centers for agrochemical services (1977) with their storage, transportation, and application facilities. Actually, even within this special business sector of the East German economy a concentration process takes place, for there were by 1973 332 ACZs (or agrochemical brigades). In the meantime, however, the labor force employed in the centers has increased from 16,693 to 24,749.[42] The average ACZ is responsible for chemical services on 25,000 ha of agricultural land. The ACZ have taken over almost 100 percent of fertilizer application, with the exception of nitrogen fertilizers, where the crop-growing farms still do 60 percent

of the work. Furthermore, the ACZs are engaged in 65 percent
of chemical plant protection in the GDR.[43]
     5. Cooperation associations (Kooperationsverbände--KOV),
i.e., associations of farming, food processing, and marketing
organizations, which are formed under the guidance of party
and state authorities of a certain district or even region for
every product or related group of products.
     The member enterprises of the KOVs do not give up their
legal and economic independence. The KOV itself usually does
not acquire the status of a legal person, but exceptions are
already known in the case of some KOVs producing and marketing
vegetables.   Currently, there may be some 400 cooperative
associations throughout the GDR, with a slight majority
engaged in the animal sector. The intensity of interaction
within the KOVs seems to vary rather strongly, with East
German authors distinguishing three or four stages of
cooperation and integration that range from a pure exchange of
experience [44]over synchronization of deliveries to joint
investment.
     It can be recognized now that the cooperative crop-growing
farms were only a transitional stage on the way towards more
stable organizational forms. Through "voluntary" decisions of
the member assemblies in the basic LPGs and through approval
by the directors of the basic VEGs, the cooperative crop-
growing farms are being dissolved, but now legal entities, the
so-called crop-growing LPGs and VEGs, immediately take over
the rights of property to (or of use of) land, machinery,
buildings, etc. For this step, some criteria on internal
organization stability have been determined.   The
establishment of a crop-growing LPG is subject to approval by
the Ministry of Agriculture. The process of creating these
"new" LPGs began in 1975 and came to a turning point in 1978.
As shown in table 13.8, it appears that in the first six
months of 1978, the crop-growing LPGs suddenly outnumbered the
KAPs and, with some 750 enterprises and an average size of
5,000 - 6,000 ha of agricultural land, became the most
important farm type in the GDR.[45] At the same time, the old
(or basic) collective and state farms acquire the status of
animal-producing LPGs and VEGs. For both special types of
collective farms, new model statutes were activated. The
state sector of agriculture now consists of 114 crop-growing
VEGs and 329 animal-producing VEGs.[46] In addition, the state
operates some 30 huge livestock-producing enterprises called
"Kombinate für Industrielle Mast" (VE KIM).
     Interestingly enough, the final breakthrough in the
reorganization of the crop-growing farms is quite coincidental
with a resolution of the politburo of the SED of February
1978, which was a clear declaration against further
enlargement and amalgamation of farms and, at the same time,
for closer cooperation of the collective and state

TABLE 13.8
New Enterprise Forms in the Collective Sector of East German Agriculture: Their Numbers and Sizes, 1971 to 1978

Year	Cooperative Crop - growing farms (KAPs)[a]		Crop - growing LPGs		Animal - breeding LPGs
	Number of Farms[b]	Average Size[c] (ha of agri- cultural land)	Number of Farms[b]	Average Size[c] (ha of agri- cultural land)	Number of Farms[b]
1971	283	2,950	n.a.	n.a.	...
1972	552	2,723	n.a.	n.a.	...
1973	1,066	3,471	n.a.	n.a.	...
1974	1,198	3,675	n.a.	n.a.	...
1975	1,210	4,130	47	6,013	...
1976	1,024	4,165	161	5,775	3,421
1977	833	4,210	329	5,178	3,165
1978	416[d]	n.a.	721[d]	n.a.	2,960

Sources: Statistisches Jahrbuch der DDR 1976, pp. 176-77; Statistisches Taschenbuch der DDR 1978, pp. 60-61; Presse-Information der DDR, 13 June 1978.

a Including inter-enterprise establishments for crop production (ZBE Pflanzenproduktion).

b As of 30 September of the given year, unless otherwise indicated.

c As the areas of agricultural land are for 30 June of the given year, the average sizes calculated by the author are only tentative indicators.

d As of mid-1978.

287

farms.[47]   It remains to be seen whether this will also mean a
moratorium on the creation of so-called "Agrar-Industrie-
Vereinigungen" (AIV) for crop production, which is a form of
territorially demarcated federations of crop-growing LPGs and
VEGs, with membership extended also to the respective centers
for agrochemical services, land improvement cooperatives, and
state-owned district works for repair of machines (KfL). The
AIV for crop production appeared in 1976, with magnitudes soon
reaching well over 30,000 ha of agricultural land. There are
eleven such conglomerates so far, each in a different
administrative district.

As in large Czechoslovak farms, the managers of the crop-
growing enterprises in East German agriculture have developed
a variety of systems of internal organization, which
nonetheless can be grouped in three basic patterns, i.e.,
organization of divisions by territory, by products and, as
the most sophisticated system, by kinds of tasks, such as[48]
plowing, chemical application, harvesting, or gathering.
Very often, so-called temporary complexes of workers and
machines are formed. As far as the management of the
agricultural production cooperatives and of the cooperative
establishments for animal production is concerned, the present
practice implies an obvious renunciation of the statutory
principles of cooperative democracy and collective management.
Instead, there is almost completely adherence to the principle
of one-man direction. Nevertheless, the head of the
enterprise delegates to subordinate managers some decision-
making responsibility and authority to give orders. Thus a
management hierarchy emerges in which there is no place for
the common members of the collective farms. In short, the
well-known problems of supervision on large farms have already
led to a veritable proliferation of management staffs, about
which the East German leaders have reportedly had second
thoughts.[49]

CONCLUSIONS

In both countries, party and state authorities maintain
substantial decision-making power in agriculture, which
enables them to pursue long-term policies towards a high
degree of production concentration and pronounced
specialization of regions and enterprises. It can be,
however, concluded that these policies have until now led to
farm sizes, that are in most cases far ahead of actual
economic necessity. Although or, conversely, because there
are few reliable investigations into this problem, it can be
assumed that very few economies of scale are obtained in
farming enterprises comprising 6,000 ha of agricultural land
or 2,000 dairy cows. On the contrary, diseconomies of scale
like supervision problems and transportation costs become

perceptible. Even if the relative scarcity of high-performance machines and other modern equipment is taken into consideration, the arguments against huge farms remain strong. Currently, the leaders in Czechoslovakia and East Germany seem to realize that their efforts for better efficiency could be harmed by further enlargements of the socialist farms.

There is some evidence that the actual development of the agricultural structure in Czechoslovakia has not always been fully consistent with official policy. Czechoslovak farm managers were very skeptical about the cooperation scheme imposed upon them from above in 1971, and they took refuge in the mutual merging of collective farms. This attitude has so far saved the collective sector of Czechoslovak agriculture from far-reaching dismemberment of its multibranch production units and, what was possibly feared most, from entanglement in joint farming with the powerful state sector. However, party and state policymakers in the GDR were able to push through their conception, unleashing a radical separation of crop-growing from animal-breeding branches and a thorough reorganization of agriculture, with cooperation relationships designed to result in an integration of the new specialized production units along horizontal and vertical lines.

East German and Czechoslovak agricultural sectors are more integrated with their respective state-wide or national economies than their counterparts in other countries of the Council for Mutual Economic Assistance.[50] The GDR has shaped an institutionalized vertical integration structure that is so far without parallel in the whole communist world. There is nothing comparable to this model in Czechoslovakia, but agriculture there has developed close contractual ties with the subsequent food processing and marketing spheres. Nevertheless, the actual intensity of vertical cooperation n East German agribusiness is lower than in some countries of Western Europe or especially in the USA. To speak of an industrialized agriculture would be more than premature for both Czechoslovakia and the GDR.

NOTES

1. In order to maintain their high livestock population, the East Germans had to purchase considerable amounts of feed grain from Western markets, especially in 1976. See Ronald A. Francisco, "The Future of East German Agriculture: The Feasibility of the 1976-80 Plan," in Roy D. Laird, Joseph Hajda, and Betty A. Laird, eds., The Future of Agriculture in the Soviet Union and Eastern Europe: The 1976-1980 Five-Year Plans (Boulder, Colo.: Westview, 1977), p. 198. At the same time, Czechoslovakia's imports of feed grain were smaller. However, it is expected that Czechoslovakia will import over

two million tons of grain in 1979, in spite of its bumper crop of 10.8 million tons in the previous year.

2. See Jaroslava Dostálova, "Vývoj, současný stav a úkoly v rozvoji koncentrace, specializace a kooperace v čs. zěmědelstvi," in 30 let vývoje čs. zěmědelství a jeho dalši perspektivy, ed. Jaroslav Kabrhel (Prague, 1975), p. 51.

3. This conclusion has been drawn in my analysis of Czechoslovak research on optimal farm sizes and actual developments. See Vladislav Bajaja, Theoretische Grundlagen und praktische Entwicklung landwirtschaftlicher Betriebsgrössen in der Tschechoslowakei (Berlin, 1975), p. 308.

4. The reasons for such a state of mind are discussed in ibid., pp. 294-96, referring to qualified Czechoslovak authors such as Suchý and Spirk.

5. Rudé právo, no. 270 (1978), p. 1.

6. State farms, as a statistical category, are directed by the district agricultural boards.

7. According to one source, the average size of state farms as of January 1978 was 7,292 ha of agricultural land.

8. See Jiři Pospichal, "Problémy organizace a řizeni oborových podnik ů státnich Statků," Zemědělská ekonomika, no. 1 (1978), pp. 1-8.

9. These data are, of course, not identical with the information that would be obtained if legal forms of ownership of land were taken into account. However, titles of personal ownership to land held by collective farm members have become almost meaningless.

10. This account of intrafarm organization structures is based upon Vladislav Bajaja, "The Organization of Czechoslovak Agriculture," a component study in the Ford Foundation project on the organization and comparative efficiency of Soviet and East European agriculture, (Glasgow, 1976), (mimeographed), pp. 54-57.

11. The farms as a whole are working in accordance with the principles of "full khozraschet." This means simply that all expenditures must be covered by their own receipts, but this is not to be taken literally with regard to the existing price and subsidy system.

12. Eugen Horváth, "Otázky organizácie vnútropodnikoveho riadenia na JRD a SM s vysokou koncentráciou výroby," Ekonomika polnohospodárstva, no. 6 (1974), pp. 171-73.

13. Published in Hospodářske noviny, no. 47 (1975), special supplement.

14. Published in Zemědělské noviny, no. 297 (17 December 1975), special supplement.

15. See J. Matoušková, "Problémy dalšiho rozvoje mezipodnikové kooperace v zemědělstvi," Zemědělska ekonomika, no. 2 (1978), pp. 88-90.

16. Among possible sources, see <u>Rolnícke noviny</u> (28 April 1971), special supplement.

17. For the latter purpose, however, there are also (with some regional disparities) 100 state-owned Machine and Tractor Stations (MTS). The MTSs operate fleets of heavy tractors and grain combine harvesters, to be employed in the UACs. They are also engaged in chemical services and other activities, such as production of special machines and space parts.

18. See J. Vysokaj, <u>K vzniku družstevnich organizaci v zemědělství. Vznik JZD sloučenim a rozdělenim a vznik společného podiku JZD</u> (Prague, 1971), pp. 78-94.

19. See Joseph Hajda, "Principal Characteristics of Agricultural Policy Trends in Czechoslovakia," in Laird, Hajda, and Laird, eds., <u>The Future of Agriculture</u>, p. 160.

20. The powers and responsibilities of the state agricultural administration and of the socialist farms in agricultural planning processes are discussed in Bajaja, "The Organization of Czechoslovak Agriculture," pp. 45-52.

21. For more detailed information, see Jaroslav Kunc, et al. <u>Koncentrace, specializace a kooperace v zemědělství</u> (Prague, 1974), pp. 42-72. One of the tasks of the district studies was to draw up an inventory of the condition of all agricultural buildings and to estimate the costs of the proposed modernization of farms.

22. See Jan Buian, "K zdokonalování soustavy plánů a metod plánování rozoje zemědělství a výzivy," <u>Zemědělská ekonomika</u>, no. 7 (1978), pp. 445.

23. The concept of the cooperation groups was based on the East German "Kooperations-gemeinschaften," that existed until 1971. These were replaced by "Kooperative Abteilungen Pflanzenproduction"; the GDR has subsequently gone on to specialized crop-growing and animal-breeding enterprises.

24. Formerly called Zlin, this busy town had until 1945 been the headquarters of the famous Bata Shoe Company (now in Toronto, Canada). For a more detailed, interesting account of the resources and activities of the UAC Slušovice, see Imrich Rubík, <u>Zemědělskoprůmyslovákombinace</u> (Prague, 1 978), pp. 106-111.

25. According to recent information, the UAC Slušovice now has 10,000 ha of agricultural land, and its output reached 1 billion kcs in 1978. See <u>Zěmělské noviny</u>, no. 3 (1979) p. 1.

26. Such a diversification of activities, which in fact constitutes a regionally important agribusiness, is nonetheless an exception. Party and state officials are afraid to grant the collective farms full freedom for entrepreneurial ventures.

27. Čestmír Suchý, "Kooperace a slučovani při vytváření velkovýrobnich forem," <u>Zemědělská ekonomika</u>, nos. 4-5 (1974), p. 322.

28. Jan Zavíral, "Rozloha není vsechno," Hospodářské noviny, no. 47 (1978), pp. 8-9.

29. Average milk production in Czechoslovakia was 2,887 liters per cow in 1977 (all sectors). See Statistické prehledy/Zemedelska ekonomika, no. 7 (1978).

30. Matoušková, "Problémy": 93.

31. See Karel Pilny et al. Zkušenosti s uplatňováním koncentrace, specializace a kooperace v rostlinne vyrobě (Prague, 1976), pp. 79-125, especially pp. 97-103.

32. Ludvik Špirk, "Kooperace a slučováni JZD v současném obdobi rozvoje konentrace a specializace," Zemědělská ekonomika, nos. 4-5 (1974) pp. 334-35.

33. Matoušková, "Problémy": 90.

34. Ibid.

35. Zemědělske noviny, no. 285 (1978), special supplement, p. 8.

36. For a characterization of the three types of collective farms and a survey of their development, see Horst Lambrecht, Die Landwirtschaft der DDR vor und nach ihrer Umgestaltung im Jahre 1960 (Berlin, 1977), pp. 44-54.

37. In 1968, a so-called "reference size" (Richtgrösse) of 5,000 to 6,000 ha of agricultural land was set up for production units in crop farming. Similarly, certain--very large, and subsequently ever larger--capacities were required for building new livestock housing. See Christian Krebs, "Entwicklungstendenzen in der DDR-Landwirtschaft," FS-Analysen, no. 5 (1974), pp. 9-10.

38. A more detailed classification is in Vladislav Bajaja, Organisation und Führung landwirtschaftlicher Grossunternehmen in der DDR (Berlin, 1978), pp. 38-80.

39. Similar relationships of cooperation exist now between the crop-growing and the animal-producing LPGs and VEGs, which gradually replace the KAPs and the basic LPGs and VEGs.

40. See Presse-Information der DDR, 13 June 1978.

41. Calculated from Statistisches Jahrbuch der DDR (East Berlin, 1978), pp. 182-83.

42. All data are from ibid., p. 167.

43. W. Pach and H. Simchen, "Erreichter Stand beim Aufbau des Netzes der ACZ, die Entwicklung ihrer Leitungen und die weiteren Aufgaben der ACZ bei der Intensivierung der Pflanzenproduktion," Feldwirtschaft, no. 10 (1975), p. 437.

44. Cf. M. Kittner et al., "Zunahmende Verantwortung der Kooperationsverbände," Kooperation, no. 3 (1977) p. 125.

45. See Eberhard Schinke, "Konzentration und Spezialisierung in Landwirtschafts-betrieben östlicher Wirtschaftssysteme," (paper presented at a symposium in Giessen, West Germany, October 1978), p. 5.

46. <u>Presse-Information der DDR</u>, 13 June 1978. The animal-producing VEGs are not to be confused with the centrally directed animal-breeding VEGs, on German "VEG (Z) Tierzucht."

47. Resolution of the politburo of the SED on 14 February 1978, published in <u>Neuer Weg</u> (East Berlin), no. 6 (1978), pp. 223-26, special supplement, as discussed in Christian Krebs, "Die LPG der DDR sollen mit volkseigenen Betrieben kooperieren," <u>Deutschland Archiv</u>, no. 6 (1978), p. 569.

48. A more detailed treatment of the internal organization of East German farms appears in Bajaja, <u>Organisation und Führung</u>.

49. The agricultural economists in the GDR have recently produced interesting research on the problems of job creation in the management sphere of crop-growing farms. Their aim is the establishment of recommended numbers of managerial staff in relation to some selected indicators.

50. Cf. Karl-Eugen Wädekin, "Die 'agro-industrielle' Integration in der Sowjetunion und Osteuropa," <u>Osteuropa</u>, no. 9 (1974), p. 677.

14
The Impact of Current Policies on Modernizing Agriculture in Eastern Europe

Joseph Hajda

What are the prospects for Eastern Europe's agricultural development in the years ahead? The answer depends on whether we recognize the central role of science and technology in the development of agricultural policies in the region, and from that recognition proceed to assess the impact of scientific discoveries and technological improvements on agricultural production.

There is ample evidence that the relationships between scientific-technological progress and agricultural development occupy a central place in current agricultural policies of Eastern European countries.[1] Science and technology are perceived by policymakers as the driving forces of modern agricultural development. The top Communist party and government bureaucracies are gripped with the problem of securing adequate food supplies by applying scientific knowledge and organizing knowledge for practical purposes. Bureaucratic structures concerned with agriculture evidence their preoccupation with food production in numerous conferences, debates, seminars, symposia, and published works dealing with various aspects of agricultural development. Specialists with a background in advanced scientific research are asked to contribute to the formative stage of policymaking. Other specialists or professionals from upper and middle levels of bureaucracy, along with outside specialists who maintain an ad hoc relationship with a policymaking institution, are called upon to provide specialized input on particular problems. The role of the specialists is so important in the agricultural policy process that their influence contributes significantly to contemporary Eastern European bureaucracies.

Before discussing implications of the scientific-technological intelligentsia's participation in goal-setting functions, let us examine the impact of scientific and

technological progress on Eastern European agricultural
production.

THE IMPACT OF POLICIES FOR SCIENCE AND TECHNOLOGY ON AGRICULTURAL PRODUCTION

The concept of scientific and technological progress
refers to the creation, dissemination, and adoption of new
knowledge and its use in agriculture with the help of new,
effective, and appropriate technology. In practice, a "mixed"
agricultural economy unfolds with new scientific knowledge and
modern technology penetrating traditional ways and affecting
the developmental process of intensified agriculture.

Table 14.1 shows that from 1971 to 1975 total agricultural
production grew more rapidly in Eastern Europe than in the
USSR or Western Europe, and that per capita growth followed a
similar trend. In fact, Eastern Europe's per capita advances
exceeded those of any other world region in 1965-75. That
rapid growth was related to national policies that focused on
the need to accelerate production growth by applying
scientific discoveries and technological improvements to farm
production. Better understanding of genetics led to improved
breeding of both seed and livestock, and the improved policies
contributed to expanding production. Production growth was
also stimulated by high-yielding varieties imported from other
lands, (for example, wheat varieties from the Soviet Union),
by implementing policies to increase consumption of
fertilizers, pesticides, and herbicides, and by expanding
irrigation programs. Policies promoting advances in
veterinary medicine led to improved animal health and to rapid
growth by the livestock sector. At the same time, policies
emphasized even more mechanization as vital for expanding
animal production, as well as for better and quicker
cultivation, seeding, and harvesting, thus reducing losses to
adverse weather. Additionally, new policies directed
attention to modern management techniques as essential for
better farming.[2]

Analysis of the data in table 14.2 indicates that five of
the six countries of Eastern Europe had considerably higher
growth rates, in total and per capita agricultural production
than did Western Europe in 1965-75. The exception, Poland,
had advances close to Western Europe's average. While
Hungary's and Romania's advances were exceptionally rapid,
growth in Bulgaria, Czechoslovakia, and the German Democratic
Republic (GDR) was not far behind the best advances in Europe.
However, the indices do not provide sufficient basis for
comparing roles of science and technology in agricultural
development. A better indication of impacts of research and
technology is given in tables 14.4 and 14.5.

TABLE 14.1
Agricultural Production in Eastern Europe, the USSR, and Western Europe, 1971–75
(with 1961–65 as the Base)

| | Total Percentage Increase | | | | | Increase per Capita | | | | |
	1971	1972	1973	1974	1975	1971	1972	1973	1974	1975
Eastern Europe	123	132	137	140	142	117	124	128	130	131
USSR	129	122	151	140	130	119	111	136	125	114
Western Europe	120	119	123	129	127	114	112	115	120	117

Source: United Nations, FAO, The State of Food and Agriculture, 1976.

TABLE 14.2

Agricultural Production in Eastern Europe, 1965-75
(with 1961-65 as the Base)

	Total Percentage Increase							Increase per Capita						
	1965	1970	1971	1972	1973	1974	1975	1965	1970	1971	1972	1973	1974	1975
Bulgaria	113	127	131	142	138	129	146	111	121	124	133	130	120	135
Czechoslovakia	102	115	125	125	138	141	137	101	112	121	121	132	134	130
G.D.R.	110	115	119	124	130	139	143	110	115	119	124	130	139	143
Hungary	104	112	131	140	144	151	149	103	109	128	136	139	149	143
Poland	103	115	113	122	130	133	134	101	109	106	113	120	122	121
Romania	110	110	135	153	150	150	154	109	102	124	140	136	134	137

Source: United Nations, FAO, Production Yearbook, 1975.

Defined and measured in terms of specific achievement and performance, the quantifiable material-technical aspect of agricultural development reflects the combined effects of national policies designed to accelerate the application of scientific and technological progress in agriculture. The indicators used in tables 14.4 and 14.5 provide a basis for analyzing and comparing achievement and performance in several categories. Wheat yields rose markedly in all countries of Eastern Europe in the 1965-75 decade. The more advanced countries of the region increased production much more than did the USSR and moved close to the European leaders in wheat production.

Data for barley yields are similar. Yields of sugar beets and potatoes increased relatively little in Eastern Europe; the more advanced countries of the region widened the gap between their yields and those of the USSR, and slightly narrowed the disparities between themselves and Western Europe. The region's growth rate in milk production was considerably better than that of the USSR. Advances in the leading countries were near-spectacular, but not enough to propel them to the top in Europe.

A declining economically active population in agriculture is a product of modernization. Labor transferring from agriculture to other sectors of the economy is an important contribution of agriculture to national economic development. The decline in the region's farm population was related to scientific discoveries and technological improvements being applied to farm production.

Table 14.5 shows that the quantitative trends in farm population decline were similar in Eastern and Western Europe in 1960-70. The more advanced countries of Eastern Europe relied in 1970 on a relatively smaller farm population than did the USSR. However, their percentage of economically active population in agriculture was not as low as that of the leading agricultural achievers and performers in Western Europe. Table 14.5 also shows that the use of nitrogenous fertilizers and tractors increased dramatically in Eastern Europe during the 1960s and 1970s, keeping pace with similar dramatic increases in Western Europe and the USSR. The scientific-technological progress illustrated in tables 14.4 and 14.5 suggests dividing Eastern European countries into three groupings, from most to least developed.

The GDR and Czechoslovakia had the lowest percentage of economically active population in agriculture in 1970, and the highest average crop yields in 1973-75. Hungary, Poland, and Bulgaria were next, in order, with Romania last.[3] The variation in yields reflects the distribution of scientific and techological capabilities in the region even before national political leaders assigned a central role to scientific and technolocial progress in agricultural

TABLE 14.3
Increase in Agricultural Production in Eastern Europe from 1971 to 1975

Country	Increase in Percentage
Bulgaria	14
Czechoslovakia	14
GDR	15
Poland	19
Romania	36
USSR	13

Source: Politická ekonomie, (Prague), 7 (1977): 365.

TABLE 14.4
Crop Yields and Milk per Cow in Europe and the USSR
(100 Kg per Ha)

	Wheat		Barley		Sugar Beets		Potatoes		Milk kilo/cow	
	a	b	a	b	a	b	a	b	a	b
Eastern European Countries										
GDR	31.5	41.4	29.5	42.4	244	295	166	199	2662	3732
Czechoslovakia	24.2	38.7	28.8	34.3	279	350	115	159	1900	2882
Hungary	18.6	34.8	18.7	30.1	246	343	79	120	2257	2595
Poland	19.7	29.9	19.4	29.5	267	304	154	185	2146	2660
Bulgaria	18.1	34.8	20.6	32.4	211	284	98	114	1499	2269
Romania	14.6	20.9	17.5	21.7	159	197	83	105	1464	1663
USSR	9.6	14.0	11.1	15.7	164	214	94	116	1713	2139
Other European Countries										
Netherlands	43.8	53.1	39.9	42.0	420	454	292	351	4183	4429
Belgium	38.5	43.3	36.9	42.5	442	456	274	329	3734	3635
Denmark	41.3	49.7	38.7	38.1	356	417	209	252	3739	4373
Germany	33.1	45.6	30.1	40.6	379	440	247	286	3517	3937
United Kingdom	40.5	45.7	32.5	39.0	342	298	228	280	3477	4158
France	29.3	43.4	28.0	36.4	378	404	172	267	2552	2836
Austria	25.5	37.1	26.6	35.0	379	467	200	241	2643	3055
Italy	20.1	26.0	13.6	24.5	327	397	104	164	2734	2440
Yugoslavia	18.0	29.8	15.1	21.4	279	400	87	98	1157	1254

Source: United Nations, FAO, Production Yearbook, 1975.
a Average 1961-65, b Average 1973-75

TABLE 14.5
Changes in Economically Active Agricultural Populations, Use of Fertilizers, and Number of
Tractors in Europe and the USSR

	Economically Active Pop. in Agriculture (Percent)		Fertilizer Use (100 tons nitrogen)		Tractors (Number)	
	1960	1970	1961-65	1974	1961-65	1974
Eastern European Countries						
GDR	17.6	13.0	3109	6713	108593	141762
Czechoslovakia	25.7	16.9	1905	4280	110000	142000
Hungary	38.1	25.0	1428	5513	54388	62361
Poland	48.2	39.0	3576	11464	97746	364763
Bulgaria	56.5	46.6	1211	3295	34789	80000
Romania	64.5	56.0	818	4900	66309	116816
USSR	41.9	25.7	14660	67460	1427000	2267000
Other European Countries						
Netherlands	10.8	8.1	2862	4320	106202	175000
Belgium	8.0	4.8	1346	1748	57643	94509
Denmark	18.1	11.2	1577	3000	145899	172660
Germany	14.2	7.5	7600	12009	1052280	1424949
United Kingdom	4.0	2.8	5814	9184	471844	473100
France	22.1	13.7	7659	15548	872931	1337200
Austria	23.8	14.8	699	1253	162939	284414
Italy	30.8	18.8	3929	6722	342675	780602
Yugoslavia	63.7	49.8	1456	3520	46041	195125

Source: United Nations, FAO, Production Yearbook, 1975.

development. Indeed, the contemporary stage of agricultural development is a radical shift from the previous stage, which was characterized by labor inputs and massive additions of fixed assets with relatively slow advances in technology. Changes in the input mix reflect greater recognition of scientific orientation and faster technological application. Additionally, new policies emphasize innovation, labor-, material-, fuel-, and capital-saving technologies, and new forms of planning, management, and organization.

The modern input mix indicates substantial shifts in the strategy of development. Designed to promote rising levels of output and living and substantial food self-sufficiency, the new strategy aims to bring rural areas into a more functional role as part of an interdependent web including an industrialized and urbanized society. The strategy, an integral part of national development policy, is based on the need to adapt to the requirements of the modern age in advanced technology, intensified production, and increased labor productivity. The importance of social progress is emphasized, particularly policies aiming at increasing the material and cultural welfare of the rural population. The value of agricultural land is recognized, and funds are allocated toward extending the area of land under irrigation.

The strategic orientation to economic growth and social progress in one complex is linked with the programs to intensify and apply scientific discoveries and technological improvements: the aim is rapid dissemination of up-to-date research results of advanced agricultural science, widespread use of modern technology, broader application of adequate management and planning tools, better organization of production, and a steady supply of trained personnel willing to work in rural areas. Such modernization is envisaged as essential for development of current national policies in Eastern Europe, and is elaborated up to 1990. The 1976-80 five-year Plan objectives are linked with long-term perspectives in all countries of the region.

PROSPECTS FOR FURTHER MODERNIZATION

It should be pointed out that the indices for gross and per capita agricultural production, crop yields, and modern inputs do not provide a sufficient data base for evaluating the quality of life. While they throw light on agricultural production in terms of achievement and performance within and among countries, the indices do not measure the extent to which the human needs of individuals are met, nor do they measure how a country's agricultural production was allocated among various types of activities and among social groups.

However, the insights developed in this analysis leave no doubt that considerable room for greater achievement and improved performance remains in all six Eastern European countries. It is generally recognized that reaching the announced goals will be a long, costly, and difficult process. Several reasons can be found to explain the lag behind the level of achievement and performance of the leading Western European countries.

One of the main reasons Eastern Europe lags behind the most advanced Western European countries is inefficient integration of science, technology, and production. Both the pace and extent of scientific discoveries, innovations, and technologial changes can be improved. However, it is more difficult to change unsatisfactory orientations toward rapid growth in labor productivity, production efficiency, and food quality.

Efforts to accelerate agricultural modernization run into political, administrative, and social obstacles. The bureaucratic establishment does not always respond to the needs to modernize, and it holds mixed views about combining the scientific and technological progress with the existing bureaucratic system. It is not easy to modify bureaucratic patterns of behavior when confronted with strongly conservative attitudes, deep-seated tradition, weaknesses in administration, and noncompliance by affected groups. The chairman of Romania's National Council for Science and Technology put it this way:

> The view was expressed in industry and in some research groups that it was not right to put too much emphasis on developing technological research in which laboratory studies went hand in hand with development, the fabrication of functional models, experimental installations and prototypes, together with engineering and actual manufacture of the products for the national economy. The other view was that instead of spending funds on research it was better to use these to import foreign products. Unfortunately, that was, in fact, the practice.[4]

It took "a clear-cut assignment from the party" in Romania to implement the new policy for the 1970s, which aimed at "designing new technology, new machines and new types of plants, developing new species of plants and productive animal breeds," and striving to "unite the forces of scientific and technical creativity with the country's productive forces."[5]

Closely related to steering science and technology toward the attainment of production goals in agriculture are expenditures for science and technology.[6] While available evidence is sketchy, it appears that Eastern European countries' structure of expenditures for basic and applied research and various kinds of technologies does not conform with the norms derived from international calculations: the structure ought to be 12 to 13 percent for basic research, 20 to 25 percent for applied research, and 58 to 62 percent for technological development. According to a recent study, Hungary's 1970 expenditures were 14.3, 32.4, and 53.3, and Czechoslovakia's (in 1971) were 15.2, 65.1 and 19.6.[7]

Low investments in technological development affected the pace and extent of agricultural development, precluded attainment of certain production goals, and contributed to Eastern Europe's lag behind the most advanced Western European countries.

Despite these and other deficiencies, the judgment of Agriculture Secretary Bob Bergland and other members of the U.S. Department of Agriculture mission who visited the USSR, Poland, Hungary, and Romania, 9-25 May 1978, was "that--for the most part--the countries are making impressive progress in expanding and modernizing farm production," and that their agricultural progress should continue in the foreseeable future, "as those nations act to meet the pent-up demand for food and to place priority on expanding livestock production."[8]

In the long run, barring intensified climatological disturbances, the task of increasing the potential for food production in Eastern Europe will depend on favorable national and international circumstances for agricultural development. To meet the problems related to current deficiencies, including inefficiencies in the use of land, labor, capital, and technology, will require continued emphasis on scientific orientation, technological innovation, and professionalizing policy inputs.

THE IMPLICATIONS FOR PROFESSIONALIZING POLICY INPUTS[9]

Eastern European political leaders and agricultural-policy analysts know that to have the desired impact on agricultural production, policies for science and technology must be formulated as long-term commitments to strengthen scientific and technological potentials. In pursuing that goal, they promote approaches that focus on accelerating the application of advanced scientific discoveries and technological improvements to agricultural production as the best way to advance development, raise living and cultural standards, and strengthen their world position. They anticipate that their policies for science and technology eventually will result in the high productivity, rational organization of production and social life, and a higher material and spiritual civilization.

The quite impressive production increases achieved in 1965-75 reflect the leaders' recognition that the long-range strategic conception of agricultural development requires rapidly expanding roles of specialists and professionals in policymaking. Specialists provide information and judgment necessary to map policies, to advance scientific research, and to increase technological innovations. They interpret policy pronouncements, affect their implementation, and judge performance in the agricultural policy arena. Increasingly, the staffs of agriculture's administrative hierarchy are composed of persons with specialized knowledge, relevant experience, and professional values. And various inducements are provided to expand the pool of experts.

The involvement of specialists in the agricultural bureaucracy is essential: advanced scientific research and technological improvements are not cheap, and policy mistakes can be very costly. Minimizing mistakes requires planners and analysts who are sensitive to scientific and technological opportunities, and who understand internal and external constraints on policies. Basically, it is a question of what can be done under existing circumstances in each country to steer policies for science and technology toward attaining short-term, medium-range, and long-term goals. Hence, effective use of science and technology in agriculture requires successful meshing of specialists' inputs with overriding political concerns.

As each country's scientific establishment grows in size and importance, the pressure to emphasize professional agricultural-policy inputs increases. Scientists and technological specialists with knowledge needed for advanced agricultural development are accorded a relatively high social status and prestige because their knowledge is needed to meet the problems. That leads to institutional adjustments to facilitate the scientific-technological intelligentsia's participation in goal setting.

To use effectively science and technology means to achieve higher production by more efficient, sophisticated science and technology, which is both capital- and energy-intensive. Rationalization is the key characteristic of moves toward modernization, and to the recognition given eminent specialists in agricultural science and technology, and to the professional development of agriculturalists. So rationalization is an instrument of change in agricultural policy. The greater recognition of specialists or professionals also indicates the extent to which empirical orientation influences policymaking in the countries of Eastern Europe.

Committed to empirical results from specific agricultural tasks, the articulate and sophisticated specialists can apply professional competence to shaping policy by manipulating the empirical content and by persuasion. Seasoned specialists with access to formal public agenda-building can participate in defining policy issues and formulating options to meet agricultural problems. Hence, specialists in agricultural science and technology influence planning and decision making at national, subnational, and enterprise levels.

However, it is evident that final decisions regarding major issues of agricultural policy do not rest with the scientific-technological intelligentsia, especially on issues involving large resource allocations; nor is the generation and evolution of values and norms left to chance or spontaneity. Political leaders shape and define the areas within which policy development takes place, and then establish purposes, goals, and priorities. Although the goal of self-sufficiency in temperate-zone products requires more intensive professionalization of policy inputs, political leaders and the bureaucratic establishment carefully screen and classify the new choices and options as desirable and undesirable.

Increasing reliance on specialists with advanced scientific and technological background does not always lead to broader participation in policymaking. Groups excluded from inside access to formal public agenda-building may have little influence. In fact, efforts to improve technical management capabilities can provide more effective controls over the specialists and agriculturalists. The chief political weakness of the specialists lies in the absence of independent, organized sources of power and influence in the political system.

The growing reliance on expert policy inputs is also related to external political circumstances that necessitate orchestrating policies in Eastern Europe, with special emphasis on policies for planning, research, and technology.

In the 1949-70 period, orchestration of Eastern European countries' agricultural policies with the Soviet Union, and with the larger international system of the Council for Mutual Economic Assistance (CMEA), was uneven. Despite public declarations about cooperation, national agricultural development took place with minimum multilateral coordination. The most successful endeavor of the CMEA agricultural commission was a cooperative effort to develop a system for classifying and testing tractors and other agricultural machinery, but its implementation was uneven.

In crop production, the commission aimed at dividing responsibilities for breeding agricultural crops, producing seeds, and testing new crop varieties. However, measures adopted by the commission had only limited effect on crop yields before 1970, as was the case with other measures adopted to increase animal production.

Cooperation in agricultural research was encouraged primarily in genetics and breeding, soil fertility, fertilizer use, crop protection, certain aspects of animal science, and mechanization. But the scope of cooperation was limited.

307

The results of CMEA activities, agricultural and nonagricultural, were discussed at the Council meeting in April 1969, and an agreement was reached to develop a comprehensive program of improved cooperation and socialist economic integration, with the aim of rapidly increasing production, achieving high levels of science and technology, and improving economic efficiency. The program was prepared by the respective CMEA authorities, and approved in July 1971.

Under this program, special attention is being paid to cooperation among the CMEA members in research in the form of coordination centers and organized contacts. For example, Czechoslovakia is responsible for promoting the activities of two international coordination centers--for the mechanization, electrification, and automation of plant and animal production processes, and for the application of econometric methods and computer technology--as well as for activities of the international poultry control and testing station. For each task incorporated into the program of coordination, a common project is developed and consultations with specialists are organized. The intent is to cooperate systematically and intensively, relying increasingly on international research teams and laboratories, and gradually harmonizing research plans and policies.[10]

Additional benefits are anticipated through information sharing, as the national systems of scientific and technological information are being linked with an international center called "Agroinform."

One of the most formidable tasks is systematically creating conditions for applying modern computer technology and mathematical methods to planning and for improving statistical information systems to serve the needs of modern management at all organizational levels. Agricultural sectors' access to computers is less than satistfactory in Eastern Europe, and not circulating relevant information remains one of the main weaknesses in agricultural management. An automated information system in agriculture is a goal of high priority.

Because the CMEA complex program of socialist economic integration calls attention to many new problems,[11] need for expert input is intensified. Although the program stresses general and common interests and goals, and by implication mutual convergence, the professionalization of policy inputs gives rise to conflicting currents of solidarity and strain in Eastern Europe. The first current manifests itself in institutionalized, collective evaluations of experiences in the agricultural sphere, and in increasing calls to apply common principles and a common approach, in other words, a common agricultural development strategy. At the same time, each of the countries makes its own distinctive contribution to the ways and methods of accomplishing the tasks of advanced agricultural development. Hence, the intensified professionalization of policy inputs tends to contribute to distinct national outlooks and heightened expectations of national agricultural development.[12]

While it is important to understand the many difficult hurdles facing implementation of the CMEA planners' vision of multilateral integration and mutual convergence, it is essential to pay close attention to the links between agricultural policies of Eastern European countries and political trends in the Soviet Union. Especially noteworthy is the way policy analysts in Eastern Europe perceive the concept of developed socialist agriculture. Although their conceptualizations are not mere extensions of Soviet concepts, policy analysts in Eastern Europe generally agree with Soviet analyses of development calling for greater recognition of the impact of scientific and technological revolution on agricultural development.

Recognized as a crucial component of development, the scientific and technological revolution requires not only greater planning and scientific-technological interaction among the CMEA countries, but also between them and the nations with the most advanced science and technology. Without such planning and interaction, it would be difficult to accelerate the application of more sophisticated scientific, technological, and managerial capabilities. According to agricultural policy analysts, such acceleration is necessary to steer development toward a steady rise in working people's living standards and cultural levels.

Assuming that Eastern European countries' internal and external circumstances will remain favorable to current policy trends, the agricultural policy outlook is for continued emphasis on greater scientific orientation, faster technological innovation, increased professionalization of policy inputs, and new advance to a higher level of agricultural modernization.

NOTES

1. For a discussion of agricultural policies in Poland, Czechoslovakia, the GDR, and Hungary in the 1960s and the 1970s see Roy D. Laird, Joseph Hajda, and Betty A. Laird, eds., The Future of Agriculture in the Soviet Union and Eastern Europe: The 1976-78 Five Year Plans (Boulder: Westview Press, 1977).

2. An assessment of the progress in expanding agricultural production can be found in ibid., pp. 2-5. The Lairds and Hajda state that the per capita increases "reflect the leaders' recognition that the past neglect of agriculture could not be allowed to continue. Significant policy changes were made, largely involving investment increases, but also including acceleration of technological change, improvement of

agricultural sciences, alteration of organizational forms, and changes in managerial structures and processes," (p. 3).

3. Similar findings appear in a much broader study of Karl-Eugen Wädekin, Sozialistische Agrarpolitik in Osteuropa: II. Entwicklung und Probleme 1960-1976 (Giessen, 1978), pp. 53-59.

4. Ioan Ursu, "The Scientific and Technological Potential of Socialism," World Marxist Review, April 1978, p. 80.

5. Ibid., p. 81.

6. In the 1976-80 five-year Plan, the GDR intends to spend 4.2 percent of the national income on scientific research and development; Czechoslovakia, 3.8 percent; and Hungary, 3 percent.

7. Pavel Mstislavskij and Viktor Durněv, "Problémy, ekonomického stimulování mezinárodní vědeckotechnické spolupráce," Politická ekonomie (Prague), 11 (1976): 973.

8. David M. Schoonover, "Bergland Trip to U.S.S.R.-East Europe Explored Farm Trade," Foreign Agriculture, 14 August 1978, p. 6.

9. In this section, I have relied on information from interviewing agricultural experts in Poland, Hungary, and Czechoslovakia in 1968; in Czechoslovakia in 1969; and in Poland and in several European locations in 1977. My interactions at Kansas State University with visiting scholars from Eastern Europe produced important insights and penetrating observations about the nature of agricultural policy process.

10. For a discussion of linkages with a national agricultural policy structure see Joseph Hajda, "Principal Characteristics of Agricultural Policy Trends in Czechoslovakia," in Roy D. Laird et al, Future of Agriculture, pp. 159-60.

11. For an examination of international socialist integration in agriculture see Zoe Klusáková-Svobodová, "Mezinárodní socialistická integrace zemědělství," Politická ekonomie (Prague), September 1975, pp. 836-49.

12. An assessment of modernization as part of national agricultural development policies can be found in Joseph Hajda, "The Politics of Agricultural Collectivization and Modernization in Czechoslovakia," in Ron Francisco, Roy D. Laird, and Betty A. Laird, eds., The Political Economy of Collectivized Agriculture (New York: Pergamon Press, 1979), pp. 130-54.

15
Conclusion

Karl-Eugen Wädekin

The system of agriculture in Eastern Europe and the Soviet Union, its achievements, problems, and weaknesses, have again aroused great interest in recent years. One of the reasons is its importance for the world market, especially in grain and high-protein feeds, accounting for much of the volume and prices in present international agrarian trade and indirectly influencing the availability of food exports to less developed countries. It would be short-sighted, though, to consider this impact on foreign trade the main point of interest. However, scholars working in the field cannot ignore the fact that this aspect plays a major role with regard to the funding of research and publication on relevant subjects. Direct political implications and interests are affected by the fact that the communist regimes have not been able to overcome the weaknesses of the agricultural sector of their countries, with the possible exception of Hungary. This has been repeatedly stated not only by Western observers, but also by representatives of those regimes themselves. In a broader perspective, for the long term, the importance of and interest in the achievements and failures of socialized agriculture rest upon the ruling communists' contention that their system offers the solution to the problems not only of society at large but also, and most particularly, to those of agriculture in developing as well as highly industrialized countries. The following words from a recent Soviet publication show awareness of the implications of such a contention.

[W]hen analyzing the contemporary condition and prospects of the cooperative sector of agriculture in the European socialist countries, one must not overlook the impact of the experience of these countries on foreign states, primarily the developing countries, in which the peasantry constitutes the predominant part of the population. The problem of advancing agriculture in these countries, and

311

of the future of the peasantry, concerns millions of people, and they are seeking an answer to similar questions in their environment. Some of the countries with a socialist orientation proclaim a cooperative path to the development of agriculture as the basis of their own agricultural policy. These countries are interested not only in the practical application of the transformation of the village on the principles of cooperation, but also in what the cooperative structure has offered the peasantry and what are its future prospects.[1]

Agriculture has been a problem sector ever since the rise of industry, i.e., since it was no longer the principal economy, with a few fringe activities of crafts and trade. This applies to all nations. It would be foolish to deny that agriculture in the United States or in other highly industrialized countries such as Sweden, West Germany, Italy, or Japan remains a problem sector, as it is in Turkey, India, Sambia, or Brazil, although for different reasons in the various categories of countries. The nature of the problem changes with the overall level of economic development, but not its severity in relation to the respective socioeconomic setting. It may no longer be a problem of output growth for achieving acceptable average nutrition standards, but then social and regional disparities, comparative costs and returns, surplus disposal, and so on, come to the fore.

In view of contentions that the inherent superiority of a socialized economy has not yet fully come to bear in agriculture, it is of paramount interest to look closely at communist agrarian systems and policies. No less than their achievements and failures, the underlying reasons for such have to be investigated as thoroughly and objectively as possible in order to find out whether the strengths and weaknesses are only temporary or whether they are part of the system itself. The relevant research must not be restricted to the agricultural output potential and its actual utilization, i.e., to the communist leaderships' ability one day fully to satisfy the population's demand for food. This leads to the question of whether communism will be able to avoid sectoral disparities of productivity and income by better means than subsidies and other transfer mechanisms at the expense of the nonagricultural population, as they are being applied presently in Western industrialized nations, not excepting those with the most favorable natural endowment, such as the United States or France.

At present the answer to such a question seems unambiguous: To the degree that some European communist countries are coming closer to satisfactory nutrition standards, in qualitative terms as well as quantitative, the volume of their subsidies channelled into agriculture increases rapidly. Whether and/or why this may be expected for the future as well is an important question not being asked by many Western observers. Yet it may become the paramount question. It is, of course, related to past and present satisfactory productivity and cost efficiency in communist organization of agriculture, which plagues ideologues as well as practicians in those countries.

Reverting to the subjects of present-day interest, one has to state that in quantitative terms the feeding of the populations in Eastern Europe and the Soviet Union is no longer a problem. Except for that of Albania, the average caloric consumption is adequate and not much, if at all, below that of most Western countries. Even the protein supply is not greatly deficient, if vegetable protein is taken into account. The fact that the supply of protein-rich and other high-quality food does not satisfy the demand (at given consumers' prices) is in the main a consequence of rising incomes and changing eating habits in industrializing and urbanizing societies. The excess demand is also due to the inadequate production capacities of the nonagricultural consumer goods industries in those countries, so that effective demand is directed to food more than otherwise would be the case.

By a similar reasoning one may point out that it is, or at least has been until now, the inability of industry to produce the needed quantities and assortment of inputs for agriculture (chemicals, machines and trucks, building materials, hard-surface roads, and other infrastructural facilities) which has prevented socialized agriculture from bringing its production potential to fruition. Adding the deficiency of the storage, processing, and distribution system for agricultural produce, one might say with good reason that the weakness of the agrarian sector is as much one of the upstream and downstream adjoining branches of the economy. So viewed, the "agrarian problem" in communist systems is only the most conspicuous aspect of the more comprehensive problem of low efficiency, i.e., of the economic cost to be paid for the overriding social and political goals. In other words, it is agriculture that pays most for an ideology put into practice.

This economic cost is so conspicuous in agriculture because it affects the food requirements, the most basic need of any population. Having to resort to imports to an increasing degree for providing these basic goods is hard to bear and suggests strategic implications for the leaders of a political system that considers itself antagonistic to those very "capitalist" countries from which most of the imports originate. It also discredits the leadership in the eyes of those over whom it reigns. Both points affect the very legitimacy of the system. Moreover, communist states are permanently short of hard currency, i.e., they are not able to compete successfully on the nonagricultural foreign markets.

This is a failure again not so much of agriculture but of the communist economy at large. Net imports of agricultural goods further restrict the ability to pay for the much-needed industrial goods and technology.

If there are good reasons, of which only a few main ones have been pointed out above, for continuing and increasing efforts in research on communist agriculture, there are also formidable obstacles to them. First of all, the communist regimes nowadays publish more or less comprehensive and reliable statistics, but these are biased, selective, and unevenly reliable in a way that often makes it difficult to extract meaningful information. One especially glaring example is Soviet statistics on grain output. The data are published in terms of "bunker" weight and leave considerable room for estimates of the true, net quantity of grain available. Other communist publications are similarly reticent to express views unfavorable to policy and ideology, especially so if system-inherent causes of failure might become obvious. There is also the language problem, if one wants to gain a comparative picture for all the communist states and not just for one of them. Knowledge of each country's special conditions, natural as well as historical or ethnic peculiarities, is needed also. Moreover, it is commonplace by now that purely economic analysis does not suffice; for agricultural more than for other economics, social factors and effects have to be taken into account, and as we have to do with highly ideologized systems and their political organization, the study of these must not be neglected either. Some of these obstacles are known for other parts of the world, too, but for the communist bloc of Europe, plus Yugoslavia, they accumulate in a unique way.

Under these circumstances, combined efforts of specialized scholars are imperative. It is this need which the conference on "The Impact of Current Policies on Agriculture in the Marxist-Leninist State," and this volume of contributions have attempted to satisfy. With the exception of Albania (mostly for lack of published sources and for lack of language knowledge of those specializing in agrarian questions), the agrarian sectors of all countries of Eastern Europe and of the Soviet Union have been dealt with. As it is nearly impossible in one volume to cover all the aspects of agriculture and the related policies in each of the countries, an effort has been made to concentrate on some characteristic developments in the individual countries and on a few cross-national overviews. To be sure, there is room for improvement, but it seems that the volume presents a considerable achievement, by the editors as well as by the contributors, towards what might be considered an ideal. Comparing its contents with what appear to be the main goals, problems, and developments of present-day interest in the region as a whole, or else which are especially important and interesting national cases, one finds

a good many of them to have been covered. Although a
selective enumeration necessarily is subjective to some
degree, this writer deems the following subjects for the
region as a whole or for individual countries the most
important ones. In enumerating he will point out those which
have been dealt with, and also those to which, in his opinion,
more research efforts should be directed.

COMMON PROBLEMS AND TRENDS

A preliminary point is the variation among the countries
concerned. They all have communist regimes, and in six out of
eight (excluding Albania) agriculture is fully collectivized,
with a tiny private sector left. Yet apart from these facts,
their natural endowment, stage of economic development, and
historical and ethnic backgrounds are very different. Even
with socialized agriculture a certain diversity of the means
for putting an overall ideologically determined uniform policy
into practice has become obvious at an early stage and has
tended to deepen in recent years. The place assigned to
agriculture and its population in the economy of each country
is symptomatic. Within the uniform policy context it differs
greatly, e.g., between the highly industrialized GDR and
Romania, who by her own leaders is classified as a less-
developed country.

The Overriding Goal: Output Growth per Land Unit

The most obvious common feature of all countries concerned
is that output growth is the overriding goal of agrarian
policy. For the Soviet Union, Keith Severin's contribution to
the present volume makes it clear that the priority given to
satisfying consumer demand for food is not likely to change in
the foreseeable future. Combined with the necessity of output
growth is the fact that it has to be achieved per unit of
land, because there are no or very few reserves of unused
land, except for those which presuppose heavy investment
outlays for soil improvement, in the first place, for
irrigation. Because of continued detracting of land for
nonagricultural uses, and in spite of extensive irrigation
efforts, the total area of arable land in the CMEA European
bloc countries barely remained stable (270.1 million hectares
by 1977 as against 270.4 in 1970). As labor surplusses have
either disappeared or are dwindling rapidly, more intensive
land use and generally higher factor productivity are the only
means by which to achieve the desired output growth. The
shift from starchy to protein-rich animal food is part of the
intensification. It puts an ever growing demand on animal
feed production and thereby on increases of fodder crop
yields, which have to be greater than the additional

315

quantities of calories for direct human consumption. An intensification of this kind also requires a change in the cropping pattern, combined with a territorial reallocation of crops and greater specialization of farms or farm sections.

The modest share of animal output in total gross output of agriculture is indicative of the efforts still required. According to CMEA statistics, it attained more than 60 percent during 1975-77 (three-year average) only in the GDR, about 55 percent in the USSR (due mainly to the price structure, possibly also to the vast areas of natural meadows and pasture) and in Czechoslovakia; in the other countries it was between 40 and 50 percent, although for Hungary and Bulgaria the great share of crop production was also a consequence of the climatically conditioned weight of valuable fruit and vegetables.

The Private Sector

The possible contribution of the private sector to output growth is an interesting issue. The present writer is devoting more space to it because it has been paid little attention in the conference papers. Formerly, private plot farming produced nearly as much animal output and in some countries even more than the socialized (collective plus state farm) sector. Abstracting from Poland and Yugoslavia, where small-scale peasant farming still predominates, this is no longer the case. In spite of recent greater tolerance and even benevolence on the part of communist politicians, the private sector since 1970 merely maintained its absolute output volume in the countries with socialized agriculture; as a percentage of total gross output, its contribution lost in importance. (Because of fewer inputs, the contribution to the net material product is greater.) The stagnation can be illustrated by three main indicators (tilled area and meat and milk output) of the private plot and rudimentary small-scale peasant production, for the USSR, Romania, Bulgaria, Hungary, Czechoslovakia, and GDR taken together. From 1970 to 1977, the total tilled area shrank by 8.8 percent. This may have been balanced by higher yields and/or a shift towards more highly priced vegetables and fruit. Meat production remained about the same, but while it increased by not quite 9 percent up to 1974, it fell back since then to a level only very slightly above that of 1970. Milk output decreased by more than 6 percent, which demonstrates a shift from milk to meat production. The number of privately owned cows dwindled faster, by more than 16 percent during the seven years, and thus implies a yield increase per cow of roughly 10 percent.[2]

A few points have to be made with regard to the private sector in individual countries. In Bulgaria, the area privately tilled expanded after liberalization towards the private sector was announced in 1973, but did so only for one year, 1973/74, and then resumed the previous downward trend, whereas the number of cows continued its slow increase, by 6 percent over the whole period. The picture for Czechoslovakia and the GDR is much determined by the collectivization of practically all remaining individual peasants in Slovakia and by the conversion of all East German type I and II collective farms into those of type III, the fully collectivized farm. It should be added that in Poland and Yugoslavia, too, the private (peasant) sector shrank by a few percentage points.

The general impression emerges that under the given sociopolitical system, a more tolerant attitude towards the private sector effects, if only for a short interlude, a growth of its output. More meaningfully, one may put it in other terms: Such an attitude and the accompanying measures merely prevented private agricultural production from continuing its downward trend. The trend as such is caused not only by the political and economic general atmosphere and the rising public farm work incomes, which compete for labor, but also by long-term demographic factors, such as rural-urban migration and the aging of the remaining agricultural population. In any case, two general statements seem justified: First, the private sector's contribution to the food economy is likely to continue decreasing as a share of the total, and, at best, to hold its stand in absolute terms; therefore no measures, short of a true liberalization after the Hungarian model towards private plot production, will make this sector contribute to an increase of the food supplies. Secondly, this conclusion holds true not only for the total of the six countries with socialized agriculture, but also for each of them in particular, despite the differing character and relative weight of their private sectors.

Farm Organization and Agro-Industrial Integration

It is frequently assumed that the public farm sectors in countries with socialized agriculture are all organized in the same way. In fact, during 1960-75, the increasing average farm sizes have led to a leveling of the previous size differences. The relative shares of state and collective farms, too, have become more similar, although they still differ considerably. The Soviet Union is the one exception, where the state farm sector has grown at a speed that made its share exceed that of collective farms; as to Soviet farm sizes, one has to take account of the special natural conditions in vast regions of the enormous territory. Looking at the average farm sizes in Soviet regions that are roughly comparable to some East European countries, one finds them not so different from these. Yet the recent steps towards the so-called agro-industrial cooperation and integration resulted in new kinds of national differences in the organization of farming, which are quite considerable. Everett M. Jacobs has

317

given an overview of these new forms (unfortunately excluding the USSR and Yugoslavia), and Vladislav Bajaja has added an in-depth analysis for Czechoslovakia and the GDR.

It is neither an accident nor a mistake that economic reforms do not figure prominently in a summing up of recent developments in the agricultural sectors of Eastern Europe and the Soviet Union. During the 1960s this subject rightfully received great attention in almost any study. The current decade saw agro-industrial cooperation and integration taking the place as a kind of substitute for reforms in the traditional meaning of the word. In the present writer's opinion, this new concept is advocated because it seemingly permits the regimes to get around some unsolved fundamental problems of an economic as well as a social nature. It seems to enable them to achieve a big leap forward into most modern technology and into an adaptation of Western agribusiness to communist systems, often with technical and organizational help of Western firms. Whether this will be economically successful remains to be seen. In most cases the infrastructural setting is not up to the demands of modern agribusiness. Moreover, socialized agriculture has not yet proven to be very susceptible to a kind of production organization that requires exact coordination and interaction of a number of intricate and closely connected processes. Where vertical linkages are weak or not functioning, a simpler, communist-type, predominantly horizontal integration will come about. It may turn out to be simply farming on still larger production units, with some specialization and capital intensity thrown in. Whether this would be worth the effort and expenses is questionable.

International Integration within the CMEA Bloc

Cooperation and integration of communist agriculture also has the international aspect of integrating the comprehensive food industries sectors of the countries concerned, i.e., not only of agriculture but also of the branches supplying inputs to it and processing and distributing its marketed output. The phenomenon is hard to evaluate, since the CMEA programs so far have not explicitly defined what is aimed at in theoretical terms, and a Western notion, such as that of the European Common Market, is not necessarily applicable to Eastern integration. Guenther Jaehne analyzes the promulgated part-goals and plans and demonstrates that by any yardstick, international CMEA integration has not advanced much in agriculture proper, but has made some progress in the other branches of the food sector. The outcome may be an intensified international division of labor and more coordination of national Plans, including some but not much, territorial specialization. These would be rewarding results, but nothing more than could be achieved by normal international trade exchange.

Planning

One of the intriguing questions, in itself and in connection with cooperation and integration, is that of planning, on the macro- as well as on the micro-economic level. More elastic and less dirigistic planning, a moving away from "command farming" was a primary goal of the reforms of the 1960s and remains one up to the present. While elaborating, imposing, and fulfilling of Plans seem to have improved, there is no sign of this being tantamount to a fundamental overcoming of the diseconomies and inelasticities of centralized planning. The larger production units of horizontally integrated farms and their closer links with the branches adjoining upstream and downstream, diminish the number of units the central planners have to take account of. For this reason, if for no other, they make planning easier and the likeliness of Plan fulfillment greater, thereby increasing the degree of central control over the objects of planning. At the same time, more elasticity in distributing Plan tasks may prevail within those large units, which become a kind of medium level of planning and directing production. Such an outcome is conceivable, but things might as well work out the other way round; no firm judgment is as yet possible. Planning communist agriculture, its inputs and output, in theory and practice is a topic deserving continuing observation and inclusion in a future collective research and publication effort, especially in an approach transgressing national borders.

Labor Productivity

Among the questions of importance for all the countries concerned, agricultural labor productivity ranks very high and with good reason received much attention at the conference. In a generally shrinking agricultural labor force (except for in Yugoslavia and Soviet Central Asia) it is labor productivity, together with that of land, which has to effect the desired output growth, and does so, although not to the expected degree. The level attained is unsatisfactory not only in comparison to that of Western medium- and large-size farms, but also according to statements of communist authors.

Frank Durgin's provocative paper draws attention to some macroeconomic and social aspects which tend to be neglected by most observers. He makes the point that the outflow of labor in Western agriculture, as it became possible and unavoidable because of the rapid rise in labor productivity, placed a heavy social cost (unemployment, social upheavals, etc.) on the nonagricultural part of society, and that this does not show in agriculture's balance sheet. Such an approach is

justified, but whether the cost can be realistically
quantified and ascribed entirely to the productivity gains in
agriculture, remains doubtful. More importantly, the Soviet
economy, with which Durgin deals, did not wholly avoid
comparable cost, although this took other forms than open
unemployment, namely that of low labor productivity or
underemployment and low wages in nonagriculture, which were at
least in part caused by the too plentiful supply of labor in
urban areas. Low standards of housing and of other communal
facilities in the towns were also part of the indirect cost.
Moreover, full employment must not be assumed for Soviet
farms. Many of their low-skilled workforce, not only in
kolkhozes but also in sovkhozes, are not employed the whole
year round in the public sector. Private plot activities make
up for the underemployment to a certain degree, but in part
they coincide in time with the labor peaks of public
employment. Apart from such underemployment within the Soviet
farms, the increasing numbers of seasonal labor recruited
(privlechennyi) from outside demonstrate that with rising
labor productivity on the farms, the problem of seasonality
becomes more pressing. The figures involved are seemingly
small, amounting to only 0.5 million in 1965, but by 1977,
already 1.1 million.[3] Soviet statistics present them
recalculated on a full annual employment basis (270-280
working days), and as most of this labor works on the farms
hardly more than fifty days, the actual number of such workers
must have been more than 5 million in 1977. Part of the
resulting cost is born by the nonagricultural enterprises and
organizations delegating such workers or by the urban communes
recruiting and transporting them. Finally, if one includes
the Soviet subsidy bill for agriculture, which at least in
part is caused by the low level of labor productivity and in
total is approaching 40 billion rubles per year (more than 20
billion for the meat and milk price subsidy alone), as does
Durgin for the U.S. agricultural subsidy, then this kind of
macroeconomic comparison of the hidden or transferred cost of
agricultural labor productivity might tip the scale against
the Soviet system.

Science, Technology and Capital Infusion

Scientific and technological progress in agriculture is
the counterpart to labor and land productivity. It looms
large in East European and Soviet discussions and measures.
Joseph Hajda's paper, dealing in cross-national fashion with
most of the countries concerned, is devoted to it. There can
be no doubt that the communist leaders spend great efforts in
this field, and most of these find their quantitative
expression in greatly increased investments. Some indicators
of the resulting progress, such as hectare yields of grain and
milk yields per cow, reveal definite improvement. It remains

320

an open question, not ignored by Hajda, whether the achievements are proportionate to the quantity and quality of inputs, whether the sociopolitical parameters are not rather unfavorable to optimum results.

This brings in the question of cost in terms of capital. Expenditures per output unit--less so per worker or land unit--have risen to impressive heights by international standards and at the same time show diminishing returns for capital. In a penetrating analysis, Folke Dovring assesses the capital intensity in Soviet agriculture, including the capital inputs in the nonagricultural branches connected with it. He finds rather great inputs compared to those of U.S. agriculture for example, and consequent low capital productivity. It would be worthwhile to apply analogous criteria to the other communist countries, too.

The investment that agriculture receives directly, or indirectly through high producers prices, is usually quantified as a share of the total investment in country's economy. This share demonstrably has become much greater in communist Europe than in any Western industrialized country and also is greater than agriculture's contribution to the national gross or net (material) product. While such an overall structural analysis makes international comparisons possible and for Eastern Europe and the Soviet Union is indicative of the greatly increased attention agriculture's needs receive in the national economic Plans, it does not provide a yardstick for comparing capital productivity in agriculture alone. It seems worthwhile to assess investment also in other terms, for example, per worker or per unit of output or land, although then international comparison will be less stringent because of the difficulties in assessing the real value of the financial means involved among countries with different price structures. On the basis of very rough calculations, the present writer has shown elsewhere that in the USSR and the GDR during the late 1960s and early 1970s the annual increase of agriculture's gross output was only about one-third of agricultural net investment, i.e., of fixed capital added, while in West Germany they were about equal.[4]

Cost Efficiency

It is self-evident that with increasing capital inputs communist agrarian policies had to become more cost conscious than previously. If nothing else, the statements, criticisms, and admonitions by the political leaders and in the specialized press of communist states bear testimony to this. The time may not be too far away when the success or failure of the agricultural sector will be evaluated more on the basis of cost efficiency than on sheer gross output growth. It is a telling fact that the net material product of Soviet agriculture stagnated during 1970-76. In other words, the

321

growth of its gross material product was offset by increased material inputs. When current food demand is met by supplies, cost considerations will be likely to receive highest priority in communist agrarian policies, much as is the case in the West. The cost squeeze looks still more threatening when labor cost is also taken into consideration. Total labor remuneration in Soviet kolkhozes increased, in spite of decreasing numbers of labor inputs, by 2.5 billion rubles (by one-sixth) from 1970 to 1976, in sovkhozes by 7 billion rubles (by 65 percent, while labor increased by 23 percent).[5] Thus the growth of the gross agricultural product was roughly equal to the rise of labor cost during the period. The picture is not likely to be greatly dissimilar for the East European countries.

Prices and Incomes

Obviously, the repeated raising of producers prices for agriculture was inevitable under such circumstances. It could have been avoided if either the numbers of the labor force had diminished faster than the remuneration per worker increased, or agricultural incomes had been kept stable or allowed to rise only slowly. The first possibility simply did not materialize; the second was not viable because of compelling social as well as economic reasons. Strikingly, the disparity of average agricultural and nonagricultural work remuneration nowadays is less than in most Western countries, or about of the same magnitude in Poland, the Soviet Union, and Yugoslavia. Yet the general level of incomes, from which such comparison starts, is much lower in the East, and this explains the stronger impact of the still existing disparities, to which urban-rural differentials of the social and cultural infrastructure have to be added.

In any case, it is a fact that all the regimes have felt compelled to raise the incomes in agriculture more rapidly than in the other sectors, thereby reducing the previous disparities considerably. Apparently, their main motives, under the impact of the necessity to increase agricultural output, were to prevent a greater outflow of labor than could be compensated by capital inputs, to offer more incentives for productive performance, and to raise the low rural living standards, which so much contradict the pretended achievements of socialism in the countryside. (One must add, though, that the annual average outflow was less than in the Western world during the 1950s and 1960s, except for certain periods and countries, especially the GDR, Czechoslovakia, and Bulgaria.) A rise of average agricultural incomes over those of the urban working class would be contrary to Marxist-Leninist doctrine. Therefore it is logical, in view of the interdependence of labor and capital inputs, that some of the huge investments seem to have been used as a substitute for rises in labor

322

incentives and are likely to continue to be used so in the foreseeable future.

Income as such is only part, although an important one, of labor incentives. The system and application of the remuneration is no less important; and this is where new approaches continue to be tried, with less than satisfactory effect so far. Although Western studies on this subject for individual communist countries exist, there is no comprehensive, cross-national overview so far to this writer's knowledge.[6] More needs to be done in a comparative approach, and the changes resulting from the enterprise reorganizations in the framework of agro-industrial integration have to be included in such investigations.

Social Change

Growing attention by Eastern as well as by Western scholars has been attracted by the social change in communist states and also by that in their rural area. The interdependence of such change with economic policies and performance, especially in agriculture, is widely acknowledged but rarely investigated in Western literature on the communist world. Its importance applies equally to all parts of the world. In the present volume, the contributions by John Allcock on Yugoslav agricultural policy and Ethel Dunn on social mobility for Soviet rural women, analyze partial aspects of it. More needs to be done in this field.

Implications for Foreign Trade

The implications of increasing agricultural imports by communist countries for international trade are deliberately enumerated last, in order not to obscure the more basic issues, which determine such trade. Moreover, the foreign trade aspects do not apply equally to the whole of Eastern Europe and the Soviet Union. While Poland, the GDR, and Czechoslovakia are heavily dependent on agricultural imports, the great absolute volume of Soviet agricultural imports looks less impressive if recalculated per head of the Soviet population ($10 to $20 per year, on a net basis, during 1970-75); Hungary exported $121 worth per head per year during 1973-75, while imports were only $68. It is generally accepted among Western observers that the Soviet grain imports will decrease from the high levels attained during 1972-76, but just to what "normal" figure is hard to predict. Chantal Beaucourt in her paper even thinks that beginning in the mid-1980s sizable net grain imports to the USSR will continue only in years following a major harvest shortfall. Future trends are of great interest and subject to possible errors of prognosis.

323

SPECIFIC NATIONAL PROBLEMS OF AGRICULTURE

Turning to individual countries and to subjects of specific interest in their agrarian sectors, which are not included in the above listing of common problems, one thinks first of Yugoslavia and Poland. The "socialist transformation" of their peasant agriculture remains a long-term policy goal in Belgrade as well as in Warsaw, although the Soviet model of collectivization was rejected a quarter of a century ago and is not likely to be accepted in the future (see John Allcock's paper on Yugoslavia). In both countries, the state farms, less so the collective farms, are assigned an avantgarde role in the gradual transformation process, although their production efficiency, especially with regard to cost, is not impressive. Also, various kinds of cooperatives are advocated, but have not proven very successful as yet, as far as their impact on the socialist transformation is concerned. Among the pressing problems of the agrarian sector, the low productivity and underemployment, together with the aging of the labor force, loom large in both countries. Some of them present a picture different from that of social change in countries with socialized agriculture. The dependence on agricultural imports is felt as a burden on the economy, most heavily in Poland (see Andrew A. Duymovic in the present volume). In Yugoslavia, regional disparities are almost as grave as in the Soviet Union, but they are concentrated in a smaller territory. Their importance exceeds that of comparable phenomena in any other of the East European countries, except perhaps for Albania. The sheer enumeration of these problems, although not complete, shows that only a few of the relevant subjects have been dealt with by the contributors to the present volume.

Bulgaria's bold venture toward horizontal and, to a minor degree, vertical integration of agriculture is of the greatest interest. Extensive exports of her agricultural products to the Soviet Union are another special feature. The gross output growth of Bulgarian agriculture was less than in any other country of the Soviet bloc during 1968-74, and after a 7.5 percent increase in 1975 it again stagnated until 1977. Paul Wiedemann's overview of the rapid build-up of "agro-industrial complexes" in that country shows that the economic results of this radical transformation have been disappointing so far.

Hungarian agriculture is the conspicuous case of socialized agriculture under a communist regime with comparatively liberal economic policies and methods and with what, in comparison to other communist states, reads like a success story. That this success is not without flaws emerges from Peter Elek's concentration on the question of profitability, with due regard to the economy at large.

Romanian agriculture, discussed in Trond Gilberg's contribution, continues to wrestle with low productivity and lagging incentive, in spite of recent attempts to concentrate on agriculture some of the attention formerly reserved for industry.

Czechoslovakia and the GDR are the most industrialized countries in the region. Their agricultural sectors are of secondary importance for their economies. Czechoslovakia has greatly reduced her grain import requirements by stepping up her own output. In view of the small size, the population concentration, and the industrial export capacity of the GDR it should be considered natural that food imports there will remain indispensable for the foreseeable future. The two countries have developed diverging ways of applying the concept of agro-industrial cooperation and integration, as analyzed by Vladislav Bajaja in his paper. Although reestablishment of convergence in this field should not be excluded, this is a remarkable development.

The Soviet Union has a vaster territory than any other country of the world and manifests practically all the aspects and problems enumerated above, except for those of peasant farms and of a relatively liberal economic policy. In view of the great distances between most Soviet production and consumption centers, transport is one of the main bottlenecks. The variety of climates and the many historical, ethnic, and socioeconomic components account for a great variety of production and living conditions in agriculture and for the resulting regional disparities. They also make a rational spatial allocation of production factors a task of utmost importance and great potential rewards. This has been pointed out in Chantal Beaucourt's paper, although more attention to the question of changing cropping patterns would have been desirable. Agrarian policy has received growing attention from Soviet leaders ever since Stalin's death. In this writer's opinion--and in contrast to Roy D. Laird's thoughts-- there was no major policy change after the demotion of Khrushchev, except that his erratic methods gave way to more considerate proceedings and that the restrictions on private plot and animal farming were lifted. The stepping up of capital supply to agriculture had started two years earlier, including fertilizer and irrigation programs; the expansion of clean fallow began in 1964, still under Khrushchev; even agro-industrial integration was envisaged in the 1961 party program, although it was almost ten years later when steps were taken in earnest to make it a reality.

CONCLUSION

It is equally amazing how many aspects of agriculture and agrarian policies in the Soviet Union and Eastern Europe have been dealt with in varying detail by the conference participants, and how many are left for further investigation and presentation. In bringing together the Western specialists, most of whom are scattered over a number of countries or over vast distances in North America, such conferences serve an important purpose. They are places not only of exchange of specialized knowledge and of discussing diverging evaluations, but also for showing what has been done, what is being done, and where future efforts should be directed. The number of senior scholars working in the field is rather small, and that of the younger generation even smaller; the research potential therefore is limited. One of the main desiderata, in this writer's opinion, is to combine comparative efforts on subjects, which are of relevance for all or most of the countries concerned, and to put the peculiarities of some of them into the perspective of the overall region and political system.

It would be utopian as well as undesirable to try to compel scholars to spend effort on subjects in which they take no interest, or which are far from their other work. Yet very likely most of them would agree to a certain commitment, if they are made to realize the importance of complementary efforts beyond the limited task each one is able to take upon himself. That is how a conference can induce combined or coordinated research already at the preparatory stage of the subsequent conference, which has tentatively and hopefully been envisaged for 1981. The Fifth International Conference and its proceedings have laid a good foundation on which to build.

NOTES

1. G. I. Shmelev and V. N. Starodubrovskaya, Sotsial 'no-ekonomicheskie problemy razvitiya sel'skogo khozyaistva evropeyskikh sotsialisticheskikh stran (Moscow: Nauka, 1977), pp. 104-5.

2. For the underlying data, see Statisticheskii ezhegodnik stranchlenov Soveta ekonomicheskoi vzaimopomoshchi, 1978, pp. 178f., 205-207, 209; for the intervening year of 1974, see Statisticheskii ezhegodnik, 1976, pp. 186f., 215, 218, 220. In the case of Hungary the number of privately owned pigs is taken as indicative of private meat output (which is not given in the source); the GDR data for meat output and cow numbers in 1977 are not comparable to the earlier ones and had to be roughly estimated, but do not markedly influence the totals for the six countries. Privately tilled land is derived as the difference between total agricultural land and the socialist sector's agricultural land. Therefore it includes a negligible share of utilled land and excludes land of public enterprises given for private usage to workers and employees.

3. Narodnoe khozyaistvo SSSR v 1977 godu (Moscow: Statististika, 1978), p. 294.

4. K.-E. Wädekin, <u>Sozialistische Agrarpolitik in
Osteuropa</u>, vol. 2 (Berlin: Duncker and Humblot, 1978), p.
137.

5. Derived from data in <u>Narodnoe khozyaistvo</u> , pp. 350
and 370.

6. Yet see, very recently, K.-E. Wädekin, "Labor
Remuneration in the Socialized Agriculture of Eastern Europe
and the Soviet Union," <u>Studies in Comparative Communism</u>, 11
(spring/summer 1978): 96-120.

About the Editors
and Contributors

RONALD A. FRANCISCO (Ph.D., University of Illinois, Urbana-Champaign), Assistant Professor of Political Science and Soviet and East European Studies at the University of Kansas, is the author of "The SPD in East Berlin, 1945-1961," and "The Future of East German Agriculture," and coeditor and contributor to The Political Economy of Collectivized Agriculture: A Comparative Study of Communist and Non-Communist Systems, 1979.

BETTY A. LAIRD is an independent research analyst working with her husband in the Soviet field and in her own interest area, Kansas history. Her most recent publications include Soil of Our Souls (with Martha Parker), 1976; To Live Long Enough: The Memoirs of Naum Jasny, Scientific Analyst (with Roy D. Laird), 1976; and (as coeditor) The Political Economy of Collectivized Agriculture: A Comparative Study of Communist and Non-Communist Systems, 1979.

ROY D. LAIRD (Ph.D., University of Washington), Professor of Political Science and Soviet and East European Studies at the University of Kansas, founded the ongoing (informal) Conference on Soviet and East European Agricultural and Peasant Affairs, and coedited The Political Economy of Collectivized Agriculture: A Comparative Study of Communist and Non-Communist Systems, 1979. He has authored many articles and a number of books, including The Soviet Paradigm: An Experiment in Creating a Monohierarchical Polity, 1970, and To Live Long Enough: The Memoirs of Naum Jasny, Scientific Analyst (with Betty Laird) 1976.

JOHN B. ALLCOCK (B.A., Leicester University, M.A., Carleton University) is a Lecturer in Sociology at the University of Bradford, where he teaches in the Post-Graduate School of Yugoslav Studies. He is secretary to the Editorial Committee of Bradford Studies on Yugoslavia and author of several articles on Yugoslav society in British, Yugoslav and German journals.

VLADISLAV BAJAJA (Dr. Agr., Justus-Liebig-University, Giessen), Scientific Associate at the Center for Continental Agrarian and Economic Research in Giessen, West Germany, has written Theoretische Grundlagen und praktische Entwicklung landwirtschaftlicher Betriebsgrüssen in der Tschechoslowakei, 1975; The Organization of Czechoslovak Agriculture, 1976; and Organisation und Führung landwirtschaftlicher Grossunternehmen in der DDR, 1978.

CHANTAL BEAUCOURT (Ph.D., University of Paris), Research Associate (on socialist economies) in the Center for International Prospective Studies and Information, publishes research results principally in Economies & Sociétés, Courrier des Pays de l'Est, Inter-Nord, and Revue d'études comparatives Est-Ouest.

FOLKE DOVRING (Ph.D., Lund University, Lund, Sweden), Professor of Land Economics at the University of Illinois in Urbana-Champaign, is the author of Land and Labor in Europe in the Twentieth Century, 1956, third revised edition 1965; The Optional Society (with Karin Dovring), 1972; "Soviet Farm Mechanization in Perspective," Slavic Review, June 1966; and "Iskusstvennoe miasa iz soi," Voprosy Ekonomiki, April 1973.

FRANK A. DURGIN, JR. (Ph.D., University of Toulouse), is Professor of Economics at the University of Southern Maine. He is the author of "Politique Agricole in URSS depuis 1950," "Toward the Abolition of the RTS," "The Growth of Inter-Kolkhoz Cooperation," "The Virgin Land Programme 1954-1960," "Monetization and Policy in Soviet Agriculture Since 1952," "Neuve Istituzioni Agricole Sovietiche," "Il Decentramente e le Leve Finanziarie Nell' Agricole Sovietica Durante L'Era Kruscheviana," "Quantitative Structural and Institutional Changes in Soviet Agriculture during the Khrushchev Era, 1953-1964," plus several other publications on Soviet agriculture.

ETHEL DUNN is the Executive Secretary of the Highgate Road Social Science Research Station, Berkeley, California. She and her husband have collaborated on two books on cultural change among the peasants of the European USSR, many articles, and translations, as well as on a study of Molokans in America. Ethel Dunn's main interest is Russian religious dissidence.

ANDREW A. DUYMOVIC (Ph.D., The University of Connecticut) is an international economist with the Foreign Agricultural Service, U.S. Department of Agriculture. He has contributed to Eastern Europe Agricultural Situation, USDA, 1977 and 1978; is the author of "Polish-U.S. Farm Trade Seen Remaining Strong,"

<u>Foreign Agriculture</u>, 1979; and the co-author of "GDR Expands Farm Trade with the United States," <u>Foreign Agriculture</u>, 1979.

PETER S. ELEK (Ph.D.), Associate Professor of Economics, Villanova University, was educated at the Universities of Budapest and Cambridge and is a founding member and Vice President of the Eastern Economic Association. He has published "The Impact on the Hungarian Model of Post-Reform Changes in Reward Policies," in <u>Economic Development of the Soviet Union and Eastern Europe</u>, Z. M. Fallenbuck, ed., 1976; "Hungary's New Agricultural Revolution," in <u>The Future of Agriculture in the Soviet Union and Eastern Europe</u>, Laird, Hajda, and Laird, eds., 1977; "Agro-mass Production and the Private Sector in Hungary," in <u>The Peasantry of Eastern Europe</u>, I. Volgyes, ed., 1979; "The Impact of Revised Economic Stimulators," <u>Eastern European Quarterly</u>, 1979.

TROND GILBERG, Professor of Political Science and Associate Director of the Slavic Language and Area Center at The Pennsylvania State University, is the author of <u>Soviet Communist Party and Scandinavian Communism</u>, 1973 and <u>Modernization in Romania Since World War II</u>, 1975, and has contributed numerous chapters to other books in the field.

JOSEPH HAJDA (Ph.D., Indiana University), Associate Professor of Political Science at Kansas State University, served in the Office of the U.S. Secretary of Agriculture, 1962, and in the White House Office of the Special Representative for Trade Negotiations, 1964-65. He coedited <u>The Future of Agriculture in the Soviet Union and Eastern Europe</u>, 1977; <u>Political Aspects of World Food Problems</u>, 1978; and <u>Analytical Perspectives on Trade Relations with China</u>, 1979.

EVERETT M. JACOBS (Ph.D., University of London, London School of Economics), Senior Lecturer in Soviet Economic and Social History at the University of Sheffield, England, is the author of numerous articles on Soviet and East European agriculture and has edited <u>The Organization of Agriculture in the Soviet Union and Eastern Europe</u>, forthcoming, 1980.

GÜNTER JAEHNE has studied in Jena/Thuringa, Kiel, West Berlin, Giessen, and at the Timirjazev-Academie in Moscow. He is a member of the staff of the Zentrum für kontinentale Agrar- und Wirtschaftsforschung at Justus-Liebig-University, Giessen. His principal publications have been <u>Landwirtschaft und landwirtschaftliche Zusammenarbeit im RGW</u>, 1968; <u>Schlachttier- und Fleischproduktion in Osteuropa: Sowjetunion</u> (co-authored with Ph. Kellner), 1978; and, together with several colleagues, <u>Prospects for Soviet Agricultural Production in 1980 and 1985 with Special Reference to Meat and</u>

<u>Grain</u>, 1978, and <u>Cereals and Meat in Eastern Europe--
Production, Consumption, and Trade</u>, 1978.

KEITH SEVERIN (M.A., Food Research Institute, Stanford
University) is an agricultural economist with the U.S.
Department of Agriculture. He has traveled extensively in the
Soviet Union.

KARL-EUGEN WÄDEKIN (Ph.D., University of Leipzig), is
Professor of Communist and International Comparative Agrarian
Policies at the Justus-Liebig University, Giessen, West
Germany, and coeditor of the monthly <u>Osteuropa</u>. He is the
author of <u>Privatproduzenten in der sowjetischen
Landwirtschaft</u>, 1967; <u>Die sowjetischen Staatsgüter</u>, 1969;
<u>Führungskräfte im sowjetischen Dorf</u>, 1969; <u>Die Bezahlung der
Arbeit in der sowjetischen Landwirtschaft</u>, 1972; <u>The Private
Sector in Soviet Agriculture</u>, 1973; <u>Sozialistische
Agrarpolitik in Osteuropa</u>, 2 vols., 1974 and 1978; and
<u>Agrarian Policies in Communist Europe</u>, forthcoming.

PAUL P. WIEDEMANN (Ph.D., London University),
Wissenschaftlicher Mitarbeiter at the Vienna Institute for
Comparative Economic Studies, is the author of <u>The
Organization of Bulgarian Agriculture</u>, 1976; "The Distribution
of Income and Earnings and Economic Welfare in Bulgaria and
Yugoslavia," <u>Southeastern Europe</u>, 1976; "Planning with
Multiple Objectives," <u>Omega</u>, 1978; "Robustness and Independent
Decision Making," <u>Journal of the Operational Research Society</u>;
and a forthcoming book on <u>Socialist Agro-Business</u>.